How Much Is Enough?

Getting the Most from Your Advertising Dollar

John Philip Jones

Lexington Books

An Imprint of Macmillan, Inc.
NEW YORK
Maxwell Macmillan Canada
TORONTO
Maxwell Macmillan International
NEW YORK • OXFORD • SINGAPORE • SYDNEY

Library of Congress Cataloging-in-Publication Data

Jones, John Philip.
    How much is enough? : getting the most from your advertising
dollar / John Philip Jones.
        p.   cm.
    ISBN 0-669-24639-5
    1. Advertising.   I. Title.
HF5821.J66   1992
659.1—dc20   91-45347
                                                            CIP

Lexington Books
An Imprint of Macmillan, Inc.
866 Third Avenue, New York, N.Y. 10022

Maxwell Macmillan Canada, Inc.
1200 Eglinton Avenue East
Suite 200
Don Mills, Ontario M3C 3N1

Macmillan, Inc. is part of the Maxwell Communication Group of Companies.

Printed in the United States of America

printing number
1 2 3 4 5 6 7 8 9 10

To Jonathan Brand

Contents

List of Tables and Figures   *xi*

Preface   *xiii*

1 Definitions, Causality, and the Structure
of the Book   1

    Five Species of Waste   *7*
    Three Causes   *12*
    The Structure of the Book   *16*
    Summary   *18*

2 Trends   21

    First Trend: Market Maturity   *22*
    Second Trend: Market Fragmentation   *28*
    Third Trend: Stagnation in Advertising Expenditure   *34*
    Fourth Trend: Growth in Promotions   *39*
    Summary   *42*

3 Is Advertising a Strong or a Weak Force?   45

    "The Power of Advertising"   *45*
    Two Theories   *47*
    Implications for Professional Practice   *53*
    Implications for Advertising Education   *56*
    Summary   *60*

4 The Culture of an Advertising Agency   63

    Programmed Anarchy   *66*
    Strangled in Its Infancy   *67*
    "Aunty Knows Best"   *71*

Too Little Culture—Or Too Much?   76
Twelve Practical Lessons   80

5 Advertising Budgets   85
The Choice Between Overspending
and Underspending

How Advertising Budgets are Set   85
Advertising Works Harder for Bigger Brands   87
Average Share of Voice: A Budgetary Planning Tool   92
Further Empirical Evaluation   96
The Practical Values of the Budgetary Planning Tool   97
Summary   100

6 Promotions   101
A Game of Double Jeopardy

A Legacy of Stagnation and Inflation   101
Short-Term Effects of Promotions and How to Measure
Them   103
Longer-Term Considerations   107
The Return on Advertising Investments   110
From Theory to Practice: Three Operational
Recommendations   112
Summary   116

7 Strategy   119
Defining the Target Group

A Rational Subject That Often Becomes Confused   122
The Brand Advertising Strategy   127
The Target Group: Where Is the Business Coming From?   130
Demographics   141
Psychographics   149
Summary   152

8 Strategy   155
The Proposition and the Ways in Which the
Campaign Should Work

The Proposition   155
Functionality   156

Added Values   162
The Ways in Which the Campaign Should Work   172
Ten Steps to an Effective Strategy   178
Hypothesized Advertising Strategies for Three Brands of
    Breakfast Cereal   180

9 From Strategy to Campaign   185

Six Steps   185
Qualitative Research: Stimulus Material   192
Qualitative Research: Pros and Cons   193
Quantitative Research   199
Summary   203

10 An Inventory of Knowledge about Advertising   205

Products and Brands   209
Market Research   216
The Creative Process   224
Advertising Budgets   230
Media Strategy and Tactics   233
The Evaluation of Advertising Effects   237
How Does Advertising Work?   244
Advertising and Industry   252
Advertising and the Consumer   257
Summary   262

11 Fifty Proposals for Action   265

Advice to Advertisers   266
Advice to Agencies   271
New Brand Development   277
Stationary Markets   280
Forecasting Advertising's Selling Power   283
The Imaginative Leap   286
Lessons from Direct Response   288
The Advertising Audience and the Media   290
Sales Effects, Budgeting, and Budgetary Deployment   293

Appendixes

Appendix A: Advertising and the Economic System   297

Appendix B: A Politician's View of Advertising:
A Speech by Enoch Powell 341

Notes 347

Acknowledgments 371

Index 373

About the Author 381

List of Tables and Figures

TABLES

2–1 Changes in Volume Usage of 150 Major Consumer Goods (1989 Compared with 1988, in Percentages)   *23*

2–2 Strongly Growing Categories of Consumer Goods (1989 Compared with 1988, in Percentages)   *25*

2–3 When Consumer Goods Markets Flattened (50 Major Categories)   *26*

2–4 Products Sold with Common Brand Names   *29*

2–5 Numbers of $1-Million Brands (Adjusted to 1979 Prices)   *30*

2–6 Main Media Advertising as Percentage of Gross National Product   *35*

2–7 Division of Advertising and Promotion Budgets by Manufacturers   *40*

5–1 Analysis of Profit-Taking and Investment Brands   *90*

5–2 Analysis of Brands with 13% + Share of Market   *91*

5–3 Share of Market Compared with Share of Voice (Brands in Balanced Packaged-Goods Markets)   *93*

5–4 Analysis of Larger Brands in Typical Balanced Packaged-Goods Markets   *94*

6–1 Effect of 10% Price Reduction   *106*

6–2 Effect of 50% Advertising Increase   *111*

7–1 Market Trends in Cold Breakfast Cereals   *132*

7–2 Segment Trends in Cold Breakfast Cereals   *134*

7–3 Summarized Data for Individual Brands of Cold Breakfast Cereal, 1990   *136*

7–4 Penetration Share and Sales Share Trends for Three Selected Brands of Cold Breakfast Cereals   *139*

7–5 Demographic Data for Overall Market for Cold
Breakfast Cereals and for Selected Brands, 1990 ... *142*
7–6 Demographic Data for Selected Brands of Cold
Breakfast Cereals (Natural Segment, 1990) ... *144*
7–7 Profiles of Lucky Charms Users by Age Group ... *147*
8–1 Toilet Soap Market Segments, 1990 ... *158*
8–2 Leading Toilet Soap Brands, 1990 ... *159*
A–1 A:S Ratios by Industry, 1989 ... *307*
A–2 Average Value of California Avocados ($ per Acre) ... *310*
A–3 The Price of Eyeglasses with and without
Advertising, 1963 ... *319*
A–4 Prices of Unilever Brands, Adjusted for Inflation ... *330*
A–5 Volume of Advertising in the United States, 1990 ... *335*

FIGURES

2–1 Main Media Advertising as Percentage of Gross
National Product ... *36*
5–1 Advertising-Intensiveness Curve ... *94*
5–2 Original and Supplementary Advertising-Intensiveness
Curves ... *97*
7–1 The Planning Cycle ... *120*
8–1 Perceptual Map of Toilet Soaps: Perceptions of User
Demographics ... *170*
8–2 Perceptual Map of Toilet Soaps: Perceptions of
Selected User Psychographics ... *171*
8–3 The King Continuum ... *173*
9–1 "Reculer pour Mieux Sauter" ... *187*
9–2 Steps from Strategy to Campaign Exposure ... *188*
10–1 Advertising Response Functions ... *238*
10–2 Advertising Response Functions for Different Brands
in the Same Category ... *242*
A–1 The Oligopolist's Objective ... *304*
A–2 Effect of Increased Demand ... *308*
A–3 The Farmers' Objective ... *311*
A–4 Long-Term Movements in the Avocado Market ... *312*
A–5 Shift in Demand Curve for Brand Alpha ... *314*
A–6 Advertising-Intensiveness Curve ... *316*
A–7 Long-Term Response of Supply to a Short-Term
Increase in Demand ... *328*

Preface

It is far easier to write ten passably effective sonnets, good enough to take in the not too inquiring critic, than one effective advertisement that will take in a few thousand of the uncritical buying public.

Aldous Huxley

The advertising business is afflicted with a deep recession that developed rapidly toward the end of the 1980s. This recession is more serious than any other since World War II, and there is no sign of recovery at the time I write these words, the winter of 1991–92. Two forces have been at work. First, there has been a cyclical downturn connected with the general business recession in the United States and other countries. Underlying this has been a second factor—a long-term and (I believe) permanent stagnation that has specifically affected advertising. The combination of these two causes has meant that the downturn in advertising has been greater than that in most other parts of the economy.

In this book, I am addressing the long-term stagnation in advertising. The advertising business cannot expect any revival unless this problem is tackled; I believe it is totally unrealistic to expect the present difficulties to be cured completely or even substantially by a revival of activity in the economy as a whole. The advertising industry must meet its difficulties by improving its efficiency: by identifying and exploiting the campaigns that are demonstrably effective and cost-efficient, and by eliminating the plentiful number of campaigns that are ineffective and therefore a waste of resources. Making such a recommendation is much easier than implementing it. This is why I have devoted this rather substantial book to how we should analyze and tackle this vast problem.

Advertising is in fact the most intractably difficult of all types of communication. There are two reasons for this. First, advertising is addressed to people who can generally recognize what it is, do not wish to be exposed to it, and can easily switch off their intellectual engagement. It is common sense that the number of people who are positively willing to watch or read advertisements is very small indeed (although those few people who accept or use or like advertising are of obvious interest to advertisers and are a group worth studying). The second difficulty surrounding advertising is that, to be successful, the advertiser must generate much more response than writers in other fields. The advertiser must go far beyond entertaining, informing, amusing, or emotionally moving the audience. He must achieve a behavioral reaction; the people who receive the message must actually *do* something as a result of it.

It follows that the successful advertiser must have, and must be able to deploy, greater skills than other types of writers—or, at the very least, skills of a different character. Aldous Huxley confirmed this point neatly, if cynically, in the quotation at the beginning of this preface. The advertiser must create a message that will be noticed by an apathetic and sometimes hostile audience. Even more important and difficult is the task of writing a message that is persuasive and powerful enough to induce some members of the audience to act on it (that is, to buy the brand in enough quantity for the margin on these sales to pay for the advertising).

It should not surprise us in any way that a large number—probably the majority—of advertisements are unable to overcome the formidable hurdles that lie in their path. This means that much of the effort that goes into advertising, no matter how serious-intentioned it may be, is going to be wasted. What is even worse, the typical advertiser operating in a hotly competitive market is often tempted to turn up the pressure to make sure that his or her advertising crosses some mythical threshold of effectiveness. This approach causes the waste to be increased, sometimes exponentially, because an intrinsically ineffective campaign will not become more effective when it is exposed at a heavier weight. On the contrary, everything we know about the sales effect of incremental pressure demonstrates that increased advertising operates with diminishing returns, that is, with *declining* effectiveness as the weight is boosted.

That is the first book that has ever been devoted exclusively to waste in advertising and to specific ways of increasing advertising's efficiency. Every reduction is the rich layers of waste not only will benefit the advertiser who makes it but is also likely to benefit society as a whole, since it liberates resources, some of which might be applied to socially beneficial purposes.

The problem of reducing advertising waste is most certainly worth tackling, but it is complex. I have approached it from a number of directions, which are discussed in chapter 1.

In brief, I have looked at how advertising budgets are determined, and I make suggestions for improvements that may enable advertisers to carry out their budgeting more efficiently. Budgeting is closely related to the measurement of advertising effects, which is something we do not know enough about. One of my main concerns is to improve our knowledge of how advertising works: to throw light on the many unknowns and—even more important—to purge the advertising community of many things that it believes to be true but that are in fact wrong.

A further group of arguments concerns the procedures for planning advertisements. Specifically I describe how advertising strategy is planned by the most sophisticated practitioners in the business. By demonstrating the punctilious and exhaustive care that goes into planning a comprehensive strategy, I hope to provide an opportunity for the average standard of professional practice to be brought up to that of the best operators.

One of the more important aspects of planning campaigns is to locate and appeal to the small number of people who are happy, or at least willing, to view or read advertisements. There are three groups of such people:

1. those who are shopping for a product in a particular category and who are willing to use advertisements as a source of information;
2. people who are genuinely amused and entertained by specific advertisements;
3. users of the brand advertised.

The last of these categories is quantitatively much the largest. This fact highlights the importance of directing the strategy to existing users of the brand, with the intention of maintaining the consumer franchise and increasing purchase frequency.

In addition to the many types of recommendation I am making in this book, there is a further way of reducing advertising waste which

I believe to be even more important: simply generating more effective advertising ideas, ideas that will be better noticed and that will be more strongly and universally acted on than most advertisements in today's marketplace.

Unfortunately, generating advertising ideas and evaluating them for their selling appeal is an aspect of advertising about which we know very little; in fact, our knowledge is weaker than in virtually all other parts of the business. It is true that research and judgment can provide a reasonable indication of whether an advertisement will be noticed by the public. But as far as the more fundamentally important question of selling power is concerned, research and judgment are both uniformly valueless. Like all practitioners and ex-practitioners, I have personal opinions about the effectiveness of advertisements—both individually and in the aggregate. However, I am not convinced that my views are more valuable than anyone else's. None of us *know* anything of predictive value. Unsubstantiated theories and unsupported judgments are thicker on the ground here than in any other branches of the advertising enterprise, and I am not anxious to add to them.

I believe that the recommendations I am making in this book—and, even more important, the recommendation which I do not feel qualified to discuss, the matter of generating stronger advertising ideas—all have the potential to improve efficiency and reduce waste in advertising. My professional experience in the field has left me with no doubt whatsoever that advertising *can* be an effective force and can contribute positively to the strength of brands. But to put in a nutshell the entire message of this book, the most pressing need is to slice away the large amounts of ineffective advertising that surround us, and to augment very significantly the quantity of the effective variety.

This book also touches on another important subject: the contribution of advertising to competitive capitalism. This topic is discussed in appendixes A and B. Overall, advertising as it is practiced today shows a credit balance when its advantages and disadvantages are weighed. But advertising has the most favorable effects when it is operated robustly, and this is not a universal characteristic of the business. It is also emphatically true that every reduction in advertising waste that we manage to achieve will tip the balance of economic and social advantages even further to the positive side. This is a point that should reassure and encourage people who are engaged in all parts of the advertising profession, a profession characterized by intense competition and insecurity, but also by excitement and vigor and much potential for enjoyment and reward for its practitioners.

The only purpose of advertising is to make sales. It is profitable or unprofitable according to its actual sales. It is not for general effect. It is not to keep your name before the people. It is not primarily to aid your other salesmen.

—Claude Hopkins

Never stop testing, and your advertising will never stop improving.

—David Ogilvy

1

Definitions, Causality, and the Structure of the Book

It is the elimination and utilization of waste, waste effort, waste time and material, that produce the great results in the industrial world.

Theodore N. Vail (1845–1920)

I must begin by explaining what this book is not. Readers who expect an anticapitalist tract expounding the waste of the earth's resources through unnecessary consumption will be disappointed. I am concerned essentially with improving the efficiency or, perhaps better, with reducing the inefficiency of professional practice in the advertising and promotional fields. The book is mainly concerned with advertising, but since in manufacturers' budgeting there is commonly a trade-off between advertising and promotions, it is impossible to ignore the latter. Promotions are in any event an important source of waste in their own right.

Although the title of the book is intended to engage and challenge the reader, the things I say are neither populist nor sensational. This should be apparent both from the tone of the writing and from the emphasis throughout the book on specific and practical suggestions for trimming advertising and promotional waste. I examine such waste in detail, with the intention of providing advertisers and agencies with some ideas for what to do about it. If even a few of my proposals are followed, I believe that there will be a benefit not only to the advertisers concerned, but also to society as a whole.

Business firms, professional organizations, and universities have never expressed interest in attacking this waste at a "macro" level, although business enterprises have obviously been concerned with improving the productivity of their own advertising and promotions, particularly during periods of profit squeeze. Journalists, politicians, and academics with dirigiste inclinations have always tended to treat advertising and promotional waste in rather a fuzzy way and have lumped it together with the supposedly moral iniquities of persuasive communication.[1]

The most important and obvious waste comes from advertisements and promotions that do not yield an economic return. This is theoretically quantifiable, but there are huge measurement problems, particularly in advertising. (The difficulty of measurement is a theme that will reappear constantly in this book.) The worst of these problems stems from the likelihood that much of the waste is concealed below the surface. An advertised product or service may have stable sales and be profitable at a given level of advertising and promotional expenditure; yet it is conceivable that its sales could be maintained and its profit increased with a lower level of advertising and promotion. But we cannot know for sure until we experiment with downweighting, and most manufacturers and advertising agencies are reluctant to countenance such experiments. They are certainly rare in the real world.

An uneconomic* (greater-than-optimal or less-than-optimal) level of expenditure is not the exclusive source of advertising and promotional waste. There is a subtler—and possibly even more important—cause that will be examined extensively in this book. This concerns the level of resources applied to writing and producing advertisements. There is of course a cost in such production, a cost that is both tangible (that is, dollar-related) and intangible (that is, effort- and stress-related). Waste is prevalent here, either from the development of campaign ideas that are weak or off-strategy, or from the use of an inadequate strategy in the first place. However, the money value of the resulting waste (assuming that we could quantify the intangible cost) is at first glance smaller than the waste from uneconomic campaign exposure. But this is by no means the whole story. There can be waste from an underinvestment as well as from a careless investment of resources.

---

*The word *economic* has a technical meaning. In this context it refers to any investment—irrespective of size—that yields a net return. The word *economical* would refer to a sparing use of investment funds. An economic investment is not necessarily an economical one.

If we devote too little resource to campaign development—too little imagination and mental commitment as well as insufficient production and research investment—in a shortsighted wish to *reduce* waste, we can cast a serious blight on the effectiveness of our media budgets, which are where the major quantities of advertising money are spent. On the other hand, increased investment in superior talent and production can generate campaigns of improved selling ability, and these have an extended and magnified effect because media budgets are then made to work harder. A piece of arithmetic will illustrate this point.

Let us assume that a brand has an advertising media budget of $10 million and a budget of $1 million to pay for writing and physically producing a campaign. If Campaign B is 10 percent more efficient than Campaign A in selling ability, then the true value of Campaign B's media budget is $11 million, as compared to Campaign A's $10 million. It therefore makes perfectly good economic sense to *increase* the production budget as long as the resultant campaign has selling ability superior to the earlier alternative. In our example, we could increase the production allocation up to double the original amount before we reach break-even.

This is of course an entirely hypothetical illustration, but the point I am making is real enough. There is a significant economic advantage in improving the efficiency of advertising development, that is, of finding a more reliable—even if more expensive—method of writing and producing effective advertisements. Paradoxically this improvement might require *greater* cost and *increased* waste in the production stage. But the end result will be increased efficiency—reduced waste—at the much more expensive stage of campaign exposure. And it is important to remember that the payoff will have not only a micro- but also a macroeffect.

Readers will be perfectly well aware that manufacturers would be interested in reducing waste only insofar as the improvements will benefit their own brands. Readers with a background in economic theory will, however, also know that the process by which businesspeople follow their individual self-interest is precisely the way in which general social welfare is eventually boosted, through the operation (to use Adam Smith's still-elegant metaphor) of an "invisible hand."

An important characteristic of advertising is that only a small proportion of it "works." Although advertising people are temperamentally too optimistic to think much about the amount of advertising exposure that is effectively lost, it is a fact that in every advertising campaign in every medium, the vast majority of individual advertisement exposures are ineffective. They either are unnoticed by consumers or achieve no behavioral or affective or even cognitive reaction from them. From everything we know about advertising and its results, it is quite unrealistic to expect anything radically different. Campaigns *can* nevertheless be effective and can yield a measurable economic return by influencing a small—sometimes even a tiny—proportion of the viewers and readers whom they address. I am very interested in ways of marginally increasing this small proportion. But I am not searching for the philosophers' stone. This book offers no proposal for a quantum improvement in how the advertising enterprise is operated. However, as already mentioned, I am very much concerned with edging it forward in modest ways, by making detailed suggestions for how to trim specific types of waste. As I hope will be obvious as this argument develops, the waste in advertising is so huge, pervasive, and endemic that even small ways of reducing this waste can yield a large dollar dividend.

Advertising plays two roles in society. First, it plays an economic role by influencing the sales of at least some individual manufacturers. Sales make a multiplier effect by generating incomes and total demand within the economy, and insofar as advertising does influence sales, it affects to at least a moderate extent the overall level of economic activity. It has this macroinfluence on the economy as a result of the sum of individual microeffects—those stemming from the productivity and growth of individual firms. Readers should be warned that the macroeffect of advertising is a controversial subject, which is given a more detailed discussion in appendix A.

In addition, advertising lubricates the competitive system by telling consumers about the differences between competing brands. Such differences are real, and they are both functional and nonfunctional. There is also controversy about the influence of advertising on competition, and this matter is also reviewed further in appendix A.

It would be difficult to visualize capitalism operating without advertising. Yet this book will argue the possibility that the economic advantages of advertising could be provided to their present degree but with greater economy of force if rather less money were to be spent on it. However, it is absolutely necessary for this smaller amount of money to be deployed more efficiently than many advertising budgets are now used. Note the assumption, which is made throughout this book, that increased productivity and reduced expenditure may go hand in hand.

Advertising's second role is incidental and might almost be described as serendipitous. Advertising provides a substantial subsidy to the media, a subsidy that is overwhelmingly, although not completely, benevolent in its social effects. The ability of the media to "inform, educate, and entertain" (to use Lord Reith's famous words, which were a guiding precept at the BBC) becomes possible in the United States because of advertising dollars. How well the media succeed in carrying out these admirable tasks is a different question altogether, although the media's effectiveness is limited more by their own problems than by advertisers' willingness to invest the money. Advertisers, of course, invest in advertising to boost their own sales, but their expenditure has the side benefit of financing the media, thereby making a transfer payment to all members of society as users of television, radio, newspapers, and magazines.

All advertisements, both the efficient and the inefficient varieties, make their contribution to the media. However, this book argues that the media subsidy is an insufficient reason on its own for us to turn our backs on the waste associated with advertising.

Reducing waste is in all circumstances socially desirable. Readers may, however, find it difficult to visualize precisely how any such reduction can benefit society as a whole. How will it happen that the resources that are freed by reduced waste will be redeployed in socially beneficial ways?

To understand the process, it is helpful to examine some economic changes that have taken place in the advertising field and what effects these have had. Here are three examples.

The first is the large increase in the volume of television advertising in the United States in the 1950s and 1960s. This contributed directly to a boost in the total amount of the resources devoted to advertising in that period (measured by advertising's share of the gross national product) and also to the decline of many newspapers and general-interest magazines, as well as to the devastation of radio as an advertising medium. The second example is the continuous reduction in the number of major American advertisers paying their agencies the traditional 15 percent commission during the 1980s. The third example, which coincided in time with the second but was entirely independent of it, is the continuous increase in the proportion of the combined total of advertising and promotional budgets that was spent on promotions "below the line." The second and third factors led to a significant pressure on agency profits, to an increase in unemployment in advertising agencies, and, indirectly, to the mergers between agencies that were such a prominent feature of advertising (and other businesses) in the 1980s.

These changes and their effects all seem to have operated in a similar way. They all started very small, but they grew continuously and incrementally, and with increasing momentum. (Mathematically even a uniform percentage increase means an accelerating effect when measured in absolute terms.) Results followed cause, like the ripples from pebbles dropped in a pool.

I believe that the effect of any reduction of waste in advertising and promotions will be felt in a similar way: it will start small but will grow continuously and at an accelerating rate. If investments "above" and "below the line" are increased in efficiency, manufacturers may be persuaded to trim them in quantity, which will have an immediate effect on manufacturers' costs. These will go down slightly, and profit will be increased. Remember that the relationship between costs and profit is geared, a small relative reduction in costs having a large relative effect on profit. More funds from undistributed and distributed profit will be available for investment, and for charity (a not unimportant beneficiary of business profit in the United States). Manufacturers and stockholders will also pay more in federal and state taxes.

Competition between manufacturers will almost certainly mean that some of the extra profit will be passed to the consumer in the form of lower prices, an effect that will contribute directly to social welfare.

Any reduction in advertising will be a blow to the media. This may not however be as serious as it appears. The more advertising-efficient media will continue to increase their advertising rates (thus taking for themselves a small share of manufacturers' increased profit). The more popular print media and cable television stations (which are substantially funded by the public) will continue to make a marginal increase in their prices to their customers, thus taking for themselves a small share of the benefit that the public will have received from manufacturers. The process of waste reduction will therefore add impetus to desirable media changes, by encouraging the success of the more efficient and popular media at the expense of the less efficient and less popular ones.

The role of advertising vis-à-vis the media is interesting and important. However, as I have already argued in this chapter, this role is secondary, the primary one being in influencing manufacturers' sales. This is accordingly the aspect of advertising and promotions that will be emphasized most in this book. The main thrust of the argument will be directed to manufacturers' marketing operations, and it will explore ways of reducing waste in these. This does not mean boosting sales at any price; it means increasing *profitable* sales and also increasing the profit yield at existing sales levels.

I shall now be specific and outline five types of marketing-related waste. These will be described in their approximately ascending order of importance. The fourth and fifth are very important indeed.

Five Species of Waste

Direct Response

The Economist carried the following news story about the British health care industry early in 1990:

> Catch them young. The Department of Health launched a campaign to attract 13-year-old girls into nursing. Strip cartoons in teen magazines will try to dispel the job's unglamorous image. The last advertising spree cost £4 million and netted 112 recruits.[2]

If we make a simple calculation using the last two figures, we can compute the very remarkable sum of £35,700 ($57,000) which the British government spent, in advertising costs alone, to recruit each of the 112 nurses brought in during the "last advertising spree." There is no conceivable way for this expenditure to have been economic, and it exemplifies in rather a dramatic way advertising's potential for waste. An unusual and noteworthy feature of this case is that these nurses were recruited by a direct response campaign, the only type of advertising whose results are precisely measurable. It is extraordinary that this least wasteful type of advertising should have been used with such profligacy. In normal circumstances the campaign would have been pretested in the marketplace and never exposed nationally.

I can only imagine that the campaign ran and the final cost was swallowed because the organization footing the bill was the British government (or, more precisely, the British taxpayer). Government departments have softer financial disciplines and less advertising expertise then private businesses have, and these factors together account for a situation in which the annual salary cost for at least two nurses was paid in the cost of advertising to recruit one.

This first type of waste advertising is therefore unproductive direct response. The example of the nurses is not generalizable and is probably untypical, for the reason just given: Test runs in the market enable the most experienced and profit-driven operators, at least, to locate and cancel unproductive advertisements before vast sums are spent on their exposure. But even in test runs, there is a significant cost in talent, labor, and out-of-pocket expense in writing and production and at least a minimal cost in exposing the advertisements in test media. The waste involved in the process is therefore too large to be ignored. On the other hand, the case of the nurses has an unambiguous price tag on it, and in the rather rare circumstances of unproductive direct response, this case provides a real and dramatic instance of the waste of resources.

Global Advertising

The second source of waste in advertising comes from the unsuccessful use of global campaigns. This is a much discussed category of advertising that has also attracted an extensive (and rather mediocre) literature. Let me make three relatively uncontroversial points about this topical but much misunderstood subject:

1. The decision to run global campaigns is governed by cost and management considerations rather than by the requirements of the countries where the campaigns will be exposed. Such campaigns are essentially producer-driven rather than consumer-induced. This is not often a formula for marketplace success.

2. There has indeed been a high failure rate, which none of the published literature on the subject has attempted to quantify. My

own experience in the field (fifteen years and twenty product categories) suggests that between one half and two thirds of global campaigns are failures according to client and agency judgments of sales success. The global campaigns are usually derived from U.S. stereotypes and are exposed in overseas markets, sometimes quite large ones. The waste involved in the failures is consequently substantial in many cases.

3. The use of unadapted global campaigns was prevalent in the 1970s among U.S. manufacturers marketing their brands in overseas territories. One piece of research shows that in 1976, as many as 70 percent of a sample of manufacturers ran "fully standardized" campaigns. By 1987, this proportion had come down to 10 percent, but an additional 55 percent of all such manufacturers were now adapting their advertising, sometimes with considerable freedom, to accommodate local inputs.[3] The reduction in the use of uniform campaigns is good presumptive evidence of failure, and the cost is obviously large, in terms both of the money spent and of the management time devoted to grappling with the problems.

The low success rate should not be taken as a comprehensive condemnation of global campaigns, many of which have been extremely successful. But the ready possibility of disaster should provide a constant and powerful inducement to test and evaluate such campaigns objectively.

New Product Introductions

The third major source of waste is the result of new product failure. This is an especially important factor in major countries like the United States, where there is continuous marketing innovation. New product development is a hazardous but high-priority activity for all major consumer goods companies. They are driven into it for defensive reasons (for example, a fear that competitors will steal a march on them) as much as for offensive ones (for example, the need to grow.) The failure rate of new products has always been high, and the actual figure depends on the criteria selected for success and failure. Estimates have put the rate as high as 90 percent or more of all new ventures.[4]

The waste incurred here involves both the cash cost of developing and exposing the unsuccessful advertising and promotional campaigns and, even more important, the value of the talent and energy of the many skilled and motivated people who worked on the projects. Advertising is sometimes the direct cause of the trouble, and advertising, at all events, cannot be strong enough to compensate for weaknesses in other parts of the marketing mix.

Although the fundamental cause of the waste in new product launches is inefficient planning procedures in developing these products, the most *immediate* problem is a failure of market research to flag the inadequacy before large sums are spent on exposure in the marketplace in a test area (and occasionally even on a wider scale). The rate of failure of new brands is a constant warning against complacency in the market research industry.

Overexpenditure on Ongoing Brands

The fourth substantial source of waste is uneconomic increases in advertising pressure for ongoing brands. *Uneconomic* means that, although there may be marginally more profit because of the increased sales generated by the extra advertising, this profit works out to be less than the cost of the advertising increase. When this happens, it is mostly because of low advertising elasticity, that is, low sales response to increases in advertising pressure. A recent estimate made by Magid M. Abraham and Leonard M. Lodish, based on increased advertising pressure in 360 split-cable television tests, shows that only about half of these produced any sales response at all, let alone any profitable sales increases.[5] More than a decade ago, a British analyst claimed that 95 percent of pressure tests had failed, judged by the criterion of increased profitability.[6]

Waste applies not only to advertising increases; it can also apply to ongoing levels of advertisers' expenditure. Many successful brands may well be overadvertised at least marginally, which means that profitable savings can be made by trimming the pressure. Such brands, which may have stable sales, an established consumer franchise, and an accepted historical level of advertising and promotional support, could well have low advertising elasticity. Furthermore, larger brands generally benefit from advertising-related scale economies, which enable them to be supported at a lower advertising-to-sales ratio than small brands in the same market.[7]

These factors make it possible to reduce by a small amount the advertising expenditures behind large and established brands. And although such reductions may represent low percentages, they can add up to large dollar sums. At the same time, the reductions may be accompanied by little or no drop in sales. The effect on sales is an *essential qualification,* because a brand's aggregate sales volume makes an important contribution to a manufacturer's general overhead. It is often acceptable—indeed desirable—to downweight advertising expenditure as long as there is not too large a resulting sales loss.[8] It is a different thing altogether—and almost invariably unacceptable—to reduce advertising if this reduction causes a major decrease in sales, even when the profit on the sales sacrificed can be shown to be less than the value of the advertising saving.

Promotions

The fifth cause of waste concerns trade and consumer promotions. Promotions (below the line) are considered by most manufacturers a separate category from advertising (above the line), but the two are closely related and are intended to complement one another. Trade promotions operate by pushing merchandise into the retail pipeline. Consumer promotions partly push goods into the pipeline (by encouraging the retail trade to display them) and partly pull the goods through it. Advertising mainly operates as a pulling force. Manufacturers normally budget advertising and promotions jointly, so that there is a direct trade-off between the two: more advertising means less promotion and vice versa.

In terms of their crude ability to shift merchandise, promotions are often very effective. It is moreover not difficult to quantify the immediate increases in sales volume that stem from them, although the long-term sales effects are more difficult to predict. Promotions are therefore attractive to manufacturers, which (as I shall shortly illustrate) spend below the line the larger share of their combined advertising and promotional budgets.

Calculating the profitability of promotions is, however, a complicated, and generally very discouraging, task. Promotions are, almost without exception, expensive, since there is no saving in direct costs for promoted merchandise, and the deflation of the net sales value caused by the (generally very significant) cost of the promotion must be paid for from the brand's contribution to overhead. The result is that a promotion, in order to pay its way and meet the shortfall in contribution, is required to generate a larger sales uplift than very many promotions succeed in doing. Thus a substantial proportion of promotions are unprofitable. The large and increasing sums of money spent on them now account for 66 percent of manufacturers' combined advertising and promotional budgets, a topic to be discussed in chapter 2. The dollar value of this 66 percent represents a historically record waste of resources, which can be explained only by manufacturers' inability to calculate the extent of this waste—or else by their indifference to their profits as long as their sales targets are reached.[9]

Although the degree of waste in advertising and promotions is not in serious dispute, much of it (as I have already suggested) is concealed. We cannot, for instance, find out whether manufacturers are over advertising until some of them are persuaded to experiment with cutting back their expenditure and to measure whether they do in fact suffer any sales loss. Because so much is below the surface, it is impossible to quantify accurately the aggregate extent of the waste in advertising and promotions; and perhaps it is not very important to spend time attempting this task. It is more important to try to think of ways of trimming waste. The guess made almost a century ago by two experienced advertisers, Lord Leverhulme and John Wanamaker, that "half my advertising is wasted and the trouble is I don't know which half" still receives wide currency and seems to receive the tacit approval of many present-day practitioners and marketing analysts.

The thing that strikes me forcibly about the Leverhulme/Wanamaker bon mot is not so much the large size of the estimated waste; my guess, and I am not alone in it, is that an estimated 50 percent failure rate is actually short of the mark.[10] I am more surprised that the advertising industry, for all its sophistication, does not appear to have improved either its success rate or its state of knowledge over the course of a hundred years of generally increasing and, in recent decades, massive advertising expenditure.

Three Causes

This book is concerned more with scaling waste down—improving matters in the future—than with making a detailed analysis of the past. Nevertheless, it is useful to look at the main causes of the present situation in the hope that these causes will provide pointers to corrective action, which are the concern of the rest of this book. There is a considerable number of contributory causes, but three strike me as being of salient importance.

Ignorance

The most important of these causes is deficiencies in our knowledge of how advertising works. It is not that we know nothing; indeed we understand a number of things about advertising with fair certainty. Our knowledge is nevertheless deficient in three ways. The first of these is the sheer amount of terra incognita. On the positive side, many analysts are optimistic enough to believe that areas of this ground will gradually be explored over the course of the next few decades; new quantities of single-source data will certainly make the job easier. But there is a long way to go.

The second source of ignorance, and one of the tragedies of our knowledge of advertising, is the amount we have forgotten. (In chapter 10, I call this *Type E knowledge.*) All agencies with a significant history should have accumulated a stockpile of things they have learned with reasonable precision. With virtually no exceptions, agencies have neglected to do this. This is a failing of their corporate culture, and it means that they are constantly forced to reinvent the wheel—at enormous expense.[11]

The third deficiency—and probably the most serious of all—concerns another category of knowledge, the actively misleading variety. A significant amount of what we think we know about advertising is almost certainly wrong. In chapter 10, this is entitled *Type D knowledge,* and it receives much attention there. The reason that it represents a greater problem than the mere unknown is that it is an especially difficult task to persuade the advertising industry to unlearn some of its most cherished received wisdom.

Attitudes

The second cause of waste is a combination of two factors, both essentially nonrational. One is the pressure of competition between manufacturing companies and between advertising agencies. Both types of organization are oligopolies, and individual oligopolists are subject to great psychological strain stemming from the activities of their competitors (and oligopolists' continual consciousness of these activities). There is the feeling that unless manufacturers and agencies keep active, they will fall behind in the race. Oligopolistic competition does not always lead to rational decisions or to the greatest economy of force. Indeed such competition works in general to cause advertising and promotional investments to be pushed up, mainly for fear of the consequences of their not being pushed up: falling behind in the competitive race. The second factor, which works in parallel with competitive fear, is the natural buoyancy, aggressiveness, and optimism of many marketing executives in advertiser companies (many of whom have a selling background and orientation), as well as a similarly optimistic outlook on the part of virtually all advertising agency people. The latter have an emotional commitment to the advertising enterprise and tend to be bullish about the likely effects of increases in advertising expenditures, and to be defensive about any threats to cut them back.

The points are illustrated in the following quotations, which give a good enough picture of an attitude that is common if not quite pervasive in the advertising industry. In each of these examples, rationality has given way to a zestful and contagious enthusiasm. While this quality can contribute to marketplace success, it is not—in default of other qualities—sufficient to ensure success on a regular basis.

> A western Massachusetts company, Adell Chemical, developed a classic marketing triumph thanks to the go-for-broke method. . . . Manufacturers of an all-purpose liquid cleaner called Lestoil, the company had never exceeded $100,000 in sales in any of the previous twenty years of its business life. Yet, after pouring every available dollar into TV commercials in Northeastern markets—a true last-stand effort—Adell's sales skyrocketed to $100,000 per day or $36,000,000 per year.[12]

> During the course of a single year, the average human mind is exposed to some 200,000 advertising messages. . . . This is why a company like Procter and Gamble is such a formidable competitor. When it bets on a new product, it will slide $20 million on the table, look around at the competition, and say, "Your bet". . . . With a given number of dollars, it's better to overspend [sic] in one city than to underspend in several cities.[13]

"How much will it cost us to clobber 30 markets for 60 days? How much? Two million? Three million? Five million? You tell me. Don't sweat the budget, open it up. Get something good and we'll come up with the money. This is a ten-million-car market, let's go get it. GM is weak. We'll never have a better opportunity than right now. It will take added advertising . . . and a lot of other things . . . but with a rising penetration in a rising market . . . now is the time to get more money."

I don't know of an agency that wouldn't kill for a challenge like that.[14]

Budget setting in many client organizations is based on a "selling pitch" by the brand management and the advertising agency, with the result that budgets are set in response to executives' persuasive ability rather than as a reflection of the profit performance of previous advertising and promotions. The attempt to maximize a brand's profit by optimizing above- and below-the-line investments is still a startlingly uncommon procedure.

The Agency Commission System

The third cause of budgetary inflation is the agency commission system, which presupposes that an agency can generally increase its income and profit only by persuading its clients to spend more money on media advertising.

The influence of the commission system in pushing up media expenditure is a background force emphasizing the natural optimism of agencies, which (as I have already argued) always tend to anticipate a large sales effect once advertising passes through a certain expenditure barrier. The commission system does, however, work in the interest of large agencies, and it provided considerable scale economies in the 1960s and 1970s. Advertisers certainly became aware of the large profits to agencies that resulted, mainly because a number of agencies had become public companies at that time.

Clients therefore rapidly moved away from the commission system—or rather from the traditional 15 percent level. The advertising industry in the United States has not shifted to a fee system based on agency compensation for salaries and other expenditures, which many people, myself included, consider greatly more logical than commission, and which is, besides, a more efficient way of protecting agencies' incomes in a time of advertising stagnation. The industry has moved instead to a continuation of commission, but on a reduced percentage (or percentages which decline as appropriations increase).[15]

This is about the worst system possible. It removes the agencies' incentive to produce work of superior effectiveness and, at the same time, fails to provide a safety net to protect them from the shortfalls in their clients' billings that often take place in the last quarter of the year. It also does not reduce agencies' bullishness and enthusiasm for increasing advertising expenditure, and it is therefore unlikely to reduce waste to any serious degree.

The difficulties in the way of tackling problems like these should not be minimized; as I have already argued, all we can hope for is piecemeal, although practical improvements. The larger number of recommendations in this book relates to ways of improving the efficiency with which we write and prepare campaigns. The operational objective is to find more reliable procedures for writing and preparing *effective* campaigns. These (as I have also explained) have a magnified importance because they are a method of making media budgets work harder. I devote less space, confined in the main to chapter 10, to the fundamental problem of extending the frontiers of our knowledge. The modest scale of this discussion is not meant to imply that this matter is in any way unimportant.

The Structure of the Book

Chapters 1 and 2 are devoted to setting the scene. Chapter 1 describes the meaning of waste in the context of this book. Chapter 2 describes four secular trends which are affecting, and which will continue to affect, the ways in which advertising and promotions are conducted. In particular, these trends will make it even more important in the future than in the past to reduce the waste that has been traditionally associated with these activities.

Although each of the remaining chapters is complete and free-standing, they are grouped to deal with specific categories of waste.

Each chapter recommends methods by which small improvements can be made.

Chapters 3 and 4 deal with two rather general and philosophical matters concerning how advertising operates. Chapter 3 debates whether advertising is a strong or a weak force. It is argued that if we regard advertising as a weak force in many circumstances, this judgment will contribute to greater economy of force—a more efficient use of resources—than in the present situation, in which we treat advertising virtually universally as a powerful force. Chapter 4 discusses the culture of an advertising agency. The chapter makes the point that any agency needs a strong culture in order to produce effective work reasonably consistently, although an agency with a weak culture can produce work of erratic brilliance. However, if the culture is too strong, this strength can be counterproductive because it can inhibit thinking which strays outside the established boundaries (some of which may be tacit rather than explicit).

Chapters 5 and 6 are devoted to budgeting and are therefore directly concerned with the economic deployment of resources. Chapter 5 describes the inefficiency of most methods of arriving at above-the-line budgets and makes suggestions for improvements. Chapter 6 gives guidelines on how to quantify the sales and profit payoff of below-the-line and above-the-line activities.

Chapters 7, 8, and 9 are devoted to suggestions for improving the methods of planning advertisements, based on the most advanced professional practice. Chapter 7 deals with the definition of target groups. Chapter 8 discusses other aspects of advertising strategy. Chapter 9 illustrates the most efficient technique of campaign development: encouraging a fertile variety and generating a wide range of creative alternatives and using qualitative research to filter them.

Chapter 10 comprises an abbreviated inventory of the state of our knowledge about advertising and a classification of the most important individual items of knowledge, judged by their reliability. There are specific proposals for closing some of the gaps: finding the answers to some of the more important things we do not know about how advertising and promotions work and how effectiveness should be judged.

Every chapter in this book contains a summary of its argument. Chapter 11 is devoted to a synthesis of these summaries—a collection of fifty specific recommendations for reducing the waste in advertising and promotions.

There are two appendixes at the end of the book. Appendix A is a review of the multiple, varied, contradictory (and sometimes surprising) ways in which advertising influences economic life; an attempt is made to balance these factors and to draw general conclusions about advertising's micro- and macroeffects. This appendix is not a part of the main argument of the book, but the economic effects of advertising are touched on in many of the chapters, and I thought it useful to have a collecting point for the various issues raised. Appendix B is the work of the well-known British politician Enoch Powell. In it, he contends that advertising performs best and exercises its most beneficial role in society when it operates robustly. He also argues that the advertising industry is ill advised to be defensive in its response to public criticism.

The book is focused throughout on advertising and promotional practice in the United States and other sophisticated markets. This does not mean that its lessons are irrelevant to less developed countries. Indeed, where resources are scarcest, the need is the most pressing to use them with the greatest efficiency possible.

Summary

1. This book is concerned with measures to reduce waste by improving the efficiency of professional practice in the advertising and promotional fields. The book is meant to be forward-looking, practical, and constructive, but not overambitious. All it aims to do is to encourage large numbers of small, specific improvements.

2. The waste discussed in the book is that resulting, first, from uneconomically high exposure levels for campaigns and, second, from inefficient planning procedures for campaign development, which reduce the effective value of media budgets.

3. The main sources of waste (in progressive order of importance) are

    a. inefficient use of direct response;

    b. unsuccessful use of global advertising;

    c. failed new product ventures;

    d. uneconomical increases in advertising pressure and excessive ongoing volumes of advertising for established and stable brands;

e. unprofitable promotions.

4. The main causes of the waste are

a. the poor state of our knowledge of advertising and promotions: that is, how they operate and what specific results are generated by them;

b. innate optimism and aggressiveness on the part of clients and agencies;

c. the agency commission system.

5. The rest of the book is devoted to specific suggestions about how waste can be reduced. These are grouped under four headings and are dealt with as follows:

Chapters 3 and 4 discuss philosophical matters relating to how advertising operates.

Chapters 5 and 6 are concerned with budgeting and the evaluation of the payoff of advertising and promotions.

Chapters 7, 8, and 9 describe the best operational procedures for campaign development.

Chapter 10 is an inventory of the state of advertising knowledge.

At the end of the book is a chapter (chapter 11) devoted to synthesizing the main lessons from the earlier chapters. There are also two appendixes.

2

Trends

P. & G. is strapped with the problem of its gargantuan size, so that a mere average 3% growth rate is tough for it to sustain. Its efforts to grow have been directed toward mature and increasingly competitive market segments.[1]

Alice Beebe Longley, stock analyst

Market maturity and intense and increasing competition are themes that will be reiterated in this book. They are familiar and topical subjects in the professional and academic literature, although they do not have quite the same vogue as the extremely fashionable concepts of entrepreneurship and globalization. Maturity and high competition may be talked about, but they are not much examined empirically. Therefore this chapter will be devoted substantially to facts about them, and about trends that stem from market maturity in particular.

What *maturity* means is a slowing in aggregate sales growth, something that happens eventually in all product categories. One after another, product categories stabilize in total volume, except for an annual increase of 1 or 2 percent caused mainly by the rise in population. This is the situation today in an advanced and sophisticated country like the United States in all except a minority of product fields. Among all advertised product categories, packaged goods and durables constitute the majority, and services and high-tech represent the minority. But category growth is more common—or rather it is less uncommon—in the latter than in the former. Procter & Gamble is one of the two preeminent American manufacturers of packaged goods. There is no doubt at all about the difficulties this company is finding in maintaining in the United States its traditional goal of an annual sales growth of 7 percent in real terms.[2] Indeed, during recent years, the generally satisfactory overall increase in the company's sales has been mainly due to its overseas operations. Its American sales were actually down in 1988 and (after a good year in 1989) rose only 2 percent in 1990.[3]

The stagnation in the total size of markets is the most important of four trends that will be described and discussed in this chapter. Each of the four listed below, will be treated in a separate section:

1. market maturity
2. market fragmentation
3. stagnation in advertising expenditures
4. growth in promotions

These are all interconnected. Maturity is, however, the most dominating of the four trends and is the prime mover driving the other three. Indeed, these might never have developed in their present strength during the past decade or so if it had not been for the overarching influence of market stagnation on the attitudes and behavior of decision makers in manufacturing companies.

First Trend: Market Maturity

When individual markets stop increasing, they do so as a result of a saturation in consumer consumption. The situation is generally irreversible; it is very rare indeed for stagnant markets to resume the growth of earlier periods except in very unusual circumstances (for example, fiscal changes, like a major reduction in sales tax, which may cause new growth in the demand for consumer durables by encouraging consumers to replace old but still serviceable equipment).

As incomes increase and consumer consumption does not, the result is that the public tends to save an increasing proportion of its income. This tendency was detected by Keynes in the 1930s and formed an important part of his analysis of the secular causes of unemployment.[4] What economists term the increasing marginal propensity to save is responsible for a gradual reduction in effective demand, because not all saving is converted into productive investment; this circumstance, in turn, calls for public investment to restore demand to the level needed to maintain full employment.

Advertising has little effect on aggregate consumption levels. This is a topic that has received some study, although it has not been analyzed as fully as it deserves to be. There is no evidence that advertising has a widespread "macro" effect, and students of the field tend to believe that other forces, in particular "underlying social and environmental conditions,"[5] are more responsible than advertising for any overall increases in demand. Moreover, advertising cutbacks (for example, the reduction in cigarette advertising during the 1970s) do little to reduce total market demand. (Macroeffects are studied in more detail in appendix A, together with other economic issues connected with advertising.)

A factor that makes it especially difficult for large individual companies to grow is the enormous size that many of them have reached already. As we can infer from the quotation that prefaces this chapter, a steady percentage increase in sales, no matter how small, becomes increasingly difficult for big firms to achieve. There is a mathematical reason. The growth in absolute terms that is called for by a steady annual percentage increase is something that becomes progressively, and eventually insupportably, larger than the increase of the year before. It is one thing to sell ten thousand extra units; it is another thing altogether to sell an extra ten million!

Another point relating to market stagnation is that changes in consumer tastes, and the health scares that regularly enliven the lives of the American educated classes, have caused a secular decline in a number of important markets, for example, cigarettes, coffee, dairy products, and hard liquor. Such declines (shown in table 2–1) have to be balanced against the numbers of still-expanding categories when we draw an overall conclusion about market trends.

TABLE 2–1

Changes in Volume Usage of 150 Major Consumer Goods (1989 Compared with 1988, in Percentages)

All categories	100
Strongly growing categories (8% growth or more)	15
Modestly growing categories (3% to 7% growth)	28
Stable categories (1% or 2% growth; no change; or 1% or 2% decline)	34
Modestly declining categories (3% to 7% decline)	13
Strongly declining categories (8% decline or more)	10

Source: Mediamark Research Inc.

The simplest way of evaluating the extent to which markets have flattened is to examine changes in the overall volume of consumption across a sample of market categories. Table 2–1 is derived from data from the large-scale annual surveys carried out by Mediamark Research Inc. (MRI). This table groups 150 different markets according to their growth or decline between 1988 and 1989.[6] In my judgment this two-year comparison is an acceptable basis for an approximation of the numbers of stable and declining markets, because once a market reaches stability, this situation normally becomes permanent, a point to which I shall return when we look at trend data (table 2–3).

Table 2–1 breaks market categories down into five different groups according to their growth rate. The largest of these groups (34 percent) comprises "no growth" categories. Of the remaining 66 percent, there are more growing markets than declining ones. However, the figures are unweighted, and this causes some distortion, since many of the expanding market categories are of relatively limited importance measured in terms of average consumer expenditure on them. This point is illustrated by table 2–2, which lists the twenty-two categories that make up the strongest growing group in table 2–1 (accounting for 15 percent of the total.)

At least half the categories in table 2–2 are relatively unimportant. In some cases they are subsegments of larger categories, and the remainder of the products within each of these larger categories in growing much less strongly. For instance, the hot breakfast cereal category (up 24 percent) was less than a quarter the size of the cold breakfast cereal category (which grew by only 4 percent); and the noncola diet soft drinks category (up 21 percent) had less than half the sales volume of regular noncola soft drinks (which also grew by only 4 percent). The exploitation of growing subsegments is in fact one of the most prevalent and successful responses by manufacturers to the lack of overall market growth. (This is a point that will shortly be examined in more detail.)

Table 2–2 also includes two seemingly large categories of consumer durables: personal computers and videocassette recorders. These are infrequent purchases, besides being markets that fall well short of 100 percent in household penetration. Thus they account for a relatively small quantity of average household expenditure, despite the likelihood that they both have good growth potential.

TABLE 2–2

Strongly Growing Categories of Consumer Goods,
(1989 Compared with 1988, in Percentages)

Category	Increase in Volume Usage
Dental rinse	75
Bottled water and seltzer	29
Personal computers	27
Hot breakfast cereals	24
Noncola diet soft drinks	21
Frozen fish and seafood	17
Mints	17
Eyewash and drops	16
Individual regular-sized candy	14
Packaged instant potatoes	14
Frozen desserts	13
Spaghetti sauce	11
Videocassette recorders	11
Packages of miniature candy	10
Artificial sweeteners	9
Canned dogfood	9
Hair-conditioning treatments	9
Regular tea	9
Tampons	9
Hair conditioners	8
Hair mousse	8
Hand and body cream/lotion/oil	8

Source: Mediamark Research Inc.

Because of the factors discussed in the last paragraph, table 2–1 overstates the overall amount of growth in markets. My own estimate is that only about 10 percent of all household expenditure is currently made in categories which are still showing strong increases. And this 10 percent could well become even less in the future.

It is interesting to isolate when most markets flattened. This happened in the United States in the 1970s and was a factor that added to the woes of businesspeople during that unhappy decade. The information in table 2–3 on the growth in the numbers of mature markets is based on trends in fifty major consumer goods categories. The data, published by the U.S. government, are expressed in the value of annual output of each market, and I have recomputed these figures to correct for inflation.[7] The data on which table 2–3 was based confirm that once a market reaches a plateau, it stays there; therefore we can rely reasonably well on the one-year shifts examined in table 2–1. Incidentally, readers will note that the proportion of growing markets in 1982 accords with the 1989 estimate in table 2–1.

The facts in tables 2–1, 2–2, and 2–3 carry important lessons for manufacturers and advertising agencies.

The first lesson is that the plateauing of markets is obviously now making it harder for manufacturers to grow—in particular, to increase their profits—than during the happier days when it was possible to ride increases in total market sales. Increasing profits are a virtual requirement for publicly held companies. In lieu of "natural," market-driven sales and profit increases, manufacturers have been forced to adopt a number of tough strategies, all of which have been plentifully evident during the past decade and more. The most obvious are

1. Searching for growing sectors within static total markets. Manufacturers, because of their frustration by the failure to find total category growth, have been relentless in ferreting

TABLE 2–3

When Consumer Goods Markets Flattened
(50 Major Categories)

	1967	1972	1977	1982
Total	50	50	50	50
Growing categories	45	41	25	8
Flattened categories	5	9	25	42

Source: U.S. Department of Commerce, Bureau of the Census: Census of Manufactures, 1986.

out and exploiting small subsegments and have generally used range extensions of existing brand names to create or enter such segments. These range extensions have been the cause of the second trend I shall examine in this chapter: market fragmentation.

2. Pruning costs, for instance "theme" advertising and research and development budgets (with the hidden danger of eating the seed corn). The stagnation in advertising expenditure is the third trend I shall describe.

3. Fighting with increasing fury for market share, using promotions as the main tactical weapon—almost invariably a high-cost and wasteful activity. This is the fourth trend analyzed in this chapter.

4. Exploring untraditional product categories, in which manufacturers' expertise has applied less well than in their original fields of endeavor. Procter & Gamble have discovered the difficulties of entering what for them were new product fields with their marketing of snacks (Pringles) and fruit juice (Citrus Hill).

5. Searching for more business overseas, often using global advertising campaigns, which (as we saw in chapter 1) may be an important cause of waste in their own right.

6. Embarking on mergers, despite their steeply rising cost, in a search of scale economies and diversification. This search has been driven by aggressive financial entrepreneurs, whose personal rewards for their enterprise are considered either dazzling or deplorable (depending on how one judges the economic value of their activities).

A second point about the plateauing of markets is a direct result of the pressure on manufacturers' profit that market stagnation has brought about. This pressure makes it urgently and increasingly important for producers to control and reduce the waste traditionally associated with all their manufacturing and marketing activities. This book argues that the largest individual source of such waste is in advertising and promotions—not only waste from the use of excessive and uneconomical quantities of money, but also waste from inefficiency in all aspects of the planning and deployment of advertising and promotional budgets.

Second Trend: Market Fragmentation

Broadly defined market categories normally show less year-by-year change in sales than many narrowly defined categories. This is another way of saying that broad categories are often made up of subcategories, some of which are stable, some rising, and some falling. In normal circumstances, the rising and falling subcategories balance out. Upward trends are especially evident in subcategories influenced by health and ecological fads, for example, high-fiber breakfast cereals, diet soft drinks, prepared foods that do not contain animal fats or tropical oils, and nonphosphate detergents.

Manufacturers have both led and responded to these trends, and they have done so by creating subsegments and also by opening them out once they have become established. As often as not, manufacturers have followed a strategy of range extension in the belief that the goodwill embodied in a brand name can be carried over into subcategories, both in the brand name's original product field and in different fields.

There are dangers in this approach. The first is that the use of a familiar name can lure a manufacturer into underspending on a new product. There is persuasive Nielsen evidence that this often happens, and that such underspending can prevent the new product from succeeding.[8] Nielsen's general conclusion is that an existing brand name's goodwill has little cash value for a product in a new field. The second, and even more serious, danger of "brand stretching" (as the process has been called) is that it can reflect badly on the original brand name and thus cast a blight on the manufacturer's core business by fragmenting its consumer franchise.[9] The third danger (which is connected to the second) is that advertising investments are often spread over a growing range of products, with the result that the fragmentation of the consumer franchise is exacerbated by a fragmentation of marketing support. The manufacturer, with more lines in his range, also has a more difficult job in selling them all to the retail trade, and the retailer's hand has therefore become perceptibly strengthened.

The process of range extension has nevertheless been a striking feature since the early 1970s, and the most obvious evidence of it is the proliferation of products, often using familiar brand names, on the shelves of every American supermarket. In most such stores, shoppers can now find six separate formulations of Procter & Gamble's Tide laundry detergent; in 1980 there was only one.

Table 2–4 examines 15 nationally distributed brand names which I have selected at random. The table shows the numbers of products on which these names were used at the beginning of the 1980s and the numbers at the end of that decade. The 15 brand names supported a total of 28 different products in the earlier period; by 1989, this figure had more than doubled, to 59.

The brands in table 2–4 are all packaged goods. Brand fragmentation has by no means been confined to such products. In 1982, there were 33 models of General Motors cars (according to MRI data); and in 1989, there were 41. During this period, GM's aggregate market share fell from 45 percent to 35 percent.[10] There were therefore one quarter more models by 1989, and each was of significantly less importance, measured by their average share of the market (0.9 percent in 1989, compared with 1.4 percent in 1982).

TABLE 2–4

Products Sold with Common Brand Names

Brand	Year	Number of Variations	Year	Number of Variations
Blue Bonnet margarine	1980	2	1989	4
Budweiser beer	1982	1	1989	2
Coca-Cola soda	1982	1	1989	7
Folgers ground coffee	1982	2	1989	3
Glad garbage bags	1980	1	1989	2
Hefty garbage bags	1980	1	1989	2
Maxwell House ground coffee	1980	3	1989	6
Michelob beer	1982	2	1989	3
Milk Bone dog biscuits	1980	1	1989	3
Miller Beer	1982	2	1989	3
Nabisco cookies	1980	2	1989	6
Parkay margarine	1980	1	1989	3
Pepsi-Cola soda	1982	3	1989	5
Purina dry dog food	1982	4	1989	6
Seven-Up soda	1982	2	1989	4

Source: Mediamark Research Inc.

The pressures of oligopolistic competition—in particular, oligopolists' constant awareness of and responses to their competitors' behavior in the market—cause new brand concepts to proliferate. One manufacturer's new brand will inevitably be widely and rapidly copied by its competitors, despite what is known about the lower market shares of "me-too" brands. Innovations in a new field normally settle at market shares twice as high as those of imitators.[11]

As might be expected, therefore, the sort of fragmentation of individual brand names demonstrated in table 2–4 carries over to product fields as a whole. At regular intervals since 1979, Sales Area-Marketing Inc. (SAMI) has been reporting the number of brands that have sales of $1 million or more (adjusted to 1979 prices) in a wide range of food and health and beauty-aid categories.[12] The numbers of brands in a sample of the more important of such markets are presented in table 2–5.

Varieties proliferate as widely as brands. There were 89 large and small brands of canned soups in 1989; these were sold in a total of 1,101 flavors or varieties. There were 77 brands of internal analgesics, and these came in a total of 792 varieties.

In the opinion of some analysts, market fragmentation is a response to changing demographics, for example, the growth of older population segments and the increase in the number of single-member families.[13] The response to such changes is called *niche marketing,* and it is often viewed as being caused essentially by the demand side of the market. While there is some truth in this

TABLE 2–5

Numbers of $1-Million Brands (Adjusted to 1979 Prices)

Product Field	Brands in 1979	Brands in 1989
Canned soup	12	17
Ground coffee	33	52
Internal analgesics	18	27
Single-strength juices	17	39
Ready-to-eat cereals	84	150
Toothpaste (foodstores only)	10	31

Source: Sales Area-Marketing Inc.

contention, it has always struck me as odd that earlier demographic shifts (for example, the massive and multifaceted baby boom in the 1960s) did not lead to the sort of fragmentation that is taking place now. I believe that the present situation is more often producer-driven (that is, spurred by manufacturers' need to grow) than consumer-induced. The end result is, of course, the same in both cases: a large number of new brands.

What has been happening is indisputable. Indeed, the well-known analyst William M. Weilbacher, a man not normally given to exaggeration, has called the phenomenon an "explosion of brands."[14] The changes have been so substantial and widespread that they have inevitably had an effect on marketing practice.

One obvious result is that brand fragmentation affects strongly the types of advertising claim used for many brands. There are two broad categories of claim made in advertisements. The first is motivators, that is, signals and arguments concerned with the reasons for consumers to use the product field as a whole (for example, refreshment for soft drinks or convenience for charge cards). The second type of claim is discriminators, that is, signals and arguments which are brand-specific. These may be rationally based (for example, the claim that Slice soda contains fruit juice). Alternatively, and more commonly, they are claims like "Coke, the Real Thing," which are nonrational—or at least impossible to demonstrate objectively—yet are claims whose meaning consumers understand perfectly well. Virtually all advertisements contain both motivators and discriminators, although as a broad generalization we can say that large brands rely most on motivators and small brands rely most on discriminators. A moment's reflection will explain why this should be so: manufacturers of large brands are focused on the market as a whole (in particular, protecting their position in it), and small brands can most easily grow by taking share from other brands.

In the United States, large brands tend to occupy smaller shares than do large brands in other countries. In 1987, an estimated 58 percent of American brands were in the 1 percent to 6 percent range, compared with 38 percent in other countries.[15] They are, in other words, crowded together with many other brands of approximately equal size. (Think of the 150 different brands of ready-to-eat breakfast cereal in table 2–5.) It therefore becomes an important advertising task to distinguish among them. This leads to the use of rational, factual, competitive, discriminating arguments, which is considered a much more *practical* tactic than attempting to differentiate among brands by means of nonrational signals, especially those concerned with psychographics or consumer lifestyles. Some advertisers in the United States attempt nonrational differentiation, but since they are usually quickly imitated by other brands in their subsegments, the result is that confusion soon reigns.

This extreme fragmentation of markets is the fundamental reason why American advertising is much more brand-specific than advertising in other countries, European countries in particular. It is also why American advertising is so widely criticized by European advertising practitioners, who do not appear conscious of the fragmentation of American market shares—and who are consequently also unaware that the style of emotionally loaded motivating advertising that is effective in Europe would be much too soft and generic and lacking in cutting edge to make an impression in the hard, competitive conditions of most American product categories.

One incidental—and not entirely beneficial—side effect of the relatively small brand shares of even important brands in the United States and the resultant extreme type of brand-specific advertising is the popularity of quantitative copy testing with American advertisers. This type of research, which is very unpopular in Europe, is supposed to be more efficient in evaluating rational copy claims than emotionally oriented advertising communication.[16] Opinion within advertising agencies (both in the United States and in Europe) is very divided on the value of quantitative copy testing, even as a measure of rational claims. Clients, however, need it, if for no other reason than to underpin advertising decisions—an essentially organizational problem concerning how decisions move up through a large company's hierarchy.

The increasing fragmentation of markets in the United States will add fresh impetus to the drive to make advertising even more rational and brand-specific. This will not make the task of developing effective campaigns any easier than it is at the moment. Any creative person can provide the reason.

The greatest problem with advertisements that rely on small rational differences between the advertised brand and its competitors is that such advertisements do not encourage the audience's emotional and intellectual engagement; they tend simply not to hold the audience's attention. (It must also be remembered that *substantial* functional differences between brands are now more difficult to achieve than ever before; this is one of the main impediments to the successful launch of new brands.) Turning off the "mental switch" is common enough at all events, since advertising is an activity that involves and engages most members of the public to such a limited degree. Boring advertising makes them even more apathetic. Advertising agencies are going to find it more difficult in the future than in the past to develop appealing personalities for the brands they advertise. A brand personality is, as often as not, based on a motivating argument that a single big brand in a market is able to preempt. By definition, such a strategy is not available for a multiplicity of small brands.

This is not all. Something that will make matters even worse is the fragmentation of advertising budgets, which has already been referred to in this chapter. Smaller brands have fewer scale economies in manufacturing and marketing than have larger brands. And such scale economies apply to advertising (as we shall see in chapter 5). The consequence is that investment of all types in smaller brands tends to be less productive, dollar for dollar, than investment in larger brands.

Perhaps the greatest danger of all—and something that stems directly from the points discussed above—is that advertisers will become increasingly disenchanted with "theme" advertising and will increase even further the amount of money they spend on promotions below the line. This activity enables them to sell a great deal of merchandise, but at a grossly uneconomical cost in many cases. There is little doubt that such a strategy increases waste, sometimes drastically.

The argument in this section provides additional force to the main theme of this book. With fragmented brand franchises, diminished scale economies, and stagnant or reduced budgets above the line, in addition to increasingly flat total markets, minimizing waste in deploying appropriations becomes an urgent problem; there is a renewed need to derive better value than ever before from each dollar spent in advertising and promotional investment.

Third Trend: Stagnation in Advertising Expenditure

In 1990, the most authoritative estimate of advertising expenditure above the line in the United States was the massive sum of $77.3 billion in newspapers, consumer magazines, television, radio, and outdoor media.[17] In round terms, this total represented $300 of advertising for every member of the American population. Advertising is not an industry of trivial importance, and the elimination of even a tiny proportion of the waste in this enormous sum would yield a payout to society in billions of dollars.

Advertising expenditure may be large, but it is not buoyant. Measured as a proportion of the gross national product (GNP)—the normal way of evaluating the overall importance of any economic activity within society—advertising has been sluggish for a number of years. In 1984, advertising's share of the GNP froze at a level below 1.5 percent, the highest mark that it had reached since World War II. The data on advertising's share of the GNP over the forty-three-year span 1948 through 1990 are detailed in table 2–6 and charted in figure 2–1.

The most interesting question raised by these figures is: Where are they pointing to in the future? Numbers do not have a life of their own, and we can make sense of the cyclical trends which seem to be present in figure 2–1 only by examining the economic forces that brought them about. When readers examine Figure 2–1, it will be clear that advertising expenditures stagnated once before. They stuck fast at 1.4 percent of the GNP over the four years 1956–60. They then dropped in 1961 and stuck again at 1.35 percent of the GNP for the five years ending in 1966. They then began a decline, bottoming out at 1.14 percent of the GNP in 1975; then they began climbing again.

The reasons for the stabilization and subsequent decline over the two decades 1956 through 1975 are not immediately apparent. I believe that two forces were at work (with a third force in the background). First, what happened to advertising was a reflection of a gradual but progressive realization by manufacturers that promotional price cutting generates stronger sales growth than do increases in advertising pressure. The second force was that during the period beginning in the mid-1950s, a few of the most sophisticated (and largest) advertisers began to evaluate the sales performance of their

TABLE 2–6

*Main Media Advertising as Percentage
of Gross National Product*

1948	1.15	1973	1.20
1949	1.25	1974	1.17
1950	1.24	1975	1.14
1951	1.18	1976	1.24
1952	1.24	1977	1.26
1953	1.28	1978	1.30
1954	1.34	1979	1.25
1955	1.39	1980	1.23
1956	1.42	1981	1.24
1957	1.39	1982	1.30
1958	1.38	1983	1.39
1959	1.39	1984	1.45
1960	1.41	1985	1.46
1961	1.34	1986	1.48
1962	1.33	1987	1.48
1963	1.32	1988	1.48
1964	1.35	1989	1.44
1965	1.35	1990	1.41
1966	1.35		
1967	1.30		
1968	1.29		
1969	1.30		
1970	1.24		
1971	1.21		
1972	1.24		

Adapted from *Advertising Age* and U.S. Department of Commerce, Bureau of Economic Analysts. Used with permission.

advertising campaigns, and to use their advertising budgets with more efficiency—greater economy of force—than before. They were not so clever at evaluating the *profitability* of their investments above and below the line, and the result was major ill effects which will be examined in chapter 6.[18] Operating in the background was the overall depressing force of marketing stagnation in a small but increasing number of consumer goods fields.

What caused advertising expenditure to start moving upward in

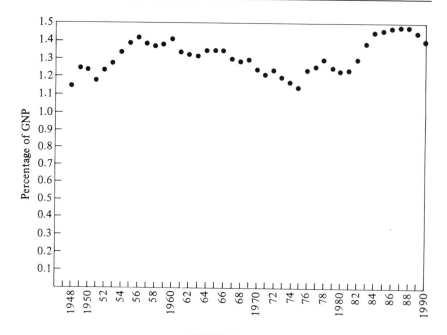

FIGURE 2–1

*Main Media Advertising as Percentage of Gross
National Product*

1976 and to continue on its upward track until 1984? The most obvious explanation is inflation (not least, media inflation), which increased the apparent value of business receipts and expenses—and
also caused profitability to diminish in importance as a goal and a
measuring stick in the eyes of many businesspeople. All economic
indicators appeared to be moving upward, and managers eventually
stopped questioning the value in real terms of their costs and benefits. (This is also a topic I shall examine in chapter 6.)

Inflation began falling in 1983, and it took a year for the meaning
of this fall to penetrate fully through the business community. Thereafter, the two secular forces I have just described began to reassert
themselves: the continuous movement of budgets into promotions
and the more widespread empirical evaluation of advertising costs
and benefits by an increasing minority of important advertisers. To
these forces should be added the two even more important trends
examined earlier in this chapter: market maturity (which was now

far advanced) and market fragmentation, with its concomitant splintering of advertising budgets and erosion of advertising-related scale economies.

Interestingly enough, the forces likely to depress advertising expenditure went almost entirely undetected for some years. Professional and journalistic commentators seemed quite unaware of what was going on until 1989, when some stories appeared—although the plateauing of advertising had already been taking place for five years. The industry was, in general, extraordinarily insensitive to trends. There were, however, isolated exceptions.[19]

In addition to the main underlying factors just discussed, a fifth and rather special change began to operate which also made some contribution to the situation.

For more than two decades before the mid-1980s, the largest advertisers in the United States relied on "day-after recall testing" (DART), a research device by which commercials were screened and evaluated in a limited number of cities before they were more widely exposed. This system was based on the assumption that relatively low levels of consumer recall could be boosted by additional advertising pressure. The use of DART therefore stimulated growth in advertising expenditure. Since the mid-1980s, however, fewer and fewer advertisers have been using DART exclusively, and there are good reasons, which I have written about in a different context.[20] Manufacturers now generally attempt to measure how well their commercials persuade the public. But persuasion measures cannot be lifted by additional advertising expenditure; the advertisement itself has to be improved first. This type of research does not therefore stimulate the growth of advertising pressure as much as DART did.[21]

There is therefore a total of five movements within consumer goods markets which are at the moment inhibiting the growth of advertising. In my judgment they will also continue to do so into the indefinite future; indeed the situation could become progressively worse.

An extraneous factor that parallels the stagnation in advertising is the crumbling of the audiences of the three television networks, which accounted for 90 percent of the prime-time audience in 1980, but only 65 percent in 1990.[22] If monolithic brands are fragmenting, so is the monolithic medium which was formerly used as their most important advertising carrier.

Some of the results of the trends in advertising are reasonably evident:

- reduced employment in the agency business[23]
- dissatisfaction with agencies (especially large agencies) on the part of many clients[24]
- pressure by clients to reduce rates of agency commission
- mergers and acquisitions in the agency field, as agency principals and outside financiers strive to rebuild advertising scale economies
- a strong move into overseas markets by agencies which hope for greater growth there than in the United States (which accounts for a huge share—probably more than 40 percent—of the world's advertising)

The present situation and the prognoses for the future all appear negative. There is, however, a speculative possibility that may lighten the gloom.

The stagnation in advertising volume of the period 1956–75 coincided with the remarkable creative revival in the advertising agency business associated with the 1960s. The old concept of the full-service agency became unfashionable; it was pushed aside by a revival of interest in the agency's creative product, a movement which was headed by David Ogilvy, Bill Bernbach, Jack Tinker, and Mary Wells, but which by the late 1960s had been followed by all the important agencies in New York and elsewhere, even those that Ogilvy had impolitely but graphically described as the "extinct volcanoes."

I believe that the advertising stagnation of the 1950s and 1960s was one of the more important forces stimulating this creative revival. Advertising had to begin working like a rapier because it could no longer afford the bludgeon of massive and increasing appropriations. Clients, under profit pressure (hence their reluctance to elevate advertising budgets), became more receptive to unorthodox creative ideas, many of which worked in the marketplace. A number of the agencies leading the charge became very successful. They were to an extreme degree advertising-driven organizations. They regarded profit as a reward for superior work, but they concentrated on the work first.[25]

I am reasonably optimistic that something similar will happen in the 1990s. I am not prepared to speculate about what form it will take, but I am happy to bet that the renaissance will come from the small rather than the large agencies. American advertising has always been prepared to give an extraordinary welcome to talented newcomers. As an educator, I have had a number of beginners with a real future pass through my classes.[26] In general, they have not been very interested in working for the larger firms in the advertising industry, because of their belief that they can fulfil their ambitions with less difficulty in small firms or else by working on their own. I also regularly observe the work of many small agencies, and much of the optimism I have for the future is based on the quality of their output.

The general conclusions that can be drawn about the stagnation in advertising expenditure are therefore gloomy—but not unrelievedly gloomy.

Nevertheless, with no projected increase in the real value of advertising investments, manufacturers and agencies will emphatically need to use what resources they have available with economy of force—ideally an increasing economy. This more efficient use of funds is yet another reinforcement of the main theme of this book. If a concentration on quality at the expense of quantity opens the door into the industry for new and unorthodox talent, and if this infusion leads to the exposure of increasingly effective advertising, and if these two things demonstrably boost the productivity of media budgets (three large *if*'s), there is no doubt at all that considerable social benefits will follow. Morale and confidence will also be rebuilt within the advertising industry, and these will lead to the recapturing of some of the *panache* of the golden days, a period which the advertising industry has not seen since the early 1970s.

One final point relates to agency compensation. The 1960s saw the first unsuccessful attempts by certain agencies (notably Ogilvy & Mather) to move to a fee system by which the clients pay the agency for the time of the staff employed on their accounts (including an agreed-upon profit). Agencies in the 1990s would be advised to pick up this ball, for the obvious reason that a fee system is more efficient than a commission (particularly a cut-rate commission) in protecting agency income when advertising budgets are generally stagnating.

Fourth Trend: Growth in Promotions

Readers will remember, from the discussion in the last section on the reasons for the stagnation in advertising expenditure, that promotional price cutting holds large and increasing attractions for manufacturers.

Donnelley Marketing publishes every year an estimate (based on questionnaires answered by a substantial sample of packaged-goods manufacturers) of how manufacturers divide their overall budgets for advertising and promotions (A&P) into their component parts.[27] The data for the twelve years 1978 through 1989 are presented in table 2–7.

The tipping of the balance toward below-the-line expenditure is the most striking feature of table 2–7; the share of total A & P accounted for by promotions rose—admittedly gradually and with interruptions—from 58 percent in 1978 to 66 percent in 1989.

I have already suggested that the most important reason for this trend is that manufacturers have become increasingly conscious that price-cutting promotions can move merchandise more dramatically than can "theme" advertising. (Whether promotions can do this profitably is another question altogether.) Added to this factor is the

TABLE 2–7

Division of Advertising and Promotion Budgets by Manufacturers

Year	Total (%)	Media Advertising (%)	Consumer Promotions (%)	Trade Promotions (%)
1978	100	42	24	34
1979	100	40	25	35
1980	100	40	25	35
1981	100	44	23	33
1982	100	45	26	29
1983	100	40	26	34
1984	100	36	27	37
1985	100	35	30	35
1986	100	34	28	37
1987	100	35	26	39
1988	100	31	25	44
1989	100	34	27	39

Source: Donnelley Marketing.

pressure of competition in stagnant total markets. In these, promotions are normally the most effective available short-term tactical weapon for increasing market shares, and also for maintaining shares against competitive threat. Interestingly enough, the move away from theme advertising into promotions has been more pronounced for large than for small manufacturers. It is the big operators that are most concerned with protecting their large market shares.

Over the period covered in table 2–7, trade promotions (intended to load the retail pipeline) have grown rather more strongly than consumer promotions (which are intended in addition to pull merchandise through this pipeline). This trend suggests that the retail trade has played a role in the move of A & P budgets below-the-line. Stronger and more concentrated retail groups require increasing "slotting allowances" to persuade them to carry branded goods. Growing promotional expenditure is the price that producers are forced to pay retailers in order to keep manufacturers' brands in distribution and on display.

The bargaining power of the retail trade is not as great in the United States as it is in certain European countries, the United Kingdom and Sweden in particular. There are no real national chains in the American food trade. However, there are many powerful regional ones, in Miami, Denver, Portland (Oregon), Chicago, Washington (DC), Milwaukee, Dallas, Philadelphia, Seattle, Atlanta, and other cities. Moreover, there has been a strong growth in concentration in at least five sectors of the retail trade (which include both food and drug) since the end of World War II.[28]

The data in table 2–7 show that 1983 was the year when the most dramatic move of funds below the line took place. As we saw in table 2–6, this was a year before the stabilization of advertising at a little under 1.5 percent of the GNP. The reason for the year's gap is not obvious, but it was probably due to the lag between the time when the decline first set in for packaged goods (monitored by Donnelley) and when other product and services categories followed.

The important question raised by table 2–7 is, of course: What does the future hold? I think it very unlikely indeed that my hypothesized underlying causes of the trends will become less important in the future. Promotions will continue to be effective selling devices and will still be perceived as such by manufacturers. Markets will remain mature, and competition will continue to be a struggle for market share, particularly between large manufacturers. The retail trade will not become more dispersed; indeed the present trend toward concentration will almost certainly increase.

This all adds up to the strongest likelihood that the trend toward promotions that has been such a strong feature since the early 1980s will continue into the indefinite future. It is a paradox that manufacturers seem unaware that the major characteristic of most promotions is not their undeniable effectiveness in sales terms, but their hidden costs. Reducing the unprofitability of promotions—cutting down their endemic waste—should be an urgent goal for the typical manufacturer, which will be using promotions even more in the future than it has in the past. This is a topic that will be discussed in detail in chapter 6.

Summary

1. In a developed consumer goods market like that of the United States, most market categories have stopped growing. The number of stagnant fields overtook the number of still-growing ones during the 1970s. In the 1990s, the proportion of consumer purchasing that will still take place in strongly growing categories probably will not exceed 10 percent.

2. The first response of manufacturers to stagnant category sales has been to search for growth by splintering brands into large numbers of variants. This approach has meant a fragmentation of consumer franchises. In addition, advertising support has also been fragmented, and scale economies have been sacrificed.

3. Advertising as a share of the GNP has been stable at a level below 1.5 percent since 1984. There is no reason to expect any upward movement in the near or distant future.

4. The balance of manufacturers' A & P budgets has been steadily tipping below the line for more than a decade. Of the current combined A & P budgets, 34 percent is spent on advertising, and 66 percent on promotions, despite the uncalculated cost—and waste—of most promotions. An examination of the underlying causes of the growing trend toward promotions suggests that this trend will continue into the indefinite future.

5. The four trends discussed in this chapter (1 through 4 above) all point strongly to the pressing need for manufacturers and advertising agencies to increase the efficiency of advertising and promotions, with the aim of increasing manufacturers' profit in the face of stagnant sales. The theme of this book is the need for a reduction of waste in advertising and promotions, and the specific emphasis is on ways to achieve greater economy of force from existing investments.

6. The fragmentation of markets and, because of it, the increased reliance on brand-specific discriminating arguments in advertisements will make it more difficult than ever for agencies to build appealing and salient personalities for the brands they advertise. This trend, together with the lack of growth in advertising budgets, will make the task of agencies progressively more difficult in the future.

7. The present stagnation of advertising expenditure and its probably indefinite continuation should force advertising agencies away from their traditional commission-based remuneration (especially since rates are being cut below 15 percent). They would be well advised to move to a fee system based on payment for staff time, a greatly more efficient way of protecting agency income when clients' budgets have stopped growing.

8. A speculative possibility is that the present troubles of the advertising industry will stimulate a remedy from the grassroots: a spontaneous emergence of innovation and unorthodoxy from young people and small agencies. This is something that has happened once before. There are signals that it is happening now.

3

Is Advertising a Strong
or a Weak Force?

*. . . all the power they obtain must be obtained by their charms and
weakness.*

Mary Wollstonecraft Godwin (writing about women)

"The Power of Advertising"*

Our knowledge of advertising, in particular our knowledge of how
it actually works, is extremely imperfect. Many aspects of it have
been studied for a long time, but with results that are far from conclusive. One sensible inference that has been drawn from all this investigation is that certain types of advertising almost certainly work
in one way, and other types in another. The case-by-case inductive
approach that has been used to a limited degree is probably the way
in which we shall eventually increase our body of reliable knowledge. But the trouble is that to date we have made very little real
progress along the path to enlightenment.

Many people have made efforts to discover a general theory.
However, the fact that none of those hypothesized have been proved
to be correct suggests that advertising's effects may eventually be
demonstrated by a multiplicity of specific theories, each relating to
small numbers of circumstances, rather than by any single, unified
theory. Broad-scale empirical work on advertising's effectiveness
supports this view, although it admits of important interconnections

*Title of special issue of *Advertising Age,* November 9, 1988.

and similarities among the ways advertising works in disparate cases.

An assumption underlying the majority of studies of advertising's effectiveness is that advertising *is* effective, and that we need only develop more sophisticated measurement tools to be able to quantify the payoff; in particular we shall do better if and when we separate more efficiently than we can at present advertising's effects from those of all the other stimuli that influence the sales of a brand. Strangely enough, nobody is much interested in the circumstances in which advertising has *no* effect, although reliable knowledge of these circumstances would be very interesting indeed to manufacturers, for if manufacturers managed to eliminate ineffective advertising, the money saved would increase profit, in some circumstances to a dramatic degree.

An instinctive (and in most cases unsubstantiated) belief in the power of advertising is a truism of the advertising business and is an article of faith devoutly accepted by observers of all persuasions, both defenders and opponents of advertising. It permeates the trade press and also the professional schools in universities where advertising is taught. Study the following randomly selected quotations:

> Turn off the advertising spigot and see what happens to sales, production, jobs, to the all-important marketing strategy that was carefully pieced together.[1]

> Advertising—the use of paid media by a seller to communicate persuasive information about its products, services or organization—is a potent promotional tool.[2]

> The marketing process depends upon advertising and promotion for its dynamic energy.[3]

> Radio and more especially television have . . . become the prime instruments for the management of consumer demand.[4]

> [I]t is tempting to put one's faith in education, and to hope that as fresh generations grow up to be more discriminating and critically-minded in their reading, viewing and spending, the mass-persuaders will be compelled to raise their sights and to reduce their reliance upon cheap emotional manipulation.[5]

> [T]he customer will be influenced by advertisement, which plays upon his mind with studied skill, and makes him prefer the goods of one

producer to those of another because they are brought to his notice in a more pleasing or more forceful manner.[6]

Readers will have no difficulty in inferring that the first three of the above quotations were written by protagonists of advertising, and the last three by antagonists. But note the similarity in the authors' belief in advertising's potency as a persuasive force. The quotations are typical of how advertising is viewed by large numbers of observers who are interested enough in the business (quite often at an emotional level) to publish their words of praise or condemnation.[7]

Readers may also guess, although they may not be closely familiar with the work of these authors, that they are all well-known commentators on advertising, or on economic matters in which advertising plays a role. The authors are, however, all either academics or journalists, and not advertising practitioners (past or present). None of them have in fact ever had to earn a living practicing the business. If they had, it would have added a measure of credibility to their words, since the authors would then have been in a position to evaluate at first hand just how powerful a force advertising actually is.

Although practitioners know an insufficient amount about how advertising operates, they are, not surprisingly, more knowledgeable than laypeople. In particular, they are constantly reminded that it operates in sometimes unexpected and subtle ways. Practitioners also have the great advantage over members of the general public— even intelligent and educated ones—that their minds are a little less confused by the myths that advertising has always generated.[8]

Two Theories

For obvious reasons, we can use the phrase "the strong theory" to describe advertising as it has been illustrated by the six quotations in the last section. The implications of this theory can be summarized along the following lines:

1. Advertising increases people's knowledge and changes people's attitudes; as a result of these changes, it is capable of persuading people who had not previously bought a brand to buy it, at first once and then repeatedly.

2. Advertising is a prime mover in the capitalist system and acts as a driving force for the engine of demand.
3. Advertising is capable of increasing sales not only of brands but also of complete product categories (for example, cigarettes); growth in markets is assumed to be common.
4. Advertising is often able to manipulate the consumer by the use of psychological techniques that destroy the consumer's defenses; in some cases these techniques are not even perceptible to the conscious mind.
5. If advertisers are to be successful, their strategic posture must generally be attacking and aggressive; they should be strongly persuasive, and increase advertising pressure with the expectation that sales and profits will rise as a direct consequence; as a rule repetition pays.
6. In general, consumers are apathetic and rather stupid.[9]

It is not too extreme an extrapolation of these points to conclude that advertising deserves (depending on one's point of view) either the most exalted praise for its contribution to the benefits of the capitalist system or the most trenchant condemnation for its contribution to its evils. According to the strong theory, advertising plays a centrally important part in the economic system of a country like the United States.

As I have pointed out, the strong theory is the theory of advertising that receives the widest support, although I believe it is accepted more by default than by active endorsement. Observers of advertising, strangely enough, do not dwell much on how advertising works (which is why we have learned so little that is reliable). When they do so, they are mostly inclined just to accept advertising as a powerful force because they have never contemplated any alternative.

There *is*, however, another theory, which has been articulated in Europe and which has been developed with increasing confidence and persuasiveness since the early 1960s. I shall call this *the weak theory*. It is associated virtually exclusively with the name of Andrew Ehrenberg, who holds a research chair at the London Business School. He is a mathematician and statistician with a formidable battery of business experiences. His theory is strongly rooted in empiricism. The words *awareness, trial,* and *reinforcement* (ATR) are used to describe it. According to the weak theory, advertising has the following characteristics:

1. It is capable of increasing people's knowledge and of stimulating the trial of a brand. But consumers are not very interested in viewing, hearing, or reading advertisements, most people who do so being users of the brand advertised (a phenomenon associated with selective perception). These advertising watchers already know the characteristics of the advertised brand; therefore, advertising's role in communicating information is of limited importance.

2. Advertising is not strong enough to convert people, that is, to persuade people whose beliefs are different from what is claimed in the advertising. Advertising is generally *not* capable of overcoming resistant attitudes. The difficulty that advertising faces is twofold. First, an advertising argument is extremely constricted (to thirty seconds—sixty words—in the case of most television commercials). Second, and even more important, people very easily switch off their mental engagement (again, through the operation of selective perception). Without enticing the audience, advertising cannot communicate. Without an interested audience, the advertiser will indeed find it difficult to lure and seduce, let alone browbeat.

3. Most product categories in countries whose consumer goods markets are mature have stopped increasing except for the amount associated with population growth; a brand can therefore increase only at other brands' expense, and manufacturers are of course aware of this.

4. As a result, much (perhaps most) advertising is used defensively. This means that it is not much used to increase sales by bringing new users to the brand advertised. It is more commonly used to retain existing users, and any advertised brand which has a significantly above-average market share benefits from the above-average frequency with which buyers buy it—something that can be stimulated by advertising. Existing users are already fairly well disposed toward a brand (because they buy it), and advertising merely reinforces this preference. The high cost of advertising is paid reluctantly, but paid nevertheless, through fear of the consequences if the advertiser were to stop or seriously reduce it. Most advertising is addressed to the existing users of a brand, not least because these peo-

ple are more likely to pay attention to the advertising for it. Achieving continuous business from existing users is a lucrative marketing strategy for many brands, particularly large ones, which have an extensive user base. Advertising is a driving force for continuity rather than for change.

5. Advertising which attempts to operate in a direction opposite to existing psychological and behavioral tendencies is in effect attempting to fight human nature. Such advertising will not be effective, and a devastating waste of resources will result.

6. We should not forget that members of the public commonly claim to be uninfluenced by advertising. Why should we assume that they are always telling lies? Most practitioners and ex-practitioners, including myself, are only too conscious of the difficulty of persuading the public to do anything at all.

7. As stated, advertising can on occasion make people aware of a new brand or a restaging of an existing brand, and it can stimulate trial. Nevertheless, people tend to learn about new brands more from promotions (particular sampling) and from word of mouth than from brand advertising.[10]

8. In general, consumers are apathetic and rather intelligent.

Some readers of this chapter may consider the whole question of whether advertising works according to the strong or the weak theory essentially an unimportant matter, comparable with the debates of the disputatious medieval Schoolmen about how many angels can stand on the head of a pin. To most of the general public, advertising is an activity of trivial importance. Even if they are conscious of the waste that is inseparable from it, they believe instinctively that it is not worth the effort to do anything about it.

However, as a student of advertising who once earned his livelihood from it, I cannot in any way share this view. Chapter 2 details the massive quantity of money that is devoted to advertising year by year. The size of the investment requires that, if advertising is to be carried out at all, it should be planned and executed with the highest skills we can bring to bear, and with the most economical use of resources. It is only in this way that the waste in the system can be brought down to less unacceptable levels; and knowledge of how advertising works is a *fundamental first step* to more efficient planning of specific campaigns. What is difficult to comprehend is how a business that has been practiced increasingly widely and in a supposedly increasingly sophisticated fashion for more than a century has taken such a time to realize basic truths.

We know a number of things at a detailed level about the degree to which people respond behaviorally to advertising. However, what we know is neither comprehensive enough nor sufficiently sharply and specifically directed to prove decisively that either the strong or the weak theory is definitive. Nevertheless, a number of pieces of good evidence can be brought to bear, and here are a few of the more important ones:

1. The vast majority of new brands fail. There is some controversy about the actual figure (depending as it does on the criterion for success or failure), but it has been estimated to be as high as 90 percent or more.[11] Advertising is directly responsible for many of the failures.

2. There is evidence from a large sample of cases that in about 70 percent of them, any sales effect (however small) generated by advertising is the direct and exclusive result of the amount of money that is spent. There is a good statistical regression linking variations in advertising pressure and sales, irrespective of campaign changes.[12] The creative content (that is, the persuasive power) of the advertisements themselves does not therefore appear to exercise any influence. Furthermore, as we shall see in chapter 6, there is much experimental evidence from tests of unusually elevated advertising pressure that such increases have a disappointing effect on sales and are rarely profitable (that is, the sales increases are very small and generate far less profit than is needed to fund the increased advertising).

3. In the market for repeat-purchase packaged goods (the product category which accounts for the largest single share of total advertising dollars), consumers' purchases show an astonishing degree of regularity and predictability. In the majority of cases, each consumer, during the course of a year, buys a group of competing brands (known technically as the consumer's *repertoire*). The proportions of total purchases represented by the different brands within the repertoire show little variation over time, and new brands join the repertoire only in the most exceptional circumstances. Most significantly, it appears that the consumer's habits are a more impor-

tant determinant of brand purchasing than either advertising or pro-motions.[13] As already mentioned, the majority of individual markets for consumer goods in developed countries do not increase in size by more than 1 or 2 percent in any year (a situation known technically as *stationary conditions*). This means that all marketing activity in such categories is entirely concerned with manipulating brands' market shares. Advertising is generally unable to increase the size of any market (nor does a reduction in total advertising cause a decline in the size of any market).

4. If advertising worked generally according to the strong theory, advertising investments would almost certainly increase continuously over time. In fact, when measured in real terms, there has been no growth, in the United States since 1984.[14]

Where does all this wide-ranging but rather fragmentary evidence take us? Readers of this paragraph and the four succeeding ones should bear in mind that they are reading here a personal view. I believe that the strong theory probably works in a small minority of circumstances (in certain defined product fields and with advertising using certain specific media). However, the weak theory has a far wider application. It operates virtually universally in fields in which advertising investments are considerable in absolute terms, that is, where consumer purchasing is high and where advertising is an important component of the marketing mix.

But it is going too far to suggest that even in these fields the weak theory operates in quite the extreme way described by Ehrenberg; it is too much to claim that advertising is *never* a prime mover, *never* a dynamic force. My particular field of study is the empirical evaluation of specific cases in which advertising may be shown to have a measurable marginal effect in the marketplace.[15] Such examples are to be found in sometimes very important product categories, and markets like these can sometimes be shown to contain minor dynamic elements within the overall pattern of stationary conditions.[16] In these cases, advertising occasionally goes beyond the reinforcement role, and even beyond the awareness and trial roles propounded by Ehrenberg. It can exploit sales growth in a more positive way; indeed such growth can provide advertising with a major opportunity to yield a dividend.

In these narrowly defined circumstances, advertising often has a pronounced effect, which can be accurately tracked and its results evaluated, sometimes even by a relatively precise estimate of the marginal increment of profit generated. But the circumstances in which such demonstrable results are apparent are exceptional, even though they are intensely interesting to advertising practitioners. It would be fair to say that these exceptions—important though they may be—serve generally to prove the rule, which is that in the majority of cases, advertising can be more persuasively explained by the weak theory than by the strong one. Ehrenberg is generally more often right than wrong.

Where advertising can be shown to have an effect, it can certainly pay for itself by achieving a behavioral response from only a tiny proportion—perhaps 1 percent or less—of the audience to which it is addressed. But such a response can be achieved only by some sort of intellectual or emotional engagement; advertising must be seen and must initially evoke some psychological response. In general, strongly persuasive advertising (often called *hard selling*) cannot always or even often achieve this. Advertising normally acts as a simple and low-key reminder stimulus to purchase, so that when the consumer is next shopping for a brand in the category (ideally in the supermarket the next day), he or she will pick up the brand advertised and not one of the two or three other brands he or she commonly uses. In most product fields, choosing one brand rather than another is not a weighty decision. It is known technically as a *low-involvement process;* a rational consideration of the pros and cons rarely takes place.

There is also evidence, certainly for existing brands and established advertising campaigns, that such advertising is capable of working on a "single-exposure" basis, and that fresh advertising exposures have little perceptible cumulative effect on the psyche of the consumer.[17] Repeated hard selling is not only distasteful; it is unnecessary. And although advertising can on occasion communicate in subtle ways, by emphasizing certain emotional stimuli rather than others (matters which are usually carefully researched), it does not use the black arts (for example, "subliminal seduction").

Implications for Professional Practice

As I have pointed out in this chapter, most advertisers and agencies appear always to have been proponents of the strong theory. For many years after World War II, the problems caused were concealed by the massive growth in consumer goods markets that took place during the long postwar boom. However, in the inflationary conditions of the 1970s and with the heated competitive climate and profit pressures of the 1980s, the folly of overpromise (perhaps unconscious overpromise) and the waste to which it contributes have almost invariably become evident sooner or later. This continuous over-promise has always seemed to me the best explanation for two unpleasant characteristics of the advertising business.

The first if the lack of stability in the relationships between clients and their advertising agencies. It is difficult to make accurate estimates of the average number of years advertisers work with their agencies, and the figures are biased to some extent by the deliberate policies of a small number of important but exceptional advertisers of building relationships to last for decades. Outside these cases, observation of the business discloses plentiful evidence of extreme volatility; there is little doubt that the average length of a manufacturer's relationship with its advertising agency is far shorter than its relationships with its other professional advisers, such as accountants and lawyers.[18] For the agency, lost business is followed almost immediately by lost jobs. This is the second unpleasant characteristic of the business.

There have been two other important influences on the numbers of people employed in the advertising industry, which have been falling gradually for two decades. The first is a lack of growth in advertising when measured in real terms (see chapter 2). This has been caused mainly by manufacturers' reducing their advertising in the main media to enable them to increase their expenditure on promotions, something that has meant, in effect, relatively less advertising and relatively more price cutting (see also chapter 2). The second influence has been the amalgamations of major agencies since the early 1980s, an important manifestation of the business's response to overall lack of growth, excessive competition, and pressure on profits.

As a result of these forces in the market, the advertising business is characterized—to a far greater degree than any other business with which I am personally familiar—by abruptly and sometimes tragically terminated careers.

This is an unhappy situation, in which the economic cost of waste is exacerbated by a social cost in the unhappiness and occasional trauma of interrupted careers. The ill effects of advertisers' and agencies' belief in the strong theory have done much to write the agenda for this book.

I shall now list four specifics. These will not be discussed extensively in this chapter, but I do point out where each argument is taken up in subsequent chapters. This list will give readers some idea of how the fabric of this book has been woven.

Deficiencies in Our Knowledge

One of the major initial problems that a manufacturer and an agency face in planning a campaign is whether *in the specific circumstances of the brand in its market,* advertising can be expected to work as a strong or a weak force. Solving this problem requires both knowledge of how advertising operates in a general sense (discussed in chapter 10) and, even more important, knowledge of the brand's short-term responsiveness to advertising pressure (discussed in chapter 6).

Budgeting

Chapter 5 is devoted to budgeting. I demonstrate in that chapter that aggressive brands in a rising sales trend tend to invest in advertising by planning that their share of all advertising in the product category (share of voice, or SOV) will *exceed* their share of category sales (share of market, or SOM). However, the more common situation is that brands are stable, and their advertising will therefore operate in accordance with the weak theory. Such brands are mostly concerned with preserving the status quo, and the average brand in such a situation should plan for its SOV to be *below* its SOM. The amount of such relative underinvestment can be established within parameters which have been set up by average brands in a broad aggregation of markets. This is all detailed in chapter 5.

Target Groups

One of the most important marketing variables controlled by the strong or weak theory (whichever applies to a particular brand) is that brand's target group. The strong theory directs attention to increasing the user base, that is, increasing penetration. The weak theory emphasizes the importance of nurturing existing users of the brand, that is, protecting the consumer franchise and increasing purchase frequency. This is a key concept discussed in chapter 7.

Advertising's Tone of Voice

As an extension of the point raised in the last paragraph, the tone of voice of the advertising—its nonfunctional signals—will differ according to whether it works in line with the strong or the weak theory. Where the strong theory applies, the advertising will spread news and be enthusiastic and aggressive. Where the weak theory operates, it will be much more quiet, protective, and reinforcing. Because of selective perception, the brand's advertising will be noticed by its existing users, a very large body in the case of major brands. This means that the advertising does not need to be strident to attract attention. These points are amplified in chapter 8.

Implications for Advertising Education

It is obvious from the issues that have been discussed in this chapter that although we know a few things about how advertising works, we have vastly more to learn. However, it is a sad fact that American universities—the organizations that in all other fields of learning are among the leading torchbearers in the pursuit of knowledge—do not contribute much to this particular debate. There seem to be three reasons for this.

The first reason is by far the most important. Rather surprisingly, the weak theory has not penetrated. It originated in Europe, and although it is believed, or at least half-believed, by some of the more important advertisers and advertising agencies in the United States, the theory is terra incognita in at least 95 percent of business and communications schools. It is not easy to comprehend why this should be so, but I have no doubt at all that it is true, and it symbolizes in rather a dramatic fashion the position of business and communications educators in relation to the advertising profession. In all substantial respects, the profession leads and the universities follow. Most people in advertising education will find nothing uncomfortable or surprising about this. But they should sometime consider the position of their colleagues in the natural sciences, and in particular in medicine. The notion that in its contributions to increasing our knowledge, the work carried out in the research laboratory and the teaching hospital is less important than that done in general practice is frankly bizarre. And yet it is accepted as the norm in advertising.

We should also remember that Ehrenberg's seminal work was carried out in an academic environment. Admittedly his work has been sponsored (both financially and through the supply of empirical data) by more than forty American and British companies, including Procter & Gamble, Colgate-Palmolive, General Foods, General Mills, and M & M Mars. But his work of analysis, synthesis, and model building was and is carried out in a place far detached physically and psychologically from the pressures of the business world.

The second reason why interested parties have not pursued the weak theory is that some people who are aware of the theory reject it on nonrational grounds. This is true in my personal observation of people in some advertiser companies, advertising agencies, and professional organizations—men and women whose resistance is due to their emotional commitment to the advertising enterprise. Advertising represents the mainspring of their lives and professional endeavors, and these people reject without serious examination any notion that devalues or undercuts it. I suspect that some university professors also share this view.

The third point is a very practical matter. Universities where advertising is studied are not fully geared (technically at least) to handle the type of research needed to advance our knowledge. The advertising faculty in communications schools have developed instructional skills, but for the most part they have never practiced in the professional world except perhaps as juniors or interns. As a result, they are not as conscious as are practitioners of the most salient issues that call for investigation. Not surprisingly, academics are unused to handling the data bearing on these issues (even if they manage to obtain access to them). Their own research activities range over many topics that interest them, and these are often related to advertising's social effects (which begs a question in that they assume that advertising *does* have social effects). Their inquiries are, however, not usually germane to improving the efficiency of professional practice.[19]

I believe emphatically—on the basis of the academic research I read every day from business and communications schools in all parts of the United States—that the interests of academic researchers are in fields far removed from those covered in the research that is carried out routinely by major advertisers and agencies, little of it published. However, these latter investigations have led to all the progress (small though it is) that we have made toward an understanding of advertising.

There is a very substantive matter that leads directly out of the dispute about the relative validity of the strong and weak theories—something with an immediate bearing on what goes on in universities in general and in communications schools in particular (as the places where the majority of advertising instruction is concentrated). This matter concerns how the controversy affects our *educational* endeavors. Are there significant differences between what we will be teaching our students according to whether our doctrine is embedded in either the strong or the weak theory? I believe that there are very significant differences indeed.

Since (as I have explained) the strong theory receives by far the wider endorsement in universities, I shall first hypothesize the sorts of beliefs that graduates who have been imbued with the strong theory take into the real world as part of their intellectual baggage.

Such graduates believe instinctively in the great power of advertising. They are likely to be imaginative and to have some talent; they are also energetic and aggressive. They are proponents of "strong selling" as a means of switching consumers from brand to brand, and—very important—they push the general policy of increasing advertising investments. If they manage to stay in the business, and if their professional status improves in it, their recommendations to their clients will gain progressively in weight and authority. Most of the advertising industry is not efficient at nor very interested in evaluating the effectiveness of campaigns scientifically and rigorously. As a result, optimism and enthusiasm may be accepted uncritically for extended periods, and the consequences of wasteful overexpenditure may take years to come home to roost.

How would the situation be different if we made an effort to teach our students (at the very least) that the weak theory exists, and that it may apply to some—perhaps the majority—of the brands on which they will be working during their professional careers? I can only hypothesize the likely long-term effect of this change in our teaching emphasis, but I have not the smallest doubt that graduates would approach their professional endeavors with a far greater realism, sense of caution, and willingness to experiment.

We should begin by emphasizing to our students that advertising is a tough and competitive business to break into, and in which to maintain a career with any upward progression. Although advertising is unquestionably exciting, interesting, and well paid, it is a calling that makes high demands on brains, imagination, and resilience. The first thing we should always do with our students is to test the strength of their motivation as well as their understanding of the realities of the business.

Students who comprehend the weak theory will have a greater technical understanding of the business than those people who know only about the strong theory. Specifically they will be skeptical of the value of hard-selling advertising. They will be open-minded about the possibility of increasing their clients' profits by *reducing* advertising investments. (The resultant effect on sales can be evaluated with reasonable accuracy by marketplace experimentation.) They will learn to operate advertising—and will also encourage their clients to operate advertising—with economy of force. They will use advertising with precision and finesse and not as a steamhammer. They will learn by experience and will base their recommendations on cool evaluation and an increasing knowledge rather than on an unremitting bullishness and enthusiasm.

The eventual result will be that the business will almost certainly operate at a lower and less heated level than at present, with less advertising overall. The force of competition will continue strongly, but it will be based more on objectively verifiable performance than it is now, and the probable result will be less neurosis among both clients and agencies. It is inevitable that waste will be reduced as a general result of these changes, and there will be less "career fallout" among advertising practitioners. These changes will certainly result in significant social benefits, in particular less waste.

The methods of working described in the two paragraphs above represent major changes, and for universities to play a part, we must of course tackle the problem of educating the educators before we educate the students. This problem brings us back to the all-encompassing role of the university, in particular in the quest for knowledge.

To my mind, it would be grossly inadequate for the university simply to learn about the weak theory (or any other theory) and then to teach it. The university cannot in good conscience earn its corn unless it participates in the frustration and the excitement of the exploration and the discovery. It is only by doing this that the university will say anything new and will provide insights that the practitioner will be interested in sharing. And I cannot see how the university can, without deep inner dissatisfaction, accept its present subordination to the practitioner, who is so clearly the person at the leading edge of knowledge. If inhabitants of the communications schools, because of weaknesses in their enterprise and skills, have to continue to accept the technical leadership of the practitioner, there is the inevitable prospect that their status will continue to sink. This lowered status will have an obvious bearing on the respect accorded to the educational programs offered by advertising departments and on the quality of the students whom these will attract.[20]

Unlike most schools of medicine, architecture, engineering, and advanced technology, the advertising departments of university communications schools are in a position of some vulnerability, and there they will remain until at least some practitioners are persuaded to beat a path to the doors of at least some universities to learn something new about the "state of the art." The traffic is much too much in the opposite direction at the moment.

Summary

1. Many opponents and proponents of advertising have only one point of agreement: they are united in a belief in advertising's great power. Most such opponents, and many of the proponents, have, however, never practiced the advertising business.

2. The strong theory of advertising can be summarized as follows:

    a. Advertising can increase people's knowledge, change people's attitudes, and persuade them to buy brands.

    b. Advertising is a driving force in the engine of demand.

c. Advertising has a macroeffect and can increase aggregate demand in entire product categories.

d. Advertising is capable of manipulating the consumer by the use of arcane psychological techniques.

e. The most successful advertising is attacking and aggressive.

f. Consumers are apathetic and rather stupid.

3. In contrast to the strong theory, a weak theory has been developed in Europe by Andrew Ehrenburg. It can be summarized as follows:

a. Although advertising can increase people's knowledge, this ability is of little practical value, since the people who pay most attention to a brand's advertising are users of that brand, who have good knowledge of it already.

b. Advertising is not powerful enough to convert people. Advertising messages are very short, and they can easily be screened out by selective perception.

c. Most consumer goods categories in developed markets such as that of the United States have stopped growing. Brands can increase sales only by stealing share from competitive brands.

d. All manufacturers are aware of the importance of protecting the market shares of their existing brands, and much if not most advertising is used defensively.

e. Advertising that tries to fight against consumers' natural inclinations and attitudes will be ineffective, and resources will be wasted.

f. Most members of the public claim to be uninfluenced by advertising. This claim is true insofar as it does not often make them change their minds.

g. Consumers learn about innovations in markets more from promotions and word of mouth than from advertising.

h. Consumers are apathetic and rather intelligent.

4. Neither theory has a universal application. However, for a number of reasons, I believe that the weak theory applies far more widely than the strong theory. Nevertheless, even in the most "classical" conditions where the weak theory applies (with large brands in highly competitive packaged-goods categories), advertising can in some circumstances operate according to the strong theory.

5. The deficiencies of the strong theory, in its causing of waste, have been an important influence on the agenda for this book. The most plausible elements of the weak theory have directed my discussion of:

> deficiencies in our knowledge (chapters 10 and 6);
> budgeting (chapter 5);
> target groups (chapter 7);
> advertising's tone of voice (chapter 8).

6. A separate and very important matter concerns how the strong and weak theories should influence the university education of men and women who wish to enter the advertising business. I believe that full awareness of the weak theory would make entrants into the profession better qualified than their counterparts today.

7. There is a real problem in making universities conscious of the weak theory. There is an even greater problem in persuading them to conduct research in marketing and advertising that is at the leading edge of knowledge. The latter problem must be solved before the former.

4

The Culture of an Advertising Agency

The way we do things around here.[1]

Marvin Bower, McKinsey & Company

Sir David Orr, a businessman of great distinction who made his early reputation in marketing and was chairman of Unilever for eight years, once emphasized something that is not immediately obvious to businesspeople who know manufacturing and trading organizations but are less familiar with advertising agencies. The agency, when compared with other types of organization, especially the manufacturing companies which are its clients, "thrives on a very different culture . . . the product company, whether in goods or services, is always more structured and hierarchical . . . [it] will also be steeped in its product, whereas the agency is more sensitive to wider trends in the market."[2]

It is generally (and I think correctly) recognized that there are advantages in advertisers and agencies being separate organizations with no overlap of ownership, for the very reason that the corporate culture of the agency is or should be different from that of its clients. This is a topic worth exploring, and this chapter is devoted to a formal, although subjective, examination of the meaning of an agency's culture. In my opinion, its culture has an important influence on the agency's stability and productivity, matters obviously relevant to the ways we can reduce waste in the advertising system.

First a definition and some amplification. The notion of *corporate culture* is widely discussed in business circles, and at least one book has been devoted to describing and illustrating it.[3] This provides details of the elements that contribute to a corporate culture, but in rather an abstract fashion, and the points raised do not in my judgement help us to understand what happens in an advertising agency.

A corporate culture is most succinctly described in the words of the management consultant which are used as part of the title of this chapter. "The way we do things around here," as it applies to an advertising agency, embraces two separate things: the type of people an agency recruits (the "social culture") and the agency's attitude toward the advertising enterprise (the "philosophical culture"). These things are not always articulated, although they have been in well-known individual cases.

The social culture defines the agency's style, sense of values, ethical principles, atmosphere, and standing in the business community, as well as the (stated or unstated) norms of behavior which an agency expects of its employees. These include the agency's definition of "client service," that is whether or not the agency is prepared on occasion to give unpalatable objective advice.

The agency's philosophical culture defines its belief in advertising, its understanding of the role of advertising and how advertising works, and most important—its own distinctive approach to the creation of effective advertising.[4] These beliefs and attitudes are intellectually based, but they all contain or have developed an overtone that can truthfully be said to transcend rationality. Indeed, a distinguished advertising researcher has detected a close analogy between competing agency philosophies and competing religions.[5] The reason that agency philosophies have developed beyond the bounds of rationality is that since the time in the early part of the twentieth century when advertising evaluation ceased being an exclusive matter of direct-response pulling power, the industry has had no robust and universally recognized criteria of effectiveness. Theories (of varying quality and usefulness) gradually took the place of objectively verifiable performance, and these theories became associated with particular agencies.

Over and beyond these matters of belief and attitude, an agency culture also covers a much simpler matter; how the agency should be organized to produce effective advertising and how this can be done efficiently and profitably. Many of the larger agencies are organized on a "matrix" system, with strong lateral lines of control and weak vertical ones on the organizational chart. This can be a formula for chaos, but the disciplines of the other parts of the agency's culture often manage to provide a cement to maintain cohesion. A culture can, in other words, substitute for a rigid hierarchy.

The culture of an agency can arise spontaneously, as part of a process in which mutually compatible people learn to work together. But far more often it is imposed from above. How this actually happens is that younger people consciously or half-consciously model their own work on that of their seniors, whom they respect professionally. This is obviously a lengthy and complicated procedure, but it is unlikely to happen unless an agency management wants it to happen. The process "cannot be delegated and it connot be created by osmosis because, though the soil may be fertile, it is up to the management to enrich the soil. I see management's main job in an agency as establishing the sympathetic climate in which creative talent can flourish."[6] It is also important for the management of an agency to establish and reinforce *both* the social culture and the philosophical culture. The former naturally embraces recruitment and training.

One very obvious aspect of an agency's culture is the extent to which the agency is account-driven (that is, dominated by the account executives) or creative-driven (that is, dominated by the creative department). As I argue in this chapter, agency cultures do not change much in their character, although they can fade or grow stronger over time. The agency's account or creative orientation is the most immutable feature of all.[7]

For an agency to have a strong culture brings advantages. The agency makes the best use of the most talented people, and this use leads to synergism, it can result in improved morale, it can make it easier to select new staff, and it results in continuity—a heritage—in a business marked by volatility as both clients and employees come and go. It cements loyalty on the part of the agency staff. Rather importantly, clients expect an agency to have a recognizable culture. The wiser ones recognize the value to them of what the agency has perhaps unconsciously absorbed from its wider professional experience, which often covers many product fields— experience that has contributed to its culture in important ways. And most client executives who work directly with advertising agencies have a background in sales and expect their advertising to be sold to them; this can be done most convincingly by an agency with depth and special expertise, elements that again contribute to its culture.

The tone of what has been said so far commends the general notion of an agency culture, but this approval amounts to only a partial truth, because there is a down side. In this chapter, both sides of the case are examined, and in order to set the scene, I shall devote a little time to describing briefly three agencies where I myself worked during my twenty-seven years of continual learning in the advertising agency business. These agencies were quite different from one another in style; they embodied essentially different cultures.

Programmed Anarchy

During an early stage of my career, I worked for two years (1955–57) in an important London agency called Colman, Prentis and Varley (CPV). I was a junior account executive, and my moves into and out of that agency were carefully planned—by me.

I was often tempted to think that CPV had no corporate culture at all. My judgment was not entirely correct, and anyway the apparent lack of a culture did not prevent the company from being for about a decade among the ten leading agencies in Britain, and not by any means the weakest of them. At the heart of the agency were three or four managers who had impressive personalities and were exceptionally skilled in orchestrating creative talent and bringing it to bear on clients' advertising problems. Even more important, there was a slightly larger number of remarkably imaginative creative men and women. In all, there was maybe a total of a dozen people in this management and creative cohort, and five of them later founded new agencies which became important and successful. But this twelve represented only a small proportion of the agency's aggregate payroll of three hundred-odd people. The rest of these (a group that included the youthful me) were hewers of wood and drawers of water.

CPV was capable of producing advertising of spectacular brilliance, although the agency did this in an erratic fashion, relying on the not infrequent flashes of inspiration which struck the best of the agency's creative individualists. The organization operated chaotically. There was much shouting in the corridors, and indeed I emerged from the agency with the conviction that superior advertising was inseparable from personal abrasiveness. The consumption of alcohol by members of the staff can hardly be comprehended when we look back at it from the drabness of today's abstemious and health-fixated society. The favorite sport of many in the agency was recreational sex, in its multiple variations. These things all contributed to the anarchy—and also to the vibrancy and the creative excitement of the organization.

There were no planning procedures and no use of research in creative development. There was no serious evaluation of advertising effectiveness. (I spent two years without looking once at a Nielsen Retail Audit report.) Even more important, there was no continuity. The most obvious direct result of how the agency operated was that when it hit hard times and began to run down, following the departure of many of its most talented people, there was no adhesive to hold the agency together and no heritage to pass on to a new generation. It eventually disappeared from sight as the result of a merger during the 1970s. It is a salutary story. And it is especially sad, because Colman, Prentis and Varley blazed like a comet during its professional apogee. But it had nothing—or at least too little—to maintain its impetus.

Perhaps, after all, CPV did have a creative-driven corporate culture, but this was too fragile and depended too much on individual personalities to work in anything but the shortest of short terms. The agency relied on brilliance. But during its heyday it did nothing at all to systematize—or even to learn from—the work of the dazzling individuals who created the agency's reputation.

Strangled in Its Infancy

I started work in Copenhagen in 1967. I was the first J. Walter Thompson (JWT) man employed by J. Walter Thompson's Scandinavian operation, and this is something that needs an explanation. The Agency was set up in Scandinavia by our buying a small Danish agency, which was to be used as a body onto which clients associated with JWT internationally would be grafted, and into which the expertise developed and used by the agency in the largest and most sophisticated world markets would be inoculated. I had earlier been transferred from J. Walter Thompson's London office to its office in Amsterdam (to import some knowledge of television, an advertising medium then new to the Netherlands), and thence to Copenhagen. It was my job in Copenhagen to bring in and service the J. Walter Thompson clients, and to act as a doctor (or nurse or midwife) to inject the serum of the agency's professional skills into the bloodstream of the reconstructed Scandinavian agency. I was being asked in effect to help create (or superimpose) an agency culture based substantially on J. Walter Thompson's own. It was a fascinating job, but this chapter is not concerned with the pleasure and benefit I derived from it.

One thing the agency obviously needed was a significant infusion of creative talent. This was not easily available in Scandinavia, so that we had to begin some difficult exploration to locate and bring in an experienced writer from a large overseas market, who would come as our creative director. We eventually discovered a suitable person in J. Walter Thompson, New York, but it took a year before we got him to Copenhagen. I had not met him before his arrival.

When the great day came, I drove to Copenhagen airport to greet him and his family. I was accompanied by an English colleague, a close friend. As we talked on our outward journey, we agreed with some relief that things would henceforth be much different from and significantly easier than they had been during our first year of operation. The former judgment was to prove correct, but not the latter. We had, of course, visualized a young American of the type with which we were most familiar: an enthusiastic product of the Ivy League, bespectacled and angular, with buttoned-down collar and an inability to stay in bed after 5 AM. In other words, we expected a person who represented the social culture of JWT. The new arrival did not look the part. My English friend and I were struck most sharply by the expression of utter forlorn dejection, the hands in the trouser pockets, and the crushed and cheerless body perched above polished shoes the size of small canoes (these were the ubiquitous symbol of the American businessman in the 1960s).

He settled in quickly, but from the first moment, problems began to arise (although this is not the whole story, as readers will soon discover). In professional affairs he was sharp and aggressive and managed only too easily to alienate account executives and administrators. The creative department, which was his private fiefdom, always appeared to be on the edge of dangerous instability. He worked late and hard and made everyone else do the same. He insisted on attending too many client meetings, not because he liked clients especially but because he did not trust anyone but himself to say the right things about "his" advertising. He personally led a haunted life—the result of everyone in the agency's continuing, in his opinion, to conspire against him. (This was not an entirely incorrect assumption.)

He soon, however, demonstrated three more positive qualities, which were, to say the least, unusual in the environment of Scandinavian advertising. First, he discovered through a process of instinct how to locate creative talent from among young people who had never written advertising before. In fact, his judgment of creative people was better than that of any other advertising person I have known before or since. This alone would have been enough to justify his position in the organization. His second strength was that, despite the apparent anarchy of his working methods and his frequent manifestations of creative temperament, he was— paradoxically— well disciplined in his thinking about advertising strategy. He had evidently absorbed some of the philosophical culture of JWT New York. My account executive colleagues and I were closely concerned with the strategy for the brands we handled and did everything possible to make this as tight and sound as possible. In detailed discussions about the positioning of our brands in the marketplace and the direction the advertising should take, we found surprisingly that our creative director was a rational and helpful colleague.

It was, however, his third quality which accounted for his largest contribution by far to the health and growth of our operation. During the four years we worked together, he was involved in a vast amount of work of routine maintenance. But he also had it within his power to write—with total assurance—a series of advertising campaigns that were astonishingly fresh, original, and relevant. He was directly responsible for at least half a dozen campaigns for major international brands of packaged goods, campaigns which were acclaimed widely outside Scandinavia and, more importantly, made a major impact on the sales of the brands within their markets. If readers think that this is a low rate of productivity, they should consider David Ogilvy's conclusion that during the *whole of his own professional career* the number of great campaigns for which he was responsible could be counted on the fingers of his two hands.[8]

What is obvious from what I have been saying is that the corporate culture which we created at J. Walter Thompson, Scandinavia, was embedded in our creative work. This made the agency unusual in the JWT world, as I shall shortly explain. My personal contribution was simple. I nurtured the clients and made sure that they accepted and ran the spectacular advertising which the agency succeeded in producing for them, and which generally had a demonstrable effect on sales. By and large we had happy and successful clients, most of whom were local branches of large and sophisticated manufacturing companies, and who were capable of evaluating our work by the highest standards.

Nevertheless, despite our professional successes, life was not easy for us because we faced two major problems. We were operating on media commission, and our clients' billings were small in absolute terms because the markets in which they were operating had small populations. This situation would almost certainly have been rectified as the agency grew, but while I was there, we were still below our "critical mass." The agency also incurred exceptionally high travel expenses since we were handling three separate national markets out of our headquarters in Copenhagen. These factors had an obvious effect on our margins.

I left Scandinavia in 1972, but kept in touch with our creative director (this book is dedicated to him). He himself remained for a number of years in Scandinavia. But shortly after my own departure the agency's priorities changed and it took (in my opinion) a disastrously retrograde step. The management became tighter and the production of outstanding advertising became a less important priority than earning comfortable margins, which I thought at the time (and still believe) should be regarded as a long-term reward for outstanding work and not a short-term operational objective. The advertising-oriented culture of the company, which had been so tenderly nurtured and which was beginning to yield such a promising dividend, was in effect suppressed. The result was an overall loss in the equation of advantages and disadvantages, because the now more efficient company had lost its engine of growth. The priorities became confused, and the agency was unable to maintain its forward drive for the simple reason that it had sacrificed its culture—something that had been directly rooted in its main professional endeavors for its clients and that was the secret of its strength.

It may occur to some readers that my story of a small agency in a remote country has more than a little relevance to agency practice in the 1990s in the major world markets. The latter part of my Scandinavian story highlights the conflict between the professional, culture-driven demands of an advertising enterprise and the profit-driven demands of a publicly owned company. In an era of agency conglomerates, with their massive debts and perpetual need to increase their profits progressively, the conflict which I have highlighted in my Scandinavian case study is an ever-present feature that will certainly not fade and has every chance of becoming magnified with the passage of time.[9] This conflict is something which has an obvious bearing on the future of advertising agency cultures—and indeed on whether they are likely to survive at all.

"Aunty Knows Best"

I worked at J. Walter Thompson, London, for three separate periods: 1953–55, 1957–65, and 1972–80. It is difficult to imagine an advertising agency which has a stronger corporate culture. The agency has never been shy about exercising its judgment and expressing strong opinions, a process described by an elderly client on whose business I worked in the early 1960s with the use of the nursery phrase, familiar to an older generation of English men and women, "Aunty knows best."

The culture of J. Walter Thompson was originally developed in New York and stemmed from the personalities of Stanley Resor and the cluster of outstanding people who, in effect, created the J. Walter Thompson company in its modern incarnation in the 1920s. The culture eddied out from New York and involved the increasing number of overseas offices that the company opened. It was only in the 1960s that the overseas offices—London, in particular—became significantly different from the New York office in their culture.

The key to understanding the company's culture as it was created by Resor et al. was the process of analyzing problems through a comprehensive and longitudinal evaluation of brands; JWT was the first agency to be interested in the shape and composition of markets. Following the stage of analysis, the advertising generated by the agency was invariably studied, rational, and soundly based. The culture of the company, as it was explained to me when I was a young man, meant "taking problems apart"[10] and developing well-considered creative recommendations. This was before the time when an agency's creative product (rather than its powers of analysis) had become the most critical competitive discriminator between itself and other agencies. Most of the advertisements produced by JWT appeared in print media until about the mid-1950s in the United States and the early 1960s in Britain, since newspapers and magazines were the dominant media for national advertisers at that time. The advertisements themselves were composed with a literary rather than an artistic orientation. They tended to be "copy-heavy." The agency was strongly account-driven— and it has continued to be, despite the evolutions that have taken place in its culture.

JWT's culture in the United States and abroad embraced both the elements I have described: the social and the philosophical. The classic expression of the former was (and is) the "Thompson man." He was given this name before the era of feminism, although a few of the most important figures in the company's history have in fact been women. This phrase describes the combination of brains, sophistication, good breeding, and good manners that characterizes most (although not all) of the account executives, creative people, account planners, media people, and researchers who work for the agency. One of the more delightful bons mots attributed to Stanley Resor is the following: "What we have discovered is that we can turn a gentleman into an advertising man, but we have been unable to educate an advertising man to be a gentleman; this is something his mother should have done a long time ago."[11] At J. Walter Thompson, there is very little shouting in the corridors, and creative temperaments are in general carefully controlled. There has always been great emphasis on agreeable personal relationships and a friendly and participative atmosphere, although this is not to imply a lack of political undercurrents flowing through the agency, or an absence of relentless, although carefully veiled, competition between personable and pleasant but also tough and ambitious opportunists.

These observations are intended not as criticisms, but merely to act as a reminder that, despite the common assumption that the "Thompson man" is different, the people at J. Walter Thompson actually have more similarities with than dissimilarities from people in other advertising agencies—something to be expected in a business as competitive as advertising. Perhaps this is another way of saying that, in comparisons of the social and philosophical cultures, the philosophical culture is, in the last analysis, the more important discriminator between one agency and another.

The early 1960s saw an important new trend in advertising: a strong revival of emphasis on the agency's raison d'être, its creative product. This trend coincided with (and was possibly influenced by) a slowing in the growth of aggregate advertising expenditure in the United States.[12] It was spearheaded and exploited by the principals of a number of thrusting agencies in New York, notably David Ogilvy, Bill Bernbach, Jack Tinker, and Mary Wells. After some delay, the movement reached London. At that time (and still today) the strongest operations in the J. Walter Thompson firmament were those in the United States and the United Kingdom. However, the ways in which the two responded to the changing conditions of the market allow an instructive comparison.

In the United States, and in the "flagship" New York office in particular, the company seemed unable to come to grips with the change in the advertising business, partly because the agency was so account-driven, partly because there was much flux at the top, and also because there were at the time important changes in its management priorities (the agency was moving toward public ownership). As a result, the management gradually allowed the traditional social and philosophical culture of the agency to fade; it was something just not fully understood by the people running the company at the time. Even today the culture has not entirely disappeared, but there is very little doubt that it was weaker in 1970 than it had been in 1960, and that in 1980 it was weaker still.

I have debated with former colleagues whether there was a difference between the philosophical culture of JWT New York and JWT London during the long years when Stanley Resor ruled the company. Both agencies took a seriously inquiring approach, but it is probable that the British put more emphasis on the theoretical underpinning of advertising than the Americans did. This emphasis was essentially a result of the British educational system. The Americans, on the other hand, were always more anxious to produce advertising solutions to problems and to see how such advertising performed in the marketplace. The American approach was more pragmatic.

By the mid-1960s, however, the London agency's philosophical culture had faded, just as New York's had. JWT London's social culture remained as strong as ever (and it began to be eroded only in the 1970s). But by the end of the 1960s, a major change had taken place at JWT London. The agency's philosophical culture had become significantly and consciously strengthened. This strengthening occurred partly in response to client pressures, but more important, it happened because the management of the company saw a reinforcement of the corporate culture as one of its key objectives.

The revitalized philosophical culture was formalized in a number of stages, and described in documents, films, videotapes, presentations, and training programs. The main emphasis was placed on five interconnected disciplines:

1. a redefinition of JWT's old concept of added values to differentiate a brand from an unadvertised product;
2. a careful analysis (based on psychological principles) of how advertising works on the consumer's mind;
3. the development of qualitative research techniques to help generate and evaluate creative ideas;
4. the construction of a new formula for drawing up advertising strategy;
5. the transformation of the old agency marketing department into a cadre of "account planners" who were to be the main developers and custodians of brand strategy, adding a further task in the 1980s: the scientific evaluation of the sales effects of advertising, using and developing innovative statistical techniques.

The agency remained in essence account-driven, and these disciplines were entirely compatible with the historical elements of the agency's culture already described. But the new disciplines represented a development and sharpening of the old. It should, however, also be added that the strengthened philosophy imposed a new restrictiveness and rigidity.

The five changes just described represented a substantial menu. Their formulation and implementation were the combined effort of an oligarchy of executives who also played a substantial part in running the company. Perhaps because of the position of these people, the culture soon became even more all-embracing, entering all parts of the agency's psyche. Very soon there was a (substantially implicit) doctrine covering media planning and budget deployment and, most important, a distinctive creative style based on building nonrational, emotionally based discriminators for the brands advertised. These were best expressed in television advertising, something that goes a long way toward explaining the agency's particular bias toward television. This extremely broad dissemination of the culture within the organization may well have been unintended, but my own careful observation suggests that it most certainly took place; and it exists to this day.

When one looks back on the JWT offices in New York and London during the 1960s and their contributions to the destiny of the company, there is no doubt that JWT London, with its strengthened culture, responded much better to a changing marketplace than did JWT New York, with its weakened culture and constant management changes. But the story is more complicated. Up to about 1960, JWT in the United States and JWT London had a similar market position. They were not only market leaders but were also commonly acknowledged to have occupied their own special niches. As agencies, they were different *in kind* from the competition, and what set them apart from the others was largely their corporate culture.

Today each of the two agencies, in its market, is one of a number of evenly balanced competitors, some of which have and some of which do not have a strong culture of their own. Neither of the JWT agencies is the market leader, although JWT London is much closer than is the U.S. agency.

It is also true that Don Johnston, the chief executive of J. Walter Thompson appointed in 1976, was acutely conscious of the way in which the culture of JWT New York had eroded during the previous decade and more. His efforts to rejuvenate the culture, mainly by introducing methods that had originated in London, deserve to be described in detail (and I may write about them at some future time). However, for the purposes of this chapter, it is enough to note that these efforts were mainly unsuccessful, for reasons unconnected with Johnston's own imagination, resolve, and drive.

The new ideas simply did not "take" in New York. But they certainly did in London. And there is little doubt that the success achieved by J. Walter Thompson, London, was strongly influenced by the agency's corporate culture. I also believe that its success, great though it has been, brought disappointment in that the agency lost the position of supremacy it had occupied in the 1950s and 1960s. I am convinced that the reason is that culture, to some extent, held it back. In particular there have been components of the culture that have narrowed the agency's thinking and made it vulnerable to the assaults of aggressive and more free-thinking competitors.

This point could be illustrated with many specific examples. And although these examples are anything but trivial, dwelling on them would inevitably mislead readers and communicate to them something that is not intended: that the disadvantages of the culture of JWT London in some way outweigh its advantages. However, some examples are introduced in the next section, where they are used to underpin some general arguments about cultures, and in particular about what readers may already be beginning to conclude: that cultures need to be rather carefully *balanced* if they are to be maximally effective. This balance is an art and not a science, and there is no research available to help us.

Too Little Culture—Or Too Much?

One thing that must continually be borne in mind when we think about advertising agencies is that an exceptionally high proportion of their staff—about 60 percent—is in the professional mainstream. These people are expected to bring their imagination and intellect with them to the office in the morning. As a result, agencies are not in the least similar to the manufacturing companies that are their clients, although they have some resemblance to the firms of attorneys and accountants, which also provide professional counsel to these clients.

Although the proportion of an agency's staff that is in what might be called the officer class is exceptionally high, the talents of this class are—strangely enough—in short supply. This is particularly true of first-class creative talent. The result is that wise managements, as part of the corporate culture they breed, cherish their staff. As sensible managements realize, without their most able employees there would be no business at all. The staff members do not remain with an agency because they have anything resembling academic tenure. They are there because they enjoy it, and the most talented people know their value in a wider marketplace. If they are unhappy where they are, they can change jobs without much trouble. Again, this is especially true of the best creative people.

It follows that it is a delicate task to impose a corporate culture from above. As I have already explained, cultures must be encouraged to grow from below, as mutually compatible people learn to work synergistically. The leadership of the agency principals must be exercised by these people working closely with the employees, leading, coaxing, and using the employees' own contributions. This approach was not difficult for Leo Burnett, David Ogilvy, or Rosser Reeves because of the great professional respect they received inside (and also outside) their organizations. These men make very good exemplars, and it would be useful now to consider briefly the corporate cultures stimulated by these three notable figures.

The most interesting corporate culture to be found in any agency anywhere seems to me to be that associated with Leo Burnett. It grew out of the challenging notion that the agency should pursue relentlessly the "inherent drama" in the product. High aspiration is an important part of the doctrine. In addition, there are some more minor parts of the culture: it embraces research (Leo Burnett was one of the agencies that pioneered the use of small-scale qualitative research in campaign development) and overall management policy, with a concentration of the agency's efforts on a small number of very substantial and like-minded clients; also— something whose importance became recognized only in the 1980s—the agency's stock continues to be privately owned.

The culture of Leo Burnett is strongly creative-driven; the thrust of the agency's efforts has been unwaveringly to improve its advertising. It is therefore surprising that Leo Burnett is not as strongly associated with the creative revival of the 1960s as are Ogilvy, Bernbach, Tinker, and Wells. The reasons are that the agency is based in Chicago, and its clients (unlike Ogilvy's and Bernbach's in their early days) are mostly manufacturers of mainstream packaged goods. These have always been considered extremely important but inherently unglamorous types of client, although if we look at the work that the agency does, for instance, for Procter & Gamble's Cheer, few people would use the word *unglamorous* to describe it.

The culture of Ogilvy & Mather resembles a coin. The obverse describes the ways in which the agency believes that advertising, particularly press advertising, should be written. The reverse demonstrates that all the Ogilvy rules are based on research covering a wide methodological spectrum (although it is not stated that some parts of this research are in fact much less reliable than others). Ogilvy & Mather is one of the few agencies that makes a major effort to catalog what it knows, and to use operationally the lessons derived. This alone is enough to make the agency noteworthy.

Like that of Leo Burnett, Ogilvy & Mather's culture is concentrated essentially on its creative product. But because the agency tells people *how* to do things, its culture has been criticized for its rigidity. David Ogilvy has answered this criticism trenchantly, although not in my opinion entirely convincingly.[13]

The culture on which Ted Bates was founded is laid out for our inspection in Rosser Reeves's best-selling book.[14] The most important element is the much misunderstood concept of the *unique selling proposition* (USP). Bates has found this an enormously useful device, although one of the related concepts, usage pull, is based on a use of research that has been demonstrated to be fallacious.[15] The USP is of course concerned almost exclusively with the agency's creative product. Its main weakness is its complete concentration on a rational brand discriminator and its ignoring of nonrational, emotional arguments for using a brand—an especially important matter when the advertiser wishes to mirror the psychographics of a brand's existing users.

A related criticism of the unique selling proposition is the way in which it concentrates on change and conversion. It is entirely concerned with persuading nonusers of a brand to become users—by no means a universal strategy for marketers in the real world. And an extension of this strategy, which readers can easily take out of Reeves's book, is that it is concerned with turning nonusers of a brand into *exclusive* users—something that is only very rarely successful in the field of repeat purchase goods.

The Bates philosophy is concerned with a method or technique of writing advertisements. But because this is a formula approach, the agency's culture is essentially account-driven, even though the USP is a creative device and Rosser Reeves was a creative leader.

Of the three cultures I have briefly reviewed, it seems to me that Leo Burnett's has withstood the test of time the best. Rosser Reeves's has been subject to the greatest criticism, although it is still in use in an amended form in the agency, which has become Backer, Spielvogel, Bates (part of the Saatchi & Saatchi organization).

My own observation of the cultures of Leo Burnett, Ogilvy & Mather, and Ted Bates leads me to think that they have not actually permeated their companies quite as pervasively as the culture of JWT London. One reason is that they have been more concentrated on one aspect of the business: the agency's creative work. The culture of JWT London has become virtually complete in its dominance of the agency's professional endeavors, a point I shall shortly illustrate.

On the other hand, the *way* in which the culture of JWT London impinges specifically on the creative product seems to me to offer an enormous benefit. The planning procedures of the agency (based as they are on respectable psychological theory) are response-oriented. The agency sets an advertising strategy, not as an advertising stimulus (as did Ogilvy and Reeves), but in terms of a desired response. As a result, there is very little doubt in my mind that the JWT approach does not confine people too much; creative people in the agency have, prima facie, great operational freedom.

Why is it, then, that there is, as I have suggested, a recognizable style of advertising from JWT London? This is not an easy question to answer. But in my judgment it has nothing at all to do with what the agency says about creative strategy. It is a clear but indirect result of the all-embracing nature of the agency's culture.

What I have in mind are at least five features of the agency's operational procedures and the subtle influence of the agency's corporate culture on each:

1. the agency's media planning, with an instinctive concentration on television, with its bias toward emotional messages;
2. the general policy of high media concentration, with most emphasis on repetition rather than on the immediate impact of a single advertisement exposure; reliance on repetition encourages gentle, emotional selling;
3. how the agency's thinking about one brand in a market can condition its thinking about a second brand from the same manufacturer, and thus inhibit the latter; the agency tends to think instinctively in motivating rather than discriminating terms;

4. how the agency's work seems much better attuned to market leaders than to smaller brands; again, there is an emphasis on motivators: advertisements for market leaders tend to rely on motivating arguments; those for smaller brands, on harder, brand- specific discriminating arguments; and finally,

5. how the agency exclusively uses small-scale qualitative research for creative planning; technically this is not uniformly excellent, and it also provides an implicit bias toward emotional advertising (or perhaps I should say a much smaller bias toward rational copy claims than quantitative research provides); this bias again influences the style of advertising, in particular by softening the edges and giving the advertising a generic rather than a competitive orientation.

What this all leads to is an extraordinary policy of contradiction. The agency first liberates its creative people from the iron shackles that some other agencies apply, but it then ties their wrists with strong but silken bonds. The result is pretty much the same as the end product of the rules of less subtle agencies.

Twelve Practical Lessons

I am going to make twelve brief points. Although these partly summarize what I have been saying throughout this chapter, some additional arguments are being added. The overall emphasis is on the practical lessons that the analysis can provide for agency management.

1. An agency culture may encompass operational methods, but it is essentially something that transcends these. It is a quality that enters the minds of highly intelligent people and influences their thinking. It follows that the procedures and ways of looking at things that form the foundation of an effective agency culture must be relevant, substantial, arresting, and durable. An agency culture that has any real influence cannot be built on platitudes and generalities.

2. An agency culture comprises a social culture and a philosophical culture. These are related to one another and work synergisti-

cally. However, the philosophical culture is ultimately the more important in distinguishing agencies from one another. When an agency management is planning how to create a culture, this is the aspect that needs the greater attention, although it is the more difficult one to plan.

3. The trait that most obviously distinguishes the culture of one agency from that of another is whether the agency is account- driven or creative-driven. An agency culture does not change much over time (although it is capable of becoming weaker or stronger), and the part that changes even less than the other parts is the agency's account or creative orientation.

4. It may be thought that an agency culture can arise spontaneously as the result of continuous cooperative work between mutually compatible people who share a common outlook. Far more often it is actively stimulated and encouraged by the personal example of the principal(s) of an agency. This can be done successfully only if the staff who are going to be imbued with the culture are receptive to it. The soil must be fertile. This was *not* true at Colman, Prentis and Varley, but it *was* true at JWT Scandinavia.

5. An agency culture can bring advantages to an agency: synergism, particularly as it relates to the widest use of the top talent; improvement in morale; easier recruitment; and stronger continuity resulting from staff loyalty. As a result, the agency is also likely to become stronger in a competitive marketplace, something which brings it great advantages. These advantages can have a financial payoff in the elimination of waste, more efficient working, and sharper focus. The agency will drill fewer dry holes. Some of these advantages can be passed on to its clients (see point 6 below.)

6. Theoretically, clients can gain from their agency's having an effective culture, and broader social benefits can follow. The main objective of an agency culture is to enable the agency to produce better advertising for its clients more efficiently (that is, with less waste.) Better advertising is unquestionably in the interest of the clients, and is also—theoretically again—in the interest of the public as a whole, since it represents a more efficient use of resources.

During the past decade there has been a strong move in the United States toward clients' paying agencies a reduced commission.[16] Some agencies manage currently to make a profit on large accounts that pay as little as 9 percent on the gross cost of space. This profit has become possible only because of considerable cost saving, in particular a reduction in the size of agency staff. It is at least possible that the cost saving yielded by the agency culture may have provided modest economies which have contributed to the reduction in overall agency expenses.

This is, however, an extremely complicated matter. I can think of more than one agency which downsized to meet reductions in its income by firing its gurus—its most important thinkers and the inventors of its planning procedures, and the very people who were doing the most to develop the philosophical culture. When times are tough, agencies and their clients have a more urgent need for objectivity and depth than for responsiveness and fast footwork, despite the general way in which hard business conditions stimulate tactical rather than strategic thinking.

7. I believe that the most impressive and effective agency cultures (for example, Leo Burnett) are oriented virtually exclusively toward the advertising the agency produces for its clients. Burnett is one of the few agencies that has been strengthened progressively, with nothing but temporary setbacks, since the early 1960s.

8. An extension of the last point is that an effective agency culture grows more commonly in an agency headed by a creative leader (for example, Burnett, David Ogilvy, Rosser Reeves, Jack Tinker, Bill Bernbach, Raymond Rubicam, and Mary Wells.) Each of these agencies was and is the "lengthened shadow of one man" (*pace* Ms. Wells). An effective culture enables this shadow to be transformed from something evanescent into something permanent.

9. A real danger is that an agency's culture may permeate too many aspects of the operation. The agency's thinking may become narrowed. Its flexibility may be reduced. Even more seriously, talented people may become impatient with what they see as their intellectual confinement, and they will quit.[17]

Advertising is a very fertile industry, and consumers in the marketplace continue to be bombarded with huge numbers of advertisements in many media, the vast majority of which are "screened out" by consumers' own selective perception. For advertising to make any impression on consumers, there is a great premium on unorthodoxy. There is therefore a heavy down side to an agency culture if it results in uniform solutions to heterogeneous problems—in particular, if the agency leaves too strong a thumbprint on its creative products (see point 10).

10. A plausible way of defining good advertising is that it enables us to penetrate into the meaning of a brand without calling too much attention to itself. Brands are extremely variegated, and this fact strongly suggests that advertisements should be equally variegated. Here lies the subtle benefit of the device used by JWT London to define an advertising strategy in terms of the desired responses of consumers to the brand. This approach contrasts with the common notion that a strategy should dictate what elements should be built into the advertising argument. But as I have suggested in this chapter, there are other elements in the culture of JWT London that tend to negate the creative freedom that the agency initially provides.

11. Unfortunately research is of little help to us in evaluating whether an agency culture is right or wrong, too strong or too weak, effective or ineffective. There is a lag in the system. A culture takes a period to develop and mature. When it has taken hold and the time comes to weigh its results, it may be too difficult to change. Like a brand, an agency culture is slow to build, slow to run down, and virtually impossible to alter.

12. As I shall examine in chapter 10, there is a disgracefully large number of things about how advertising works that are totally unknown, only partially known, or completely misunderstood. It is notable how few agency cultures devote attention to the weak state of our knowledge. David Ogilvy is viewed by most of the advertising profession, first of all, as a creative innovator. A handful of people (myself included) think of him primarily as a man preoccupied, almost obsessed, with the need to answer fundamental questions about how advertising operates.

Advertising Budgets

The Choice Between Overspending and Underspending

A Scotch mother is the greatest asset a boy can have who desires a career in advertising. Then economy and caution are instinctive with him.[1]

Claude C. Hopkins

How Advertising Budgets Are Set

Claude Hopkins was a seminal figure—in David Ogilvy's estimation, the "father of modern advertising."[2] Yet general advertising practice in the 1990s, especially where packaged goods are involved, is only feebly influenced by Hopkins's methods, in particular by his reliance on direct-response pulling power as a measure of advertising effectiveness. Indeed Hopkins's often-repeated emphasis on objective evaluation of performance raises only the faintest echo in the advertising business today. His temperament, which is so neatly captured in the quotation that prefaces this chapter, seems to be the antithesis of that of contemporary practitioners, whose optimism, enthusiasm, and sheer blind belief in the advertising enterprise are well demonstrated in the quotations describing professional attitudes toward advertising budgeting in chapter 1. These words by modern advertising people are distant indeed from the "economy and caution" of the guru Hopkins.

In the eyes of the advertising profession today, advertising expenditure is not often seen as a major outlay that should be expected to yield a *measurable* return; it is more often regarded as a tribute paid to the gods of business. In 1989, I raised in a national forum the unorthodox, although perhaps not completely illogical, notion that manufacturers could increase their profits in stationary markets by reducing their advertising investments.[3] The response I received was immediate and rather as I had anticipated. The barrage of disagreement with my view was trenchant. I was also not very surprised by the strongly emotional nature of the arguments against me, nor at the fact that these arguments were quite uncontaminated with empirical support.[4]

In chapter 1, I introduced the idea that inefficient budgeting is the largest single source of waste in advertising. I argue in this chapter that the mind-set of Claude Hopkins would be the most salutary possible corrective to what is all too prevalent in current professional practice: determining the size of a brand's advertising budget through a combination of optimism and mindless rules of thumb unrelated to the brand's position in the marketplace. Readers should remember that the advertising budget and the creative content of the advertisements themselves are the twin variables of decisive importance to every advertising campaign.

The advertising budgets for most brands in all countries are derived from the brand's sales volume. The majority of manufacturers use the "case rate" system or one of the large number of its variants.[5] The case rate system ties a brand's advertising budget to its sales, by allocating a certain number of advertising cents or dollars to each case of the brand sold. As a result, sales and advertising move directly in step. Despite its popularity, this procedure raises three important and surprisingly obvious questions.

First, what does this system tell us about whether a brand's actual advertising budget is the right sum for generating optimum sales and maximum profit? The answer to this question must be "nothing," because the procedure is directed inward to the brand's costs and not outward to the market, the place where the brand's sales are determined.

Second, are advertisers fully aware that the advertising budget has a double influence on profit? We are used to thinking about the long-term influence on profit of the extra sales generated by advertising. But since advertising and profit are both residual expenses, there is also the immediate and direct influence of budget changes on profit in the short run. When the advertising budget goes up, profit is immediately reduced. On the other hand, any advertising cutback goes straight to the bottom line (hence the prevalence of fourth-quarter advertising cancellations to counter the effect of anticipated short-falls in sales). And do advertisers realize that in many cases, the short-term influence of advertising on profit is a *geared* effect? If the brand's net earnings ratio is smaller than its advertising-to-sales ratio, an increase or decrease in advertising will have a *greater* pro-portional effect on profit.

Third, are there any realistic options available to most advertisers other than overspending or underspending on advertising? These two unappealing alternatives generally represent our sole choices until better budgetary methods are developed, believed in, and used. The sums of money involved underline the importance of this third question. The average major advertiser spends tens of millions of dollars on advertising above the line for each of many individual brands, and hundreds of millions on all brands combined. Therefore marginal improvements in productivity are likely to provide a very significant payback indeed when measured in absolute dollar terms.

What this all amounts to is an enormous need for more efficient advertising budgeting, and this means that we badly need some tools to help us. However, if they are to be of the faintest practical use to those people who actually manage brands, such tools must be rela-tively simple in all respects; there must be no confusion about how they are constructed or how they can be used to tackle specific brand situations. And they must also be more than theoretical "constructs"; they must be recognizably derived from the experience of brands in the real world. There is no shortage of what are called in England "black boxes"—the props used by magicians; but the problem is that we are unable to discern, comprehend, or accept the contents of most of them.

This chapter describes a simple empirical tool that will help deter-mine a brand's advertising budget. A budget should in fact be influ-enced by a number of factors, some more important than others. Four of these factors are described and discussed briefly in this chap-ter. Our simple empirical device is one of these.

Advertising Works Harder for Bigger Brands

Our budgetary tool came out of an examination of large and small brands, a piece of work that was undertaken to throw light on a hypothesis that large brands are less advertising-intensive than small brands; that is, that per dollar of sales value, there is *less* advertising spent on larger brands than on smaller ones. Another way of expressing this point is that a given number of advertising dollars spent on large brands produces more sales than a similar number spent on small brands.

Impressionistic, case-by-case data suggested that there was something in this hypothesis, but there was a need for much more information to check whether it was generally valid. If the hypothesis could be proved, it would obviously tell us something of actionable value for the marketing strategy for large brands, so that the investigation was intrinsically important enough to be described here. However, the details given in this chapter are intended mainly for another purpose: to sketch in just enough background information for the reader to understand fully the budgetary tool, which happened to emerge quite serendipitously from the research into large and small brands.

The investigation was carried out in cooperation with J. Walter Thompson. In the fall of 1987, the agency's offices around the world were sent a questionnaire calling for a limited amount of clearly defined and solidly based factual data. Two hundred and forty-two completed questionnaires came back to New York, each referring to a single product category in a single country.[6] Data were sent in from twenty-three countries around the world.[7] The investigation was relatively simple. Nevertheless no inquiry covering the same ground had ever been carried out anywhere before.

Basic information was collected relating to a total of 1,096 advertised brands. This number of readings represents an excellent gross sample size, as long as it is not broken down into too many subsamples for the examination of special groups based, for instance, on product types, brand sizes, or blocs of countries. In this chapter, when the sample is fragmented in any way, the statistical dangers are pointed out, and when the data are given in percentages on a total of less than 100, the percentages are put in parentheses.

The majority of the brands covered—although certainly not all of them—were repeat-purchase packaged goods. The markets for such goods are almost invariably oligopolistic and they are generally stationary. (As discussed in chapter 2, I estimate that in the United States 90 percent of the sales of all brands are made in markets that show very little overall growth.) Sales and advertising expenditures for individual brands also tend to remain stable.[8] The advertising-to-sales ratios of such brands are normally in the 4 percent to 8 percent range.

The best way to examine advertising intensity is to estimate the advertising-to-sales ratio fairly precisely on a brand-by-brand basis. This approach needs reliable estimates both of the brand's advertising expenditure and of its sales value. While it is not difficult to arrive at an estimate of advertising expenditure, it is virtually impossible to make a tight estimate of sales on the basis of the retail audit or consumer panel data on which we have to rely if we want to examine a broad spectrum of brands. It is therefore necessary to find an alternative system of evaluating the importance of advertising in relation to sales.

Fortunately, there is an alternative method of calculating advertising intensity, and this was the method used in this investigation: it is simply to compare a brand's share of the market (on a volume or value basis, volume being used here) with its share of voice (the brand's share of the total value of the main media advertising in the product category).

The rationale for this method of calculating advertising intensity is that the cost structure of one brand in a market tends to be similar to that of any other. The manufacturers of competitive brands are also conscious of one another's advertising expenditures; this is a characteristic of oligopolistic competition. The result is that brands of a similar size tend to spend similar amounts on advertising, and also that a brand which is twice the size of another tends to spend twice as much on advertising.

The comparison of brands of different sizes introduces the concept of a normal approximate similarity between a brand's share of market and its share of voice. There are obviously some erratic exceptions, and nothing can be done to allow for these. But there are also *consistent* exceptions, which relate to brands of different sizes. The purpose of this study was to examine these consistent exceptions.

The first step was to break down the data into two categories:

- *profit-taking brands* (or underspenders): those whose share of voice is the same as or below their share of market[9]
- *investment brands* (or overspenders): those whose share of voice is clearly above their share of market

In table 5–1, all the brands have been put into groups covering three percentage points of market share (1% to 3%, 4% to 6%, and so on). The reason is that the sample cannot be reliably broken down to allow an analysis based on single percentage points of share. As can be seen in this table, profit-taking brands are in a minority among those with small market shares; but the proportion consistently increases as the brands get larger. The trend is uninterrupted: from 27% for brands with a 1% to 3% share of market, to 59% for those with a share of 16% or more.

TABLE 5–1
Analysis of Profit-Taking and Investment Brands

	All Brands	Profit-Taking Brands (Share of Voice Equal to or Smaller than Share of Market)	Investment Brands (Share of Voice Larger than Share of Market)
Total	1,096 = 100%	= 44%	= 56%
Share of Market			
1% to 3%	224 = 100%	= 27%	= 73%
4% to 6%	218 = 100%	= 37%	= 63%
7% to 9%	153 = 100%	= 41%	= 59%
10% to 12%	112 = 100%	= 45%	= 55%
13% to 15%	(77 = 100%)	(= 56%)	(= 44%)
16% and over	312 = 100%	= 59%	= 41%

Note: This analysis is confined to advertised brands.

The picture is remarkably clear, and there are three forces at work that are responsible for it.

The first is that new and burgeoning brands (which are of course nearly always small) normally receive advertising investments deliberately calculated to exceed their market share percentages. Indeed, A. C. Nielsen has long recommended this budgetary policy on the basis of an extensive empirical knowledge of successful and unsuccessful new brands.[10] This factor accounts for many small-share brands having relatively high shares of voice.

The second factor is the all-too-common practice of "milking" older and often quite large brands. This is a tempting strategy for manufacturers, because significantly reducing advertising and promotional support can bring about a sometimes dramatic increase in a brand's earnings in the short run (although sales will almost certainly be adversely affected, an effect that will eventually lead to the demise of the geese that lay the golden eggs). Manufacturers are sometimes persuaded to adopt this strategy because of a belief in brand-life-cycle theory. This belief is essentially self-fulfilling, because the very act of cutting down support when a brand's sales are turning down, in the expectation that such a downturn is inevitable, will actually cause the downturn to be accelerated.[11] An examination of the 389 larger brands in our sample (table 5–2) shows that a third of the profit-taking brands are in a slightly falling sales trend, which suggests that many, if not most, of these are being milked.

TABLE 5–2
Analysis of Brands with 13% + Share of Market

	All Brands	Profit-Taking Brands (Share of Voice Equal to or Smaller than Share of Market)	Investment Brands (Share of Voice Larger than Share of Market)
Sample size	389	226	163
	100	100	100
Brands with			
Slightly rising share (%)	43	39	49
Static share (%)	26	28	24
Slightly falling share (%)	31	33	27
Premium price (%)	32	28	37
Average price (%)	51	54	46
Below-average price (%)	17	18	17

Note: This analysis is confined to advertised brands.

The third factor causing a consistent disparity between shares of market and shares of voice is the most interesting and possibly the most important of the forces at work. Many large brands flourish in the marketplace with shares of voice consistently below their shares of market. (According to the data in table 5–2, two thirds of large profit-taking brands are holding or improving their market shares.) This indeed means that for such brands, advertising works harder, dollar for dollar, than it does for most smaller brands, creating a clear advertising-related economy of scale for such large brands. This scale economy can be expressed for any brand by the dollar value representing the difference between its appropriation with a normal relationship of share of market and share of voice, and the smaller dollar amount actually spent on it. This is one of the real strengths of the branding phenomenon. Another of its strengths clearly visible in table 5–2 is that 28 percent of the profit-taking brands are able to command a premium price in the market.

The cause and operating mechanism of this scale economy are not known with certainty, but they are thought to be related to a characteristic of consumer purchasing behavior: a tendency for large brands to benefit from above-average purchase and repurchase frequency. In a book published in 1986, I coined the term *penetration supercharge* to describe this phenomenon, and it is one which appears to have a wide application.[12]

Average Share of Voice: A Budgetary Planning Tool

These findings provided satisfactory confirmation of my original hypothesis that large brands are less advertising-intensive than small ones. But the next step in the investigation— the calculation of *average* shares of voice for brands of different market shares—provided the practical budgetary tool referred to earlier in this chapter. Its derivation and practical use are now described. Also, as the result of an additional analysis, a very important and practical example is given of the device in action.

Table 5–3 concentrates exclusively on typical packaged-goods markets which are reasonably balanced competitively. These provide data with the maximum of internal consistency, which give relatively clear results.[13] There were 666 brands that could be classified in this way, and these were grouped into families covering three percentage points of market share. For each brand, the difference between share of voice and share of market was calculated, and these differences were averaged within each family of brands. These differences vary according to the size of the brand. Again there is a fairly consistent picture. Brands in the 1% to 3% range overinvest in advertising by an average of five percentage points, and brands in the 28 to 30 percent range underinvest by an average of five percentage points. The size brackets in between follow an approximate continuum, but with some discontinuities.

TABLE 5–3

Share of Market Compared with Share of Voice
(Brands in Balanced Packaged-Goods Markets)

	Share of Voice Minus Share of Market (Percentage Points)
Share of market	
1% to 3%	+5
4% to 6%	+4
7% to 9%	+2
10% to 12%	+4
13% to 15%	+1
16% to 18%	+2
19% to 21%	No difference
22% to 24%	−3
25% to 27%	−5
28% to 30%	−5

Sample size = 666 brands in 117 markets.

These data can be set out diagrammatically (figure 5–1), and although the trend line is not a perfect fit, there is a reasonable-looking curve, which descends in a convex path. This convexity provides a hint that the gap between share of voice and share of market tends to increase as share of market grows. I describe figure 5–1 as the *advertising-intensiveness curve* (AIC).[14]

The AIC can be used for operational purposes. The advertising appropriation for any brand in a balanced packaged-goods market can be tested according to the averages embodied in this curve. The brand's market share can be located on the curve, and the advertising share of voice for all brands of that same size can be read off. This

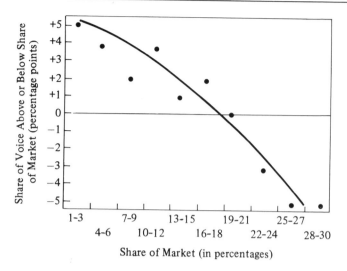

FIGURE 5–1

Advertising-Intensiveness Curve

figure can be converted without much trouble into an advertising expenditure calculated in dollars or any other currency. And such a money estimate will provide a normal expenditure level with which the brand's actual expenditure can be compared, and from which operational conclusions can be drawn.

A further analysis was carried out which also yields operational conclusions (table 5–4). All the brands with market shares of 13 percent or more in these balanced packaged-goods markets were isolated, and the brands in upward, static, and declining trends were broken out, with their average shares of voice compared with their market shares.

TABLE 5–4

Analysis of Larger Brands in Typical Balanced Packaged-Goods Markets

Share of Voice Minus Share of Market	
13% + brands with rising trends ($n = 83$)	−1 percentage point
13% + brands with static trends ($n = 53$)	−3 percentage points
13% + brands with declining trends ($n = 64$)	−4 percentage points

Allowing for the small sample sizes, it can be concluded at least tentatively that the average larger (13% +) brand with a rising sales trend will be profit-taking, that is, underinvesting in advertising by one percentage point. But there are signs that, with a greater underinvestment, the sales increase will be imperiled, and if the underinvestment opens out to four percentage points, the sales increase will turn into a decline for the average brand.

These estimates are averages, and it is to be expected that the figures for individual brands will vary to some degree from them. In particular, weaker brands can be expected to stand less underinvestment, and stronger brands rather more underinvestment.

I have published data describing one specific strong brand, and these are briefly summarized here.[15] The brand is Lux, a major international toilet soap manufactured by Unilever. The brand has an aggregate volume brand share in thirty leading countries of 17 percent and an overall share of voice of 14 percent. With this share of voice, Lux is holding its market share and, on occasion, increasing it marginally. Note that this is a slightly more optimistic performance than the overall averages for all brands would suggest. Evidence from markets where the brand's advertising has been cut back indicates that loss of share will result from a share of voice of less than 12 percent. The threshold level of underinvestment for this brand is therefore five percentage points below its market share, again indicating a better performance than the overall averages.

Lux is one of the most remarkable brands in any product field. It has occupied a major share of its category for more than sixty years, and in many countries it has achieved extraordinary levels of consumer penetration and purchase frequency. Its ability to beat the odds in its underinvestment is clearly a function of its massive strength in the marketplace.

It must be reiterated that the data presented here demonstrate that profit taking by planned underinvestment in advertising is a normal (and successful) policy *only for large brands*. The others— specifically those with a market share of under 13 percent—are, on average, in an investment situation, with a higher share of voice than share of market.

Readers should also be reminded that a significant minority of substantial and sophisticated advertisers and agencies have for a long time considered share of voice an important influence on a brand's position in the market and hence a partial determinant of its budgetary strategy. Indeed share of voice has been incorporated as an independent variable in many econometric models that have been used in the marketplace, some quite productively. Such practical experience means that analyzing share of voice and its derivative, average share of voice (described in this chapter), is more than an armchair exercise or piece of academic speculation unconnected with the real world. Average share of voice is an original concept with a practical application.

Further Empirical Evaluation

The AIC was first drawn up from a reasonably strong data base. It has also been tested by the use of (at least) five further data sources. Three major advertising agencies have been involved: Backer, Spielvogel, Bates; Leo Burnett; and J. Walter Thompson. Two of the new data bases covered a range of advertised goods and services, similar to the battery of information used to construct the original AIC. The other three new data bases related to individual product categories in two separate but highly developed countries, the United States and the United Kingdom.

While all five of the new data sources yielded a regression similar in general shape to the original AIC, there is an important difference between the original curve and those derived from the three individual product categories. The curves from these categories have the general shape of curve A2 in figure 5–2. (Curve A1 is the original AIC.)

The specific ways in which curve A2 differs from A1 are that:

1. A2 cuts the horizontal zero line further to the left than does A1. This means that manufacturers start underinvesting in the more sophisticated countries with brands of smaller sizes than is the case in other countries.
2. The degree of investment for smaller brands is less pronounced in the more sophisticated countries (A2). This is a function of the relatively *greater prevalence of smaller brands* in large countries than in small countries.[16]
3. The falloff in the curve is steeper in the more developed countries (A2). This seems to suggest a greater tendency to milk larger brands in more mature markets.

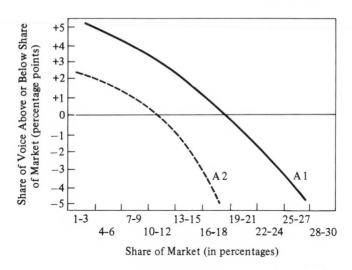

FIGURE 5–2

Original and Supplementary Advertising-Intensiveness Curves

These three points are made tentatively because the data on which they are based are thinner than those from which the original AIC was built. But the likelihood that more sophisticated countries yield a slightly different AIC from less developed countries suggests that if we wish to use the AIC operationally, it is wise to supplement the basic AIC with a specially constructed AIC for any category we are looking at. This is not a difficult procedure, but whether it can be done effectively depends on the number of brands from which observations can be made. For instance, it would obviously be an easier procedure with soft drinks in the United States (where there is considerable brand fragmentation) than with disposable diapers (where the market is dominated by three brands).

The Practical Value of the Budgetary Planning Tool

The AIC has two important features. First, it gives us a *measure,* that is, a useful objective comparison between our brand's advertising expenditure in its own marketplace and the expenditures of many other brands of a comparable size in different marketplaces.

Second, it provides us with a change of viewpoint, a shift away from the usual inward-directed system based on the brand's case rate. We move outward to the market, where the brand's sales are made. As a result, it becomes psychologically easier for us to accommodate other market-based criteria. A single rule of thumb will give way to a sensible use of judgment in weighing facts from different sources. None of these facts is good enough on its own, but each brings something important to the party.

Let us look at four such facts, beginning with the AIC.

1. Average Share of Voice

Average share of voice is the measure discussed in this chapter. The AIC is generally useful in determining the overall expenditure bracket for a brand of any size, as it has been determined by a broad range of brands of a similar size. The particular value of the AIC is to help determine the specific level of underinvestment that may be acceptable for larger brands, subject to area testing. I am of course thinking of controlled programs of underinvestment which are well short of milking the brand.

2. Marketplace Trends

The advertiser should evaluate trends in category sales, trends in the brand's sales, the competitive situation, trends in total category advertising, the current level of the brand's advertising, and trends in the advertising budgets of specific competitors. Although these pieces of information are all important, major changes in any year tend to be the exception and not the rule: most packaged goods markets are reasonably stable in most respects. The value of studying stationary markets is to determine normal levels of the main marketing variables, including advertising budgets. But the existence of normal levels does not imply immovable stasis; indeed gradual changes are always possible and often take place in the long run.

3. The Brand's Response to Advertising Pressure

Many long-established brands have built a useful track record of experience of varying levels of advertising pressure. In a substantial minority of cases, econometric studies have produced a specific advertising elasticity—an estimate of the marginal increase in sales that will follow a 1 percent increase in the advertising pressure put behind the brand. This is an input of extraordinary value and importance, and it should also be emphasized that experimental marketplace testing of different levels of advertising pressure to determine such coefficients, despite the fact that it is still a relatively uncommon procedure, is something that will increase in importance in the future. It should be on the agenda of all major advertisers. This very important concept is discussed in more detail in chapter 6.

4. *The Cost Structure of the Brand*

The cost structure of the brand tells the advertiser what level of advertising is affordable, while a given level of profit is maintained. If factors 1, 2, and 3 all add up to a higher expenditure than does factor 4, the advertiser is in an obviously difficult position and must rethink the short-term profit target for the brand and decide whether it will make sense to accept reduced (or zero or negative) profit for a finite period, in the expectation that the brand will pay out and recoup the investment at a targeted future date. This is a worst case scenario, but it is a less unattractive option than spending what the brand can afford in the strong likelihood that it will be too little to be effective.

It is, however, possible, to say the least, that factors 1, 2, and 3 will lead to a *smaller* expenditure than will factor 4. In this case, there is a good reason now to conduct some carefully evaluated area testing of advertising downweighting.

The evaluation will of course measure the effect of any advertising reduction on the brand's sales volume. From this effect the loss of profit can be computed. Anything more than a marginal loss of sales may endanger the brand's "critical mass," with its ability to generate scale economies. However, this is by no means a certain outcome. If competitive brands also follow the path of budget reduction, the eventual outcome will probably be no loss of aggregate sales in the market and reasonable stability in the shares of the individual brands.[17] Even if our brand goes it alone, there may be no serious reduction in its overall sales. But the important point is that area testing can help us evaluate in advance the likely extent of a reduction in sales and how far the loss of profit on any fall in sales will offset the (normally substantial) amount of money saved by the advertising cutback.

Some advertisers may fear that an advertising cutback on their part may be met by an opportunistic advertising increase on the part of their competitors. This is a possibility, but its consequences need not be much feared. The advertising elasticity for most brands tends to be low, so that the sales response to additional advertising pressure is very limited. This point is illustrated in chapter 6. The result is that our brand is unlikely to lose much share to competitors which have opportunistically increased their budgets.

Summary

1. The case rate method for determining a brand's advertising budget is an inefficient system despite its virtually universal use. It is inefficient because it is concerned with a brand's costs and not with the wider marketplace where the brand's sales are generated.

2. The AIC method described in this chapter is derived from average advertising expenditure levels for brands of different sizes. It is an objective, market-based guide for setting advertising budgets, and it is relatively simply to apply.

3. No single system should be used to determine a brand's budget, no matter how soundly based it may be. This chapter proposes that at least four factors should be taken into account, and that the budget should be determined judgmentally from a consideration of all four.

4. The four factors are
   a. the AIC, supplemented where possible by a special AIC drawn up for the product category of the brand under examination;
   b. a full evaluation of marketplace trends;
   c. a calculation of the brand's advertising elasticity, if it is possible to arrive at this;
   d. an analysis of the brand's cost and profit structure.

5. If the consensus of factors a, b, and c points to a *higher* budget than does factor d, the sales and profit targets of the brand should be rethought so that the time period before the brand is expected to generate full profit can be extended. The most likely operational outcome is an experimental program of increased advertising pressure in an area.

6. If factor d points to a *higher* budget than the consensus of factors a, b, and c, there should be no general downweighting without experimental area testing of reduced advertising pressure.

Promotions

A Game of Double Jeopardy

The only way to a position in which economics might give positive advice on a larger scale to businessmen, leads through quantitative work. For as long as we are unable to put our arguments into figures, the voice of our science, although occasionally it may help to dispel errors, will never be heard by practical men.

Joseph A. Schumpeter

A Legacy of Stagnation and Inflation

Chapter 2 gave details of the gradual stagnation in consumer goods markets in the United States and the influence of this stagnation on the fragmentation of brands, the plateauing of advertising expenditure above the line, and the growth of promotions below the line.

Chapter 6 focuses on promotional activity, and it addresses promotions from the point of view of their effectiveness, and in particular their profit yield. In order to provide a perspective, I also look at "theme" advertising above the line and also attempt to judge the profitability of that activity. As I argued in chapter 2, the main cause of the progressive increase in the proportion of combined advertising and promotional (A & P) budgets that is going below the line is the general and progressive flattening of consumer goods markets. In the absence of aggregate category growth, manufacturers find that promotions have a more immediate effect on market share than has theme advertising. This effect does not necessarily hold for profitability, and this chapter argues that promotions are a major source of waste because in general they are planned with sales (rather than profit) in mind.

The increase in the share of A & P funds going into promotions began to take place before 1980. The decade of the 1970s was a time of high inflation, and one of the side effects of this dismal and pernicious phenomenon was that it also contributed to tipping the balance of A & P investment below the line. Inflation meant that business gradually became accustomed to a situation of declining profit when measured in real terms.[1] Profit itself was regarded (at least for a while) as an inefficient measure of the performance of an organization: "'Profit,' it cannot be said often enough, is an accounting illusion . . . the announcement of 'record profits' is being greeted with skepticism by the Stock Exchange and with hostility by the public at large."[2]

It was during the 1970s that managers got into the habit of boosting the list prices of their goods and simultaneously making deep promotional price cuts. Profit was therefore sliced away before firms could benefit from it.[3] The habit of mind associated with this procedure has not been totally eradicated. Indeed, it offers the most plausible explanation for a tacit and possibly unconscious shift of goals on the part of many businesspeople. Despite a good deal of talk about the importance of profit, the actual pursuit of profit appears to have given way de facto to a search for growth in naked sales volume.

Market maturity and inflation led to much puzzlement and frustration. But they certainly did not lead to any slackening of the competitive impulse. Competition—and in particular, competitive response—has become increasingly aggressive as manufacturers react in frustration to what they see as the inertia of markets. Their yardstick of success is their brands' market shares. Much of the initial competitiveness and the reaction that it generates cancel one another out, but the drive continues unabated because manufacturers have an atavistic fear of any relaxation.

Sales volume and market share are regarded as the keys to the future. This view is not entirely fallacious insofar as volume can represent a source both of future repeat business and of manufacturing and marketing scale economies. But the concentration on sales volume has resulted in a remarkable neglect of the price that manufacturers pay and the profit that they are therefore obliged to sacrifice as a result of the marketing plans they embark on so optimistically.

This is not all. In addition to the massive and, in many cases, concealed costs that manufacturers pay for their attempts to increase their short-term sales volume at their competitors' expense, there is a second series of even more worrisome ill effects that are manifested over the longer term and that are described and discussed in this chapter. These short- and long-term outcomes represent a double jeopardy that managers, unthinkingly and unwittingly, encounter as a routine part of their marketing operations.

Short-Term Effects of Promotions and How to Measure Them

As I have already argued, manufacturers have put large and increasing quantities of money into promotions because many of them believe that a given sum spent on promotions has a greater and more immediate proportionate effect on sales volume than theme advertising has. Historically, the responsiveness of sales to promotional activity is not much in dispute, but there are enormous concealed problems in the proper measurement of such effects. A promotion is a device that enables a manufacturer to buy tonnage sales on a once-and-for-all basis. Repeat purchase is only rarely stimulated. And although a promotion does normally have a measurable short-term effect on sales, the down side is that in the great majority of cases, manufacturers pay a price that is frankly exorbitant. I can conceive of them doing this only because they have not calculated rigorously enough what they are really paying for the tonnage they are buying.

This chapter is concerned with, among other things, helping them to make this calculation.

What promotions mean in the majority of circumstances is price reduction. This procedure is disguised even by manufacturers' own terminology. Promotions are often described as "investments," when they are in reality income sacrificed; they should appear on the income side of the ledger (as a reduction, a negative item), and not on the expenditure side (as money consciously and explicitly paid out). Trade promotions, which (as we saw in chapter 2) accounted for 39 percent of total A & P budgets in 1989 (compared with 27 percent that went into consumer promotions), virtually always mean rebates, even when described by such names as *slotting allowances, advertising rebates,* and *display incentives.* Of consumer promotions, the most important are coupons and various types of temporary price reduction (TPRs), that is, price rebates printed on the label, banded packs, free samples, and so on. These devices, those directed both at the trade and at the consumer, are mostly variations on the theme of price cutting.

As any student of microeconomics knows, the sales effect of price cutting can be quantified—with a good deal of trouble and given enough data to allow the calculation of a coefficient of price elasticity. This is a number, and it means simply the percentage by which the sales of a brand will increase in the short run as a result of a 1 percent reduction in price. Note that the number is preceded by a minus sign, demonstrating that lower prices cause sales to go up, and vice versa. The calculation is made from a laborious examination of historical price and sales data that establish an average sales change associated with a price change, and this should be arrived at from a range of prices. Exogenous variables have to be accounted for, as well as time lags between price change and sales change. The data on prices must also be corrected for inflation.

The elasticity can of course be calculated for sales to the retail trade and also for sales to the consumer, and there are some interesting differences between the two. However, these are not the concern of this chapter. The main focus here is on the consumer, but it should be remembered that trade and consumer promotions can be connected; in particular, the profit from a trade promotion is not always retained by the retailer, who sometimes passes it to the customer (for example, by doubling the value of manufacturer's coupons). Incidentally, consumer promotions are all, to some extent, also directed at the retail trade insofar as they are intended to encourage retailers to display the merchandise promoted. Display is an important sales stimulus in its own right, and it can also reinforce other stimuli.

Price elasticity is essentially a measure of how easily the consumer will accept a competitive brand in substitution for the brand being examined. Low price elasticity means that substitution is difficult and that a change in price will not affect the demand for the brand very greatly. The opposite also holds: if elasticity is high, price change greatly affects demand. As the number of competitors grows (something that tends to happen over time even though markets do not grow much in absolute size), we would logically expect price elasticities in general to rise.[4]

Calculations of price elasticity are not simple, and manufacturers only rarely have on their staffs statisticians capable of making the estimates. However, the calculations have been made in hundreds of cases. They are almost invariably based on a relatively narrow range of price variations, so that they should not be extrapolated too far outside this range. They can nevertheless be used for sales optimization and profit maximization, a process in which I myself participated as long ago as the early 1960s.[5]

A number of estimates have been published of the average price elasticity of groups of brands. The most recent major study, by Gerard J. Tellis of the University of Southern California, reviews and summarizes the figures for 367 different brands which appeared in the academic literature published between 1961 and 1985.[6] The most striking feature of Tellis's survey is the high level of the average price elasticity: −1.76. This means that, for an average brand, a 1 percent reduction in price would boost sales by 1.76 percent. Manufacturers do not of course vary their prices in 1 percent increments; a more realistic 10 percent price reduction would lift sales by 17.6 percent, an impressive figure. However, this sales increase alone provides an extremely incomplete picture of the effect of the price reduction, a point that will be demonstrated and discussed later in this chapter.

In table 6–1, I have made a number of calculations of the sales effect of a 10 percent price reduction, based on price elasticities of −1.6, −1.8, −2.0, and −2.2. Tellis has argued that typical marketplace elasticities may be much higher than the −1.76 average he worked out from his 367 cases. However, the empirical support for his hypothesis of higher elasticities is much more tenuous than that for his −1.76 average.[7] Estimates based on European experience suggest that even Tellis's average of −1.76 may be too high.[8] I have therefore limited the calculations to the range of coefficients listed above, which cover not only Tellis's average, but also elasticities on both sides of it.

If we look solely at the sales projections in table 6–1, these provide ample support for the view that promotions can shift merchandise. It

TABLE 6–1

Effect of 10% Price Reduction

Variable Cost as Percentage of NSV	Price Elasticity	Effect on Sales (%)	Effect on Net Profit If 5% of NSV (%)	Effect on Net Profit If 10% of NSV (%)
40	−2.2	+22	+20	+10
50	−2.2	+22	−24	−12
60	−2.2	+22	−67	−34
40	−2.0	+20	No change	No change
50	−2.0	+20	−40	−20
60	−2.0	+20	−80	−40
40	−1.8	+18	−20	−10
50	−1.8	+18	−56	−28
60	−1.8	+18	−92	−46
40	−1.6	+16	−40	−20
50	−1.6	+16	−72	−36
60	−1.6	+16	−104	−52

is therefore perfectly easy to understand the attraction they hold for a brand manager, particularly one who finds himself or herself in the uncomfortable situation (which I have witnessed on many occasions) of running a brand whose shipments during the year have been slower than planned and whose sales target has to be met by December 31—and particularly a brand manager whose career is on the line.

But the attractive volume figures are not the whole story. We must look at how costs have been affected. In order to do this, we have to make certain assumptions about the cost structure of the brand that is being examined. In table 6–1, alternatives have been worked out on the basis of ratios which are reasonably typical for real brands:

- variable cost representing 40%, 50%, and 60% of net sales value (NSV)[9]
- net profit representing 5% and 10% of NSV

As has already been pointed out, the table examines four different levels of price elasticity, and a single price reduction, of 10%.

The most obvious feature of the profit calculations is that most of the sales increases provided by the price reductions yield a lower profit than before the sales rise. Indeed, some of the resulting profit reductions are *disastrously large*. The reasons for this unappealing outcome are

1. an increase in variable costs (raw materials, packaging, labor, and so on) required by the extra sales volume, in conjunction with
2. a deflation in the NSV which applies to *all sales resulting from the lower consumer price* (that is, all sales of the brand offered on the promotional terms; unpromoted merchandise will be sold at list price, on which it will earn normal profit).

A certain amount of promotion is undertaken for defensive reasons, for instance, to maintain high distribution and display for brands in an increasingly concentrated retail trade.[10] This approach is understandable, although manufacturers should also be able to provide a countervailing force to retailers' strength, by the obvious method of ensuring that their consumer advertising will pull the merchandise through the retail pipeline; and, perhaps equally important, by ensuring that retail buyers will be aware of this process.

Although promotional actions are conducted from a mixture of offensive and defensive motives which cannot often be separated from one another, I believe that the former are generally the more important. Indeed, it seems clear to me that in the majority of circumstances, manufacturers who promote heavily are deliberately exchanging profit for volume; in other words, they are making less profit on greater sales or, to make the point more crudely, slicing into their own margins in order to dump their merchandise.

Longer-Term Considerations

Earlier in this chapter, I referred to the even more worrying long-term legacy of promotions. I had in mind three separate points, points that are in fact all related to one another.

First, there is overwhelming marketplace evidence that the majority of promotions have only a limited long-term effect. A price-off promotion causes sales to rise, but they then return to their original level once the promotion stops.[11] The "blip" on the Nielsen consumer purchases graph looks like the silhouette of a top hat.[12] The reason is very simply that the strategy for such a promotion aims to move merchandise by bribing the retailer and the consumer. When the bribe stops, the extra sales also stop.

It has been argued by some commentators that a proportion of promotional money has a long-term franchise-building effect.[13] There is a limited degree of truth in this argument when it relates to promotions that encourage repeat purchase. However, all trade promotions and the most important consumer promotions (TPRs and coupons) have just about the smallest long-term effect of any below-the-line activity. With TPRs in particular, there is no stress on building a consumer franchise by emphasizing the competitive benefits of the brand or building warm nonrational associations with it, which might encourage the public to buy the goods on a more-or-less continuous basis. As a consequence, such promotions lead to volatile demand, in contrast to franchise building (for instance, by consumer advertising), which leads to relatively stable demand. A promotion often also results in what Nielsen calls a "mortgaging" effect, by bringing forward sales from a later period; thus full-price sales in the period following the promotion may be even less than they would otherwise have been. Mortgaging effectively prolongs the period during which the manufacturer is paying a heavy promotional subsidy to the consumer.

This all leads to a not insignificant weakening of the brand. A parallel point, for which there is patchy evidence, is that brands which are supported more by advertising than by promotions often carry, without too much trouble, a higher-than-average list price and tend therefore to be more profitable.[14] The consumer pays the premium price because the advertised brands have given more psychological added values than have heavily promoted brands.[15] This point is related to the third legacy, to be discussed later.

The second long-term disadvantage is that promotions fuel the flames of competitive retaliation to a far greater degree than other marketing activities. As a result, diminishing returns set in with frightening rapidity.[16] When the competition is drawn into the promotional war, it can cause the sharp sales increases predicted by the original price elasticity coefficients to be significantly muted—with an even more disastrous effect on the profit outcome of the promotions.

The long-term result of such retaliation has sometimes been that all profit has been eliminated from total market categories. There is no shortage of examples of this self-destructive effect. Two dramatic instances which I can remember from my own professional career are the market for laundry detergents in Denmark during the 1960s and the once-large market in Britain for fruit concentrates which the housewife mixed with water to make soft drinks. In both markets, heavy promotions eventually caused strong brands to degenerate into virtually unbranded (and unprofitable) commodities.

The third long-term legacy of promotions is the one that is most talked about, particularly by advertising agencies. Promotions are said to devalue the image of the promoted brand in the eyes of the consumer. This theory accords with common sense, although there is no very extensive evidence to support it. Indeed, the argument may not be quite as powerful as it appears, because once a brand has established a consumer franchise and a brand image, it takes a long time for these to decay, as the image is maintained more by people's personal familiarity with and usage of the brand than by external marketing stimuli. However, promotions have occasionally, but undoubtedly, had an unfavorable influence on consumers' brand perceptions. There is good (unpublished) evidence that this happened to Burger King in the late 1970s and early 1980s, when the brand was in a promotional war with McDonald's.

As a general rule, the image of a brand can never be improved by promotions—a matter directly related to the stability of the consumer franchise. In Unilever language, there is a vicious circle described as "promotion–commotion–demotion."[17]

The image can, on the other hand, be strengthened by consumer advertising. This strengthening represents a long-term effect in addition to short-term sales generation, and it leads to an increasing perceived differentiation of the advertised brand from rival brands. This differentiation in turn reduces their ability to substitute for it, thus leading to greater stability (that is, less elasticity) of consumer demand for the advertised brand. This outcome can represent a significant advantage, discussed further in the concluding section of this chapter (although certain informed observers are skeptical about whether the creative quality of present-day campaigns actually leads to as much image building as past advertising was capable of doing). Advertisers' general ability to reduce the elasticity of demand is examined in some detail in appendix A.

The Return on Advertising Investments

We now come to the very difficult matter of evaluating advertising investments, since readers will undoubtedly be asking themselves the question: If promotions involve such massive short-term costs and bring about such worrisome long-term problems, can advertising investments promise anything better?

Setting to one side the potentially favorable long-term effect of advertising which provides something like an added bonus, we can on occasion quantify advertising's strictly short-term effect. This is based on a calculation of the advertising elasticity of a brand. This calculation is also a number, and it measures the percentage increase in sales that can be expected from a 1 percent increase in advertising weight. The coefficient is preceded by a plus and not by a minus sign, since (it is hoped!) an increase in advertising will result in an increase in sales.

Estimating advertising elasticity involves complex regression calculations, but (as for price elasticity) the computation has been carried out in hundreds of cases. The spread of research based on single-source scanner data will make it easier to make such calculations in the future.

The most recently published examination of advertising elasticity was based on 128 cases, which provided an average short-term advertising elasticity of +0.22.[18] This figure agrees well with earlier published studies.[19] The reader will be struck by the large difference between this advertising elasticity coefficient of +0.22 and the average price elasticity of −1.76. It is, however, extremely dangerous to draw conclusions about the apparently much greater effectiveness of promotions. The key difference between promotions and advertising is that promotional price reductions cost the manufacturer much more money than advertising increases, so that it is highly misleading to evaluate their relative effectiveness by their sales effect alone.[20]

Table 6–2 looks at the sales and profit outcomes of a 50% advertising uplift. In this table (as in table 6–1), I have been concerned

TABLE 6–2

Effect of 50% Advertising Increase

Variable Cost as Percentage of NSV (%)	A:S Ratio (%)	Advertising Elasticity	Effect on Sales (%)	Effect on Net Profit If 5% of NSV (%)	Effect on Net Profit If 10% of NSV (%)
40	4	+0.1	+5	+20	+10
50	4	+0.1	+5	+10	+5
60	4	+0.1	+5	No change	No change
40	4	+0.2	+10	+80	+40
50	4	+0.2	+10	+60	+30
60	4	+0.2	+10	+40	+20
40	4	+0.3	+15	+140	+70
50	4	+0.3	+15	+110	+55
60	4	+0.3	+15	+80	+40
40	6	+0.1	+5	No change	No change
50	6	+0.1	+5	-10	-5
60	6	+0.1	+5	-20	-10
40	6	+0.2	+10	+60	+30
50	6	+0.2	+10	+40	+20
60	6	+0.2	+10	+20	+10
40	6	+0.3	+15	+120	+60
50	6	+0.3	+15	+90	+45
60	6	+0.3	+15	+60	+30
40	8	+0.1	+5	-20	-10
50	8	+0.1	+5	-30	-15
60	8	+0.1	+5	-40	-20
40	8	+0.2	+10	+40	+20
50	8	+0.2	+10	+20	+10
60	8	+0.2	+10	No change	No change
40	8	+0.3	+15	+100	+50
50	8	+0.3	+15	+70	+35
60	8	+0.3	+15	+40	+20

solely with the sorts of operational changes in marketing variables that a manufacturer is accustomed to making. Business does not operate with 1% advertising variations any more than it does with 1% price changes. From my own experience of advertising pressure testing and the difficulties of measuring its effects, 50% is the minimum uplift in the advertising appropriation that will get the needle to swing. The profitability estimates in table 6–2 are based on:

- variable costs of 40%, 50%, and 60% of NSV;
- advertising to sales (A:S) ratios of 4%, 6%, and 8% of NSV;
- advertising elasticity coefficients of +0.1, +0.2, and +0.3;
- net profit representing 5% and 10% of NSV

What is strikingly obvious in table 6–2 is that, despite the relatively small sales effects of the extra advertising, these sales produce good profit increases in the majority of cases. This outcome is quite different from the effect of the price reductions analyzed in table 6–1, where the sales increases are all substantial, but nearly all of them are accompanied by serious reductions in profit.

But before we rush headlong out of promotions and into advertising, making advertising agencies our friends for life, let me remind the readers that the world is a confusing place, and that there are some additional complications to be examined. These are discussed in the next section of this chapter, in which I attempt to provide readers with a set of signposts—easy to read but rather less easy to follow—which are intended to help them through a maze which has two entrances, one labeled *promotions* and the other, *advertising*.

From Theory to Practice: Three Operational Recommendations

The basic discipline described in this chapter, the use of mathematical techniques to help project the sales volume and profit which are likely to follow specific marketing actions, is intended to sharpen the efficiency of marketing practice. This discipline is currently rather rarely applied in the United States, although somewhat less rarely in Great Britain. The main reason for the very slow adoption of the methods described in this chapter is that not many manufacturers are prepared to go to the considerable trouble of developing the tools, that is, estimating the price elasticity and advertising elasticity for their brands. This estimation is more than a once-and-for-all process, because the actual outcome of promotional and advertising activities may differ slightly from predictions, so that manufacturers must expect to have to monitor their price and advertising elasticities continuously and to adjust them as necessary.

It will be obvious to readers that their first basic task is to carry out a good deal of homework to produce the tools, that is, the elasticity coefficients. Everything I shall say in this concluding section is predicated on the assumption that this work will be done.

We now come to three operational recommendations.

Price Elasticity and List Price

The first possibility a manufacturer should consider is a permanent price increase for its brand. At the lower levels of price elasticity, the loss of sales that would result from a 5 percent of 10 percent price increase is so small and the increased revenue from the higher price so significant that the price reduction will often lead to a net increase in the profit earned by the brand. Indeed, this is a realistic possibility for brands with elasticities of -1.0 and less. If the elasticity is below -0.5, the chance of a major profit increase is very good indeed.

Price Elasticity and Promotional Planning

The second recommendation is that manufacturers do everything possible to evaluate the sales and profit results of each specific promotional action and accumulate (and eventually use in promotional planning) a battery of results data.

It is not necessary to repeat the lessons contained in this chapter about the danger of overpromoting and sacrificing profit for volume, lessons that point to the danger of implementing promotions in anything but a carefully planned and well-disciplined fashion. In order to test the tightness of the planning for each brand's promotional program, manufacturers should estimate how much promotional activity is necessary for strictly defensive purposes:

1. to maintain competitive levels of display in supermarkets
2. to counter the more aggressive promotional actions of the largest and most direct competition

Promotional expenditure in excess of what is needed for these defensive purposes should be scrutinized with maximum rigor. This is very much a judgment call. However, the projections of sales and profit from specific price reductions provide the best available data on which an evaluation of the probable results of the manufacturer's own actions can and should be based.

I am aware personally of only a small handful of manufacturers that make any effort to improve by formal study their knowledge of the effects of promotions on their brands. An old adage that is only too easily forgotten is that manufacturers should always strive to achieve a double benefit from their marketing programs: first, additional profit, and second, increased knowledge and expertise.

Advertising Elasticity and Advertising Planning

The third recommendation to manufacturers is to use the best available professional talent to compute the advertising elasticity of each brand they market.

A common problem, however, is that the mathematics, no matter how skillfully executed, may show a complete absence of sales effect attributable to the advertising. There could be two reasons: continued mathematical insensitivity and inadequacy or (against the manufacturer's own judgment) an absence of any sales effect to be discovered.[21] This is the most important of the complications referred to at the end of the section entitled "The Return on Advertising Investments."

There is no fundamental reason to be disheartened by the discovery that a well-loved campaign has no effect on sales in the marketplace. The fact of the lack of success may be disappointing, but the accurate intelligence of the failure should be welcomed.

The absence of any evidence of effectiveness does, however, put the manufacturer in a difficult position. If the manufacturer is forced reluctantly to conclude that the emperor does not have many clothes, the most pressing task that must be addressed is what must be done to achieve some measurable effect which can then be evaluated for its financial implications. This means embarking on an energetic program of experimentation, covering alternative advertising campaigns, budgets, media, and phasing, and this experimenting should go on until the manufacturer and its agency manage to throw up some perceptible results (or are forced to give up in despair). There will be a large research cost because extensive market testing must be evaluated not only for short-term sales-generating effects, but also for any long-term job that the advertising may be doing.

A concealed or long-term effect of advertising may involve something that can be monitored by surrogate measures (for example, the advertising may be slowly modifying consumers' perceptions of brand attributes). But what the advertising is doing may very possibly be well below the surface. For instance, it may be doing a protective job for the brand in a competitive environment, and this may only be measurable when a cutback causes an erosion in market share—a very serious outcome which may take a long time to manifest itself. This possibility means that experimentation, particularly if it involves downweighting, must be evaluated over an extended period of time.

But what should be done if, after advertising has been given every chance, there is no perceptible short-term or long-term effect? Quite simply, the manufacturer should cut its losses. It is by no means unknown for a brand to be maintained in effective distribution by a minimal level of promotional support and with only enough theme advertising to keep the brand name intermittently in front of the sales force and the retail trade—sometimes even with no theme advertising at all. It is too much to expect growth from brands which are only modestly supported in this way, but they may be quite capable of maintaining a low level of profitable sales, in some cases for decades. I was myself associated with such a brand, Lux Toilet Soap. It is sold extremely widely and is the market leader in a number of countries around the world. It has, however, received no theme advertising support in the United States since 1967, and in 1990 it still maintained a small but measurable (and profitable) market share.

A final but rather important point relates to brands for which advertising *does* have a demonstrable marketplace effect. In this effect, it will probably influence the consumer by strengthening the image attributes of the brand and hence its perceived differences from the competition. The process, which is stimulated by image-building advertising and nourished by repeat purchase, is likely to result in a reduction in the price elasticity of demand for the brand, by the process of making competitors less easy to substitute for it. The result is that a strengthening of image attributes will make the demand for the brand less responsive to promotional price cutting. In the last analysis, this is the reason why larger and stronger brands have the balance of their promotional effort more tipped toward theme advertising than have smaller and weaker brands.

Summary

1. The flattening of markets and the effects of inflation in the 1970s spurred a progressive increase during the course of the 1980s in the proportion of A & P budgets that were spent below the line on sales promotion, as well as a corresponding reduction in the proportion spent above the line on theme advertising.

2. In the majority of cases, promotions operate in the same way as price cutting. Aggregated data on the results of changing prices, based on the statistical study of price elasticity, demonstrate that price cutting commonly results in significant sales increases. However, based on realistic assumptions about the cost structure and profitability of typical brands, the sales increases associated with price cutting are only rarely profitable. The loss of profitability is sometimes dramatic.

3. In addition to this unproductive short-term effect, promotions also bring long-term problems:

   a. The short-term effect is normally confined to the period of the promotion, and this effect often takes place because of a "mortgaging" of future sales.

   b. Promotions stimulate active competitive retaliation, which causes manufacturers to increase promotional activity; at the same time, the efficacy of the promotions is being progressively reduced.

   c. Overpromotion tends to debase the image of a brand in consumers' eyes.

4. In contrast to promotions, theme advertising tends to generate only small short-term increases in sales. However, since the cost to the manufacturer of increasing its advertising is normally much more modest than the cost of price cutting, advertising has a much better chance of operating profitably, despite its relatively limited effect in stimulating sales.

5. The operational recommendations in this chapter hinge on

manufacturers' ability and willingness to compute the price elasticity and advertising elasticity of each of their brands:

a. A low price elasticity may make it possible to implement a permanent increase in the list price of a brand.

b. Manufacturers should study all aspects of the results of each promotion and learn progressively about promotional effectiveness. Manufacturers should estimate the amount of promotional activity they need to carry out for strictly defensive purposes and should endeavor to trim the promotional budgets intended for aggressive marketing. The underlying principle they should follow is to evaluate promotional actions according to their effects on profit as well as on sales volume.

c. Manufacturers should be equally tenacious in uncovering a brand's advertising elasticity. Because of the elusiveness of some advertising effects, there may be no apparent response either to given levels of advertising or to changes in advertising pressure. But before accepting this lack of response as a proven fact, the advertiser may have to carry out extensive experimentation. If there still appears to be no advertising effect at all, the manufacturer should be as relentless in cutting its losses as it should be in cutting its losses from uneconomic promotions.

Strategy
Defining the Target Group

*I try to get a picture in my mind of the kind of people they are—how they
use this product, and what it is (they don't often tell you in so many
words) . . . what it is that actually motivates them to buy something or
to interest them in something.*[1]

Leo Burnett

Chapters 7, 8, and 9 concentrate on the creative content of advertisements, that is, the intrinsic quality of campaigns, in contrast to
their extrinsic quality, which is governed by the weight of their exposure. The creative content is the end product of three processes: (1)
planning and writing a strategy; (2) developing, screening, and refin-
ing creative ideas; and (3) applying craft skills to turn ideas into finished advertisements.

These processes are complementary, and none of the three could
do a satisfactory job on its own without the other two. They are nevertheless not *equally* important. What matters more than anything
else is the development of ideas, and this is not so much the product
of analysis and reasoning as of imagination, flair, and intuition. Idea
generation (and the craft with which it is so closely connected) is a
unique process. For this reason, and also because of its importance,
the creative enterprise really must be studied on its own, and I plan
to devote a book to it, a book that will be focused entirely differently
from this one.

In this book, chapters 7 and 8 are concerned with the empirical and
describable planning procedures before advertisements are written.

Chapter 9 deals with the evaluation and screening of strategic directions and the advertising ideas that are derived from them. In all these activities, efficiency has a significant payoff in terms of reduced waste.

All these chapters are meant to be severely practical. They describe the best methods used in the professional field and are intended to help advertisers and advertising agencies improve their efforts to develop campaigns of superior selling ability. The campaign content is the qualitative variable on which the quantitative variable—the media appropriation—depends for its effect. It follows that the better the quality of the campaign, the more productive the media investment, and the less waste in the advertising process.

The most helpful way to study how advertising campaigns are developed is to use a simple device called the *planning cycle,* devised by Stephen King, formerly of J. Walter Thompson, London, and which has been used in many offices of that agency for two decades. The planning cycle helps us isolate the roles of the research and creative processes during each of five phases. These phases are framed by five simple questions, shown in figure 7–1.

The questions in the planning cycle are intended to help advertisers and agencies guide a brand through the stages of planning, writing, exposing, and evaluating an advertising campaign. For most brands, the cycle is used as an annual procedure; for some brands it is used more frequently, and for others, less often.

The first two questions—"Where are we?" and "Why are we there?"—are research-based, and are answered from quantitative and qualitative data, some research being collected once only and some longitudinally. The reason that these questions must be answered is that it is important to understand fully the brand's position

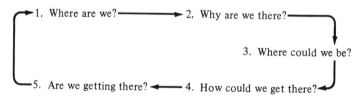

FIGURE 7–1

The Planning Cycle

in the market before we draw up the brand's advertising strategy. This is done in response to question 3: "Where could we be?"

Question 4—"How could we get there?"—is concerned mostly with the creative process of planning and generating campaign ideas. But research is also involved; we need it to help us evaluate, screen, and refine our ideas. The most useful types of research for these purposes are described in chapter 9.

The fifth question—"Are we getting there?"—involves evaluating the effect of the campaign in the marketplace, in order to improve its productivity in the future, or to provide guidance for new campaigns. This fifth stage is essentially research-based.

An important feature of the planning cycle is that the questions follow a sequence and they are in a loop, which tells us that when we get to question 5, it is time to start at the beginning again. This is an admirable reminder that an agency's relationship with the brands it handles is continuous. It does not stop when the advertising has been exposed to the public. There is also some feedback in the process, by which the answers to one question sometimes cause the answers to the preceding question to be reconsidered.

To write an effective strategy, we must determine our brand's position in a competitive environment and work out the best way to protect and improve this position. Although the analysis of facts is an essential background activity, the actual development of an advertising strategy is an exercise in judgment.

In this chapter, the first of two devoted to strategy, we concentrate on the target group of consumers to whom we shall direct our advertising. They are our source of business. The purpose of the chapter is to accustom readers to weighing the main variables—the overall trends in our market, the trends in our market segment, and the position and trends of our own brand—and on the basis of these data, to determine the target group. In particular, proper weight must be given to the importance of attracting new users (increasing our brand's penetration) and nurturing existing users (encouraging an increase in purchase frequency). In all aspects of strategy, tightly disciplined planning means control of subsequent waste, because the creative expression of the strategy is steered away from potentially unprofitable paths.

The objective of the chapter is not so much to teach facts as to inculcate a way of thinking.

A Rational Subject That Often Becomes Confused

Writing a strategy is a rational process and calls for the analysis of data and the ability to make logical deductions. When we proceed to develop advertisements from our strategy, as I have already explained, the actual writing of our advertisements is an exercise in applied imagination and craft. The difference in the mental qualities required for writing the strategy and for writing the campaign is an important matter, and it means that the two jobs are normally done by different people. The strategy and the campaign are, however, intimately linked, because the strategy is the device that enables us to point imagination and intuition in the right direction.

Strategy is like a diving board over a swimming pool. It should be strongly constructed and should be built over the deep end of the pool, so as to give the diver the best possible chance of making a safe and pretty dive. However, the dive itself depends on the skill of the person on the diving board. For the diver, read the creative man or woman who will be writing the advertisement.

The word *strategy* comes from military science and is most simply defined as "generalship, the art of war."[2] Much more has been written about military strategy than about business strategy, the "art of business."[3] Both are slightly complicated and are made up of a number of layers, or subsidiary strategies. This chapter discusses three separate strategies which together add up to the business strategy. These are the company plan, the brand marketing strategy, and the brand advertising strategy. This chapter is most concerned with the third of these. Since military strategy has many helpful affinities with business strategy, it is worth making a short digression to discuss the art of war, because this will help us understand some of the subtleties of the art of business.

The first and most important point about military strategy is that is concerns armies in conflict. It is therefore centrally concerned with our relationship to the enemy. There is an obvious analogy with business strategy, insofar as this is embedded in the competitive environment. Indeed much of the language of marketing and advertising is derived (perhaps unconsciously) from military thinking. The adjectives *offensive, defensive,* and *aggressive* are in everyday use. Manufacturers often conduct "marketing warfare" and aim to "seize a market" and "drive out competitors," who are then forced to "hoist the white flag." Advertisements are planned to work as a "campaign," and to have an "impact" on the consumer. In planning media exposure, we plan "strikes" or "hits."

The second point about military strategy is that it is planned at more than one level. The highest level, grand strategy, represents the plan of the nation in arms. There is an analogy here with the company plan. Below the level of the nation in arms is a range of military formations of descending size, which are guided by pure strategy, which embraces all phases of military planning that fall short of actual contact with the enemy. When this contact takes place, strategy becomes tactics. The relationship between strategy and tactics is such that a good strategy saves much bloodshed and effort in its tactical execution. Ideally, the enemy will be maneuvered into such an impossible position that it will see no alternative but to surrender. We can never quite see such perfect use of maneuver in business, but there is nevertheless an analogy, in that in business a well-planned strategy enables the resources deployed in its execution to be used more economically and effectively, and waste to be reduced.

It is often difficult to draw a clear line to define where military strategy ends and where tactics begins. The same is true in business. However, it is always worth making the effort to draw such a line for the reason just given: The more we concentrate on the strategy and the stronger we make it, the less effort will be needed to execute it well.

The third characteristic of military strategy is that it is multidimensional. It embraces logistics (deployment of resources), psychology (exploitation of our own strengths and, no less important, the enemy's weaknesses), and time (the goals have to be accomplished within a finite period). Business strategy also has these constituents. In advertising, we pump media investments into campaigns, which represent the execution of our strategy. Our advertising arguments themselves are almost invariably written with some knowledge of psychology. And the execution of our strategy is accomplished within a defined period. Another point is that effective logistical and psychological planning depends on good knowledge, or intelligence, in military jargon. Again there is an obvious affinity with the use of market research in business.

In the same way that a nation has a grand strategy, a firm has a company business plan. This sketches the role that the company plans to play in the market or markets in which it operates (including those it intends to enter in the near future). The plan details how the company will use its resources (capital, labor, know-how, and goodwill) to the best effect. And it often, although not invariably, maps out how the firm will be perceived by its customers, business partners, and the public as a whole in a broad business and social context. The plan sets objectives and proposes in general terms how these will be met.

Below the level of the company plan are the plans for the individual divisions of the corporation (in the case of diversified firms). And below these are the plans for the individual brands in the company's portfolio. Most firms have a number of brands in each market, and these must be handled separately. But they must conform overall to the company plan; otherwise there will be a risk that brands will cannibalize one another. The marketing strategy for an individual brand (together with the advertising strategy, which stems from it) aims to establish the brand's place in the competitive scene. The importance of the competitive situation cannot be emphasized too strongly, and most of the elements of the marketing strategy should be explicitly framed in competitive terms. A brand marketing strategy comprises four elements, listed below. These are sometimes referred to as the *four P's*.[4]

1. *Product.* This includes, first, the functional characteristics of the brand in comparison with its competitors, and specifically how its functional strengths and weaknesses are perceived by consumers. Second, it includes a description of the market segment in which the brand is positioned, as well as the demographic and psychographic (lifestyle) characteristics of the users of brands in this segment and of the users of our brand in particular. Third, it describes the brand's nonfunctional added values. Advertising is an important element here because added values are created substantially by advertising. The brand's positioning is also influenced by advertising to a considerable degree. These elements of the marketing strategy must therefore be closely linked to the brand advertising strategy, which will shortly be described.

2. *Price.* Again, the price must be seen alongside those of competitive brands. There are two important points that need emphasis. First, this part of the strategy covers the brand's prices both to the

trade and to the consumer. The difference between the two represents the brand's distributive margin. (Advertising is often able to reduce the size of this difference, a phenomenon illustrated in appendix A.) The second important point is that price is rarely fixed, even for short periods. Trade and consumer promotions are mostly price-related. Indeed nearly all trade promotions, since they are discounts of various types, effectively reduce the trade price, that is, the price charged to the wholesaler and retailer. And the majority of consumer promotions (money-off packs, coupons, banded packs, and so on) also operate on price, but on consumer price this time.

3. *Retail distribution* (sometimes called *place,* to maintain the consistency of the "four P's"). This describes the extent of the brand's geographical distribution, the types of retail outlet that handle it, and a measure of the present and targeted levels of effective distribution.[5] Distribution is related to the brand's trade and consumer promotional programs because it is impossible to get a brand into distribution (and extremely difficult to maintain it on display in the stores) without competitive levels of promotion.

4. *Promotion.* This embraces plans for advertising (above the line) and also for promotions (below the line). Publicity and public relations are included among the below-the-line activities. The brand advertising strategy, which is the main concern of this chapter and of chapter 8, is the central element of this part of the marketing strategy.

The marketing strategy should of course be regularly reviewed. However, it should be very rarely changed or even modified, and then only when the competitive position of the brand has altered. However, many clients tend to tinker with it if the brand falters in the marketplace.

Below the level of the brand marketing strategy, and deriving from it, is the brand advertising strategy (and on occasion, a number of parallel strategies dealing with publicity, merchandising, direct mail, and so on). The brand advertising strategy can be defined as *the objectives for an advertising campaign, defined in three specific terms: the audience, the proposition, and the ways in which the campaign should work.*

The meaning of these phrases will shortly be clarified and illustrated, but it is worth pointing out immediately that the words *ad-*

vertising strategy have very different meanings depending on who uses them. Different advertising agencies—organizations that often pride themselves on the comprehensiveness and efficiency of their working procedures—use a variety of different formulas, some much fuller and more helpful than others.

An example is provided by a well-known collection of advertising case studies, which publishes the actual strategies for twelve campaigns, all the work of first-class agencies, together with the advertisements that resulted.[6] The advertisements themselves are generally impressive, but surprisingly, the strategies on which these were based seem to be mostly very inadequate. The majority of them omit important ingredients. Even worse, many cross over the border into the field of creative execution and dictate the elements that should go into the advertising. In other words, they do not hold the line between strategy and tactics. In certain cases, one agency framed a strategy in one way for one client and in quite a different way for another.[7]

There is obviously a paradox here. How can it be that an indifferent strategy can lead to an effective advertisement? We can press the point and ask a second question: Is a strategy really necessary?

The answer to the first of these two questions is that an effective advertisement can sometimes be produced serendipitously, *but this is something we cannot rely on.* We must avoid wasting effort, time, and resources in following blind alleys. The answer to the second question is yes, a strategy is indispensable if we are to conduct advertising on a businesslike basis; in other words, as something better than a hit-or-miss affair. If we are to reduce some of the inevitable waste in the process of developing advertising, we must plan the strategy as soundly as possible before we begin to generate idea. We must make sure that all our ideas—the good and the bad—are at least relevant. Developing a good but irrelevant idea is purely wasteful.

The advertising strategy, like the marketing strategy, is only rarely modified. A well-planned advertising strategy ensures that things will not be forgotten. It reduces the risk of creative people's drilling dry holes and wasting their time and their talent, something that is in short supply and that always needs nurturing and protecting. Most important, good creative people, for reasons that are difficult to explain, respond well to a tightly written strategy; in the words of an

Old Testament prophet, "In our chains we shall be free." Creative people understand the limits on what they can and cannot say. In many circumstances, the closer these limits are, the more intense the imaginative and intellectual effort that is stimulated, and the more arresting the creative solution that emerges in response to the strategy.

The most important reason for an advertising strategy is nevertheless the one described earlier in this chapter. It is a component of a company's business plan and is therefore a tool of management—a method of setting priorities—that is already in place. Its purpose is to help decision making. Also, rather importantly, the objectives which form part of the advertising strategy provide a series of targets. With targets established, we are able to measure how closely the advertising comes to hitting them. This measurement in turn helps us set realistic future targets. This point holds good for all advertisers who are in business to make a profit, whether they are manufacturers of nationally distributed brands of detergent or owners of local bicycle stores.

A final point must be made before we describe the specific components of an advertising strategy. Although it is most importantly a device to point creative people in the right direction, the advertising strategy also provides a valuable service to the account executives, who normally work closely with the agency researchers. A good strategy makes it easier to explain advertising proposals convincingly to a client. This is especially true on the (only too rare) occasions when the client is faced with a genuinely unorthodox creative idea. In these circumstances, the best weapon available to convince the client of the advertising's relevance and likely effectiveness is research evidence that the advertising seems to do its job in meeting the objectives explicitly stated in the strategy.

The Brand Advertising Strategy

The advertising strategy should not be a lengthy document; it should never exceed a page or two in length. If it is longer, creative people will not use it. In general, creative people work best with a tightly written strategy. On rare occasions, an effective strategy can be expressed in one or two *words*.[8] It should, however, be the end product of much thought, or more explicitly, it should be derived from an analysis of facts, reflection on their meaning, and judgment in their interpretation.

Some agencies use forms with preprinted subheads as standard strategy documents. From my experience, these tend to encourage people to treat their content rather perfunctorily. A useful advertising strategy is the end product of serious intellectual mastication, and the way it is written should not be laid down too rigidly; the elements need varying amounts of emphasis for different brands.

The strategy is normally produced by the advertising agency's account executives (in cooperation with a number of agency colleagues). The client provides the basic brief and input when the strategy is drafted. It must of course also be accepted by the client in its final form before creative work is begun. This means that it acts as a discipline for the client as well as for the agency.

In a small but probably increasing number of cases, the client goes further and determines all aspects of the strategy herself or himself. The reason is disenchantment on the part of some American clients with the ability of their agencies to carry out sound strategic thinking. This is less true in London, where account planning encourages agencies to dig relentlessly into the competitive strengths and weaknesses of brands, and specifically into consumer perceptions. Chapters 7, 8, and 9 are in fact based on the methodology used by many British agencies, although the illustrative data in chapters 7 and 8 are from the United States.

It is important to remember that an advertising strategy is a selective document. An advertisement cannot work effectively if it is expected to do too many jobs. The strategy should concentrate on what matters most, but there is an opportunity cost, since we pay for what we include by the sacrifice of what we omit. This price must be paid, but naturally we must choose what to include (and therefore what to omit) with scrupulous care.

Strategies are occasionally criticized for being rather dull documents. But it should be stressed that the main quality that a strategy should possess is logical soundness. On the other hand, it is extremely important that the advertising which is derived from the strategy not be dull; otherwise it will not do its first job of attracting and engaging its audience.

An advertising strategy should cover three subjects, which (as already explained) should be linked with other parts of the business strategy, in particular with the brand marketing strategy:

1. *The target group.* This should define the people to whom the advertising is addressed. This group is derived from, but is often a narrower version of, the target group covered by the marketing strategy (which embraces both above-the-line and below-the-line activities). Selecting the target group is a more complicated matter than it appears, and the whole of the rest of this chapter is devoted to this process. The target group is the most important part of the advertising strategy. It is the strongest common bond with the other elements of the brand's marketing strategy; in particular, the needs and values of the target group are the main influence on how the manufacturer plans the functional and nonfunctional properties of the brand. Also, because of the target group's influence on the product, these people essentially control the advertising proposition.

The target group has a twin function in advertising strategy. First, it enables us to pick the most economical media, and thus to reduce waste in the way we deploy the media budget (which is where most money is spent). Second, and this is actually the more important reason, it helps the creative people "tailor-make" the advertising to the brand's market. This function is precisely what Leo Burnett had in mind when he wrote the words that preface this chapter.

2. *The proposition.* This describes the sorts of things we should be saying about our brand. It is not necessarily a single argument; it is more commonly a single-minded and coherent amalgam of a small number of signals and selling points which are derived from the brand's position on its competitive map—its main differences from (and similarities to) competitive brands, as perceived by consumers. It should also determine to what extent the advertising should be motivating (that is, concerned with general arguments for using the product category), and to what extent discriminating (that is, brand-specific.) The richest discriminating arguments contain motivating elements, but these are not universal, or even common; many, perhaps most, discriminators are concerned with detailed points of difference and nothing else.

There are three important points about this part of the strategy. The first is the special importance of selectivity, a point already emphasized. Since an advertisement cannot effectively communicate too much, it should concentrate on a small number of signals about the brand, and as far as possible these should be mutually supporting. The second point is that the terms *signal* and *selling point* should not be interpreted in exclusively rational terms. Although signals about a brand commonly include rational arguments (these occasionally being of prime importance), signals and selling points also embrace both emotional persuasion and sensory appeals (for example, ways of stimulating the appetite). Such signals are often nonverbal; they can be communicated very effectively by pictures, and by music and sounds.

The third point is a reminder of the difficulty of keeping the strategy separate from the execution. This means that we should avoid including in this part of the strategy any components (for example, symbols, slogans, and demonstrations) that are properly the concern of the men and women who will be writing the advertisements, and who should express their own views about whether and how to use such devices rather than be forced to follow rigid instructions.

3. *The ways in which the campaign should work.* This part of the strategy covers (a) how *directly* the campaign is expected to work and (b) what type of gestalt, or total reaction, the campaign should evoke. This includes the consumer's responses to the media and the media vehicles used in the main campaign, as well as responses to the types of promotions used. Campaigns are mainly concerned with behavioral response (that is, advertising should prompt action and, in particular, buying), but this is not the whole story. Behavior is commonly accompanied by reinforcements or shifts in consumers' knowledge and attitudes.[9] These are influenced by all elements of the marketing mix, and they should be described in the strategy.

The Target Group: Where Is the Business Coming From?

When we embark on an advertising strategy, the first question we must ask ourselves is: Where is the business coming from? This question immediately focuses attention on our existing and potential consumers and, most important, on what brands these people are now using. The map on which we fight our marketing battles is a topography of competing and complementary brands, and we must determine at the very outset where our brand is located on this map.

There is research to help us, and this must be described before we continue the description of target groups. The most immediately useful information comes from large-scale, regularly repeated surveys of consumers, with demographic data, and with information on the brands they use and the media they watch and read. Two research organizations publish annual surveys of this type: Mediamark Research Inc. (MRI)[10] and Simmons Market Research Bureau (SMRB).[11] Since both companies collect a massive quantity of data which they sell to numbers of subscribers—in effect, all the major advertisers and advertising agencies in the United States—their services are described as *syndicated research*. The data are proprietary and not in the public domain, but I have obtained permission to quote in this chapter some real information for illustrative purposes. I shall use MRI data exclusively, since MRI provides both brand penetration data and shares of market (based on volume consumption). SMRB concentrates on penetration, and its data are used in conjunction with share-of-market figures derived from other sources: retail audits and consumer panels. A target group cannot be described accurately without information on the penetration and market shares of our brand and its competitors.

The market I shall feature is that for cold breakfast cereals in the United States, and the data come from nine continuous years of MRI surveys, 1982–1990. The breakfast cereal market is large, very fragmented, mature, and divided into functional segments. The 1990 MRI survey shows that breakfast cereals had been bought during the previous six months by 89.9 percent of all female homemakers (and by 82.9 percent of the smaller number of male homemakers). The average household (with a female homemaker) that used cold breakfast cereals had consumed 5.1 individual servings during the previous week.

Ninety-four different manufacturers' brands were counted, ranging in share from Cheerios, with an 9.4% share of volume sales, to much smaller brands, each holding 0.1% of the market. Because there is such a large number of different brands, average market shares are smaller than in many other product categories. (In certain other fields, market leaders account for more than 20% per brand.)

The 94 brands listed are the most important of the 150 substantial brands mentioned in chapter 2. A storekeeper to whom I talked told me that in 1990 he was confronted by 270 brands of breakfast cereals, large and small. Out of these, he stocked 72.

The maturity of the breakfast cereals category can be seen in table 7–1, which examines trends in household penetration and frequency of use (a measure closely related to purchase frequency). These two measures describe and explain virtually all movements in consumer purchasing.

Table 7–1 demonstrates that while frequency of use did not change significantly over the course of nine years, penetration of breakfast cereals as a whole had risen. The increase appears to be small: from 87.6% in 1982 to 89.9% in 1990. However, these proportions must be applied to a growing population, and the result is that the number of households with a female homemaker who bought cold breakfast cereals rose from 66,928,000 in 1982 to 74,948,000 in 1990. This rise represents an increase of 12% in cereal buyers (compared with an 8% growth in the number of households). This 12% rise in the number of cereal buyers represents an average compound growth of a little less than 1.5% per annum. Since there had been no great change in usage frequency, we can

TABLE 7–1

Market Trends in Cold Breakfast Cereals

Year	Household Penetration: Percentage of Female Homemakers Buying during Previous 6 Months	Average Number of Servings Per Week Per Buying Household
1982	87.6	5.2
1983	86.3	5.1
1984	88.1	4.8
1985	87.6	4.9
1986	88.5	5.0
1987	89.6	4.9
1988	89.5	4.9
1989	90.3	5.0
1990	89.9	5.1

infer an increase in volume sales in line with the penetration growth.[12] Much of the growth had come from premium-price brands, so that the increase, when measured in dollars, is more pronounced than when it is expressed in volume.[13]

The category as a whole was therefore not quite flat, since sales had grown a little faster than population, and because people were moving to more expensive brands. However, the most important feature of the category growth is that it was confined to certain defined market segments.

The breakfast cereal market (like many others) is made up of brands which are functionally different from one another. The main segments into which the brands are normally grouped are as follows:

1. *Regular.* This segment represents the oldest brands in the market, for example, Kellogg's Corn Flakes, Kellogg's Rice Krispies, and Nabisco Shredded Wheat, plus clones and many differentiated competitors, for example, Cheerios and Wheaties. The brands in this segment are only slightly sweetened and rely on the taste of the basic cereal ingredient.

2. *Presweetened.* There are brands with a specific appeal to children: Cap'n Crunch, Kellogg's Frosted Flakes, Kellogg's Fruit Loops, Lucky Charms, Trix, and many others.

3. *Natural.* These are high-protein brands that often contain nuts and fruit. This is a relatively new segment and is much smaller than the others. Typical brands are Kellogg's Mueslix, Kellogg's Nutri-Grain, Kellogg's Raisin Bran, Post Fruit & Fibre, and Quaker Oat Bran.

The trends in the penetration of these three segments can be seen in table 7–2, from which it is clear that the regular segment was the largest, and also that it had shown no growth since 1982. The presweetened segment was smaller but had grown by more than a third (assuming that sales growth was in line with penetration growth). This increase was caused partly by demographic change. After many years of decline, the population of children under the age of ten began to move upward in 1982. By 1987, the numbers were 9 percent above those in 1981.[14] The natural segment was tiny in comparison with the other two but had increased by more than a half since 1982, again assuming that penetration growth was an indication of sales

TABLE 7–2

Segment Trends in Cold Breakfast Cereals

Year	Household Penetration: Percentage of Female Homemakers Buying During Previous Six months		
	Regular	Presweetened	Natural
1982	81.5	38.2	8.8
1983	79.5	38.3	9.2
1984	80.1	37.1	16.9
1985	79.6	37.7	10.2
1986	79.8	40.3	10.8
1987	80.0	47.2	10.7
1988	80.5	47.6	12.7
1989	81.4	52.7	13.7
1990	79.6	52.3	14.2

growth; the growth in dollar sales had been faster than this because brands in the natural segment are priced above the market average.

The general conclusion is that the entire increase in the category had come from the presweetened and natural segments, and that the most dramatic relative increase (although not the biggest absolute growth) had been in the latter.

There was much competitive activity during the 1980s. MRI counted 94 manufacturers' brands in 1990, up from 65 in 1982. As might be expected, most of the new introductions were in the presweetened and natural segments.

All the individual brands covered by the 1990 MRI survey are listed in table 7–3 (pp. 136–137), together with the estimates of the penetration and market share of each. Note in particular the last column of figures, the "Volume/Users Index." This column expresses each brand's share of volume as a percentage of its share of users. (Share of users is derived from the total sum of all the individual brand penetrations. The percentage of each individual brand penetration is calculated from this total.) If the index is below 100, the market share is weak in comparison with its penetration. In other words, the brand's purchase frequency is low. If the index is above

100, then the market share is strong in comparison with its penetration, representing relatively high purchase frequency.

We now return to the description of target groups and in particular to the basic question of where our business is coming from. There are four main sources of *new* business for any brand:

1. *New users entering the product category.* This is, of course, only possible when we are operating in an expanding category, and today such categories are relatively rare in consumer goods in the United States. They do, however, exist, and there are some markets which attract new users every year (for example, feminine hygiene products, which gain new users as girls reach puberty; hair colorants, which attract people whose hair is turning gray).

2. *New users entering our market segment—generally from other segments.* This is often feasible because there are many markets in which there are increases in some segments, more or less balanced by declines in others. New entrants into a segment will rarely come in as exclusive buyers. More commonly they will become infrequent buyers of brands in Segment B while remaining users (although now slightly less frequent users) of brands in Segment A.

3. *New users from other brands within the segment.* This is the most promising opportunity for new and small brands—to try and lure some of the infrequent users of larger brands (who may continue to use the larger brands but now even less often). The strategy for the new brand should detail the existing brands from which it is hoped the business will come. This will dictate the functional characteristics that the new brand should have and also the demographic characteristics of its target group. The most obvious examples of targeting competitive brands are those that the advertising explicitly names as such. This technique of "comparison advertising" has been used for two decades and shows no signs of disappearing despite many strongly expressed doubts about its effectiveness.

4. *Increased usage frequency by our own buyers.* This is a common strategy for all large brands. If at the moment consumers buy a brand an average of five times a year, and if an advertising campaign that is focused on usage frequency boosts this average to six times, the result will be a 20 percent sales lift, without the need to persuade a single extra person to buy the brand.

There is a further important source of business for many brands,

TABLE 7–3
Summarized Data for Individual Brands of Cold Breakfast Cereals, 1990

BASE: FEMALE HOMEMAKERS (83,366,000)	ALL			SHARE OF USERS	SHARE OF VOLUME	VOLUME/ USERS INDEX
	'000	%	UNWGT			
TOTAL USED IN LAST 6 MONTHS	74948	89.9	8245			
BRANDS:						
ALMOND DELIGHT	5156	6.2	558	1.4	1.3	93
CAP'N CRUNCH (REGULAR)	6926	8.3	711	1.9	1.6	84
CAP'N CRUNCH CRUNCHBERRIES	3545	4.3	374	1.0	.9	90
CAP'N CRUNCH PEANUT BUTTER CRUNCH	2779	3.3	264	.8	.6	75
CHEERIOS	23903	28.7	2529	6.5	9.4	145
HONEY NUT CHEERIOS	12693	15.2	1362	3.5	4.1	117
BRAN CHEX	3262	3.9	351	.9	.6	67
CORN CHEX	4846	5.8	556	1.3	.8	62
HONEY GRAHAM CHEX	1703	2.0	195	.5	.3	60
RICE CHEX	6181	7.4	679	1.7	1.2	71
WHEAT CHEX	4095	4.9	471	1.1	.9	82
CINNAMON TOAST CRUNCH	4919	5.9	544	1.3	1.1	85
CIRCUS FUN	387	.5	38	.1	.	.
COCOA PUFFS	3875	4.6	389	1.1	.8	73
COOKIE CRISP	2025	2.4	210	.6	.5	83
COUNT CHOCULA	1034	1.2	126	.3	.2	67
CRISPY WHEATS 'N RAISINS	2763	3.3	318	.8	.5	63
FIBER ONE	1745	2.1	184	.5	.6	120
FRANKENBERRY	1162	1.4	117	.3	.1	33
GHOSTBUSTERS	1887	2.3	221	.5	.3	60
GOLDEN GRAHAMS	5652	6.8	605	1.5	.8	53
HONEY BUCKWHEAT CRISPS	191	.2	21	.1	.1	100
KELLOGGS ALL BRAN	5157	6.2	582	1.4	1.7	121
KELLOGGS ALL BRAN EXTRA FIBER	1517	1.8	162	.4	.5	125
KELLOGGS APPLE CINNAMON SQUARES	1216	1.5	135	.3	.3	100
KELLOGGS APPLE JACKS	6151	7.4	632	1.7	1.7	100
KELLOGGS APPLE RAISIN CRISP	1462	1.8	151	.4	.3	75
KELLOGGS BRAN BUDS	636	.8	78	.2	.1	50
KELLOGGS COCOA KRISPIES	3331	4.0	318	.9	.7	78
KELLOGGS CORN FLAKES	20405	24.5	2139	5.6	8.1	145
KELLOGGS CORN POPS	3790	4.5	395	1.0	.8	80
KELLOGGS CRACKLIN OAT BRAN	4719	5.7	522	1.3	1.4	108
KELLOGGS CRISPIX	3347	4.0	409	.9	.7	78
KELLOGGS BRAN FLAKES	3917	4.7	470	1.1	1.1	100
KELLOGGS FROOT LOOPS	9465	11.4	924	2.6	2.3	88
KELLOGGS FROSTED FLAKES	13453	16.1	1406	3.7	4.4	119
KELLOGGS FROSTED MINI-WHEATS	5737	6.9	580	1.6	1.5	94
KELLOGGS FROSTED KRISPIES	1258	1.5	131	.3	.5	167
KELLOGGS FRUITFUL BRAN	1682	2.0	183	.5	.3	60
KELLOGGS FRUITY MARSHMALLOW KRISPIES	1308	1.6	132	.4	.2	50
KELLOGGS HONEY SMACKS	3013	3.6	295	.8	.8	100
KELLOGGS JUST RIGHT	2317	2.8	268	.6	.5	83
KELLOGGS MUESLIX	4273	5.1	485	1.2	.9	75
KELLOGGS NUT & HONEY CRUNCH	4031	4.8	433	1.1	1.1	100
KELLOGGS NUTRI-GRAIN ALMOND RAISINS	1475	1.8	178	.4	.2	50
KELLOGGS NUTRI-GRAIN CORN	302	.4	37	.1	.1	100
KELLOGGS NUTRI-GRAIN NUGGETS	1270	1.5	135	.3	.3	100
KELLOGGS NUTRI-GRAIN WHEAT	887	1.1	129	.2	.3	150
KELLOGGS NUTRI-GRAIN WHEAT & RAISIN	1395	1.7	177	.4	.3	75
KELLOGGS PRODUCT 19	6094	7.3	632	1.7	2.6	153
KELLOGGS RAISIN BRAN	12114	14.5	1280	3.3	3.3	100
KELLOGGS RAISIN SQUARES	1583	1.9	181	.4	.2	50
KELLOGGS RICE KRISPIES	15716	18.9	1650	4.3	4.1	95
KELLOGGS SPECIAL K	6321	7.6	740	1.7	2.0	118
KELLOGGS STRAWBERRY SQUARES	1503	1.8	153	.4	.2	50

BASE: FEMALE HOMEMAKERS (83,366,000)	ALL '000	%	UNWGT	SHARE OF USERS	SHARE OF VOLUME	VOLUME USERS INDEX
OTHER KELLOGGS	1486	1.8	163	.4	.5	125
KIX	3485	4.2	366	.9	1.1	122
KRETSCHMER WHEAT GERM	806	1.0	115	.2	.2	100
LIFE	2927	3.5	349	.8	.6	75
CINNAMON LIFE	2491	3.0	279	.7	.3	43
LUCKY CHARMS	6471	7.8	638	1.8	1.2	67
NABISCO FRUIT WHEATS	1235	1.5	147	.3	.3	100
NABISCO 100% BRAN	1278	1.5	151	.3	.4	133
NABISCO REGULAR SIZE SHREDDED WHEAT	5654	6.8	606	1.5	1.4	93
NABISCO SPOON SIZE SHREDDED WHEAT	7580	9.1	825	2.1	1.6	76
NABISCO SHREDDED WHEAT & BRAN	1896	2.3	217	.5	.5	100
NATURE VALLEY 100% NATURAL	1018	1.2	130	.3	.1	33
OATMEAL RAISIN CRISP	2030	2.4	234	.6	.6	100
POST ALPHA BITS	2666	3.2	287	.7	.3	43
POST BRAN FLAKES	2024	2.4	229	.6	.5	83
POST CRISPY CRITTERS	742	.9	63	.2	.2	100
POST FRUIT & FIBRE	2606	3.1	303	.7	.5	71
POST GRAPENUT FLAKES	1671	2.0	159	.5	.3	60
POST GRAPE NUTS	6973	8.4	734	1.9	1.5	79
POST HONEYCOMBS	2290	2.7	245	.6	.3	50
POST OAT FLAKES	1684	2.0	201	.5	.4	80
POST PEBBLES (COCOA)	2014	2.4	208	.5	.4	80
POST PEBBLES (FRUITY)	2664	3.2	286	.7	.5	71
POST RAISIN BRAN	8581	10.3	871	2.3	2.2	96
POST SUPER GOLDEN CRISP	1447	1.7	148	.4	.3	75
POST TOASTIES	1366	1.6	130	.4	.4	100
QUAKER OH'S CRUNCHY NUT	1815	2.2	196	.5	.3	60
QUAKER OH'S HONEY GRAHAM	1409	1.7	151	.4	.2	50
QUAKER 100% NATURAL	2054	2.5	279	.6	.4	67
QUAKER PUFFED RICE	1825	2.2	209	.5	.4	80
QUAKER PUFFED WHEAT	2016	2.4	206	.5	.4	80
OTHER QUAKER	1662	2.0	213	.5	.6	120
RAISIN NUT BRAN	3479	4.2	364	.9	.8	89
RALSTON MUESLI	1315	1.6	151	.4	.3	75
ROCKY ROAD	167	.2	24	.	.	.
S'MORES CRUNCH	939	1.1	107	.3	.2	67
TOTAL	4982	6.0	587	1.4	1.8	129
TRIX	3722	4.5	391	1.0	.8	80
WHEATIES	6609	7.9	648	1.8	1.6	89
GENERIC (NO LABEL)	1075	1.3	110	.3	.4	133
STORE'S OWN BRAND	2558	3.1	247	.7	1.7	243
OTHER	5210	6.2	565	1.4	3.4	243

TYPES:

NATURAL	11867	14.2	1422			
PRE-SWEETENED	43609	52.3	4527			
REGULAR	66346	79.6	7319			

INDIVIDUAL PORTIONS/LAST 7 DAYS

L NONE	9003	10.8	1072			
L 1	5036	6.0	540			
L 2	6964	8.4	751			
L 3	5818	7.0	684			
M 4	6173	7.4	703			
M 5	5084	6.1	544			
M 6	4966	6.0	547			
M 7	8794	10.5	1000			
M 8	2373	2.8	271			
H 9 OR MORE	20738	24.9	2133			
L TOTAL	26820	32.2	3047	35.8	6.9	
M TOTAL	27390	32.9	3065	36.5	30.2	
H TOTAL	20738	24.9	2133	27.7	62.9	

but this is concerned not with any changes, but with the *maintenance* of existing purchasing patterns:

5. *Protection of existing penetration and purchase frequency.* This is an important objective for large brands which are being assaulted by newcomers (as in point 3 above). It is also important for all brands, large or small, in declining categories or segments. If a brand holds its penetration and purchase frequency in a falling market, its market share will go up.

We can now look at three brands of breakfast cereal with these five points in mind, and we shall begin to draw conclusions about the target groups for their advertising. The brands chosen are Kellogg's Corn Flakes, Lucky Charms, and Post Fruit & Fibre, manufactured by three different manufacturers, respectively Kellogg's, General Mills, and General Foods (Philip Morris). The history of the penetration and market share of each brand is given in table 7–4, which shows pronounced differences among the three brands, differences that have an important bearing on their target groups, the likely source of their future business.

Kellogg's Corn Flakes

Kellogg's Corn Flakes (KCF) is the second largest brand in the entire cold cereal category. It has a long history and continues to hold an important place in the largest market segment, the regular brands. As we have seen, however, this segment has not been growing.

In this static segment and with continued competitive pressure, KCF has suffered some loss of brand share. Since this fall has been accompanied by a decline in penetration, the brand has lost share because of a reduction in the number of users and not because of any decline in purchase frequency.

These facts suggest that the Kellogg's Corn Flakes advertising should adopt a defensive stance to stop further erosion. The most important priority should be to protect the brand's current penetration level (and perhaps recover it a little), and at the same time to maintain the existing satisfactory level of purchase frequency. This analysis points to existing users of the brand as the primary target group. Finding new users from competitive brands within the same segment (especially lapsed users of KCF) should be the secondary

TABLE 7–4
Penetration Share and Sales Share Trends for Three Selected Brands of Cold Breakfast Cereals

Year	Share of Total Household Penetration (Percentage of Female Homemakers Buying during Previous 6 Months)	Share of Market (Volume Usage)	Volume/Users Index
Kellogg's Corn Flakes			
1982	6.3	8.7	138
1983	6.5	9.3	143
1984	6.0	9.0	150
1985	5.8	7.3	126
1986	6.1	8.5	139
1987	5.9	8.0	136
1988	5.7	8.0	140
1989	5.4	7.3	135
1990	5.6	8.1	145
Lucky Charms			
1982	1.8	1.6	89
1983	1.9	1.7	89
1984	1.6	1.2	75
1985	1.8	1.4	78
1986	1.7	1.5	88
1987	1.8	1.4	78
1988	1.7	1.3	76
1989	1.7	1.4	82
1990	1.8	1.2	67
Post Fruit & Fibre			
1982	—	—	—
1983	—	—	—
1984	0.9	0.7	78
1985	0.9	0.8	89
1986	1.2	1.3	108
1987	1.1	1.1	100
1988	1.0	0.7	70
1989	0.9	0.9	100
1990	0.7	0.5	71

target. Both the primary and the secondary groups have similar demographic characteristics, which will be described shortly.

Lucky Charms

Lucky Charms is a medium-size brand, ranked twelfth in penetration out of the total of ninety-four manufacturers' brands covered by the 1990 MRI survey. It is positioned in the modestly growing presweetened market segment and has maintained a reasonably steady position since 1982. However, the brand is weak in one important respect. Its usage frequency is below average, a fact suggesting that it is a second or third brand in the homemaker's buying repertoire. The low volume/users index is a sign of vulnerability and strongly suggests that the advertising should address existing users in order to persuade them to use the brand more often. These people should be the primary target group. Finding new users from competitive brands within the presweetened segment should be the secondary target. Both primary and secondary target groups have similar demographic characteristics, to be described shortly.

Post Fruit & Fibre

Post Fruit & Fibre is a relatively new brand, launched nationally in 1984. It is positioned in the small but rapidly growing natural segment.

The penetration and share of market of Post Fruit & Fibre are both relatively low, and the figures have varied rather erratically year by year. This fluctuation is possibly connected with the vicissitudes in the popularity of fiber-rich foods; they have certainly lost some of their initial appeal. Nevertheless Post Fruit & Fibre has gained a foothold, and the total natural segment continues to be buoyant. Thus the brand should continue to reinforce its position and to be actively marketed with growth in mind. It should aim to capture users from new entrants into the segment, and the advertising strategy for the brand should aim to boost the brand's penetration, and thereafter to encourage usage frequency once new consumers have begun to buy it. (We shall shortly look at the demographic characteristics of the natural segment as a whole.) One possibility is a brand restaging; the functional characteristics of the restaging will influence the proposition, although not the brand's target group.

These examples are intended to demonstrate an approach, a method of applying judgment to information on trends in category and segment sales, and to facts about our brand and its closest competitors. For our brand, we must arrive at a sensible definition of what we want the advertising to accomplish in terms of penetration and usage frequency. And to do this, we must define the target group in terms of what brands these people are now using. Then we can move forward to define our target group according to its demographic and psychographic characteristics. Demographics is the subject we cover next.

Demographics

In tables 7–5 and 7–6, the demographic classification used by MRI is set out on the left side of the figures. MRI uses a neat and precise method to describe the demographic characteristics of the users of different brands. However, some explanation is needed to help readers become comfortable with the precise meaning of the MRI tables.

Start with the Lucky Charms data in table 7–5. There are four vertical columns of figures, identified as A, B, C, and D. A is the most important column, and it specifies the number of female homemakers who bought Lucky Charms during the previous six months. These are the *absolute* penetration figures and not the penetration share figures used to describe trends in table 7–4.

The top (that is, total) figure in the column (6,471,000) is a repeat of the figure in table 7–3. Column C computes this figure of 6,471,000 as a percentage of the total population of female homemakers, 83,366,000 (seen at the far left of table 7–5). The first percentage in column C is 7.8% (6,471,000 as a proportion of 83,366,000), and this is another figure that appeared in table 7–3. This 7.8% represents the brand's six-month penetration percentage.

As we move down columns A and C, the same analysis is applied to each demographic subcategory. Look, for instance, at the 18–24 age group. There are 855,000 female homemakers in this group who bought Lucky Charms, out of a total of 7,596,000 homemakers in the age category. This means that the Lucky Charms penetration percentage (column C) is 11.3%, a figure much greater than Lucky

TABLE 7-5
Demographic Data for Overall Market for Cold Breakfast Cereals and for Selected Brands, 1990

BASE: FEMALE HOMEMAKERS	TOTAL U.S. '000	ALL A '000	B % DOWN	C % ACROSS	D INDEX	HEAVY USERS A '000	B % DOWN	C % ACROSS	D INDEX	KELLOGGS CORN FLAKES A '000	B % DOWN	C % ACROSS	D INDEX	LUCKY CHARMS A '000	B % DOWN	C % ACROSS	D INDEX
ALL FEMALE HOMEMAKERS	83366	74948	100.0	89.9	100	20738	100.0	24.9	100	20405	100.0	24.5	100	6471	100.0	7.8	100
WOMEN	83366	74948	100.0	89.9	100	20738	100.0	24.9	100	20405	100.0	24.5	100	6471	100.0	7.8	100
HOUSEHOLD HEADS	28345	24380	32.5	86.0	96	4581	22.1	16.2	65	6335	31.0	22.3	91	1546	23.9	5.5	70
HOMEMAKERS	83366	74948	100.0	89.9	100	20738	100.0	24.9	100	20405	100.0	24.5	100	6471	100.0	7.8	100
GRADUATED COLLEGE	12896	11520	15.4	89.3	99	3424	16.5	26.6	107	2540	12.4	19.7	80	760	11.7	5.9	76
ATTENDED COLLEGE	14718	13254	17.7	90.1	100	3811	18.4	25.9	104	3226	15.8	21.9	90	1537	23.8	10.4	135
GRADUATED HIGH SCHOOL	35709	32344	43.2	90.6	101	8941	43.1	25.0	101	8889	43.5	24.8	101	3225	49.8	9.0	116
DID NOT GRADUATE HIGH SCHOOL	20043	17829	23.8	89.0	99	4563	22.0	22.8	92	5770	28.3	28.8	118	949	14.7	4.7	61
18-24	7596	6839	9.1	90.0	100	1571	7.6	20.7	83	1457	7.1	19.2	78	855	13.2	11.3	145
25-34	19963	18175	24.3	91.0	101	6302	30.4	31.6	127	3991	19.6	20.0	82	2350	36.3	11.8	152
35-44	17118	15917	21.2	93.0	103	5463	26.3	31.9	128	3926	19.2	22.9	94	2057	31.8	12.0	155
45-54	12257	10948	14.6	89.3	99	2722	13.1	22.2	89	3207	15.7	26.2	107	703	10.9	5.7	74
55-64	10967	9898	13.2	90.3	100	1915	9.2	17.5	70	3314	16.2	30.2	123	*290	4.5	2.6	34
65 OR OVER	15464	13172	17.6	85.2	95	2765	13.3	17.9	72	4511	22.1	29.2	119	*215	3.3	1.4	18
18-34	27560	25014	33.4	90.8	101	7873	38.0	28.6	115	5447	26.7	19.8	81	3205	49.5	11.6	150
18-49	51245	46820	62.5	91.4	102	14968	72.2	29.2	117	11083	54.3	21.6	88	5760	89.0	11.2	145
25-54	49338	45039	60.1	91.3	102	14487	69.9	29.4	118	11124	54.5	22.5	92	5110	79.0	10.4	133
EMPLOYED FULL TIME	35817	31821	42.5	88.8	99	8239	39.7	23.0	92	7184	35.2	20.1	82	3239	50.1	9.0	117
PART-TIME	9658	9059	12.1	93.8	104	2878	13.9	29.8	120	2434	11.9	25.2	103	969	15.0	10.0	129
SOLE WAGE EARNER	11247	9961	12.9	85.9	96	1586	7.6	14.1	57	2269	11.1	20.2	82	630	9.7	5.6	72
NOT EMPLOYED	37891	34068	45.5	89.9	100	9621	46.4	25.4	102	10787	52.9	28.5	116	2263	35.0	6.0	77
PROFESSIONAL	7232	6551	8.7	90.6	101	1851	8.9	25.6	103	1549	7.6	21.4	88	597	9.2	8.3	106
EXECUTIVE/ADMIN./MANAGERIAL	5447	4744	6.3	87.1	97	838	4.0	15.4	62	841	4.1	15.4	63	*344	5.3	6.3	81
CLERICAL/SALES/TECHNICAL	19699	17657	23.6	89.6	100	5015	24.2	25.5	102	4034	19.8	20.5	84	1795	27.7	9.1	117
PRECISION/CRAFTS/REPAIR	1091	952	1.3	87.3	97	*245	1.2	22.5	90	*213	1.0	19.5	80	*74	1.1	6.8	87
OTHER EMPLOYED	12005	10976	14.6	91.4	102	3169	15.3	26.4	106	2981	14.6	24.8	101	1399	21.6	11.7	150
H/D INCOME $75,000 OR MORE	5950	5256	7.0	88.3	98	1538	7.4	25.8	104	1071	5.2	18.0	74	568	8.8	9.5	123
$60,000 - 74,999	5600	5059	6.8	90.3	100	1604	7.7	28.6	115	1169	5.7	20.9	85	*469	7.2	8.4	108
$50,000 - 59,999	6353	5813	7.8	91.5	102	1697	8.2	26.7	107	1570	7.7	24.7	101	690	10.7	10.9	140
$40,000 - 49,999	9623	8767	11.7	91.1	101	2615	12.6	27.2	109	1976	9.7	20.5	84	1092	16.9	11.3	146

	A	B	C	D	E	F	G	H	I	J	K	L	M	N	O	P	Q
$30,000 - 39,999	12677	11605	15.5	91.5	102	3143	15.2	24.8	100	2842	13.9	22.4	92	1010	15.6	8.0	103
$20,000 - 29,999	13762	12454	16.6	90.5	101	3614	17.4	26.3	106	3105	15.2	22.6	92	1077	16.6	7.8	101
$10,000 - 19,999	16448	14645	19.5	89.0	97	3798	18.3	26.5	93	4887	24.0	29.7	121	914	14.1	5.6	72
LESS THAN $10,000	12953	11348	15.1	87.6	97	2729	13.2	21.1	85	3785	18.5	29.2	119	652	10.1	5.0	65
CENSUS REGION: NORTH EAST	17159	15165	20.2	88.4	98	4322	20.8	25.2	101	4520	22.2	26.3	108	1421	22.0	8.3	107
NORTH CENTRAL	20276	18598	24.8	91.7	102	4979	24.0	24.6	99	5138	25.2	25.3	104	2166	23.5	10.7	138
SOUTH	29397	26824	35.8	91.2	101	7787	37.5	26.5	106	7536	36.9	25.6	105	1530	23.6	5.2	67
WEST	16534	14362	19.2	86.9	97	3650	17.6	22.1	89	3211	15.7	19.4	79	1355	20.9	8.2	106
MARKETING REG.: NEW ENGLAND	4405	3834	5.1	87.0	97	924	4.5	21.0	84	1111	5.4	25.2	103	*275	4.2	6.2	80
MIDDLE ATLANTIC	13768	12183	16.3	88.5	98	3672	17.7	26.7	107	3605	15.7	26.2	107	1198	18.5	8.7	112
EAST CENTRAL	11792	10880	14.5	92.3	103	2979	14.4	25.3	102	3200	15.7	27.1	111	1191	18.4	10.1	130
WEST CENTRAL	13275	12136	16.2	91.4	102	3370	16.3	25.4	102	3339	16.4	25.2	103	1343	20.8	10.1	130
SOUTH EAST	15926	14687	19.6	92.2	103	4331	20.9	27.2	109	4232	20.7	26.6	109	729	11.3	4.6	59
SOUTH WEST	9589	8601	11.5	89.7	100	2266	10.9	23.6	95	1997	9.8	20.8	85	502	7.8	5.2	67
PACIFIC	14611	12627	16.8	86.4	96	3196	15.4	21.9	88	2921	14.3	20.0	82	1234	19.1	8.4	109
COUNTY SIZE A	34874	30829	41.1	88.4	98	8915	43.0	25.6	103	7922	38.8	22.7	93	2739	42.3	7.9	101
COUNTY SIZE B	24866	22682	30.3	91.2	101	5824	28.1	23.4	94	6129	30.0	24.6	101	1617	25.0	6.5	84
COUNTY SIZE C	12578	11416	15.2	90.8	101	2995	14.4	23.8	96	3125	15.5	24.8	102	1002	15.5	5.1	66
COUNTY SIZE D	11047	10022	13.4	90.7	101	3004	14.5	27.2	109	3230	15.8	29.2	119	1114	17.2	8.0	103
MSA CENTRAL CITY	29246	26021	34.7	89.0	99	6805	32.8	23.3	94	6666	32.7	22.8	93	1570	24.3	10.1	130
MSA SUBURBAN	34920	31386	41.9	89.8	100	8809	42.5	25.2	101	8561	42.0	24.5	100	3000	46.4	5.4	69
NON-MSA	19199	17561	23.4	91.5	102	5124	24.7	26.7	107	5179	25.4	27.0	110	1901	29.4	8.6	111
SINGLE	10575	9040	12.1	85.5	95	1849	8.9	17.5	70	2247	11.0	21.2	87	666	10.3	6.3	81
MARRIED	52106	48096	64.2	92.3	103	15343	74.0	29.4	118	13393	65.6	25.7	105	4746	73.3	9.1	117
OTHER	20686	17812	23.8	86.1	96	3547	17.1	17.1	69	4766	23.4	23.0	94	1059	16.4	5.1	66
PARENTS	31945	30236	40.3	94.7	105	11882	57.3	37.2	150	7289	35.7	22.8	93	4457	68.9	14.0	180
WORKING PARENTS	20048	18932	25.3	94.4	105	7261	35.0	36.2	146	4537	22.2	22.6	92	2936	45.4	14.6	189
SOLE PARENT	7497	7084	9.5	94.5	105	2536	12.2	33.8	136	1768	8.7	23.6	96	949	14.7	12.7	163
HOUSEHOLD SIZE: 1 PERSON	13337	10785	14.4	80.9	90	841	4.1	6.3	25	2961	14.5	22.2	91	*221	3.4	1.7	21
2 PERSONS	26259	23109	30.8	88.0	98	4900	23.6	18.7	75	6909	33.9	26.3	107	969	15.0	3.7	48
3 OR MORE	43771	41054	54.8	93.8	104	14997	72.3	34.3	138	10535	51.6	24.1	98	5281	81.6	12.1	155
ANY CHILD IN HOUSEHOLD	35220	33234	44.3	94.4	105	13092	63.1	37.2	149	7978	39.1	22.6	93	4736	73.2	13.4	173
UNDER 2 YEARS	7198	6674	8.9	92.7	103	2522	12.2	35.0	141	1228	6.0	17.1	70	918	14.2	12.8	164
2-5 YEARS	13967	13300	17.7	95.2	106	5805	28.0	41.6	167	3111	15.2	22.3	91	2207	34.1	15.8	204
6-11 YEARS	16745	16034	21.4	95.8	107	7100	34.2	42.4	170	4298	21.1	25.7	105	2444	37.8	14.6	188
12-17 YEARS	14871	13875	18.5	93.3	104	5320	25.7	35.8	144	3548	17.4	23.9	97	1974	30.5	13.3	171
WHITE	71865	64745	86.4	90.1	100	17487	84.3	24.3	98	17543	86.0	24.4	100	5959	92.1	8.3	107
BLACK	9557	8563	11.4	89.6	100	2830	13.6	29.6	119	2485	12.1	25.8	105	384	5.9	4.0	52
SPANISH SPEAKING	4446	4018	5.4	90.4	101	1338	6.5	30.1	121	1038	5.1	23.3	95	*414	6.4	9.3	120
HOME OWNED	55898	50819	67.8	90.9	101	14165	68.3	25.3	102	14274	70.0	25.5	104	4077	63.0	7.3	94

TABLE 7-6
Demographic Data for Selected Brands of Cold Breakfast Cereals (Natural Segment, 1990)

BASE: FEMALE HOMEMAKERS	TOTAL U.S. '000	ALL A '000	B % DOWN	C % ACROSS	D INDEX	NATURAL A '000	B % DOWN	C % ACROSS	D INDEX	KELLOGGS RAISIN BRAN A '000	B % DOWN	C % ACROSS	D INDEX	POST FRUIT & FIBRE A '000	B % DOWN	C % ACROSS	D INDEX
ALL FEMALE HOMEMAKERS	83366	74948	100.0	89.9	100	11867	100.0	14.2	100	12114	100.0	14.5	100	2606	100.0	3.1	100
WOMEN	83366	74948	100.0	89.9	99	11867	100.0	14.2	100	12114	100.0	14.5	100	2606	100.0	3.1	100
HOUSEHOLD HEADS	28345	24380	32.5	86.0	96	3513	29.6	12.4	87	3100	25.6	10.9	75	773	29.7	2.7	87
HOMEMAKERS	83366	74948	100.0	89.9	100	11867	100.0	14.2	100	12114	100.0	14.5	100	2606	100.0	3.1	100
GRADUATED COLLEGE	12896	11520	15.4	89.3	99	2555	21.5	19.8	139	1605	13.2	12.4	86	488	18.7	3.8	121
ATTENDED COLLEGE	14718	13254	17.7	90.1	100	2613	22.0	17.8	125	2351	19.4	16.0	110	528	20.3	3.6	115
GRADUATED HIGH SCHOOL	35709	32344	43.2	90.6	101	4776	40.2	13.4	94	5645	46.6	15.8	109	1049	40.3	2.9	94
DID NOT GRADUATE HIGH SCHOOL	20043	17829	23.8	89.0	99	1923	16.2	9.6	67	2513	20.7	12.5	86	*541	20.8	2.7	86
18-24	7596	6839	9.1	90.0	100	732	6.2	9.6	68	1057	8.7	13.9	96	*161	6.2	2.1	68
25-34	19963	18175	24.3	91.0	101	3059	25.8	15.3	108	2737	22.6	13.7	94	449	17.2	2.2	72
35-44	17118	15917	21.2	93.0	103	2996	25.2	17.5	123	2814	23.2	16.4	113	730	28.0	4.3	136
45-54	12257	10948	14.6	89.3	99	1824	15.4	14.9	105	2176	18.0	17.8	122	507	19.5	4.1	132
55-64	10967	9898	13.2	90.3	100	1347	11.4	12.3	86	1457	12.0	13.3	91	*321	12.3	2.9	94
65 OR OVER	15464	13172	17.6	85.2	95	1909	16.1	12.3	87	1873	15.5	12.1	83	438	16.8	2.8	91
18-34	27560	25014	33.4	90.8	101	3791	31.9	13.8	97	3794	31.3	13.8	95	609	23.4	2.2	71
18-49	51245	46820	62.5	91.4	102	7843	66.1	15.3	108	7932	65.5	15.5	107	1627	62.4	3.2	102
25-54	49338	45039	60.1	91.3	102	7879	66.4	16.0	112	7726	63.8	15.7	108	1686	64.7	3.4	109
EMPLOYED FULL TIME	35817	31821	42.5	88.8	99	5154	43.4	14.4	101	5321	43.9	14.9	102	1206	46.3	3.4	108
PART-TIME	9658	9059	12.1	93.8	104	1724	14.5	17.9	125	1587	13.1	16.4	113	*493	18.9	5.1	163
SOLE WAGE EARNER	11247	9661	12.9	85.9	96	1357	11.4	12.1	85	1320	10.9	11.7	81	406	15.6	3.6	115
NOT EMPLOYED	37891	34068	45.5	89.9	100	4988	42.0	13.2	92	5206	43.0	13.7	95	907	34.8	2.4	77
PROFESSIONAL	7232	6551	8.7	90.6	101	1294	10.9	17.9	126	896	7.4	12.4	85	*321	12.3	4.4	142
EXECUTIVE/ADMIN/MANAGERIAL	5447	4744	6.3	87.1	97	836	7.0	15.3	108	763	6.3	14.0	96	*159	6.1	2.9	93
CLERICAL/SALES/TECHNICAL	19699	17657	23.6	89.6	100	3066	25.8	15.6	109	3215	26.5	16.3	112	762	29.2	3.9	124
PRECISION/CRAFTS/REPAIR	1091	952	1.3	87.3	97	*173	1.0	15.9	111	*119	1.0	10.9	75	*22	.8	2.0	65
OTHER EMPLOYED	12005	10976	14.6	91.4	102	1511	12.7	12.6	88	1915	15.8	16.0	110	*434	16.7	3.6	116
H/D INCOME $75,000 OR MORE	5950	5256	7.0	88.3	98	1080	9.1	18.2	128	869	7.2	14.6	101	*210	8.1	3.5	113
$60,000 - 74,999	5600	5059	6.8	90.3	100	1216	10.2	21.7	153	994	8.2	17.8	122	*206	7.9	3.7	118
$50,000 - 59,999	6353	5813	7.8	91.5	102	1211	10.2	19.1	134	1201	9.9	18.9	130	*264	10.1	4.2	133
$40,000 - 49,999	9623	8767	11.7	91.1	101	1553	13.1	16.1	113	1665	13.7	17.3	119	*275	10.6	2.9	91

$30,000 - 39,999	12677	11605	15.5	91.5	102	1742	14.7	13.7	97	2024	16.7	16.0	110	524	20.1	4.1	132
$20,000 - 29,999	13762	12454	16.6	90.5	101	2118	17.8	15.4	108	2017	16.7	14.7	101	•410	15.7	3.0	95
$10,000 - 19,999	16448	14645	19.5	89.0	99	1596	13.4	9.7	68	1895	15.6	11.5	75	•322	12.4	2.0	63
LESS THAN $10,000	12953	11348	15.1	87.6	97	1351	11.4	10.4	73	1448	12.0	11.2	77	•394	15.1	3.0	97
CENSUS REGION: NORTH EAST	17159	15165	20.2	88.4	98	2732	23.0	15.9	112	2525	20.8	14.7	101	554	21.3	3.2	103
NORTH CENTRAL	20276	18598	24.8	91.7	102	2805	23.6	13.8	97	2897	23.9	14.3	98	701	26.9	3.5	111
SOUTH	29397	26824	35.8	91.2	101	3290	27.7	11.2	79	4222	34.9	14.4	99	899	34.5	3.1	98
WEST	16534	14362	19.2	86.9	97	3039	25.6	18.4	129	2470	20.4	14.9	103	451	17.3	2.7	87
MARKETING REG.: NEW ENGLAND	4405	3834	5.1	87.0	97	777	6.5	17.6	124	665	5.5	15.1	104	•116	4.5	2.6	84
MIDDLE ATLANTIC	13768	12183	16.3	88.5	98	2108	17.8	15.3	108	2019	16.7	14.7	101	555	21.3	4.0	129
EAST CENTRAL	11792	10880	14.5	92.3	103	1568	13.2	13.3	93	1717	14.2	14.6	100	•353	13.5	3.0	96
WEST CENTRAL	13275	12136	16.2	91.4	102	1994	16.8	15.0	106	1843	15.2	13.9	96	•509	19.5	3.8	123
SOUTH EAST	15926	14687	19.6	92.2	103	1634	13.8	10.3	72	2125	17.5	13.3	92	•468	18.0	2.9	94
SOUTH WEST	9589	8601	11.5	89.7	100	1086	9.2	11.3	80	1542	12.7	16.1	111	•283	10.9	3.0	94
PACIFIC	14611	12627	16.8	86.4	96	2700	22.8	18.5	130	2202	18.2	15.1	104	321	12.3	2.2	70
COUNTY SIZE A	34874	30829	41.1	88.4	98	5481	46.2	15.7	110	4652	38.4	13.3	92	934	35.8	2.7	86
COUNTY SIZE B	24866	22682	30.3	91.2	101	3229	27.2	13.0	91	3572	29.5	14.4	99	781	30.0	3.1	100
COUNTY SIZE C	12578	11416	15.2	90.8	101	1645	13.9	13.1	92	2227	18.4	17.7	122	•426	16.3	3.1	108
COUNTY SIZE D	11047	10022	13.4	90.7	101	1511	12.7	13.7	96	1663	13.7	15.1	104	•465	17.8	4.2	135
MSA CENTRAL CITY	29246	26021	34.7	89.0	99	3889	32.8	13.3	93	3726	30.8	12.7	88	798	30.2	2.7	86
MSA SUBURBAN	34920	31366	41.9	89.8	100	5482	46.2	15.7	110	5005	41.3	14.3	99	1162	44.6	3.3	106
NON-MSA	19199	17561	23.4	91.5	102	2495	21.0	13.0	91	3382	27.9	17.6	121	658	25.2	3.4	110
SINGLE	10575	9040	12.1	85.5	95	1223	10.3	11.6	81	1131	9.3	10.7	74	•234	9.0	2.2	71
MARRIED	52106	48096	64.2	92.3	103	7986	67.3	15.3	108	8731	72.1	16.8	115	1761	67.6	3.4	108
OTHER	20686	17812	23.8	86.1	96	2658	22.4	12.8	90	2252	18.6	10.9	75	610	23.4	2.9	94
PARENTS	31945	30236	40.3	94.7	105	4892	41.2	15.3	108	5239	43.2	16.4	113	1038	39.8	3.2	104
WORKING PARENTS	20048	18932	25.3	94.4	105	2989	25.2	14.9	105	3396	28.0	16.9	117	716	27.5	3.6	114
SOLE PARENT	7497	7084	9.5	94.5	105	1034	8.7	13.8	97	1025	8.5	13.7	94	•125	4.8	1.7	53
HOUSEHOLD SIZE: 1 PERSON	13337	10785	14.4	80.9	90	1289	10.9	9.7	68	1222	10.1	9.2	63	501	19.2	3.8	120
2 PERSONS	26259	23109	30.8	88.0	98	3849	32.4	14.7	103	3390	28.0	12.9	89	627	24.1	2.4	76
3 OR MORE	43771	41054	54.8	93.8	104	6728	56.7	15.4	108	7502	61.9	17.1	118	1478	56.7	3.4	108
ANY CHILD IN HOUSEHOLD	35220	33234	44.3	94.4	105	5455	46.0	15.5	109	5686	46.9	16.1	111	1137	43.6	3.2	103
UNDER 2 YEARS	7198	6674	8.9	92.7	103	1029	8.7	14.3	100	1035	8.5	14.4	99	•154	5.9	2.1	68
2-5 YEARS	13967	13300	17.7	95.2	106	2039	17.2	14.6	103	2144	17.7	15.4	106	•345	13.2	2.5	79
6-11 YEARS	16745	16034	21.4	95.8	107	2786	23.5	16.6	117	2739	22.6	16.4	113	515	19.8	3.1	98
12-17 YEARS	14871	13875	18.5	93.3	104	2585	21.8	17.4	122	2664	22.0	17.9	123	628	24.1	4.2	135
WHITE	71865	64745	86.4	90.1	100	10743	90.5	14.9	105	10870	89.7	15.1	104	2409	92.4	3.4	107
BLACK	9557	8563	11.4	89.6	100	835	7.0	8.7	61	1077	8.9	11.3	78	•173	6.6	1.8	58
SPANISH SPEAKING	4446	4018	5.4	90.4	101	501	4.2	11.3	79	529	4.4	11.9	82	•171	6.6	3.8	123
HOME OWNED	55898	50819	67.8	90.9	101	8133	68.5	14.5	102	8887	73.4	15.9	109	1871	71.8	3.3	107

Charms's total penetration of all demographic groups (7.8%). The ratio between the 11.3% penetration of the 18–24 age group and the brand's overall penetration of 7.8% is expressed as an index number, the figure in column D. This index number is 145 for the 18–24 age group, indicating that 11.3% is 45% higher than 7.8%.

The index number in column D is very useful because it shows the importance of any demographic subcategory among all users of the brand. If the number for any group is close to 100, this group represents *average* purchasers. A good example is Lucky Charms usage by the $20,000–$29,999 income group, with a 7.8% penetration (the same as the overall penetration for the brand). If the number is greater than 100, the category is of above-average importance, as is the case with the 18–24 age group for Lucky Charms, indicated by its index of 145. Index figures is the 90 to 110 range are close to the average; figures under 90 are below average, and figures over 110 are above average.

The column so far unexplained is B. This presents what is often called *profile percentages*. The total number of users of Lucky Charms (6,471,000) is used as the base (100.0%) on which the profile of each demographic category is calculated. Take the age category, which is expressed in two separate combinations of ages. The first series is 18–24, 25–34, 35–44, 45–54, 55–64, and 65 and over; the second series is three mixed combinations: 18–34, 18–49, and 25–54. If we take the first of these series, the figures in column B represent each of the six age groups as percentages of the total of all users of Lucky Charms. We see the result in table 7–7, which is extracted from (and is precisely the same information as we see in) table 7–5. The individual numbers and percentages in table 7–7 add up to the totals at the top of the column.

Once readers are familiar with the meaning of the MRI figures, it is an easy matter to pick up the study of Kellogg's Corn Flakes, Lucky Charms, and Post Fruit & Fiber. Tables 7–5 and 7–6 provide all the information necessary to analyze the demographic characteristics of the target group for each of these brands.

Kellogg's Corn Flakes

As described earlier in this chapter, the primary target group is existing users of KCF, to prevent any further erosion. These people are described in the Kellogg's Corn Flakes columns of table 7–5.

From the index numbers in column D, it is clear that KCF has a

TABLE 7-7
Profiles of Lucky Charms Users by Age Group

Ages	Number of Users (Column A)	Percentage (Column B)
All ages	6,471,000	100.0
18–24	855,000	13.2
25–34	2,350,000	36.3
35–44	2,057,000	31.8
45–54	703,000	10.9
55–64	290,000	4.5
65 and over	215,000	3.3

well-distributed group of users, since none of the figures are very far from 100. The brand does, however, have an above-average penetration among the following subcategories:

- homemakers aged fifty-five and over
- the less well educated
- homemakers not employed outside the home (mainly pensioners)
- those in more rural localities
- lower income families

These categories represent groups of particular importance to the brand, but it is not true that KCF users are concentrated exclusively in these groups. For instance, KCF has 7,825,000 homemakers aged fifty-five and over, a strong pocket of concentration. The brand nevertheless has 60 percent more users (12,581,000) among the younger age groups.

When we use this demographic analysis for creative and media planning, we can conclude that KCF is used by all types of people, but at an above-average rate by the demographic groups listed above. These therefore deserve extra attention in the creative and media plans for the brand. (In the creative plans, these demographic groups should, for instance, be represented in the models used in the advertising.)

Lucky Charms

As already described, we are primarily interested in targeting existing users of Lucky Charms, since we wish to persuade them to buy the brand more often than they do at present.

There are fewer users of Lucky Charms than of KCF, and the users of Lucky Charms are more polarized demographically. Note that the index numbers are generally more extreme than for Kellogg's Corn Flakes, and that the following subcategories are especially important for Lucky Charms:

- homemakers who attended college
- the eighteen to forty-four age groups
- part-time workers
- families in the $40,000–$59,999 income bracket
- homemakers in the Central regions
- parents of children of all ages (an especially important concentration)
- rural families
- Hispanics

Our conclusion for the demographic targeting of Lucky Charms is that, although the brand is used to varying degrees by all groups of the population, it has important pockets of high concentration, for example, the eighteen to forty-four age group and, especially, parents. Note that users (children) are separate from buyers (parents). This demographic analysis provides a clear focus for our creative and media plans.

Post Fruit & Fibre

We earlier concluded that the advertising for Post Fruit & Fibre should be directed aggressively to attract new buyers who are coming into the growing natural segment of the market. Table 7–6 shows the demographic characteristics of the natural segment as a whole. It also covers Kellogg's Raisin Bran (the largest brand in the segment) and Post Fruit & Fibre.

There is a reasonable degree of polarization among all users of natural cereals, and in some respects this is more pronounced among users of Post Fruit & Fibre. This pronounced polarization suggests that Post Fruit & Fibre has made progress by intensive concentration on some of the narrowest demographic groups who were most likely to be interested in natural cereals:

- homemakers who have attended college
- the thirty-five to fifty-four age group
- upper income families

- professional families
- families in the Middle Atlantic and West Central regions
- families living in smaller towns and in the country

Since it is now appropriate for the brand to broaden its appeal, Post Fruit & Fibre should aim for a profile approximating that of the natural cereals market as a whole. For instance, the brand should now devote extra attention to top-income families and those on the West Coast.

The type of demographic analysis made for these three different and important brands could be extended to virtually all brands in the cold cereal category. It is hoped, however, that these examples are clear enough to enable readers to grasp the analytical method and to apply it themselves.

We must now devote some attention to a different although related way of measuring the users of a brand.

Psychographics

The study of psychographics is much more recent than the study of demographics. Psychographics is concerned with a more qualitative evaluation concerning consumers' lifestyles, habits, and attitudes. The concept is interesting and useful, mainly because it helps creative people understand the subtleties of the target group. It helps them understand *why* members of the target group are there, and this understanding provides a potent lead to ways of selling to them. However, there are significant difficulties with the concept, mainly concerned with definition and measurement, something which readers can infer from Leo Burnett's words that introduce this chapter.

At its simplest, a description of the typical lifestyles of a brand's target group can provide a useful ingredient to an advertising strategy and can be used in a green-thumbed way to fertilize creative thought. We can arrive at such a psychographic picture of a brand from qualitative research among members of the target group. (The best types of research for this purpose are discussed in chapter 8.)

It is even possible to use judgment to extrapolate the psychographic qualities of the target group, on the basis of their known demographic characteristics, and such an extrapolation will shortly be attempted for Kellogg's Corn Flakes, Lucky Charms, and Post Fruit & Fibre.

Psychographic analysis has, however, been carried much further than is possible with the technique described in the last paragraph. The research disciplines of the social sciences have been used, and more than one attempt has been made to classify the whole body of American consumers into groups, each defined fairly tightly in terms of their psychographic characteristics. The most familiar analysis of this type, known as *values and lifestyles* (VALS), puts the population into four subtly defined and self-contained groups and nine subgroups. These are put together on the basis of the responses of a large sample of consumers to more than fifty questions of opinion, plus details of the respondents' demographics.[15]

The VALS grouping is as follows:

Need-Driven Groups (materially deprived people with little education)

- *survivors*—economically the bottom 4% of the American adult population: Old, fearful, remote from the economic and cultural mainstream.
- *sustainers*—7% of the adult population: younger than survivors, angry, resentful, street-smart, often involved in the underground economy.

Outer-Directed Groups (people happy to maintain the social and economic status quo)

- *belongers*—35% of the adult population: Aging, unadventuous, happy, patriotic.
- *emulators*—9% of the adult population: Young, ambitious, striving for upward mobility.
- *achievers*—22% of the adult population: Middle-aged, confident, content, those who have achieved material success.

Inner-Directed Groups (highly educated people whose ambitions transcend the economic and social status quo)

- *"I am me"*—5% of the adult population: Young, narcissistic, impulsive, moving toward Inner Direction.
- *experiential*—7% of the adult population: Youthful, adventurous, artistic, intensely oriented toward inner growth.

- *societally conscious*—8% of the adult population: Oriented to clear goals, mature, successful, aiming to improve society.

Combined Outer- and Inner-Directed Groups (A very small cluster of people who have achieved a happy medium)

- *integrated*—2% of the adult population: Understanding, mature, flexible, able to see all sides; they have a vision of where their lives are going.

This analysis is intellectually attractive. Nevertheless there is an important reason why we should *not* rely too much on an all-embracing system like VALS in defining the target group in the advertising strategy. Multibrand buying is normal in most product categories. This means that consumers buy different brands in the same market segment and also often cross over between segments. It follows that if we try to match buyers of a brand to any self-contained psychographic group, we shall be ignoring occasional buyers who come to the brand from other brands and other market segments. We shall be operating with blinders on because the VALS typology assumes that in many cases the use of individual brands is exclusive to individual categories of buyers, when in fact a brand is bought by many different types of buyers, although at different purchase frequencies.

A similar argument holds for demographic classification, and this is why I have emphasized that a brand is never (or at least only very rarely) used exclusively by any single demographic group.

But despite these qualifications about taking psychographic analysis too far, it is nevertheless useful to add a psychographic extension to our demographic description of a brand's target group. For the three brands of cold breakfast cereal we have been studying in this chapter, such an addition might be hypothesized as follows:

1. *Kellogg's Corn Flakes.* The target group are traditionalists, people who buy the trusted and true, home-lovers, family-centered people, those with passive lifestyles, and Outer-Directed people, particularly Belongers and Achievers.

2. *Lucky Charms.* The target group are families whose lives revolve around the children; narrowly focused, hard-working people; families who are more concerned with continuing their present lifestyles than with expanding their horizons; people with conventional

tastes; and Outer-Directed people, particularly Emulators and Belongers.

3. *Post Fruit & Fibre*. The target group are families on an economically upward path, fitness enthusiasts, people with active lifestyles, experimenters, those who lead busy social lives, and Inner-Directed people of all types.

These hypotheses, based on judgment and not research, lead us to the two remaining parts of the advertising strategy (covered in chapter 8): the proposition and the ways in which the campaign should work. They will help us in particular to define the proposition. At the end of chapter 8, I shall complete my hypotheses about the advertising strategies for KCF, Lucky Charms, and Post Fruit & Fibre.

Summary

1. A business organization plans its strategy at a minimum of three levels: the company plan (embracing all its brands), the individual brand's marketing strategy, and the brand's advertising strategy. The third of these grows out of the second, which in turn grows out of the first.

2. At all levels, strategy is written in competitive terms. It is concerned essentially with the position of the company and the brand in a competitive environment.

3. The brand advertising strategy can be defined as *the objectives for an advertising campaign, defined in three specific terms: the audience, the proposition, and the ways in which the campaign should work.* Writing an advertising strategy calls for the ability to analyze facts and the capacity to judge their meaning and relevance.

4. The most important question we must ask when we define our target group is: Where is our business coming from? A brand has five sources of business:

a. from new users entering a growing market

b. from new users entering a growing market segment from a different segment

c. from attracting users from other brands within its market segment

d. from increased usage frequency by its own buyers

e. finally—a strategy for brands under pressure—retaining existing users and maintaining their purchase frequency

Of these five sources of business, a, b, and c are exclusively concerned—and e is partly concerned—with penetration; d is exclusively and e is partly directed at purchase frequency.

5. Defining our target group calls for an evaluation of overall trends in the market, trends in our market segment, and the position of and trends in our own brand. From this evaluation, we must determine how much we wish to increase penetration by attracting new users (and we must define which brands these people are now using) and how much we wish to increase purchase frequency by current users.

6. This initial definition of our target group in terms of what brand(s) they are now using enables us to describe these people demographically with the use of MRI or SMRB data.

7. With the use of qualitative research (and sometimes even by a simple extrapolation of demographic data) we can add an extra psychographic dimension. Both the demographic and the psychographic descriptions of our target group are valuable inputs when we come to write the remaining two parts of the advertising strategy, discussed in chapter 8.

8. Strategy is very important because it points creative work in the best direction and helps to reduce waste. However, readers should always keep in mind that idea generation is an even more important part of the process of developing advertising campaigns; but idea generation must be described and evaluated in a book different in focus and presentation from this one.

8

Strategy

The Proposition and the Ways in Which the Campaign Should Work

There must be something about it that made the manufacturer make it in the first place. Something about it that makes people continue to buy it. . . . [I aim at] capturing that . . . and making the thing itself arresting.[1]

Leo Burnett

The Proposition

Proposition is no longer a fashionable word to describe the signals and arguments that are built into an advertisement. However, it still seems to me the best word to use because it is so succinct and down-to-earth—a reminder that advertising is a part of the selling process, a description of the manufacturer's offer. In the sophistry and prolixity of the debates about the economic and social effects of advertising, people tend to forget that advertising is a part of a mundane process in which goods and services are made available to the public in exchange for payment—Wordsworth's "getting and spending" at its most humdrum.

James Webb Young, the most thoughtful and experienced of the practitioners who have written books about advertising, had no hesitation about using the word *proposition:*

(1) Be crystal clear in your own mind as to what your proposition is.
(2) Have reason to believe that it is an appealing proposition to the particular group of people you are addressing.[2]

Martin Mayer, an investigative journalist who has published the best-informed review of the advertising industry ever written by an outsider—*Madison Avenue, USA,* a book whose general argument still holds up remarkably well after more than thirty years—devoted two chapters to the concept of the proposition and assumed that the word was used universally, which indeed it was in the 1950s.[3]

One of the reasons that the word got into disrepute was its specific use by Rosser Reeves for his unique selling proposition (USP). As discussed in chapter 4, the USP is a restrictive concept, now in disfavor for the important reason that it encourages us to throw many babies out with the advertising bathwater. I intend to use the word *proposition* in a much fuller sense, as a description (although a selective one) of the elements that distinguish the brand advertised from all other brands. Concentration on the centrally important functional and nonfunctional elements prevents attention from being diverted to the periphery, with all the waste implied by such a diffusion of effort.

A brand can be defined as *a product that provides functional benefits plus added values that some consumers value enough to buy.* It follows from this definition that the proposition must cover as precisely as possible both the brand's functional properties and its added values (that is, its nonfunctional attributes). The tighter the proposition (the more exactly it is written), the less the waste of resources and effort there will be in developing advertisements from it.

Functionality

Functionality is in theory objectively demonstrable (for example, with the use of scientific tests). However, there are complications. These concern the dissonance that sometimes occurs between what the scientists show (including occasionally what they are unable to show) and what consumers perceive. Here are four examples that illustrate this point.

Many brands of dishwashing liquid are advertised for the way they care for hands even though the product's main purpose is obviously to wash dishes clean. The reason why the advertising emphasizes mildness to hands is that people believe that if the liquid works efficiently to clean dishes, it is harsh to the skin (something which is not necessarily true scientifically). It is the consumer's erroneous impression that determines the way in which the proposition concentrates on the hands and not the dishes.

The second example concerns brands of instant coffee. These are invariably advertised for their genuine coffee taste, although the most obvious functional characteristic of all instant coffee is its convenience in use. The benefit featured in the advertising is the end product of reliable research that demonstrates that a convenience appeal has negative associations: convenience coffee is seen as something used by lazy and self-indulgent housewives. Buyers are able to convince themselves to buy it if it tastes as good as ground coffee, a beverage that is known to be much more difficult to prepare.[4] Hence the advertising concentration on genuine coffee taste.

The third example relates to the introduction of cake mixes into the British market. Research demonstrated that housewives understood clearly what a cake mix was, but they were skeptical that the resulting product was as good as homemade. The advertising therefore concentrated on the end result, and not on the more obvious product benefit of convenience.

The fourth example is the common technique of preempting an argument when such a claim is not unique to the brand advertised. The slogan for a washing powder that "nothing washes whiter" allows that other brands may wash equally well. (This was an ingenious "weasel" produced in response to a legal prohibition on superlative claims.) The time-honored slogan of the British department store John Lewis, "never knowingly undersold," admits the possibility that prices in other stores may be just as low as at John Lewis. In any field, the first advertiser who makes a preemptive claim reaps an individual benefit from what is in reality a generic argument that could be made for many other brands.

What these examples show is that a brand's proposition may not be as obvious as it appears from an objective description of the brand's ingredients and functional characteristics. These characteristics are merely the starting point for constructing a proposition. We must move on to determine, on the basis of consumer perceptions, the best attributes to build into the advertising. As already suggested, the most promising functional end benefit is not always obvious, and therefore some advertisers use the deplorable phrase "*end* end benefit" in order to encourage the brand management and the agency to ferret out what really matters about the brand in the eyes of the consumer.

As we shall see in the discussion of "upstream" testing in chapter 9, qualitative research is helpful; indeed it is all that is available for a new brand that has not yet come onto the market. The most reliable method, however, is also the most expensive and time-consuming: producing advertisements based on alternative propositions and area-testing them. More than twenty years ago I was working on a major brand of health drink sold in Britain. We narrowed down the brand's functional appeal to two alternative end benefits: the brand's ability (1) to protect against colds and chills, and (2) to help children grown healthy and strong. These alternative propositions were developed into finished campaigns which were exposed separately in the marketplace over extended periods and were carefully monitored for their effect. The first proposition was the hand's-down winner.

The first thing we need to know is the basic facts about the functional characteristics of our brand and its competitors. Table 8–1 uses 1990 data from Mediamark Research Inc. (MRI) for the toilet soap category in the United States. The table breaks this market down into its main functional segments, based on volume usage by men and women separately. The advertising for this and other packaged goods is mostly directed at women, in their capacity as purchasers of all brands for their families. Different family members may,

TABLE 8–1
Toilet Soap Market Segments, 1990

Category	Share of Volume Women Users (%)	Share of Volume Men Users (%)
Total	100	100
Personal care—family orientation	24	21
Personal care—beauty orientation	33	20
Body freshness—deodorant orientation	24	33
Body freshness—deodorant + freshness	13	20
Other brands (including "price" brands)	6	6

Source: Mediamark Research Inc.

however, have different preferences, although in many cases (as will be apparent from table 8–2), large numbers of men use brands of soap which have a feminine orientation, like Caress and Dove, just because the bars are in the house.

Table 8–2 looks at the ten leading brands in the toilet soap category. These together account for rather more than three quarters of total volume usage by both men and women, although the table also shows that half the brands are used more by women than men and the other half vice versa.

Although toilet soap is a product obviously intended for washing the skin, this function is so universally understood—the product is so commonplace—that the end benefit embodied in the proposition for every advertised brand simply has to reach out beyond this simple function. The specific ways in which this has been done for different

TABLE 8–2

Leading Toilet Soap Brands, 1990

Category	Share of Volume Women Users (%)	Share of Volume Men Users (%)
Personal care—family orientation		
Ivory	15	16
Tone	3	2
Personal care—beauty orientation		
Camay	4	2
Caress	5	3
Dove	15	10
Body feshness—deodorant orientation		
Dial	11	15
Safeguard	6	6
Zest	6	7
Body freshness—deodorant + freshness		
Coast	5	7
Irish Spring	5	10

Sourch: Mediamark Research Inc.

brands have in turn dictated how the total market has become segmented.

The original brand of toilet soap was Procter & Gamble's Ivory, launched in 1879, and within a few years well established and nationally advertised. It was created and built on a proposition of purity. The soap was (and remains) 99.44 percent pure; it is white and unscented and floats on the water. The end benefit for the consumer is that Ivory contains no harmful chemicals to damage the skin. And with no perfume, it appeals to men as much as to women. Ivory has attracted imitators, but none has come near its success, with its fifteen percentage points of share in the female market out of the total segment share of 24 percent.[5]

After Ivory had become an established brand, competitors entered the market offering quite different types of benefit. A number of specifically beauty-oriented brands got a strong foothold in the 1920s, although Camay (also from Procter & Gamble) is the only one of these original brands that has retained a significant market share. The functional characteristics of brands in this category are their specific ingredients to keep a woman's complexion soft and wrinkle-free. The soaps have a cosmetic perfume; and the bars come in pastel shades. The end benefit is especially relevant to women: the promise of a softer, smoother complexion because of the special ingredients in the soap.

The third market segment, deodorant soaps, was created shortly after World War II by Dial, a brand originally from the Chicago meat packer Armour, a company that until then had not diversified outside its original field. Its venture into soap was an overnight success. The brand is now marketed by the Dial Corporation. The end benefit of Dial was (and still is) that it prevents perspiration smell because of its germ-killing ingredients. The brand attracted many competitors. However, with its current fifteen percentage points of the male market, Dial manages to keep its leading position, although not quite such a dominant position as Ivory in its own segment.

The fourth segment, the freshness-oriented soaps, came like Adam's rib out of the deodorant soap group. This fourth segment has developed fairly modestly since its beginning in the late 1960s; all new brands are modeled on a European brand not sold in the United States, Henkel's Fa, which was first marketed in Germany. The brands in the freshness segment offer a combination of refreshment and deodorizing. The end benefit to the consumer is the rather intangible quality of the wide-awake and confident feeling that comes from this type of product's deodorant ingredients and its very pronounced citrus perfume. The bars in the category also have a distinctive appearance: they are marbled (striated, in technical language). The segment is the smallest of the four, and the only two reasonably successful brands in it are Procter & Gamble's Coast and Colgate-Palmolive's Irish Spring.

The advertising proposition for each of the brands in the toilet soap category is dictated to a considerable degree by the functional properties that I have just described. Each brand's proposition emphasizes the functional qualities of the segment as a whole in which the brand is positioned; for example, for Ivory, purity so as not to harm the skin; for Dove, complexion care; for Dial, deodorizing properties to prevent smell; and for Coast, freshness and confidence. But this is not all. The proposition for each brand also has to *distinguish* it from the others with which it competes directly within its segment.

The signals and arguments that place the brand in the consumer's eyes in its market segment are motivators. All advertising must make something of these; and advertising for very large brands (for example, Ivory and Dial) relies very heavily on motivators. The reason is that the success of such brands depends essentially on the success of the segment in which each is positioned. However, in addition to motivators, the advertising for any brand must contain specific discriminators if such advertising is to perform a successful job for the brand as well as for the category as a whole.

Discriminators can be of two varieties. They can, like motivators, be functional. Functional differentiation is not uncommon; but it is not the strategy selected (or available) for the majority of brands. The only striking example in the toilet soap market is the claim that the Dove bar is one quarter cleansing cream: a claim that has done more than anything else to build this important brand. In other markets, most brands that feature functional dicriminators are those that employ unique selling proposition (USP) advertising, a style much less common in the 1990s than it was in the 1950s and 1960s.

Because of the speed of competitive response in oligopolistic markets, the type of extreme functional differentiation perceptible to nonusers is simply not available to many brands. However, users of a brand tend to be more conscious of unique functional features, no matter how small these may be.

An alternative and more common way of differentiating a brand from its competitors is by means of its nonfunctional qualities. Brands can be set apart by their personality; that is, their added values.

Added Values

Added values—the nonfunctional attributes of a brand—come from four main sources:

1. *Consumers' experience of the brand;* that is, its familiarity, known reliability, and reduction of risks. The brand becomes an old friend.
2. *The sorts of people who use the brand.* Such people sometimes—although not necessarily always—appear in the advertising. Use of a brand makes a public statement about the user; this is sometimes called the *necktie quality.*
3. *Belief that the brand is effective;* a quality of particular importance with proprietary medicines and cosmetics.
4. *The appearance of the brand;* which is the most important role for design and packaging and is a strong influence on how the design and packaging are presented in advertisements.

Added values are nurtured and developed in two ways. The first way is by people's having used and been satisfied with the brand. Satisfaction encourages repeat purchase, and every time this happens it reinforces the multiple satisfactions that consumers receive from the brand. The second way that added values are made to grow is as a result of the advertising. The advertising also provides the important additional advantage that the brand becomes increasingly differentiated from its competitors. This differentiation helps to protect the brand's price, a point that is argued and demonstrated in appendix A.

Effective advertising describes—or more commonly reminds the audience of—the brand benefits. It demonstrates the brand. And it allows users to picture people like themselves.

Users of one brand sometimes differentiate themselves from users of other brands because of shared social values. An example is how users of brands associated with New York City (such as banks) tend to believe that New Yorkers live in a tougher environment and have to work harder than other people do. Another example, which relates to a number of different product fields, is consciousness of ecology. This applies to users of brands (for example, paper products) that can be recycled; and to users of brands of cosmetics and toiletries that are not associated with animal experiments. Users of many brands see themselves as members of an exclusive club, with its own rules and attitudes. The nonrational signals in the advertising should encourage viewers and readers to nod their heads in agreement with the values depicted. Such agreement obviously contributes to stabilizing a brand's consumer franchise.

As a general rule, users of a brand pay more attention to its advertisements than nonusers do, and there are more users of a large brand than of a small brand. Therefore advertising for a large brand works more strongly than advertising for a small brand, since the *cost* of an advertisement for a large brand is the same as that for a small one. In the words of an economist, a large brand generates advertising-related scale economies.

Consumers' familiarity with and use of the brand is reinforced by advertising campaigns that often run for years, so that consumers manage to develop a subtle and multidimensional picture in their minds of what a brand stands for. There is more than one research technique that can be used to reveal this picture.

What Is a Brand?

The procedure used in this well-known research method is to ask consumers a hypothetical question: "If this brand were to come to life and become a person, what sort of person would he or she be?" It is important to recognize that this research explores the personality and image of the *brand*. These are sometimes (although by no means always) similar to the psychographics of the target group, discussed in chapter 7.

The most important example of differences between the two relates to the *aspirational* quality of some brands. A brand may be looked up to, as something especially suitable for a very select group of people; yet it may actually be used by a broad mass market. The Lux Toilet Soap movie-star campaign and the celebrated British campaign for After Eight chocolates are good cases in point.

Another example of the difference between brand imagery and user psychographics relates to various abstract qualities that may be intrinsic in a brand. A well-known American cleaning product which traditionally does not feature its users in its advertising is viewed by consumers as having a cold personality. This trait is not a characteristic of the actual users of this brand, but it is important that its advertising strategy should be written in full knowledge of this problem.

We learn about these things by using the research technique of having consumers use language they understand—that is, words that describe human personalities—as a means of revealing their perceptions of something that they normally cannot either understand or articulate: the personality of brands. The technique has been used by J. Walter Thompson in Europe and the United States for two decades. Representative interviews are often filmed verbatim for the direct enlightenment of client and agency people. Here are three typical examples of the technique. The Campbell's and Korvette's examples were filmed.[6]

1. *Campbell's* (combined comments of three men and one woman):

Oh, a lovely woman, a lovely lady, lovely lady.

Mrs. Campbell is kind of grandma, you know, a place to go eat on Sunday. Lots of kids around all the time. Table is always ready; a lot of food in the refrigerator.

I would think she is a very warm, genial lady who sits in her kitchen and brews delicious soups and cares about your nourishment and cares about your children and has a flock of grandkids, and has her ration of liver spots on the backs of her hands.

It's over the river and through the woods to grandma's house when you go see Mrs. Campbell.

Oh, I don't think she has much leisure time. I just don't think there's another minute left in the day for all the things that perhaps she'd like to do, but she's just so busy.

Everybody goes when they're invited to Mrs. Campbell's house.

I like Mrs. Campbell.

2. *Ronzoni Spaghetti* (comments of one woman):

My name is Italia Piccolo and I am the proud mother of twelve children, twenty-four grandchildren, and six great grandchildren. We all live here in Sicily. Our village is very tiny and most everyone here knows one another. You could call us one big happy family. My husband, Antonio, is one of many grape farmers, being that our village produces its own wine as well as most everything else we eat and drink. It is something that everyone here takes great pride in.

As for me, I have made my family my entire life, and without shame I can say that I have enjoyed every moment of it, especially Christmas, when all forty-four of us share dinner together.

3. *Korvette's Stores* (combined comments of two men and one woman):

I'd have to say that it's probably a man wearing . . . and likes to wear the latest in polyester knit pants; you know, big bold plaid . . . open-neck shirts . . . dark, dark tan because he likes to stay in Miami a lot.

A sort of a hustler: Mr. Korvette is a hustler in my imagination.

I see a man who's kind of grown to paunch.

He's been married to the same woman for forty years, I would think something like that; and he has three or four kids. And they're all over-weight.

In recent years he's become more conservative. He's probably realized, "Look, I've got to be more like other guys, if I'm going to make it."

I would think the word Korvette is not flamboyant. It's tacky, really tacky.

There are two general points about this type of research. First, the investigations are fairly small-scale and are qualitative; and people express a variety of different opinions about any brand. Yet, in every case that I have studied, there has been a good degree of consensus among the views of many different people. The same signals seem to emerge repeatedly, although expressed in different words.

The second point is that there are many cases in which consumers' perceptions of brands are seriously unfavorable, and most pieces of such research contain one or two negative elements. Since these could never have stemmed from the advertising, the unfavorable impressions must have come from other communications about the brand: from consumers' experience of its functional qualities, from publicity about the brand, from word-of-mouth, or from comments in the media. Negative comments are less common for small corporations than for large ones; and they are less prevalent for packaged goods than for monolithic operations like banks and oil companies. The negative reactions to many brands are often the mirror image of their positive strengths. Even Mrs. Campbell,who is perceived in an almost uniformly favorable light, has a potential problem because of her age. This could involve difficulties for a highly innovative product launched under the Campbell's name.

The Korvette's interviews were made before that retail chain went out of business. They are typical of what consumers thought at the time, and it is clear that these comments from the public would have been of diagnostic value if they had been collected and acted on early enough.

Projective Techniques

Projective techniques are derived from clinical psychology. They cover a range of quantitative and qualitative methods. The underlying principle is that consumers are encouraged to describe the image of brands as they perceive them, using the visual and verbal language that is used in familiar but unconnected fields. The techniques were introduced tentatively in the 1950s and are today widely used in the United States. I am grateful to Edward Rosenstein for guidance on the methods used. He is a leading user of the techniques and was involved in developing them at Foote, Cone & Belding, Batten, Barton, Durstine & Osborn, and Saatchi & Saatchi-Compton.[7]

The early work in this field (first carried out widely during the 1960s, but still done occasionally today) uses a long list of words to describe brands. Samples of 150 to 200 consumers are asked which of these words they would use to picture each brand in a product category. The research yields much usable differentiation among brands, but consumers are much more inclined to apply the words to the functional characteristics than to the nonfunctional qualities of brands, with the result that the research is not very good in achieving the main objective of differentiating between brand personalities.

In the 1970s, a richer research vein was struck, with the technique of picture sorting. Such research takes a number of forms; here are four of the most popular types. The first two are linked and are normally used together.

1. A good number of pictures of people are cut out of magazines. Seventy is about right. These should cover a range of places and settings, but the people shown need not be demographically representative. A sample of about 250 members of the public are then interviewed, one at a time. They examine the pictures and apply to each as many words as they like, from a long list of words describing personal attitudes. As a result, researchers can build a library of pictures, together with a measure of how these are perceived by consumers according to preestablished attributes.

2. A second stage of research introduces a new batch of consumers to the pictures, but without the verbal descriptions this time. The labels for, say, ten brands in a product category are put on a table, and a reasonable number of users of the category (100 to 150) are asked to sort from the seventy pictures which people describe each of the ten brands. The respondents are encouraged to put as many pictures as they wish alongside each brand. This sorting enables researchers to match brands with perceived personality attributes (which have, of course, been tied to the pictures in the first stage of the research). The research can be taken further. After a number of such tests, it is possible to isolate the similarities among the images of different brands in entirely different fields. As a result, we can predict reasonably reliably that a user of brand A in one field will use brand X in another field, on the basis of the perceived similarity of personality between A and X.

3. Borrowed imagery can be explored in further ways. Members of focus groups, in which there is an important dynamic in the personal interaction among the respondents, can be encouraged (after careful initial preparation) to associate pictures of people with the brands these people use. The pictures of people are used as prompts; the brand name is the consumers' unprompted response. This technique is effective for brands whose use says something publicly about their users (the so-called necktie categories), for example, cigarettes, automobiles, department stores (for women), and baseball teams (for men). By comparing personality attributes across product categories, we can (again) predict what brands in a second category will be bought by users of a brand in one category.

4. There is a range of further qualitative techniques, some of which are suitable for some types of product, some for others. In one, a drawing of a female shopper confronts a range of blank boxes representing brands in a particular product category. A blank bubble for words comes out of her mouth. Each respondent is told that her friend has changed her regular brand. The respondent is asked what had she changed it to and why. A second technique uses an unrecognizable silhouette of a man holding a recognizable beer can. Respondents are asked to describe the man. A third technique is to persuade people to describe a brand as a house, and to run through its physical characteristics.

These variegated research methods are obviously of value only if it is true that brands offer consumers subtle and multidimensional satisfactions. I believe that this is much more generally true than untrue. If we remember that brands have been used by massive numbers of consumers on a weekly or even a daily basis for decades—and some were used by their parents and grandparents before them—we can begin to understand that the package of Tide or Colgate or Kellogg's or any other major brand on a supermarket shelf is merely the visible symbol of a collection of functional and nonfunctional satisfactions and associations. These include memories of and connections with the brand (many positive and a few negative), and they also include credible promises based on consumers' personal knowledge of the brand. These are all elements that the advertising should highlight. The result should be that favorable attitudes toward the brand should be sometimes planted and always reinforced in the minds of consumers. But to do an effective job, the advertising must press the right buttons. Projective techniques help us find them.

Values and Lifestyles

Readers will remember from chapter 7 the description of the values and lifestyles (VALS) analysis and how it can be used to define the psychographic characteristics of the advertising target group.

VALS has a second use, because the language that describes the attitudes, the consumption patterns, and the types of activities that occupy the people in each of the VALS lifestyle groups can help us define the added values of a brand directed at such a group. The analysis helps, in short, to match the psychographics of the target group to the personality of the brand. The practical procedure is to study the (plentiful) descriptions of the attitudes, consumption patterns, and activities of the various lifestyle groups, and to search for harmonies with the personality of our brand.[8] For instance (one of a large number of examples I could have chosen), "happy, permissive in personal living, but full of doubts about the way the system works" is a partial but thought-provoking description of the mental attitudes of the Experiential group. It seems to me entirely possible that there is a brand in some market whose personality echoes such a mind-set. And this fit between brand and consumer could be replicated in other markets.

Another independent contribution of VALS is that it helps us locate market trends. The drive for many of the leading movements in the marketplace almost certainly comes from the Experiential and Societally Conscious groups. Examples include the "green" movement and protection of the environment; antismoking; energy conservation; "back-to-nature" and the diet trend to foods with fewer preservatives; and low cholesterol, low sodium, low sugar, and other aspects of what passes in the 1990s for healthy eating. These movements have all influenced the attitudes and strategies of consumer goods manufacturers, and they all originated essentially with the Inner-Directed groups of consumers.

It is even likely that opinion leadership in a changing society will come more from the relatively small Inner-Directed groups than from the much larger Outer-Directed ones. The average age of the Inner-Directed groups is much lower, and they are more dynamic and restless in their attitudes. The psychological features of the Inner-Directed groups should be studied carefully by new-product project teams, in particular those concerned with precursor brands, especially innovative concepts that are considered important but risky long shots.

Perceptual Mapping

Perceptual mapping is a useful analytical device for presenting brands in juxtaposition to their competitors, according to defined criteria. The measures and the relative positions of the brands on the map are derived from research, but the map is merely an expository device. The criteria described mostly relate to how consumers perceive the brands. This perception helps us find the uncommon and salient qualities of a brand that should be embodied in its advertising proposition.

There is no end to the perceived functional and nonfunctional characteristics that the maps can cover. Each characteristic is set out on a continuum, with the ends representing opposite extremes (for example, harshest-mildest, strongest-weakest, youngest-oldest). Since maps are two-dimensional, perceptual maps measure two attributes.

Figures 8–1 and 8–2 cover various nonfunctional characteristics of the ten leading brands of toilet soap. Figure 8–1 describes two aspects of brand imagery: the perceived ages and sexes of users of the brands. I have drawn up the map on judgment, by extrapolating brand imagery from MRI data on the demographics of the actual users. (We do not of course know for certain whether user demographics predict user imagery, and we need to carry out qualitative

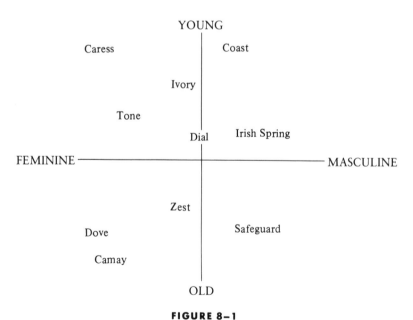

FIGURE 8–1

Perceptual Map of Toilet Soaps: Perceptions of User Demographics

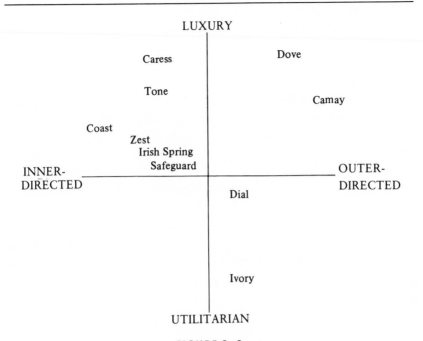

FIGURE 8-2

*Perceptual Map of Toilet Soaps: Perceptions of Selected
User Psychographics*

research to confirm the hypotheses embodied in the map before we
act on them.) Figure 8–2 describes two purely psychographic aspects
of brand imagery: inner and outer-directedness (based on VALS) and
the luxury–utilitarian continuum. Figure 8–2 is also judgmental and
is derived from MRI demographics.

The relative positions of the different brands marketed by each of
the main manufacturers are worth a comment. Procter & Gamble
markets Camay, Coast, Ivory, Safeguard and Zest; Lever Brothers
markets Caress and Dove; the Dial Corporation markets Dial and
Tone; and Colgate-Palmolive markets Irish Spring. Procter & Gamble, with the most complex of the brand portfolios, is obviously efficient in keeping its individual brands separate from one another.
This efficiency prevents cannibalization. The positions of the two
Lever Brothers brands are particularly interesting. Both Caress and
Dove are luxury products; both are oriented to skin care, with a
strong feminine emphasis; and in formulation, both, unusually, are

nonsoap detergent (NSD; Zest is the only other major NSD bar on the market). On the face of it, Caress and Dove are uncomfortably close to one another in their positioning. Yet, as we can see from Figure 8–1, they have been neatly separated according to the important criterion of the perceived age of their users. MRI data show that Caress is strongly oriented to younger women and Dove to older women. Thus the two brands are complementary and not competitive.

Another thing worth noting about Figure 8–1 is that the brands in the market have a somewhat more feminine than masculine orientation. The reason has already been given: Most packaged goods, including toilet soaps, are bought by female homemakers, who follow their own brand preferences to a large degree. The brands they buy are used by the men in the house, just because the bars happen to be in the bathroom.

The Ways in Which the Campaign Should Work

The proposition controls the content of an advertisement. This is important, but the target group and the proposition are not the whole of the strategy. The third element, the part that sets out the ways in which the campaign should work, influences its *style*.

A major factor is how *directly* a campaign is meant to work. A new and aggressive brand that is intended to take market share from large, established brands will probably have a campaign that works in a very direct way to demonstrate in particular the functional features of the new brand. On the other hand, the strategy for large and established brands is normally to protect their penetration and purchase frequency. This means that they will probably be supported by campaigns that work indirectly to reinforce existing users' perceptions of the brands' functional and nonfunctional qualities.

In the 1970s, Stephen King, author of the planning cycle discussed in chapter 7, developed a useful device to describe how directly or indirectly a campaign is planned to work.[9] This tool is called the *King continuum,* and it is shown in figure 8–3.

The King continuum comprises six different roles set out in the form of a hierarchy. Campaigns fit into one or two of these (although the roles planned for a campaign are not necessarily next to

Role of Advertising	MOST DIRECT
	C
Direct action	O
Seek information	N
	T
Relate to needs / wants / desires	I
Recall satisfactions / reorder / short list	N
	U
Modify attitudes	U
Reinforce attitudes	M
	MOST INDIRECT

FIGURE 8–3

The King Continuum

each other on the continuum). The roles selected enable us to focus on the specific job to be done by the campaign. This is an essential addition to the proposition; to the "what" of the proposition, there is now added a "how."

The best way of illustrating the roles on the continuum is to demonstrate the product categories and types of brand which are particularly relevant to each.[10]

Direct Action

"Do it now." Call an 800 number on television, fill in the coupon, call the company with your credit card in hand, take one off the display, and so on. This stage is obviously relevant to goods sold by direct response; to much retail advertising; to promotional advertising of packaged goods; and to advertising for new brands of packaged goods (in order to encourage the consumer to try them out).

Seek Information

"I want to find out more about that": Go to a showroom, send for a brochure which has more information, talk to dealers, and so on. This role applies mostly to products with a high ticket price. The advertising plays an important part in getting the brand onto the buyer's list of alternatives.

Relate to Needs/Wants/Desires

"What a good idea!" The advertising is less direct; there is no call for immediate action since the role of the advertising is to link the brand to a specific need that has been determined. The goal tends to be trial because someone is new or almost new to the brand. Advertising in this category tends to be rational (more than emotional), to have strong "reason why" copy, and to focus on motivators and discriminators (rather than on brand personality). This role applies to products which are widely but not frequently used: brands that are bought regularly but only part of the time (for example, tampons and headache remedies); and brands that are bought very intermittently (for example, elastic bandages and sunburn treatments). The category applies to cosmetics and toiletries, which come in a broad range of varieties which appeal to different people. It also applies to established products for which new uses have been found (for example, baking soda and cotton swabs).

Recall Satisfactions/Reorder/Short List

Bring to the top of mind: "Ah, that reminds me . . . " This is James Webb Young's role of "familiarizing"—helping people recall the satisfactions they had in using our brand, getting our brand back on their short list, increasing frequency of usage, and reminding people familiar with the brand that we're still around. This role mainly relates to brands in competitive markets that are bought repeatedly, and the advertising is generally used to reinforce the brand personality.

Modify Attitudes

"I never thought of it that way." This role is very difficult and it often takes a long time to see results. It often applies to brand restagings and new advertising campaigns. It also applies to attempts to recapture lapsed users (for example, former users of Kellogg's Corn Flakes, as discussed in chapter 7).

Reinforce Attitudes

"I always knew I was right." This role applies to continuous advertising for big, regularly purchased brands in large markets. This is traditionally brand leader advertising, aimed at holding penetration and purchase frequency. The style of advertising is often strongly emotional and relies heavily on brand personality.

Readers will appreciate that the last four categories are especially relevant to important brands of packaged goods. Reinforcement is a consistent theme for all established brands in this (and other) fields. But it commonly works in conjunction with the other roles: relating to consumers' needs, recalling satisfactions, and even modifying attitudes. Modification is invariably a gradual process because it is impossible for advertising to change consumers' perceptions radically. Modification and reinforcement are not therefore as incompatible as they might seem at first glance.

Reinforcement of attitudes is so pervasive in advertising campaigns that it can even operate in conjunction with direct stimuli. This commonly happens with military recruitment campaigns, which encourage inquiries (a direct effect) and at the same time reinforce the image attributes of the particular branch of the service advertised (an indirect effect).[11]

An important additional point concerns the speed with which advertising works. Effective advertisements are of course a minority of the total. I am convinced (although my view is not universally accepted) that the small number of advertisements that work have an immediate effect. They include those that operate directly, and that work with no delay to trigger telephone calls, coupon responses, visits to showrooms, and purchases from the shelf. Advertisements that work indirectly also work immediately, by tripping a (metaphorical) switch in the consumer's mind. But the behavioral outcome of this mental operation, which is visible only at the supermarket, may have to wait until the consumer's next shopping trip, when the brand advertised will be selected in preference over competitors.

Advertising does have a lagged effect in addition to its immediate effect, but I believe that this comes more from the accumulation of nonfunctional added values in the consumer's mind, and also from repeat purchase, than from what consumers can remember of the campaign. This is another way of saying that campaigns may be evanescent, but brands are permanent. Throughout my analysis of advertising strategy, readers will note that I have directed most consideration to the *brand*.

A final point relates to consumers' overall response to the brand and the campaign; what we might call the *communications gestalt*.

In writing a campaign, all good creative people realize that what consumers *take out* of the advertising is the only thing that matters. This is not always precisely what was intended. Every experienced advertising professional can tell war stories about miscommunication; a phenomenon that should not surprise us in any way, as most members of the public do not consider advertisements important enough for their full attention. Miscommunication is even prevalent in the most explicitly competitive type of advertising: "comparison advertising," which names competing brands.[12]

But an effective advertisement must do much more than avoid being confusing. A campaign that works must encourage the intellectual and/or emotional engagement of its audience. Attention value alone is not enough. And it is this engagement—easy to describe but very difficult indeed to achieve—that turns an advertisement from a film or a design into an engine that stimulates a behavioral reaction from consumers, with profit to the advertiser at the end of it. The viewer or reader must be triggered by some quality in the advertisement into bringing something to the communication to clinch its effect. Herein lies the genius of the creative mind.

The consumer responds to an advertisement as an isolated stimulus, and different communications vehicles enable the manufacturer to focus communication in a tailor-made way for each vehicle. However, the consumer's response is also affected by many other communications about the brand—by what he or she knows of it, where it is sold, who uses it, and how it is promoted to the trade and the consumer. Most important, there is an implicit communication about the brand in the advertising company it keeps, in the media and media vehicles in which it appears; to a large extent the medium is indeed the message. Yet dissonance of all types is only too common in the real world.

An automobile advertisement tries to persuade us that the brand is now better built and more reliable than ever before; at the same time the advertisement offers a massive price rebate, as if to demonstrate that the manufacturer does not believe its own quality claims. Another car advertisement, for an exceedingly traditional make of automobile with dated styling, tries to persuade younger buyers that the car is now for them—simply by saying that it is now for them. A highly exclusive brand focused on the upper end of its market runs advertisements on prime-time network television, shoulder to shoulder with the most undiscriminating mass-market brands. A highly sophisticated product concept is promoted in advertisements of a stupefying banality. These instances are in no way exceptional. We can see these and similarly disheartening examples on television virtually every evening.

During the 1970s, a parable was circulated widely within J. Walter Thompson that illustrates vividly the meaning of communications gestalt.

There were once two farmhouses, with a field in front of each. In the field belonging to the first farm there was a crude black wooden sign, and on it the words "Fresh Eggs" were painted. The lettering was the work of an unskilled sign writer, probably the farmer's wife, and although the message was readable, it would have won no prizes in a graphic arts competition. The letters were crooked, the spacing uneven. In the field in front of the second farm was a sign also reading "Fresh Eggs," but this one was clearly the work of an expert designer, and a disciple of the Bauhaus. It was a highly polished piece of work and would not have been out of place in an annual publication devoted to examples of graphic excellence.

It was very clear to visitors that the first farm sold the fresher eggs. Even if the eggs were not in fact fresher, they *seemed* so to people who looked at the two signs.

It would be equally instructive to repeat the exercise, but with a message which reads "Flying Lessons." There is little doubt that the farm that sells the fresher eggs would not offer the safer flying lessons! In a literal sense, the flying lessons are no more connected with the "Flying Lessons" sign than the eggs are with the "Fresh Eggs" sign. Yet this is not so obvious to consumers, to whom any brand projects a total impression.

In order to pull together the principles discussed in chapters 7 and 8, the next section outlines ten steps to an effective strategy. I then return to the three brands of breakfast cereal discussed in chapter 7—Kellogg's Corn Flakes, Lucky Charms, and Post Fruit & Fibre—and I hypothesize a complete advertising strategy for each.

Ten Steps to an Effective Strategy

General Points

An effective strategy reduces waste in the process of developing advertisements because it helps to prevent the misuse of expensive and scarce creative resources. The strategic process is separate from the creative process, but the former provides direction for latter.

A strategy should be written with knowledge of a brand's competitive position. The brand's situation within its market substantially governs its target group and proposition, as well as the role of its advertising.

A strategy is always verbal and rational, and it normally contains many words. This does *not* mean that the ensuing advertising should be densely verbal or exclusively rational. Many points in the strategy can be communicated in the most effective way by pictures, and by music and sound.

Target Group

1. Determine your target group in terms of your planned source(s) of business:
   a. from new users entering a growing market.
   b. from new users entering a growing market segment from a different segment. Which different segment?
   c. from attracting users from other brands within your market segment. Which other brands?
   d. from increased purchase frequency from your own users.
   e. from retaining existing users and maintaining their purchase frequency.
2. With the use of MRI or Simmons data, define your target group demographically.
3. Using qualitative research (or, if this is not available, using judgment based on an extrapolation of demographic data), define your target group psychographically.

Proposition

4. Study the functional characteristics of your brand and its competitors; if possible, use research on consumer perceptions of the brand's

functionality. Determine the functional features that should be demonstrated in your advertising. In the main, these will be motivators.

5. Determine the extent to which functional features differentiate your brand from its competitors. Do not give up easily. If there is no important functional discriminator, find out whether it is possible to create one. Alternatively, is it possible to preempt a *general* functional discriminator? (Major functional differentiation, although reasonably common, does not apply to the majority of brands; and the proportion to which it applies is declining.)

6. Using qualitative research, determine the nonfunctional qualities—the personality—of your brand. This is a big and important step, and more than one psychological technique should be used. Plot the market on a series of perceptual maps.

7. Your brand's personality will be (by definition) unique. Determine the source of this uniqueness. This is what should be communicated in your advertising, and it normally represents your most important discriminator.

8. Consider all questions of *balance;* in particular the balance of motivators and discriminators in your advertising. As a general rule, larger, older brands rely more on motivators than smaller newer brands do. But all advertising should be a mix of both motivators and discriminators, and this mix strongly influences the tone of voice of the advertising. This tone should be unique to the brand and should be defined as far as possible in the strategy. There is also the balance of the rational and the emotional. A strategy does not have to be exclusively rational or exclusively emotional. Indeed, emotional signals can provide a powerful reinforcement of the rational elements in the strategy.

Ways in Which the Campaign Should Work

9. What is the role of the advertising? How directly should it work? Plot the role or roles on the King continuum.

10. Include additional points about the communications gestalt, in particular, how media and promotions should work in conjunction with the creative content of the campaign. The last procedure of all should be to review carefully the strategy as a whole, to make sure that it does not contain any internal dissonances.

Hypothesized Advertising Strategies
for Three Brands of Breakfast Cereal

Kellogg's Corn Flakes

TARGET GROUP

1. First, existing users of Kellogg's Corn Flakes (KCF). Second, uses of other brands in the regular category (for example, Cheerios, Nabisco Shredded Wheat, and Wheaties), *in particular lapsed users of KCF.*

2. *All* demographic groups, with extra emphasis on older home-makers; the less well educated; homemakers with no outside jobs; rural families; and lower income families.

3. Traditionalists; people who buy the trusted and true; home-lovers; family-centered people; those with passive lifestyles; and VALS Outer-Directed people, particularly Belongers and Achievers.

PROPOSITION

4. A combination of taste and nutrition: delicious, crunchy, gen-uine corn taste with no added artificial ingredients, fresh, golden; and balanced food value—contains vitamins and minerals.

5. Superior freshness supplies some functional differentiation. (Since Kellogg's is the largest manufacturer of breakfast cereals, its supplies in-store are normally fresher than brands from other firms.[13]) However, this point is not strong enough to be the central discriminator for the brand.

6. Original, authentic, tried and true, reliable, trustworthy, friendly, part of a happy, loving family, and nutritious enough to set you up for the day.

7. The most important discriminator for KCF is that it was the first brand; all others are imitators.

8. The advertising should present an even balance of motivators and discriminators. The tone of voice should communicate the au-thority of KCF as the original brand in the market.

WAYS IN WHICH THE CAMPAIGN SHOULD WORK

9. For existing users, reinforcement of attitudes. For new users, some modification of attitudes: "I never looked at KCF quite this way before." For lapsed users of KCF, recall the past satisfactions

(and reappraisal of present brands): "New brands I have experimented with make me realize how much I enjoy KCF."

10. A mass market brand that is psychologically suitable for mass media. Promotions should be geared to increased purchase frequency by existing users; trial by new users; and retrial by lapsed users.

Lucky Charms

TARGET GROUP

1. First, existing users of Lucky Charms. Second, users of other brands within the presweetened segment (for example, Cap'n Crunch, Kellogg's Froot Loops, and Kellogg's Frosted Flakes).

2. Better educated homemakers, those aged eighteen to forty-four, homemakers with part-time jobs, those with $40,000 to $59,999 incomes, those who live in the Central regions, parents of children of all ages, rural families, and Hispanics. Note that users (that is, young children) are separate from buyers (that is, homemakers); the advertising should appeal to both.

3. Families whose lives revolve around their children; narrowly focused, hard-working people; people who wish to continue their present lifestyles rather than expand their horizons; people with conventional tastes; and VALS Outer-Directed people, particularly Emulators and Belongers.

PROPOSITION

4. Frosted oat cereal with colored marshmallow bits; crunchy; sweet and tasty; and (to mothers) a wholesome cereal with 100 percent whole-grain oats and eight essential vitamins and iron. Deliciousness plus nutrition.

5. The colored bits represent a reasonably important functional discriminator to which the nonfunctional discriminator can be linked.

6. "Fun in a box", and a breakfast cereal like a snack. The colored bits are a talking point for kids: the way these bits represent charms opens a fantasy world to the young.

7. The main nonfunctional discriminator is the fantasy built around the Lucky Charms and the cartoon characters portrayed on the box. (The actual charms are the colored bits in the cereal.)

8. The advertising signals should be tipped toward discriminators, especially the nonfunctional discriminator. The tone of voice should be lively and competitive.

WAYS IN WHICH THE CAMPAIGN SHOULD WORK

9. For existing users, reinforcement of attitudes in order to increase purchase frequency. The campaign should make children recall the fun of eating Lucky Charms; to mothers, it should reiterate the nourishment in the cereal.

10. A mass-market brand that justifies psychologically the use of mass media. The strategic objective of increased purchase frequency should dictate the type of consumer promotions used.

Post Fruit & Fibre

TARGET GROUP

1. First, new buyers who are coming into the natural segment from the regular segment. Second, users of other brands within the natural segment (for example, Honey Nut Cheerios, Kellogg's Nutri-Grain, and Kellogg's Raisin Bran).

2. Better educated homemakers; the thirty-five to fifty-four age group; upper income families; professional families; Middle Atlantic, West Central, and Pacific regions; and those who live in smaller towns and in the country.

3. Families on an economically upward path; fitness enthusiasts; those with active lifestyles; experimenters; those who lead busy social lives; and VALS Inner-Directed people of all types.

PROPOSITION

4. Good for you because it contains a number of high-fiber cereals (whole wheat, bran, and oats) plus thirteen vitamins and minerals. Delicious because of the fruit (three different fruits in each variety) and the crunchiness of the oat clusters. Part of a healthy diet. *Any functional improvement made as a result of a brand restaging should be emphasized.*

5. The specific cereal and fruit combination is unique and represents an important functional discriminator.

6. Part of a healthy lifestyle. A "necktie" brand for people for

whom fitness and sensible eating are a protection against the pressures of their successful lives.

7. Because fitness brands have proliferated in this and other categories, psychographic differentiation is difficult. The functional differentiation of the brand should therefore be emphasized as far as possible.

8. The advertising argument should be evenly balanced between motivators and discriminators. The tone of voice should be sophisticated, to engage an educated audience.

WAYS IN WHICH THE CAMPAIGN SHOULD WORK

9. The role of advertising is, first, to relate to the needs/wants/desires of potential new users; and second, to reinforce the attitudes of existing users, in order to boost purchase frequency.

10. Because of the "necktie" nature of the brand, there is a psychological need for the advertising to appear in specialist (probably print) media vehicles used specifically by the target group. These should be used in addition to mass media employed for reasons of coverage and cost efficiency. Promotions should be geared to brand trial.

From Strategy to Campaign

Advertising researchers hope to set up questions or sets of questions which will not in themselves carry any emotional charge, but will draw answers indirectly revealing the true answers to questions which—if asked directly—would have put people on their guard. The practice of this technique requires experience, a high order of cleverness, and a clear intelligence.[1]

Martin Mayer

Six Steps

The strategy for our brand has now been thought out, written, and agreed on by both client and agency. The most exciting part of the advertising process now begins: the search for an advertising idea. It cannot be emphasized too strongly that an advertisement needs an idea to engage the consumer and to stimulate an effective response from him or her. An advertisement will not work if it is merely a statement of the proposition, no matter how much polish is used in its presentation. If the proposition itself is not enclosed within a concept that captures the mental interest—and also the self-interest—of at least some consumers, it will be ineffective. And the result will be a waste of most of the brand's advertising budget.

The critical importance of advertising ideas raises three points of difficulty. The first is something I discussed in the preface. Generating an effective idea calls for a high degree of imaginative talent—something that is in short supply—besides much practiced craft. Jeremy Bullmore (former Chairman of J. Walter Thompson, London) makes a distinction between advertising and an advertisement. The former is the only thing that really matters. Advertising must have the depth and staying power to resonate with the consumer's experience of a brand to build added values in his or her mind. On the other hand, an advertisement all too often represents an arresting idea which is not necessarily embedded in the brand. What this all means is that the creative process is a tough and uncertain endeavor. This is probably why it is so exciting; it appeals to our gambler's instinct.

The second consideration is that the number of alternative ideas that can be generated from a single proposition is very large. This may not appear to be a problem, but effectively it is, because of the third difficulty, which is a very major matter. Most people's judgment is a poor guide to discriminating effectively between ideas, to selecting those with positive selling ability in preference to those which will be no good in the marketplace.[2] The advertising world finds this point impossible to accept and either defies or ignores it. We know this because clients and agencies spend much more time in evaluating ideas in rough forms than in generating them in the first place. What makes the situation even worse (in the opinion of some informed practitioners) is that despite the endless review of creative proposals, people are increasingly reluctant to use (and thus to sharpen) their judgment; and they therefore tend to use research increasingly blindly.

Research is, however, unable to provide us with anything approaching a reliable forecast of the selling ability of an advertisement. Nevertheless, research does have its uses, but only as a guide (not a substitute) for judgment. It can detect problems. And with major problems corrected, a campaign's chances of success can always be improved, at least marginally. This chapter is devoted to the best types of research to use to sift and improve creative ideas. It is therefore a logical continuation of the discussion of strategy in chapters 7 and 8.

Referring to the planning cycle (chapter 7), readers will remember that the progress from strategy to campaign takes place when we answer the questions: Where could we be? and How could we get there? There is sometimes a direct connection, a straight line, between strategy and campaign, and agencies often proceed from one to the other without any intervening steps. However, if research plays a role in developing the campaign, feedback is introduced into the system. Research may cause us to backtrack, to reevaluate our ideas because of problems of comprehension or consumer appeal.

After correcting these, we can move forward again with greater strength and confidence. This point is illustrated diagrammatically in figure 9–1. The neat French aphorism can be translated less neatly as "Pull back to position yourself for the best jump forward."

The ways in which we use research are, however, more complicated than is shown in figure 9–1. A more realistic picture can be found in figure 9–2. (Feedback, as illustrated in figure 9–1, can be assumed to occur at steps 2, 3, 4, and 5. This complication has been omitted to keep the diagram comprehensible.)

Since the early 1960s, research has been applied to the "downstream" steps: numbers 3, 4, and 5. In the United States, step 5 is often handled quantitatively, but the research used here serves not as a way of improving the creative, but as a management screening and evaluative mechanism by large-budget advertisers.[3]

During the early years of advertising research—the 1950s and 1960s—it was also common at steps 1 and 2 to test alternative strategies quantitatively. This was done by evaluating monadically a range of verbal propositions according to their ability to stimulate purchase intention or to trigger direct response.[4] This procedure gradually lost favor because of the growing recognition that in the consumer's eyes there could be a large difference between a proposition and an advertisement. A strong proposition could lead to a weak advertisement, and vice versa.

Since the mid 1980s, there has been a revival of interest "upstream," to step 2. This step is essentially concerned with interpreting the advertising strategy and is known in the United States as developmental research. It is actively pursued by many sophisticated practitioners on both sides of the Atlantic.[5] The important difference from what was done in the 1950s and 1960s is that *qualitative* techniques are now used.

Two real examples will clarify the difference between upstream and downstream research.

Strategy　　　　　First Idea　　　　　Second Idea

FIGURE 9–1

"Reculer pour Mieux Sauter"

Step 1	Step 2	Step 3	Step 4	Step 5	Step 6
Strategy	Possible Creative Directions (Interpretations of the Strategy) (One Winner)	Alternative Creative Executions (One Winner)	Developed Executions (One Winner)	Final Execution	Campaign Exposure

FIGURE 9–2

Steps from Strategy to Campaign Exposure

Note: At steps 2, 3, and 4, the number of alternatives is normally two to four. The three shown here are merely illustrative.

FINDING THE MOST FRUITFUL CREATIVE EMPHASIS (UP-STREAM): CROWN PAINTS. In 1988, Crown, the second largest brand of household paint on the British market, introduced a new gloss paint with a genuinely innovative formula. A new thickening system gave the paint a creamy consistency, in contrast to the consistencies of the existing brands, which were either thin and runny, or jellified.[6]

The new formula provided a wide range of functional advantages over competitive paints: It was easier to apply. It provided better results for the amateur do-it-yourselfer. It provided a thicker coat of paint. It gave a smoother finish on rough surfaces. It needed no undercoat (a clear advantage but one that was not unique). It had less smell than other paints.

The difficulty was to determine which element or elements of this complicated proposition should provide the main direction for the advertising campaign. The problem was addressed by producing and researching qualitatively six different "concept boards," each with a different creative emphasis and presenting the paint with four alternative descriptive names in addition to the brand name Crown. A concept board is a device, resembling a press advertisement, which presents a proposition clearly, but which plays down important elements that distinguish a finished advertisement: stopping power, persuasiveness, and production values. The emphasis of a concept board is on "clear and forthright communication."[7]

There was some overlap between the arguments about the brand on the concept boards, but the main emphasis of each was as follows:

1. how quick and easy the paint is to apply
2. the many technical features the paint possesses and its top quality overall
3. how quick and easy the paint is to apply and what high-quality results it produces
4. details of the many special features of the paint
5. the extra-glossy finish of the paint on any type of surface
6. the many technical features of the paint and how significant an innovation it represents

The creative development was at step 2 in figure 9–2. Qualitative research was now carried out. In groups, it was found that the third of these concept boards was the most promising. Paint users believe instinctively that gloss paint that is easy to apply must be poor in quality. Concept board number 3 led to the proposition that Crown's technical expertise now made it possible to combine ease of use with high-quality paint and a professional end product.

This proposition in turn led to the choice of the name Crown Solo, and to an advertising concept based on the idea that Crown is the "Gloss Paint That Rewrites the Book." The television commercial written for the launch featured a larger-than-life product demonstration filmed in an airship hangar. The traditional prejudices about gloss painting—written in words painted in black on a huge monument erected in the center of the hangar—were physically painted over with one coat of Crown Solo. The most important of the prejudices that were obliterated with paint was the supposed rule "You will always use an undercoat."

The overall result of the brand launch was an increase in Crown's volume share of the white gloss paint market from about 20 percent to approximately 30 percent, an upgrading in Crown's average selling price, and evidence of positive consumer perceptions of the brand. Perhaps more interestingly, Crown Solo acted as a spearhead for Crown as a whole: other paints in the range also increased in sales.

These favorable outcomes were clearly the result of the launch of a product with measurable functional benefits over the competition, allied to advertising that managed to combine these functional benefits with the consumer's desideratum of ease of use. If the latter argument had been used on its own, or with a greater prominence, its credibility would have been eroded, and doubts would have set in about the down side: potential loss of quality. It was the initial upstream creative research which enabled the campaign to find the important but elusive point of balance.

SELECTING THE BEST ALTERNATIVE CREATIVE EXECUTION (DOWNSTREAM): RED MOUNTAIN INSTANT COFFEE. Red Mountain from Brooke Bond Oxo (a Unilever company) was a relatively small brand in the British instant coffee market, a category dominated by Nescafé (from Nestlé) and Maxwell House (from General Foods). In the early 1980s, the total category was large and buoyant, but Red Mountain had a market share of only 2.4 percent and household penetration of 2.9 percent.[8]

Red Mountain is of high functional quality. It is freeze-dried to provide genuine ground coffee taste. In this, it resembles Gold Blend, the premium Nescafé variety. However, because of Brooke Bond's weak position in the instant coffee market (unlike the company's position in the tea market), Red Mountain was perceived in the early 1980s almost as a store brand. It was relatively cheap, and consumers saw it as serviceable but not classy.

When it was decided in 1985 to try and modify how consumers viewed Red Mountain, the strategy was directed at raising the profile of the brand in the minds of buyers, and at differentiating Red Mountain on the basis of its taste to enable it to compete more effectively with the brand leaders. One important part of the plan was to develop an advertising campaign that would generate interest on its own account. Coffee advertising in Britain was notoriously trite and predictable until the launch of the Red Mountain campaign.

The planning proceeded to step 3 in figure 9–2. Two creative alternatives were worked out in the form of narrative tapes and visuals.

The first was a parody of the family scene in conventional packaged-goods advertising. The difference was that the family (including the cat) responded in an exaggerated way to the taste of the product. The housewife fainted with pleasure at how much her family enjoyed her coffee.

The second alternative showed a smart dinner party. The hostess prepared the coffee in the kitchen by pouring hot water onto Red Mountain in a jug. But within earshot of her guests, she mimicked a percolator for ground coffee by emitting an extraordinary series of lifelike onomatopoeic sounds.

In qualitative research using consumer groups, both creative alternatives produced positive responses, but number 2 generated much more powerful playback of the central intrinsic benefit of natural coffee taste. The research into Number 2 described quite clearly *how* the advertising worked with consumers. The idea of the campaign was gritty and humorous, and at the same time it was a near-perfect extension and enhancement of Red Mountain's advertising proposition.

The campaign was exposed in the summer of 1986 and had an immediate effect, which has not flagged over the subsequent years. The advertising boosted the brand's consumer penetration (which reached 17 percent in 1987). Market share and consumer perceptions of the brand also improved significantly. The success of Red Mountain can be firmly attributed to the advertising campaign, and there is no doubt at all that the qualitative research played a key role in persuading client and agency to follow the creative route that was to become so effective in the marketplace.

In both these cases, the client–agency team made the decision to follow a particular creative direction. The research results did not make the selection for them, but in both cases the qualitative research provided valuable diagnostic insights.

The important difference between the two cases concerned the stage of development of the creative idea when it was tested. With Crown, the alternatives researched were advertising propositions with different degrees of internal balance, and with the winning proposition, the agency had to undertake a major program of creative work to turn the proposition into an advertisement. In the case of Red Mountain, the alternative campaigns had actually been worked out, and the winning approach merely had to be turned into finished advertising with the production values of a commercial polished enough to go on the air. Upstream research was important for Crown because of the broadness of the proposition; there had to be some initial selectivity, and the testing enabled this to be done. Downstream research was important for Red Mountain because the campaign could have gone in one of two (or more) ways, and the agency needed help.

A side benefit of conducting research upstream is that the client becomes involved in and committed to a strategic direction early in the advertising development, and the result is a stronger continuous cooperation between client and agency.[9]

Qualitative Research: Stimulus Material

The material used as the stimulus or prompt in qualitative research can vary considerably in its degree of finish.

For television, the following material can be used (in ascending order of finish)[10]:

1. *Script:* Written audio and sound effects, plus verbal description of the video.
2. *Narrative tape:* Recorded audio of the soundtrack and verbal description of the action of the film. (The danger of this type of material is that to respondents, the advertisement may turn into a longish radio play rather than a 30-second television commercial.)
3. *Concept board/storyboard/tape and boards:* The last of these is a recorded audio of the soundtrack, plus drawn boards of the main visual sequences. (This was the material used for the Red Mountain research.)
4. *Animatics:* Videotape films composed of soundtrack, plus drawings of key frames. These do not move as in live-action or cartoon films but dissolve or are cut from frame to frame.
5. *Photomatics:* Videotape films composed of soundtrack, plus still photographs of key frames. Like animatics, they dissolve or are cut from frame to frame; occasionally they provide a limited amount of movement (for example, mouths can be shown opening).
6. *Stealamatics*[11]: Videotape films made from soundtrack, plus film footage "borrowed" from finished commercials for other brands and also from movies. The video has moving action like any other film.

All these devices can be used for the research. Numbers 1, 2, and 3 are cheap and quick to produce, but their remoteness from any finished commercial means that they must be explained carefully by the research interviewer or moderator. And the lack of production values can sometimes produce misleading results, especially with advertising which relies on nonrational communication, that is, the special extra ingredients provided by actors, photography, and music. This is especially true of advertisements for beer, soft drinks, fragrances, and many luxury products.

The more finished devices, numbers 4, 5, and 6, are generally the most reliable but are relatively expensive in time and money. Stealamatics are more commonly used in the United States than in Britain. They provide full production values. But unfortunately these values can be misleading because they apply to (and may be associated in some consumers' minds with) brands other than the one under test. When the test film is finally turned into a finished advertisement, there is no guarantee that the stealamatic's production values can be duplicated. As an executive creative director of a major American agency tells us, "Now you have a vignette spot with twenty seconds that you have to think up from scratch and the client is already sold on twenty of the finest scenes ever aired in the last five years. So that is a curse."[12]

For researching print advertising, the stimulus material is usually closer to the form of a finished advertisement than is the case with television films. Concept boards or layouts can be researched. Illustrations can be drawn or photographed (to varying degrees of finish in either case). Headlines can be hand-lettered or typeset. Body copy can be typeset or typed and shown separately from the layout.

In the stimulus material for both television and print advertising, the general rule to follow it that emotional and sensory communication requires material with a higher standard of finish than is needed for more rational and verbal messages. This is a tacit acknowledgment that emotional advertising is more difficult to research reliably than factual communication.

Qualitative Research: Pros and Cons

Qualitative research is usually exploratory or diagnostic. It involves small numbers of people who are not sampled on a probabilistic basis. They may, however, be selected to represent different categories of people from a given target market or section of the community. In

> *qualitative research no attempt is made to draw hard and fast conclusions. It is impressionistic rather than definitive.*[13]

There are two main types of qualitative research: individual interviews (known in the United States as one-on-ones) and focus groups.

One-on-ones are carried out by experienced interviewers with, normally, a professional background in psychology. The interviews are structured; a written guide is used, but not a rigid questionnaire. The questioning is open-ended, and each interview may last up to an hour. A high degree of skill is needed in conducting and interpreting the research. Respondents' answers are often tape-recorded.

A focus group is run by a moderator, also an experienced person, often also with a background in psychology. Most groups comprise six to twelve respondents in the United States (seven to eight in the United Kingdom). The discussion is structured loosely, and one of the moderator's jobs is to direct the discussion so that it covers the ground that should be covered, while allowing latitude in how this should be done. Occasionally, focus groups in the United States use mechanical devices to measure respondents' interest in various sequences in television commercials as these are screened.[14] (These devices are only used for quantitative research in Britain.) Focus group discussions are commonly recorded, on audiotape or videotape. It is also normal practice to hold the sessions in a room with a one-way mirror, so that client and agency people can be inactive participants. (Members of the group are told about the mirror first.) Sessions normally last between one and two hours.

On rare occasions, qualitative research is carried out by other methods than those described above. Examples are interviews with one researcher and two informants (dyads) and minigroups of three to six people. These systems are used for specialized purposes and will be ignored in the present discussion.

One-on-ones and groups are both expensive. Single groups are very rarely used. In order to iron out the effect of erratic answers from small numbers of respondents and to provide some geographical spread, four or more groups are normally used to answer a specific problem. Four groups (each of ten respondents) normally have a total price tag in the $15,000 to $25,000 range. Forty one-on-ones can cost twice or three times as much.[15]

When concepts and advertisements are put into research at steps

2, 3, and 4 in figure 9–2, the work is usually qualitative. Small samples of twenty to fifty people are drawn from the population representing the brand's target group, defined by what brands they use at present and by their demographics. Even the representative nature of the sample, however, cannot provide projections which can be relied on to represent the opinions of the total target group, because the questioning procedure is not standardized, and also because the margin of error would be very large as the samples are so small.

The topics that are investigated in detail are the respondents' views of each concept or advertisement as a whole (a holistic evaluation is very important) plus some (not necessarily all) of the following: detailed likes and dislikes; opinions of the visual scenes and situations, commentary, music, and sound effects; anything that is difficult to comprehend; attitudes toward the people in the advertisement; and similarities to other advertisements. In addition, the respondents are asked to compare all the concepts or advertisements being researched. The main emphasis of the inquiry is on exposing difficulties and problems, and on uncovering as far as possible underlying attitudes as well as those at the top of the respondents' minds. The emphasis of the research is on pure comprehension and response; it is the job of the researcher to interpret the responses for their underlying meaning.[16] The wise moderator is a listener, and keeps his or her active participation to a minimum.

Qualitative research helps the process of developing advertising in four important ways.

First, it is an aid to creative people, who have learned not to look upon it with hostility. Since the techniques were developed in the 1960s mainly to help the creative process, it was common at that time for agencies to pay for the research. This is less usual today because of current pressures on agency profits. Creative people find qualitative research useful because it does not pose a threat; it does not operate like a pass-fail examination. It is open-ended and *diagnostic* and helps them improve their ideas.

For a successful restage of Mazola corn oil in Britain in 1984, the agency developed a commercial devoted to the purity and natural ingredient of the product. The video in the commercial was, for part of the time, devoted to cooked food and, for part of the time, to starkly symbolical figures of farmers, "in silhouette, against stunning, dramatic skylines." The people were shown lifting plants from the ground and admiring the natural produce. The research demonstrated quite clearly that it was the symbolism of the farmer figures and the soil and nature that communicated the purity of the product: "I found it quite comforting, that one. It made me think that I should be using 100% Pure Corn Oil. The feeling of getting back to the land and eating things that are good for you."[17] (This was a respondent speaking.)

It is an advantage that the respondents' own words come out of the research. In many cases, the words from qualitative research have found their way into finished advertisements, where they have played a uniquely persuasive role.

Research after the national exposure of a campaign can also be diagnostic. This is true even for simple regular monitoring of consumers' brand associations by quantitative research. Andrex, the leading brand of toilet tissue in Britain, has been advertised for two decades with a popular and successful campaign featuring puppies, and in which the copy stresses the strength and softness of Andrex and the length of paper on the roll. Buyers are aware that Andrex is more expensive than other brands. However, continuous tracking of the attribute "value for money" shows that consumers rate Andrex very favorably according to this criterion. Since value for money is never mentioned in Andrex advertising, the brand's high score on this attribute means that buyers weigh the brand's superior product features against its high price, and that Andrex comes out on the positive side as offering good value for money. In terms of consumer perceptions, this is the explanation for the brand's considerable and continued success in the marketplace.[18]

The second benefit of qualitative research is that it is far better than quantitative research in handling, without too much bias, *emotional, nonrational, nonverbal* advertising. Brands in advertising-intensive markets invariably differ from one another by their added values as well as by their functionality. Qualitative research is emphatically the best way of evaluating how the advertising contributes to building these added values. There is, however, an important difference between one-on-ones and focus groups. While they are both better than quantitative techniques, one-on-ones are much more sensitive to qualitative nuances than groups are. The personal interaction between respondents in groups often distracts attention from the advertisement which is supposedly being evaluated.

As a creative director in a leading American packaged goods agency says:

> I'm a thirty-year-old guy in a Focus Group. I'm trying to be macho because there are a couple of good-looking women in the room. They show the Pepsi spot where the lady hugs the chimpanzee at the end of the spot because it got her soda. Do you think I'm going to say the reason I like the spot is because of the way the chimp hugged the lady? I really think that you're not going to open up emotionally in a room like that.[19]

The third benefit of qualitative research is something I have already mentioned briefly. It is very effective in *locating weaknesses* in a concept or advertisement. It is also capable of handling problems in a constructive, green-thumbed way.

The British campaign for the yellow pages directories that ran in the early 1980s concentrated on specific problems which members of the public experienced in locating where to find something. Each television commercial in the campaign was directed to a single problem. The campaign was intended to make people view the yellow pages positively, not just as a place to locate unwelcome addresses like dentists' and plumbers'. One new script in the campaign featured a professional family searching for a birthday present for their young daughter and deciding to buy her a pony. This script was presented to focus groups as an animatic. It immediately ran into serious problems because of its "upmarket humor, tone of voice and subject matter." In another animatic in the series, a brief sequence of a small boy admiring a new bicycle evoked a warm reaction among the respondents. The objections to the "pony" advertisement were neatly defused by the substitution of a bicycle for a pony.[20]

The fourth major advantage of qualitative research is that it is *rich and fertile*. This is more true of groups than one-on-ones because of the dynamics of the personal interaction among the members of the group. As a brand manager in a leading United States packaged-goods company says, "I think groups have a role to play. It's like a cattle herd. Get a lot of data fast."

But the reliability of the data cannot be accurately gauged. This brand manager is happy to use groups to discuss brands where the balance between functionality and added values is heavily weighted toward functionality. But "if I really want to understand what's going through my consumer's mind and when it relates to advertising and they don't feel comfortable talking about it in a group, I would lean heavily toward one-on-ones."[21]

The wealth of data from focus groups is such that the report of one investigation, which covered six groups and a total of forty-nine respondents, covered several hundred pages, including verbatim comments by the people interviewed—a rich source of enlightenment and ideas for the creative people at the advertising agency.[22]

Despite its unquestioned advantages however, there are problems with qualitative research.

First and most important, the success of an advertisement in any type of research is not a predictor of success in the marketplace. The stories of Crown and Red Mountain should not be taken as evidence that qualitative testing always produces such a favorable outcome. All that can be hoped for generally is that if we manage to correct any weaknesses, we will improve the odds of success. Locating before the event what will work in the marketplace is a goal that has always eluded us. And the present state of the art of advertising research has not moved us very far along the path to enlightenment.

Second, qualitative research into advertising is carried out by "forced exposure." People are asked to devote their attention to the advertisements being researched. There is little measurement of whether there is anything about the advertisements that would have engaged consumers under conditions of normal exposure. Qualitative research is a poor measure of advertisements' stopping power.

The third point has been mentioned already. The findings of qualitative research cannot be projected to the whole of the population group sampled. However, this is not a matter whose importance should be exaggerated. When a piece of research is being interpreted and a problem arises with a concept or advertisement, even if it is raised by only a handful of respondents, it is worth doing something about. In most cases, three or four people who are troubled by an advertisement or by a feature in an advertisement should be enough to raise a signal flare. Another point is that similar findings produced by a number of independent groups always provide a powerful confirmation that those findings are valid. This is especially true if the groups are located in different parts of the country.

The fourth problem relates to focus groups alone. There is the ever-present danger of a group's being dominated by a single powerful and vociferous individual. This domination obviously inhibits the contributions of fellow group members. A researcher in a leading packaged-goods agency describes focus groups discussing a blockbuster network television program in this way: "It got outrageous quantitative scores. When you talked about it in groups one person would say 'I thought it was stupid.' The next thing you know, the whole group is saying it's stupid."[23]

Allied to this point is the danger that some participants will try to become advertising experts, with quasi-technical views on how the advertising ideas should be expressed or improved. The result is generally a waste of the time and effort spent on the research. Wise and experienced moderators learn how to steer respondents away from "expert" opinions and to concentrate on responding as *consumers*.

When there is any question of evaluating the communication of elusive verbal or visual signals, it is generally far better to use one-on-ones than groups, so as to avoid internal prompting among group members.

When we weigh the advantages and disadvantages of qualitative research, there is a balance on the positive side. However, the balance is not so strong that qualitative research can always be accepted at its face value. It always needs to be carried out and interpreted with skill and care. Like all research, qualitative research is an aid to judgment, not a substitute for it. In most individual cases, the concepts and advertisements for which such research is used are improved as a result. Qualitative research is generally far more often productive than unproductive. But the same conclusion cannot be drawn with certainty about quantitative copy testing.

Quantitative Research

Quantitative research is concerned with large numbers of people, usually members of some carefully drawn sample that is representative of a larger population. The data obtained are quantified on some basis to indicate the numbers and proportions of sample members who fall into different response categories. A degree of statistical significance is usually attributed to quantitative data and within the confines of a known margin of error, its conclusions are generalized to the population universe represented by that sample.[24]

Much quantitative research is conducted in the United States (although considerably less in Europe) into the impact and effectiveness of television advertisements. Such research takes two forms:

1. *Natural on-air exposure* with subsequent telephone interviewing. This is the method used for Burke Day-After Recall and by On Air Lab (OAL). Note that the commercial must have appeared on the air and money must have been spent on media exposure. The "cow has left the barn" before the research takes place.

2. *Forced exposure:* The advertisements are specially screened and the respondents personally interviewed, sometimes immediately, sometimes after a three-day delay. Interviewing takes place in a theater in the cases of Advertising Research System (ARS) and McCollum/Spielman; in a shopping mall with Motivation Learning Potential (MLP).

The sample size is 200 adults in most cases. Burke was originally concerned exclusively with recall measures. Since Burke's heyday in the 1950s, 1960s, and 1970s, there has been a movement away from recall as the sole measure and a growing interest in monitoring persuasion.

An important aspect of quantitative testing is that major packaged-goods companies have developed an inventory of test data for their commercials, in some cases going back three decades. Average scores have been worked out, and total batteries of scores are often grouped into quintiles (that is, the total range is divided into five 20 percent groups of ascending scores). In addition, attempts have been made to associate sales results with test scores, although with little success.

It is easy and alluring to compare the score achieved by a tested commercial with the scores in the collection of previously tested commercials; and it is equally tempting to make a decision on the basis of this comparison: "go" if the commercial beats the average; "no go" if it does not.

Quantitative testing is commonly, although not universally, used by major advertisers in the United States at the downstream stage of advertising development, especially at step 5 in figure 9–2. Finished commercials are tested either by forced exposure or on air in a number of cities (commonly four) before being run nationally or in substantial areas of the country. As already mentioned, quantitative testing is more rare in other sophisticated advertising markets, notably Britain. British practice is influenced by the long-standing and deep-seated skepticism of the research community there toward quantitative copy testing; and also by the prevalence of account planning, a method of agency operation which is forcefully directed at the consumer, and which has relied traditionally on qualitative and not quantitative research.

Quantitative testing is a highly problematical endeavor. I have published my views on it in a different context and shall do no more in this chapter than raise the salient issues.[25] There are four strong objections. The first and most decisive point is that although the scores look neat and actionable, there is no proven connection between any quantitative numbers and a commercial's selling ability. There is one exception. Commercials with scores in the bottom quintile tend not to perform well in the marketplace.[26] But this is an insignificant objection because an experienced agency, with the expertise and craft to be expected of such an organization, can teach itself to achieve reasonable test scores.[27] Numbers in any of the top four quintiles are nonpredictive. The reason that quantitative scores are generally unable to forecast the sales success of commercials is endemic: a function of the research methods themselves, and in particular the superficiality of the questions asked.

Allied to this last problem is the second point, which is that quantitative research, because it is not diagnostic, is not of much help to creative people in their job of improving advertising.

The third objection is that the research also suffers from other intrinsic (but possibly correctable) flaws. The samples of respondents are entirely unselective. On-air testing is contaminated by as many as nineteen extraneous factors, not least by the type of television program with which the commercial appears.[28]

A fourth important point is that the methods discriminate heavily against emotional, nonverbal copy.[29] A speculative reason why the systems are much more common in the United States than in Europe is the more emotional nature of European advertising. In view of the relative prevalence of small-share brands in the United States, most packaged-goods advertising on the western side of the Atlantic concentrates on differentiating the advertised brand from its competitors on the basis of rational copy claims.[30] Quantitative copy testing is concerned with rational messages above all else.

The most interesting question raised by quantitative copy research is why large, effective, and experienced advertisers still continue to rely so heavily on it. The best explanation derives from the hierarchical, pyramidal structure of large American companies. Quantitative research is not used developmentally, as a means of improving the advertising. On the contrary, it is used as a tool to help with management decisions, in particular with the decision whether or not to run particular advertisements. In large, highly structured companies, the test scores provide evidence that can be used by junior executives to support their recommendations as these are sent up the company ladder.

As a brand manager in one of the leading advertiser companies in the United States describes it:

> Between me and the President of this company, there are six levels of management. One given day, because he feels like it, the President might want to see my advertising. Now how many pieces of advertising ever produced will everyone of us in the line of management like? The level up has more experience with advertising, and in a lot of cases the egos get bigger as you go up too. So copytesting allows me to merchandize good advertising up the line so it isn't he who has the most stripes wins.[31]

This is all understandable. But if advertisements which score below average are rejected despite the likelihood that they would be as effective in sales terms as commercials that score above average, then the effort, imagination, skill, and resources expended on the low-scoring commercials will be entirely wasted. Even more important, with a notable shortage of outstanding conceptual ability in the advertising agency business, it is, to say the least, counterproductive for the best agency talent to be wasted in developing commercials aimed at achieving high but meaningless and nonpredictive test scores. There is an obvious opportunity cost.

The fact that such strange things take place seems to me the most plausible reason why unorthodox and arresting advertising is so very rare in the United States. The corporate culture of the largest advertisers simply does not allow for breakthroughs. Clients are focused on their organizations when they evaluate advertising. The agencies' attention is directed at their clients and their own peers. Clients and agencies both seem to be distracted from what should be their all-important focus on consumers. Test scores seem to have developed an existence of their own, with their norms and quintiles. A gap seems to have opened up between the scores themselves and what they purport to represent: measurements of aspects of the consumers' psyche.

A group creative director in a leading agency should have the last word:

> We talked about the Maxwell House Linda Ellerbee stuff which God knows how it tested but it moved the brand to number one. They threw away a lot of nice creative—"Good to the last drop," pretty music, nice storyline, and a lot of charm, a lot of executional attention, quality—to this videotape garbage and it's selling the hell out of the coffee. There's definitely a difference between the real world and kind of what we do to impress each other.[32]

Summary

1. There are six steps from an advertising strategy to final campaign exposure. Research is often used at steps 2, 3, 4, and 5 in figure 9–2. At each of these steps, the research may cause a backtracking, "reculer pour mieux sauter."

2. During the last twenty years and more, research has been used mainly for the downstream stages, that is, increasingly to refine creative executions, to make small improvements. Since the mid-1980s, there has been some redirection of interest upstream, to strategic or developmental research using qualitative techniques. This is concerned mainly with the varying emphases to be given to individual parts of the advertising proposition.

3. A wide range of stimulus material can be used for qualitative research, ranging from the simplest scripts to the most complex stealamatics.

4. Qualitative techniques are used for steps 2, 3, and 4. Such research is diagnostic and helpful to creative people. It is fair in its evaluation of emotional and nonverbal communication. It is efficient in locating weaknesses. It provides a wealth of data.

5. However, no research can be relied on to predict a commercial's success. Qualitative research is carried out by forced exposure,

which means that it is weak in judging advertising's stopping power. And the findings cannot be projected to describe accurately the whole of the population that has been sampled.

6. Both one-on-ones and focus groups are used for qualitative research. One-on-ones are more sensitive to image-oriented advertising, but they are less rich and fertile than groups. Groups are less objective in that they can be distorted by the participation of strong and vociferous individuals. Groups are, however, much less expensive and take less time to implement than one-on-ones.

7. Quantitative copy testing is widely used in the United States with finished commercials before they are exposed nationally or seminationally. There are severe objections to the procedure. Directly and indirectly it is responsible for large amounts of waste. Quantitative testing is much less popular in other sophisticated advertising markets because of methodological objections and for reasons connected with the characteristics of those markets.

An Inventory of Knowledge about Advertising

Let every sluice of knowledge be opened and set a-flowing.

John Adams

The Americans have all a lively faith in the perfectibility of man, they judge that the diffusion of knowledge must necessarily be advantageous, and the consequences of ignorance fatal.

Alexis de Tocqueville

The material in this chapter can be understood by readers who do not know much about advertising. The chapter is, however, addressed to advertising professionals and academics, as the people who should be conscious of what we know about advertising and disturbed by what we do not know or what we misunderstand, and who are in a position to improve the situation.

The individual pieces of knowledge (or lack of knowledge) about advertising in this inventory are described with very little detail because the ground covered by the chapter is extensive. In discussing each piece of knowledge, I have made a personal qualitative judgment of its intellectual respectability. I have relied on my subjective evaluation because there is a general lack of objective criteria to guide us in any appraisal of the body of what is known and not known.

I believe that all knowledge about advertising can be classified into five types. These are all quite different from one another and are listed below. This classification is the basic analytical tool used in the chapter, and the types of knowledge are described here, at the beginning, so that they will be easy to find if the reader wants to refer back. I have also given them titles—types A, B, C, D, and E—for the obvious reason that they will be mentioned on virtually every page of this chapter, so that we need some shorthand.

1. *Knowledge Type A:* Things we know about advertising with a reasonable degree of certainty. There are two subtypes, but I shall normally lump these together: things that we know fairly completely (Type A-1) and things that we know parts of, but for which we also know the precise limits of our knowledge (Type A-2).

2. *Knowledge Type B:* Things we know in an incomplete or impressionistic way, and which we ought to be anxious to know more about. This category is different from A-2, which refers to narrowly defined types of knowledge. B describes larger pieces of knowledge which are only partly understood and occasionally also large complex matters, some parts of which we can understand better than others.

3. *Knowledge Type C* (to be more precise, lack of knowledge Type C): Terra incognita.

4. *Knowledge Type D:* Things which we think we know, but which are probably wrong. This category encompasses myth, much instinctive belief, and most received wisdom.

5. *Knowledge Type E:* Things which many people know, but which many (not necessarily the same) people commonly ignore.

The only fully respectable category is, of course, Type A. On the other hand, B and E can be considered quasi respectable. Of the remaining classifications, C represents a complete gap, and D is disreputable. Sometimes in this chapter there are anomalies, that is, pieces of knowledge which are, for instance, partly Type A and partly C. I shall do my best to explain these as we come to them.

Although my classification of knowledge is, as explained, subjective, it is based on the use of empirical data. The endnotes for this chapter list more than 100 different carefully selected sources, and certain of these have their own sometimes extensive bibliographies. Readers should understand, however, that I have sometimes chosen to believe some facts in preference to others, and that on certain rare occasions, I have even classified in the more respectable categories some pieces of knowledge for which there is very little empirical support at all. In other words, I have throughout this chapter evaluated source material with all the intellectual rigor I can muster, but I have not excluded the possibility that some things may be right even though data are not available to prove them.

Empirical support means marketplace evidence or, in rare cases, evidence from laboratory experiments. Except for the occasional reference to the views of named practitioners on narrowly defined topics, I do not include as respectable knowledge the general views of experts. The reason is not any refusal to believe that their opinions are often valuable, but that there is sometimes a notable (and rather charming) lack of consistency in what they say. Take the following five examples from a single extremely well-known book, *Reality in Advertising*, written by a distinguished practitioner, Rosser Reeves. In each case, he obviously thought what he had written to be an exact and true statement. In very many instances, however, what he said is highly questionable.

"There is no general economic theory on what advertising does and how it works."[1] This is indeed a piece of Type A knowledge.

"Recently a group of marketing men, almost idly, at a luncheon table, listed thirty-seven different factors, any or all of which could cause the total sales of a brand to move up or down."[2] This may be true in certain instances; in many others, however, it is a half-truth at best. Most econometric experiments in the marketplace suggest that in the majority of individual cases, the number of important variables is much smaller than thirty-seven; there are, of course, exceptions. As a generalization, I would put this statement in Type B.

"If you run a brilliant campaign every year, but change it every year, your competitor can pass you with a campaign that is less than brilliant—providing he does not change his copy."[3] It is quite impossible to justify such a sweeping statement; everything depends on the old and the new campaigns. A good deal is known about the effects of campaign changes, and brilliant new campaigns are not infrequently accompanied by volume sales increases of 20 percent or more. Most ongoing campaigns are associated with annual sales increases of generally much under 10 percent. In certain product fields (for example, motor cars and shaded cosmetics), annual product innovations require frequent campaign changes anyway. As a generalization, the statement lacks any credibility, despite the confidence with which it was written. It is Type C knowledge.

"Now we know, for the first time, how many people remember our advertising. Even more important, we know just how well it is working—how many new customers it is winning over to our brand."[4] This statement is an almost perfect fallacy.[5] Use of a brand is one of the strongest determinants of knowledge of the advertising for it.[6] Advertising cannot in this context be said to be winning customers over to the brand; rather, the use of the brand can be said to be winning over customers to awareness of the advertising for it.[7] This statement is a classic example of Type D knowledge.

"A study of campaign profiles, over a long period of time, shows us that many of the most respected advertising campaigns in America are merely show windows . . . these campaigns merely display the merchandise. They merely present it to the consumer and ask that it sell itself."[8] I believe that Reeves stumbled on an important truth here, and this statement is therefore Class E knowledge. There is good evidence from Nielsen that in about 70 percent of cases, the effectiveness of a campaign appears to be directly—and perhaps solely—related to its weight in the marketplace relative to other campaigns in its category.[9] There is no evidence from the professional literature that advertisers and agencies are in any way conscious of this rather fundamental general pattern. For instance, serious creative innovation, using marketplace experimentation with alternative campaign ideas, is virtually unknown among manufacturing companies (with one or two notable exceptions; Procter & Gamble is the most prominent of these).

The first of the five points made by Rosser Reeves is a matter of great importance. Many people believe that a single theory may eventually be propounded to explain advertising in all its manifestations. This is an assumption which accounts for the wrongheadedness of a great deal of research in the field, investigations aimed at uncovering uniform "macro" patterns which do not in fact exist. I am convinced that the most fruitful route for the researcher who wishes to explore advertising and get some useful results is to work inductively, from the particular to the general, a procedure which has been compared to how the entomologist collects insects: in different species, and always searching for groups with underlying similarities.[10]

It may eventually be possible for us to develop a general theory of advertising. But such a theory must explicitly encompass (and it must also list and codify) the many different ways in which advertising works or may work. This use of the phrase "general theory" is similar to Maynard Keynes's: he explicitly distinguished his own general theory (of macroeconomics) from the more limited special theories which preceded it, and which he included as integral (but incomplete) parts of his own theoretical battery.[11]

Products and Brands

We have Type A knowledge of what brands are: how they differ from unbranded product and what are the relative contributions of functional performance and added values to consumers' brand choice. We have Type B knowledge about the things which contribute to added values. There are serviceable qualitative and quantitative research techniques that provide good knowledge on a brand-by-brand basis. The reason why all this knowledge falls short of Type A is that it varies a great deal among brands, and we do not know quite enough to formulate reliable general patterns. The greatest single contribution to added values in most circumstances is made by consumer advertising.[12]

With one exception, we have Type A knowledge of how new brands originated and how consumer advertising developed historically. The one exception is the influence attributed to the wholesaler during the early development of branding and advertising. This single element represents Type D knowledge, and the reason is that the debate has for so long been distorted by covert political overtones.[13]

New Brands

We have Type A knowledge of the high failure rate of new brand introductions.[14]

We have Type B knowledge of the reasons for this failure. The most important single reason is an inability to provide functional superiority over competitive brands, as evaluated in blind product tests.[15] But we know less about any general patterns of other contributions to failure. There is a suspicion (based on private discussions with businesspeople), that Type D knowledge is quite prevalent, and in particular that too little attention is paid to competitive functional performance, and too much to other factors, notably the advertising, the potential importance of which is commonly overestimated.

We have Type A knowledge of the general distribution and sales patterns of new brands: instore distribution starts at reasonably high levels even for brands which are doomed to fail, as long as the brand comes from a respected manufacturer.[16] But only the brands which are going to succeed grow to the highest levels of distribution. In the planning of distribution growth, simple predictive models can be developed which are of operational value. Sales patterns of new brands show a remarkable regularity, and much is known about the length of the initial sales cycle, which describes the drop from the initial sales peak represented by the first consumer trial to a normal ongoing level. We also know about the extent of the actual drop from peak to stable plateau, and predictive models can also be developed to help plan and control this drop.[17]

We have Type B knowledge of the value of correct market positioning for a new brand. There is a strong indication that positioning based on functional differentiation is a more valuable device than attempting to segment users by demographic or psychographic criteria. The reason is that, in most markets, because of regular multibrand purchasing, *the same* homemakers tend to buy a number of different brands which differ widely from one another in functional and nonfunctional respects.[18]

We have Type A knowledge that it makes little difference to the success of a brand launch whether the brand has a new name or an "umbrella" one. The amount of money spent on the launch is a more important determinant of whether it will succeed, and there is convincing evidence that the goodwill supposedly carried by the umbrella name is not enough to compensate for an inadequate launch advertising investment.[19]

Our knowledge of initial product pricing for new brands is Type B. There are certain methods of assessing consumer responses to likely price ranges for a new brand, but these are merely a guide to judgment.[20] What prevents our knowledge of pricing from graduating to Type A is that not all manufacturers accept the principle of pricing on the basis of what the market will bear; they tend to be preoccupied with ensuring that production costs will be adequately covered in the short run. Three-year payouts are normally necessary, but businesspeople sometimes find the pressure of costs so great that they are forced to attempt to shorten the payout time.

There is also reasonable Type B evidence that consumers will accept a premium price for a new brand if it is functionally superior to the competition. But the consumer will resist a higher price if it is not.[21]

We have Type A knowledge of the general sales level to be expected of successful second and third brands in a market, in comparison with the sales level of a successful pioneer brand.[22] These followers are often loosely and incorrectly described as "me-too." (In order to succeed at all, a second brand must have some degree of functional differentiation.)

We have Type A knowledge of the reliability of test markets to predict a national outcome. There is a direct relationship between length of time in test and our ability to make correct forecasts on the basis of the test market experience.[23]

Prima facie, we have reasonable knowledge of the process of launching new brands. But although what is known is interesting, these things are some way removed from the central issues. They resemble symptoms as detected by a physician, which will help in a diagnosis of what went wrong. It would be of much greater interest to us to know how to avoid going wrong in the first place.

In other words, what we know about new brands is of very limited value if we are faced with the creative task of inventing a new brand—and of evaluating, before money is spent on marketplace testing, how well the brand will succeed in a real competitive environment. Our *fundamental* knowledge of new brands is in fact entirely inadequate. The state of knowledge about the fundamentals of invention and forecasting is therefore in the Type C category. It is the first of the big unknowns that will be addressed in this chapter and in chapter 11.

Our general inability to launch successful new brands is substantially a failure of research (and will be mentioned again in the section entitled "Market Research"), and it is the first of the seven most striking failings in our overall knowledge of marketing and advertising processes.

There is Type B evidence that American industry has been taking steps to address the weaknesses in this centrally important planning function.[24]

There is also a good deal of energy expended in developing proprietary research techniques, mostly based on what is known as "forced purchase" (that is, compelling consumers to make hypothetical brand choices), which aim to predict the success of new brands. Some of these techniques are promising, but their overall yield so far is closer to Type C than to Type B knowledge.

Ongoing Brands

There is good Type A knowledge of all substantive matters concerned with patterns of regular consumer purchasing in stationary markets. Most markets for repeat-purchase packaged consumer goods are characterized by stationary conditions in the short and medium run; this is Type A knowledge. In particular we know that homemakers buy a repertoire of brands—each being bought with its own degree of irregularity.

Sales of a brand in any period can be determined from five variables: the size of the population; the brand's penetration, or the number of people who buy it (this is the prime determinant of market share); its purchase frequency; the number of packs bought per purchase occasion; and the average size of the pack. Mathematical models can be constructed on the basis of penetration and purchase-frequency data, which will predict with extraordinary precision a range of other important variables: the frequency distribution of purchases, the patterns of repeat buying, and the patterns of multi-brand buying.[25] This battery of data, derived from the work of Andrew Ehrenberg, is the single most important body of marketing knowledge which exists for ongoing brands. But to all intents and purposes its existence (let along its importance) remains substantially unrecognized by the American professional and academic communities.

The main conclusion from this body of information is that the variables listed in the last paragraph disclose regularity and uniformity. This means that established brands in virtually all markets are guided by a seemingly unthinking repetition of purchasing habits, which effectively guarantee, at least in the short run, that sales levels and patterns will be maintained. Even the cancellation of consumer advertising will generally have no immediate effect.

We have faint knowledge (somewhere between Type B and Type C) about what this regularity of buying patterns means for the role of advertising for ongoing brands.[26] The notion of a protective, reinforcing role aimed at maintenance of the status quo is regarded as unorthodox. It is certainly rare for practitioners to plan explicitly to use advertising in this way. The unstated assumption of virtually every advertising agency on Madison Avenue is that advertising should be planned to work aggressively, to upset the status quo. This is a good example of Type D knowledge, and the fact that it is Type D is confirmed by Type A evidence that radical changes in buying patterns only very rarely take place in mature markets.

There is Type A evidence that there are advertising-related scale economies accruing to large brands. When a brand's market share reaches about 15 percent (which is typically accompanied by a four-weekly penetration of plus or minus 30 percent), a measurable increase begins to take place in its purchase and repurchase frequencies. I have coined the term *penetration supercharge* to describe this phenomenon.[27] This is a matter of considerable importance which is unrecognized by most practitioners and academics. And there is also Type A evidence that such scale economies can be quantified and expressed by the ability of large brands to be supported by advertising budgets which are smaller than the levels suggested by these brands' market shares. Marginal savings in advertising can of course mean very significant increases in net profit. (See chapter 5 of this book.)

The connection between the penetration supercharge and these budgetary scale economies is something we know only impressionistically; it is Type B knowledge.

The notion of a "hard core" of regular buyers of any brand is Type D knowledge.[28]

The existence of the "leaky bucket" (that buyers regularly quit a brand) is also Type D knowledge.[29]

The idea that promotional and seasonal sales increases are caused by an increasing use of a brand by existing users is in very many circumstances yet again Type D knowledge. (They are normally a function of temporarily increased penetration.[30])

There is Type A knowledge that an ongoing brand will maintain its position in the medium and long run only if it keeps a competitive level of functional performance.[31] Successful brands benefit from improvements in their formulations on a regular basis, and certain enlightened manufacturers carry out comparative blind product testing for their major brands against their competitors as part of an ongoing program.[32]

There is Type A evidence that existing mature brands do not normally encounter difficulties with their retail distribution. One slight exception is that out-of-stock problems commonly cause a loss of potential sales, which is often more serious for faster selling brands than for slower selling ones. Such problems should direct manufacturers' attention to monitoring inventories, maintaining deliveries, and (wherever possible) increasing case sizes.[33]

We have general knowledge, which is somewhere between Types A and B, about pricing in a market. We have Type A knowledge that the consumer's price awareness tends to be imperfect.[34] We have Type A knowledge of price elasticities based on a range of 367 elasticities in a large number of product fields. These have been calculated within a reasonably tight span of observations. The elasticities range very widely, although they cluster around the average, which is -1.76. This means that within the levels of price for which the prediction holds, a price increase of 10 percent (for the average brand) will bring about a reduction of 17.6 percent in consumer sales.[35] Despite the unquestioned operational value of such a calculation, it is relatively rare for manufacturers to embark on the econometric investigations which are normally necessary to derive such figures for their own brands. I incline therefore to classify our knowledge of pricing for ongoing brands as Type B.

With regard to investments on ongoing brands above and below the line, we have Type A knowledge of the effect of absolute amounts of advertising pressure, which will be considered in the section entitled "The Evaluation of Advertising Effects." We also have Type A knowledge that there is a secular tendency for most manufacturers, but not retailers, to reduce very gradually (but, when examined over long periods, very markedly) the share of their sales volume which goes to advertising.[36]

We have Type A knowledge that this long-term movement has been accompanied by a gradual increase in expenditure below the line, which now accounts for at least 66 percent of most manufacturers' combined advertising and promotional investments, and in many cases for even more than this. (This topic is discussed in chapter 2 of this book.) Even Procter & Gamble now spends more money below than above the line. We also have Type A knowledge that promotions bring no long-term benefits in expanding a brand's consumer franchise, except in the relatively rare cases of brands which are in a strongly rising sales trend.[37]

We know about the reasons for the growth in promotions. (These are discussed in chapter 6.) At least four reasons have been adduced, but their relative importance is unknown, so that our overall knowledge of this subject is no better than Type B.

First, there has been a gradual but very real increase in the strength, concentration, and bargaining power of the retail trade. There is Type A knowledge that this has taken place, but opinions differ about how it has affected manufacturers.[38]

Second, there is thought to have been a concentration on short-term goals on the part of marketing managements (in response to inflationary pressures during the 1970s), allied to a notable failure of nerve.[39]

Third, certain advertising practitioners have expressed the opinion that the trend of expenditure from above to below the line has followed certain long-term changes in manufacturers' branding policies:

- a slowing in the rate of new brand introductions[40]
- a reduction in emphasis on functional differences between brands (a result of the rapid pace of competition and the rapidity with which functional improvements are copied)[41]

Fourth, promotions appear to deliver greater sales than "theme" advertising does, although individual manufacturers have often not managed to work out the profitability, or rather the lack of profitability, of the extra sales generated by promotions. We have Type B knowledge of all this, and I shall pick up this point in the section entitled "The Evaluation of Advertising Effects."

The final matter concerning ongoing brands is a belief in the inevitability of cyclical decline. This is one of the classic expressions of Type D knowledge. Such views are universally believed in academic circles and are common even among practitioners, who should be aware that what makes such a belief dangerous is not just that it is wrong (something we know from Type A knowledge), but that it is alarmingly self-fulfilling.[42]

Overall, the state of knowledge about ongoing brands is in advance of that about successful new brand activity. The one important and rather mysterious gap concerns the lack of awareness (or perhaps the emotional rejection) of the large body of facts bearing on the regularity of consumer buying behavior and the role of advertising in supporting mature, stable brands in stationary markets. I am inclined to put this particular body of doctrine—or at least how it is regarded in the United States—in the Type E category. Whether or not this is the best place to put it, I regard this particular branch of knowledge as the second of the seven most striking things which need radically to be taken in hand. In this case, I am not suggesting the need for original empirical work or even a synthesis of existing knowledge. More important is the process of thinking through what the doctrine should bring to the advertising strategies of existing and new brands, testing hypotheses in the marketplace, and taking steps to inject into the bloodstream of practitioners something of the meaning and implications of this most important body of knowledge.

Proceeding from this point, too little is known empirically of the patterns of buying behavior in dynamic market conditions. There are impressionistic flashes—typical of Type B—but we need to know much more at a solid factual level.[43]

Market Research

Market research is the only scientific tool available to the advertising practitioner. A great deal is known about it, but the quality of our knowledge is variable.

To carry out useful research, we need to do at least five things, and this is true no matter what type of research we are doing. With specific types of research (notably advertising research, which will be discussed later in this section), certain of the five things are especially problematical.

First, we must choose and describe our sampling frame: the universe we are going to cover, which generally means the types of people we are going to interview. There is generally no shortage of data to help us do this, and our knowledge of the procedure is of Type A. The only problem (and it is sometimes an extremely serious one) arises when we have to select *on judgment* between alternatives which appear to have equal merits. For instance, with advertising research, do we interview users or nonusers of our brand? Or do we interview both? Or doesn't it matter—can we rely on simple demographic descriptions to locate the people we should talk to? The answer depends on the state of the brand: its importance in the market place, the characteristics of its users, and any market forces which appear to be affecting it over time.

We have to use our brains to evaluate these things, and market researchers, like all other people, would prefer to follow rules (which are often wrong) to using judgment (which is less often wrong but is harder work). Because of the occasional entry of such uncertainties, I judge our knowledge of sampling frames to be somewhere between Types A and B.

Second, we must select a sample and try to arrange that we do not get too many refusals if we are using the probability method (or variants of it). Although it is a process which requires considerable technical expertise, a great deal is known about sampling and the margins of error for samples of different sizes and types.[44] Sampling knowledge can be placed in that rarest of categories, Type A-1.

The third problem is the worst of the five: it concerns the questions we ask. There are difficulties with all questioning techniques. Even in the investigation of simple facts, there is a persistent tendency for respondents to overclaim. This tendency is so consistent that we can normally "aim off," or modify, our results to compensate for it. As the questions become more difficult, are more judgmental, and occasionally imply hidden meanings, the difficulties of extracting the truth multiply. I am not saying that such difficulties make the research so hard to plan and implement that it is not worth the effort. But I *am* saying that in order to get useful insights into matters which are neither obvious nor simple we should ask a range of questions, some direct and some oblique, to encourage people to reply as fully as they like in their own words, and we should interpret what they say very carefully indeed. Researchers do not often do these things because it makes the research very complicated to plan, tabulate, and interpret.[45]

A basic problem is that people find it difficult to answer questions outside their range of direct experience. Research is concerned essentially with the status quo. It has been said that if the development of household lighting systems had depended on market research, houses would be lit today by kerosene lamps of a highly advanced design. One of the unfortunate side effects of research, which stems from the fact that all advertisers use it in more or less the same way, is that it leads to extraordinary similarities in their behavior: they manufacture similar brands, and (until recently at any rate) they invariably used the same advertising techniques. I am convinced that a correlation analysis would disclose a strong relationship between the employment of the "slice-of-life" technique for television advertising and the use of day-after recall testing.

It follows from all this that I am often skeptical about semantic scales for opinion questions. Not only are these questions rigid and different from the way we ask questions in real life, but they make the unrealistic assumption that people have an opinion on every subject they are being asked about. It is too easy for a respondent to appear to have a defined view by agreeing with a statement of assent or dissent. As a result, they can produce misleading answers.

All in all, I would rate our knowledge of questioning techniques no higher than Type B.

The fourth problem with research is a matter of interpretation: our assessment of the direction of causality. Does X cause Y? Or does Y cause X? Or are they perhaps both caused by Z? Or is there any causal relationship at all—is any connection that there may be between variables purely coincidental? The development of the technique of regression analysis has improved our knowledge of causality, but only on the occasions when we take the considerable trouble of quantifying the relative importance of the independent variables. Regression analysis generally provides knowledge of Type B and, on rare occasions, Type A. In simpler matters, however, there are often baffling and unexpected difficulties in the interpretation of data. Take the matter of tracking studies into consumers' brand awareness and belief in image attributes. The assumption often made about such research is that changes in these variables are a result of advertising (plus other marketing stimuli), and that they precede and influence brand purchasing. It can more plausibly be argued that changes in these variables are the *result* of brand purchasing.

In summary, I would classify our knowledge of the direction of causality somewhere between Types A and B. On occasion, however, Type B manifests itself, as in the case of the tracking studies mentioned in the last paragraph.

The fifth and last point about research is that most research reports are not well written. This failing affects the degree to which the conclusions penetrate our consciousness and, as a result, how much they influence our actions in the marketplace. One especially irritating feature of many research reports is the sloppy solecism of calculating percentages on totals much smaller than 100. The perpetrators are clearly unconscious of the fact that they are making projections, and in all circumstances, the ability to make such projections depends on whether the smaller total is a true and complete reflection of the larger; the smaller is in effect a sample of the larger.

This matter of the interpretation of research is less a result of knowledge than of competent writing. If the average research report (of the very many hundreds I have seen) were to be handed in by one of my graduate students, it would deserve a bare passing grade. There are, of course, exceptions.

Special Types of Research: Retail Audits and Consumer Panels

Retail audit research is normally good and reliable. Samples are adequate. There are no questioning problems (questions are not asked; the data are simply collected by counting). The presentation of the data is admirably simple and practical. Nielsen is indeed something which we hold in special esteem. There are only two problems with it. First, it does not cover the complete retail trade through which the specific products which are being measured are sold. But we know its specific limits in this regard. Second, since consumer sales are aggregated, we cannot trace the behavior of individual consumers. Nielsen therefore needs to be supplemented with consumer panel data. All in all, however, I would put the rich and multidimensional knowledge of markets which comes from retail audit data in category A-2.

Consumer panel research does not have such a substantial data base as retail audit research, but it avoids the problem of the incomplete coverage of sales in the market (purchases from all types of retail outlets are recorded). The reliance on postal data collection means that the sample is not entirely controlled, and there is therefore some problem with its reliability. There is also a tendency toward overclaiming (for which we can compensate in the interpretation of the findings). All in all, however, I would put our knowledge from consumer panel research somewhere between the A-2 and B categories.

As and when we develop—and have available for analysis and use—a range of statistical batteries based on "single-source" data, it will provide a body of knowledge in the A-2 category. Quantitative techniques—model building and regression analysis—are almost certainly the branches of market research with the most promising future. Single-source data (which relate individual consumers' purchasing to their media exposure, including detailed exposure to television day parts and channels) will be the richest source of such quantitative research—Type B knowledge, which is being constantly improved.

Simmons (SMRB) and Mediamark (MRI) both provide consumer penetration figures for a wide range of brands. These are related to media exposure patterns, which obviously help in the construction of media plans. These are all data in the A-2 category. MRI supplements its penetration figures with serviceable estimates of market shares of the same brands, based on estimates of volume consumption. This is also A-2 knowledge.

Special Types of Research: Media Research

Meter-based audience measurement, recording the number of sets switched on to specific programs, provides A-2 information on network television, and on some spot (i.e., regional as opposed to national) television. A total of twenty panels is in operation in local spot markets, but the number of markets covered is less because of panel duplication in a number of areas.

The use of "people meters" by the Nielsen Television Index means that network research into audience composition is now approaching the A-2 category. These devices make it relatively easy for one television viewer to record, by punching a button, who else is in the same room. However, this type of research will be perfected and will definitely enter the A-2 category only as and when "passive" meters come into use. These will record the number of people in the room where the television set is switched on by an automatic process, and without people's having to press buttons.

The Nielsen panel for network audience measurement now comprises twenty-one hundred homes. But one unresolved problem is the monitoring of cable programs. There is no industry agreement on the size of the samples needed for this monitoring, except that it needs to be large.

Where we do not have people meters to measure audience composition, diaries are used. This is the method employed by Nielsen and Arbitron in spot markets. This method and the diary-recorded coverage of radio programs (by Arbitron) are of a second order of reliability. I would in general rate all our knowledge from television and radio research as Type B. A special problem with both people meters and diaries is that no attempt is made to distinguish between the audience of the programs and the audience of the commercials, taking account of people who are out of the room, or who "zap" the advertising.

Research into the readership of print media is generally of reasonably good quality. The samples are large enough to provide reliable data for demographic subgroups and also (most important) for users of named brands. There is still controversy about the questioning techniques (although the differences in opinion between experts are not as great as they were in the early 1980s). But despite this problem, I would rate the standardized measures of readership, in particular those derived from Simmons and Mediamark as Type A-2 knowledge. Simmons has extended its coverage to newspapers as well as magazines.

The computer-based techniques for estimating net reach and "opportunities to see" for alternative schedules generally provide Type A knowledge, although the selection between the alternatives—which is a process of optimization—must be made judgmentally.

The simple statistical techniques for estimating net reach (for example, the Sainsbury formula) provide Type B knowledge.

Our knowledge of outdoor and billboard advertising is Type C.

Special Types of Research: Advertising Research

By *advertising research,* I mean not the quantitative and qualitative research used to formulate advertising strategy, but the research techniques used to evaluate individual advertisements either before they are exposed, or after trial exposure, or after exposure before a substantial audience. (At the end of this section, I shall mention and evaluate briefly the techniques used for monitoring the cumulative effects of campaigns.)

There are two uses for research into individual advertisements. First, there is a mainly diagnostic and generative role which takes place before the advertisement is prepared, or during the course of its construction. Second, there is a "quality-control" role, which normally takes place before the advertisement is used as part of a campaign. This role is meant to ensure that the advertisement meets action standards, which may or may not be spurious, but which are an agreed-on decision-making tool for brand management.

In its diagnostic role, the research is invariably qualitative and is intended to help generate thought, to act as a sounding board for tentative ideas, and to assess interest and clarity of communication. This type of research is on occasion criticized for lack of rigor and for general shoddiness, but the advantages generally outweigh the disadvantages, and the knowledge acquired deserves to be classified as Type B.[46] For once, such impressionistic knowledge may be preferable to "harder," more complete knowledge; for the very reason that it is incomplete, it may trigger the imagination of the creative person. Its often vivid one-sidedness may nudge him or her forward, in fresh and possibly productive directions.

The knowledge acquired by quality-control research is much more questionable. There is a variety of techniques. The most common for television advertisements are "in-home" monitoring and "forced exposure" (where respondents are shown the commercial in a theater or shopping mall). The research purports to measure intrusiveness, recall, and persuasion.

The subject has long been controversial, but tests of this type remain in common if not quite universal use by larger advertisers, especially those that operate in the more competitive categories.[47] As discussed in chapter 9 of this book, the fundamental objections to the technique(s) are:

1. There is a substantial number of factors which have been proved to contaminate the data. These include the type of copy claim (the method discriminates in favor of simple factual claims and against more complex emotional messages), the program environment, and the time of day.[48]
2. Rather decisively, there is *proven* lack of connection

between factual recall, on the one hand, and preference and buying behavior, on the other. [49]

3. Standardized testing contributes to the perpetuation of advertisement stereotypes, and in general it inhibits creativity.

An important philosophical point is that such tests are based on the supposition that advertising operates by engineering *change*. They ignore the possibility that much—maybe the majority—of advertising works by the reinforcement of current purchasing patterns.

Most of the problems stem from the fact that the tests simplify—in most cases grossly oversimplify—what is normally a complicated process. The questioning is just not subtle enough to get near the truth. Advertising communication can at times be subtle and multidimensional (confirmed by a good deal of Type B evidence), and what it says to people cannot normally be uncovered by a few simple questions asked on the telephone. Indeed, although such tests provide neat answers which are eminently actionable, they operate by offering an inflexible choice between limited alternatives, and by expecting this choice to substitute for reason and judgment. They are a classic manifestation of Type D knowledge, and their popularity resembles the search for the philosophers' stone. No alternative is readily available to evaluate the selling power of an advertisement. This is an important gap, unknown territory, or Type C knowledge.

As far as print advertising is concerned, experimental work carried out in the 1960s undermined the theoretical basis of the standardized research into both recognition (Starch) and recall (Gallup and Robinson), by demonstrating the working of unconscious selective perception, which makes people screen advertisements into or out of their conscious memories. This happens through the influence of a number of factors—not just the creative content of the advertisement itself.[50]

Far more people actually see advertisements than remember seeing them, so that recognition and recall measures are a function of, among other things, people's interest in the product field. It has also been demonstrated that there are at least nineteen factors which contaminate recognition and recall scores. I am inclined to put normal recognition and recall data for print advertising into Type D. But if the data are broadly aggregated with the aim of comparing different advertising techniques, they can on occasion yield Type B knowledge. This statement may appear anomalous, but the research is used in these circumstances rather like a catalyst in a chemical experiment. We do not have to accept the various readership scores in an absolute sense, and such aggregation can be used to focus attention on sometimes important differences between different types of advertisement. We can measure and can believe the *differences* and not be worried much about the absolute measure we are using to make the comparison.

As we move from the evaluation of single advertisements to complete campaigns, the most efficient technique now available to evaluate the progress of campaigns in the marketplace is continuous tracking studies.[51] This procedure should be supplemented wherever possible by the construction of models that isolate the specific contribution of the advertising to sales. Despite the problem with tracking studies of assessing the direction of causality (a matter already discussed in this section), the findings often provide diagnostic insights into what is going right (or wrong). However, this type of research is based on the assumption that the decision has been made to expose the campaign; it is not geared to help us make that decision in the first place. Our inability to find a way of predicting the selling power of an advertisement is a notable weakness of our research knowledge. It represents the third of the seven most substantial gaps in our knowledge of advertising.

As a summary of our state of knowledge of the various fields of research, there are weaknesses to be corrected, as well as one major gap to be closed: the problem with advertising research just mentioned. Nevertheless, our knowledge is generally not bad; indeed what we know about the various research processes compares favorably with our knowledge of any other single aspect of advertising which is discussed in this chapter. Moreover, improvements in research techniques take place regularly, although slowly.

The Creative Process

Most practitioners believe that there are two parts to the creative process: the strategic and the tactical steps. I believe there are not two but three. And although the second and third overlap, there are advantages in separating them because of important differences in the extent of our knowledge of the second and third steps. I shall discuss each of these processes in turn: the strategy, the creative leap, and the craft skills. After describing the salient characteristics of each, I shall examine the state of our knowledge concerning them.

The Strategy

Writing a soundly based and "green-thumbed" strategy involves analytical and intellectual activity, requiring knowledge of the brand and the market; objectivity; and depth. The process can be described as mentally "vertical," which means allowing logic to guide us along a direct route of "high probability."[52] Different, similarly skilled people, when confronted with the same problem, generally end up by drawing broadly similar strategic conclusions.

The knowledge available to use in drawing up an effective strategy is in general more Type A than Type B. (See chapters 7 and 8.)

Some practitioners carry out research into strategic alternatives, but this is a controversial procedure. There is Type B knowledge that it is much more reliable to test strategic propositions (expressed as verbal statements) when the advertising arguments are factual and product-related, than when they are emotional and mood-oriented.[53] Some practitioners, however, reject the possibility of efficient proposition testing even for factual claims.[54] However, as we saw in chapter 9, qualitative (but not quantitative) techniques can be helpful).

It is fairly clear then that in the important matter of drawing up a brand's advertising strategy, we are able to call on substantial amounts of Type A and Type B knowledge. The next stage in developing a campaign raises more problems.

The Creative Leap

The creative leap is less an intellectual and more an imaginative and intuitive process. It is mentally "lateral" rather than "vertical"; the birth of an arresting idea normally results from tangential thinking. Different, similarly skilled creative people, when confronted with the same strategy, invariably make their creative leaps differently. Six people will develop six different (and often equally relevant) advertising executions of the same strategy. These naturally vary in qual-

226 · How Much Is Enough?

ity. However, there is Type B evidence that human judgment, even that of experienced professionals, is a poor way of discriminating between alternatives.[55]

The creative leap is the most important single activity in the whole field of advertising, and it is the aspect of the field about which we know the least. With the prominent exception of James Webb Young's *A Technique for Producing Ideas*,[56] it is ignored in the vast library of professional and academic literature, partly perhaps from a mistaken belief that the intellectual and imaginative faculties which are needed to create a campaign are not different in kind from the analytical qualities needed to draw up a strategy.

Since there is such a thin literature which bears directly on the subject, I am able to rely only on my personal experience, and on extrapolations from literature from outside the advertising field.

The most fruitful single idea which is germane to advertising creativity is Arthur Koestler's concept of "bisociative fusion." This describes how, when we reach a creative "block," we have to search around the subject and move into completely unrelated areas.[57] When we alight on an idea which can be made to relate to the point we reached when we were blocked, the fusion of the new with the old causes a fresh new idea to be sparked. This is a pregnant concept, which jibes well with James Webb Young's contention that there is no such thing as a completely fresh idea; the human mind is capable only of rearrangements of existing ideas.[58]

Koestler developed a number of allied notions which are both stimulating and productive:

- incompleteness (that "stepping stones . . . should be spaced wide enough apart to require a significant effort from the audience")
- unexpectedness
- humor
- participation, and the importance of persuading the receiver of a message to take a step toward the sender of it[59]

Some of these ideas were picked up in a short but influential paper by the English market researcher Timothy Joyce.[60]

Very little is known about how we can encourage the mind to sweep over a strategic problem in search of an idea to fuse with our original block. The only notable contribution is a method of disciplining our unconscious to do the work on our behalf. This is the idea contained in James Webb Young's tiny monograph *A Technique for Producing Ideas.*

Many people find Edward do Bono's concept of "lateral" thinking stimulating, but I find his books much too oriented to the relatively static matter of problem solving and too little directed to the dynamics of idea generation.[61] In recent years, there has been a rash of books of a type similar to de Bono's, but they are subject to the same limitations. That by von Oech is the best.[62]

It will be apparent from this discussion that our knowledge of the creative leap is somewhat better than Type C. In view of the importance of the process, this is little short of scandalous. I am going to classify this subject as the fourth of the seven major gaps in our knowledge of advertising, but it is probably the single most important one.

Craft Skills

There are relatively simple and easily described techniques for making effective use of a thirty-second television film, a press advertisement, a radio advertisement, or a billboard.

There are two types of craft skills. These are the skills of the agency and those of external artistic talent: filmmakers, photographers, designers, and so on.

I shall not talk much about the nonagency craft skills, except to note that in the major advertising capitals (especially New York and London), there is Type A-1 knowledge that such skills are in plentiful supply. The advertising industry has created a need for these skills since the 1960s, if not before, and the market has responded splendidly.

As far as the agency's craft skills are concerned, there is often a good deal of overlap between these and the creative idea itself. It is, however, useful to try to draw a line, because by doing so we shall be able to locate more efficiently the gaps in our knowledge.

In the audiovisual media, especially television, the craft skills in major agencies tend to be impressively high. By this I mean the imaginative conception of the visual elements in the commercials, as well as the flow and economy of the verbal arguments. I am talking only of the best work in the most sophisticated advertising markets, but I would say that our knowledge of such techniques is mostly, although not invariably, Type A. One weakness, which is related to the matter of advertising strategy and which often needs to be remedied, is that not enough emphasis is given to volume use of the advertised brand. This is very important to food advertisers, demonstrating for instance the importance of recipe advertising. (Our knowledge of the value of recipe advertising is somewhere between Type A and Type B.[63])

Agencies have developed their craft skills with television to an advanced degree because they have devoted so much of their clients' money to the medium (the ten top agencies in both New York and London spend about two thirds of their clients' total budgets on television). They have also learned a great deal from qualitative research, which is used as a routine procedure in campaign development at most professionally competent agencies. (On the other hand, simplified quantitative research, notably day-after recall, has had a baleful effect on the *content* of the television advertising for many large brands, although such advertising may be executed with superlative craft skill.)

The situation with press media is worse than that with television. The problem here is that agency creative people do not believe unanimously that we have, in fact, an agreed-on body of knowledge. The difficulty stems from the fact that the most useful books on the subject, all written by practitioners with first-class experience, stem substantially from their authors' experience of direct response.[64]

As far as direct-response advertising is concerned, there are indisputable rules regarding press executions: the length and style of the headlines, the use and style of subheads and paragraph titles, the length and style of the body copy, the use of illustrations, the use of captions, simplicity of typography, and the avoidance of reverse type. Direct-response experience dictates firmly which things work best (Type A knowledge).

However, it is obvious from a study of packaged goods and other general advertisements in the mass print media that the rules of direct-response presentation are only rarely followed. In fact, it is quite exceptional to find a advertisement which demonstrates any evidence of them. A small-scale investigation carried out by Tom

Amico, a student at Syracuse University, demonstrated that, out of a sample of 223 advertisements in major magazines, 89 percent broke at least one of the direct-response rules (which were at one time respected by the practitioners of general advertising), and 45 percent broke at least three of them (Type B knowledge).[65]

This seems an absurd situation, but there are two reasons that it is possible. First, print advertising is a low-priority activity for most major agencies in the main advertising centers. Press advertisements represent a minor element in most large campaigns (except of course for cigarettes). The second and possibly more important point is that agency professionals tend to separate direct response from main-line or general advertising, and to argue that the two have little in common. This lack of commonality is widely regarded as Type A knowledge. It is not. It is Type C at best. Indeed it is probable that direct-response and general advertising should follow *the same* principles of communication, in which case we are really talking about Type E.

But we do not know with real certainty. It is astonishing that, after the experience of a hundred years of direct response, our knowledge of whether its lessons apply over the whole advertising field should be so limited. This matter represents the fifth of the seven major types of advertising knowledge we need to augment radically. Its importance lies in the considerable opportunities which may be opened up to improve our professional skills. If we can learn to test general advertisements through direct response, we shall have discovered a research tool of great value.

Use of television advertising by direct-response practitioners is developing strongly. Two-minute commercials were originally considered the minimum usable length, and out of the two minutes, twenty seconds were thought necessary to communicate the advertiser's address and telephone number. However, at the end of the 1980s, sixty-second commercials began to be used effectively for direct response, with ten seconds of the commercial devoted to the address and telephone number. One of the forces driving advertisers toward the use of sixty-second commercials was the difficulty of buying two-minute spots.

The device of featuring an identified person at the end of the commercial who purportedly answers the viewer's inquiry has a significant influence on the advertiser's cost per response.[66] (This is all Type A knowledge.)

Advertising Budgets

Because advertising and promotional budgets are often of an order of magnitude similar to the profits earned by a brand, reductions (and increases) can have a major effect on a brand's earnings. For instance, with some brands, a 50 percent reduction in advertising and promotions can cause a 50 percent increase in profitability, with the proviso that sales will remain unchanged despite the reduced investment. In the short run—say, within the calendar year of the budget reduction—it is often reasonable to expect that sales will hold. This is especially true if the reduction comes more out of advertising than out of promotions. But of course the advertiser will be "eating its seed corn," and many (although not all) brand managements are aware of the hidden dangers. This is all type A knowledge.

As discussed in chapter 5, when manufacturers determine their advertising budgets above the line, they almost invariably concentrate attention on their *costs,* that is, what they can afford to spend and also maintain profit in the short run. This concentration leads them to determine appropriations according to some "percentage-of-sales" formula. Doing this means that they give too little attention to whether the budgets they arrive at are realistic investments for specific sales goals. Our knowledge of manufacturers' cost-oriented attitude toward budget determination is Type B.

The practices of 130 American and European advertisers in setting their budgets were studied in the mid-1970s. It was discovered that there was a massive reliance on the cost-based methods (share of past or anticipated sales).[67] But a small minority of advertisers—a higher proportion in Europe than in the United States—were beginning to use econometric modeling techniques. This procedure has grown in importance, and we have Type B knowledge that a minority—maybe 10 percent—of major advertisers in the United States now use such methods, at least on an experimental basis.

For new brands, advertisers normally base their budgets on what has been spent on other brands launched in the market (which have achieved varying degrees of success). This is a reasonably sensible procedure, but there is normally no attempt at a scientific evaluation of all the variables. This type of knowledge is at the lower end of Category B.

Taking into account both ongoing and launch budgets, manufacturers have available to them as many as fifteen different methods for budget determination. (This is known from Type A knowledge.[68]) The diversity of these methods is perhaps an indication of advertisers' fundamental dissatisfaction with the whole procedure.

I shall now discuss briefly three specific ways of setting above-the-line budgets.

Cost-Based Methods

As a method of planning expenditures to achieve sales objectives, the cost-based method (for example, share of past or anticipated sales) as in general in the "folklore" category of Type D knowledge. Because expenditures are determined by costs and not results, no attempt is made to isolate and specify advertising's contribution to the latter. In the absence of rational argument, recommendations about advertising levels rely on emotional appeals, especially fear of the competition. The pressure of oligopolistic competition on budgets operates in only one direction: upward. And this pressure is not discouraged by advertising agencies, which operate on the commission system. Such, anyway, was the situation until a different series of pressures—those stemming from the bargaining power of the retail trade—led to a siphoning of expenditure during the 1980s from above to below the line. Despite even this countervailing pressure, the system still tends to boost budgets because of manufacturers' fears of being capped by their competitors. (This is all Type A knowledge.)

In one review of sixty-nine tests of changes in advertising weight, there was the clear inference that more than half the brands were already at or above optimum advertising levels.[69] There was also an earlier study of forty cases made by Ogilvy & Mather, New York. In these, an advertising response function was calculated with the use of a construct called the *Hendry model* (in which the extent of the projection outside the range of observations is unstated). There was evidence from this analysis that sizable numbers of manufacturers overadvertise. In about half the cases studied, the advertising level was approximately optimal. In the remaining half, three times as many advertisers were found to be spending too much money than were spending too little.[70]

If the cost-based methods for determining expenditures are qualified and adjusted by the use of forecasts from empirical data about their likely effectiveness in the marketplace, they can become a more useful tool, and our knowledge improves to Type B. But this is the case with only a relative minority of advertisers who have developed experienced-based guidelines for estimating the effects of different pressure levels. Procter & Gamble are in this category; their "case rate" system is qualified by a general knowledge of the effectiveness of many "going" levels of expenditure.

Methods Based on Competitive Expenditures in the Market

To evaluate the sorts of expenditure levels which "work" in a market—to study the advertising expenditures and sales performances of competitive brands and to evaluate and judge what is needed for one's own brand—is to use Type B knowledge.

This method marks the beginning of the use of econometric techniques, and in certain circumstances, our knowledge can improve to Type A-2. I refer here to the dynamic difference, a sometimes valuable regression analysis based on two variables: changes in a brand's share of advertising in a market (when measured against its previous year's market share) and changes in its share of market itself.[71]

There is also the advertising-intensiveness curve, which measures the average share of voice for brands of different sizes. This was described in chapter 5. As a contribution to budget determination, it provides knowledge in the A-2 category.

More Complex Econometric Methods

The econometric techniques used for the calculation of advertising elasticities are reasonably well developed, and they are implemented at least experimentally by an important minority of advertisers. The most important method used is regression analysis based on historical data, supplemented in many cases by marketplace experimentation. Aggregated data on ranges of advertising elasticities have been collected and published in both Europe and the United States. The most recent such collection was published in 1984.[72] This important subject was discussed in chapter 6 and will be raised again in the section entitled "The Evaluation of Advertising Effects."

For below-the-line expenditures, a few manufacturers keep excellent records; and for well-established brands, there are enough back data to make serviceable projections of the sales results of specific promotional actions, insofar as these represent effective reductions in the retail price.[73] Such manufacturers (for example, Procter & Gamble) have Type A knowledge of promotional budgeting. But firms like these are in the minority. For all others, the budgetary determination for promotions is near-guesswork, somewhere between Type B and Type C knowledge.

Because of the importance of its geared effect on profitability, which has already been described, I believe budgeting to be one of the two most important advertising activities (the other is the development of the creative idea). In its operation, the Type D knowledge that budgets should be determined by the cost structure of the brand is so prevalent as to be almost universal. Better methods *are* available. More efficient budgeting forms part of the seventh of the most serious gaps in our knowledge (discussed in the section entitled "The Evaluation of Advertising Effects").

This weakness in our knowledge does not end here. The *same* difficult choice, between the easy alternative of accepting myth and the more arduous one of following scientific principles, faces us when we attempt to evaluate the short-term effect of advertising pressure. Such an evaluation should in turn substantially determine the weight of television "flights," and the principles involved will be discussed in the section entitled "The Evaluation of Advertising Effects."

Media Strategy and Tactics

Media planning is a part of the advertising process which combines analytical rigor in strategy with freedom and opportunism in tactics. The principles of these two are different, and the procedures are quite separate.

Media Strategy

There is an important distinction between the strategic process of discriminating between *media* (television, versus radio, versus magazines, and so on) and the process of discriminating between *media vehicles* (one television day part versus another, one magazine versus another, and so on).

When agencies develop a media strategy (as opposed to a media vehicle strategy), discussion centers on four sets of arguments. The people who make the evaluation and the recommendations are, incidentally, the agency account group as a whole, and not just the media planners. The four sets of arguments are

- the creative requirements of the campaign;
- the psychological attributes of the various media;
- quantitative and cost-efficiency arguments;
- the myths surrounding the different media.

We have Type A knowledge that these are the factors which are evaluated by agency account groups. As might be expected, however, the quality of the information surrounding the different arguments is extremely variable.

The first of the factors is the creative requirements of the campaign. These are evaluated judgmentally. A campaign idea is invariably expressed in terms of an individual medium. The argument for that particular medium therefore depends on the campaign. The essential point is that the *overall judgment* of the potential of the campaign is the deciding factor, and this has much more to do with the judgment of creative than with the judgment of media matters. We have Type A knowledge of how agency account groups operate in evaluations of this nature.

Our knowledge concerning the second set of arguments, the psychological attributes of the different media, is very limited. General research into people's *use* of media is badly needed—data, for instance, on the hours people spend with each medium; whether they are doing anything else at the same time; why they look at, listen to, or read different media; and what specific rewards each medium provides. Research like this is not particularly difficult to execute. Simple quantitative techniques can provide data from which useful insights into consumer attitudes can be obtained indirectly. Quantitative research should, however, be supplemented and extended by qualitative research. Research on these lines was carried out by J. Walter Thompson in the United Kingdom in the 1970s. This research may or may not be relevant today.[74]

The British evidence provides a rather cursory confirmation of the sorts of conclusions about the psychological attributes of different media which might have been provided by common sense. For instance, it seems that women tend to be more *involved* with magazines than with television, but there are of course fewer of them in the audience for magazines than in the audience for television. The evaluation of the psychological characteristics of different media is made at present with something between Type B and Type C knowledge.

The exploration of people's use of media represents the sixth of the seven most serious gaps in our knowledge.

We have very good knowledge on which theoretically to base the third set of arguments, those concerned with quantities and cost efficiency, and this knowledge will shortly be examined. However, when we are choosing between media (as opposed to vehicles), these arguments are themselves not of primary importance. The reason is that the qualitative delivery of the advertising—its persuasive and selling power in one medium—cannot be compared in any exact way with its selling power in another medium. There is therefore no point in attempting to use the things which can be measured (for example, net reach and cost per thousand) with the aim of influencing a decision which is mostly determined by unmeasurable factors. Our knowledge of the limitations of these quantitative arguments in media choice is Type A.

There are two special circumstances in which the economic arguments have a bearing on the choice between media: when we are selling to a narrow target audience and when there is a very limited advertising budget. These conditions put an immediate restriction on the number of media alternatives which can be considered. Our knowledge of these things is also Type A.

The last of the four inputs which helps determine media choice is altogether more questionable. I am talking here about the role played by myth, plentifully reinforced by received wisdom.

Some of the individual examples of myths—for instance, that television is the most effective medium for mood and emotion, and women's magazines are particularly suitable for recipe advertising, and that radio works well for retail advertising—are all half-truths, possibly Type B knowledge. The danger of using such arguments is that they can lead to an uncomfortable rigidity of thinking. In extreme circumstances, media decisions may be so weighted by the myths that more respectable types of argument are submerged.

The myths surrounding television tend to be richer than those surrounding other media.

When we turn our attention to strategic choices between media *vehicles,* the clouds surrounding our knowledge clear away, and science begins to play a role in the decision making. This decision making is of two types.

First, it is possible to make comparisons of different vehicles based on an assumed parity in their advertising delivery. An optimization of reach and "opportunities to see" within the confines of the advertising budget is made judgmentally, but this is done with the use of "hard" data: Type A knowledge. The only limitation on the value of this particular scientific procedure is the imperfection in the audience research on which the estimates of viewership and readership and "opportunities to see" are based (a matter discussed in the "Market Research" section).

Second, research into the effect of advertising pressure (to be discussed in the section entitled "The Evaluation of Advertising Effects") can help to determine how advertising weight should be deployed over time, for example, the weight of television "flights."

Media Tactics

Media and media vehicle choices are made on judgment, with the aid of substantial amounts of Type A and Type B knowledge (plus the less welcome intervention of myth, Type D knowledge). Once the strategy is set for the media and the vehicles, its execution depends on up-to-date knowledge of a rapidly changing marketplace and also on the aggressiveness and the "lightness of footwork" of agency media buyers. Their goal is simple: to minimize costs per thousand. The breadth and depth of their knowledge of the marketplace is considerable (Type A). This is true in particular of the large agencies in the most sophisticated countries. We have a "guesstimate"—somewhere between Type B and Type C knowledge—that large American advertisers with considerable buying power can purchase airtime and press space at prices 5 percent to 10 percent below those paid by smaller advertisers.[75]

The Evaluation of Advertising Effects

The classic problem with attempting to evaluate the effect of advertising is how to isolate its influence from all the other forces in the marketing mix.

The Short-Term Effect of Advertising

The short-term effect of advertising can be demonstrated in at least three different ways. First, the normal procedure in firms is to evaluate sales measured by shipments from the factory, alongside retail audit and/or consumer panel estimates. Other variables are also commonly examined, such as tracking data on brand awareness and image attributes for all brands in the market. The evaluation of the effects of advertising is made on judgment. This procedure is what determines the vast majority of decisions either to increase, or to continue as before, or to reduce, or to cancel advertising campaigns. But the analyses cannot isolate the variables in any controlled, scientific way. The normal evaluation of advertising effects is therefore essentially Type B knowledge.

There is also Type B knowledge that substantial numbers of tests of increased advertising pressure yield no result in terms of extra sales, or *a fortiori* extra profit.[76]

Second, there is the construction and application of market models, a process which requires experience, judgment, substantial data inputs, and the willingness to experiment. In general, our knowledge of these procedures is Type B.

With the use of models describing advertising response functions, it is possible to isolate the *immediate* effect on sales of a single advertisement exposure or a small number of exposures, including the incremental effect of progressive exposures within the purchase interval. This is often a virtually instantaneous effect, and cases have been published which provide reasonably "hard" data on it. These models all monitor sales effects.

There is an important matter of principle regarding incremental pressure, best illustrated with the use of a piece of geometry. There are two main ways in which incremental "doses" of advertising can be shown to operate, and these are demonstrated in figure 10–1. The curve on the left is known as the concave-downward function. Its

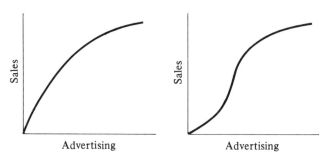

FIGURE 10–1

Advertising Response Functions

shape demonstrates that equal marginal increments on the horizontal axis (representing progressive "doses" of advertising) are associated with decreasing marginal increments on the vertical axis (representing sales stimulated by these advertising "doses"). This pattern means diminishing returns from the beginning. The curve on the right is, for obvious reasons, known as the *S-shaped function*. With their curve, at low levels of advertising—up to the bend in the S—equal marginal increments of advertising on the horizontal axis are associated with *increasing* marginal increments of sales on the vertical axis. Then, at the bend of the S, the curve changes to the shape of the concave-downward function, representing a change to diminishing returns. The place where the change in the slope of the curve takes place is known as the *inflection point.*

Note that it is nowhere suggested that increasing returns are anything but limited and temporary. The surest evidence of the truth that there is a limit to increasing returns is that there is always a ceiling on advertising expenditures; this must mean that manufacturers acknowledge that there must be a limit on increasing returns.

There is a total of eighteen well-known published cases that provide reasonable Type B evidence (better than this in certain cases) that response patterns like those in the diagrams exist with real brands. The cases demonstrate that twelve show diminishing returns, and seven show an S-shaped response.[77] (The reason why these cases provide nineteen examples is that one covers a group of brands, most of which show diminishing returns, but one of which does not.) A total of eighteen cases is too small for any quantitative extrapolation. We cannot therefore generalize about the prevalence of the two types of response pattern. Our knowledge of patterns at the macrolevel is therefore Type C.

The operational importance of this analysis is that, with the concave-downward curve of diminishing returns, an extremely strong case can be made for a policy of media dispersion: drip feeding advertising at continuous low pressure. The reason is that low pressure is relatively more productive and efficient than high pressure, because efficiency progressively declines as pressure increases. With an S-shaped response function, on the other hand, the best policy is to concentrate media weight up to the inflection point: the bend in the S at which diminishing returns begin to operate. This is why we must know where the inflection point is, and we can of course expect it to differ for different brands.

This type of generalization about the media implications of the different response functions may appear flimsy, but it is in fact extremely robust: Type A knowledge.

The analysis therefore provides specific guidelines for the degree of the concentration (the density of the flights) which should be applied to any advertising schedule; and this is a matter of considerable practical importance to media planners. This description provides the theoretical background for a debate, which has been waged in most major agencies in the United States, about the most effective frequency levels for individual brands. This level is normally deemed to be three (or more) "opportunities to see" within the brand's purchase interval. Our knowledge of agencies' widespread awareness of the effective frequency issue is Type A.

There is, however, a basic problem with this most practical application of the theory: our knowledge of actual response functions for individual brands is very thin, somewhere between Type B and Type C. The theory is excellent, but the empirical basis for applying the theory is not generally good enough because of the shortage of skill, resources, and energy to carry out the necessary econometric work. This lack of skill and resources, alongside the weak state of knowledge about scientific budget determination, represents the seventh and last of the most pressing of our problems with the state of advertising knowledge.

When advertising is working extremely directly, the response will probably conform to the concave-downward pattern, and if it is working extremely indirectly, then the S-shaped response function is likely to operate.[78] This statement represents tentative knowledge (somewhere between Types B and C), although it does manage to explain why direct-response media schedules are always dispersed (because of diminishing returns), and also why three exposures in the purchase interval are normally required for packaged-goods brands in competitive markets (to exploit increasing returns below the inflection point.)

The third device that helps us understand short-term pressure effects is the use of models constructed to measure the effect on sales of changes of absolute amounts of advertising within a budgetary period, not as short a period as the purchase interval, and in most cases a year. The use of such models can lead to a computation of the short-term advertising elasticity, which can be calculated only by regression analysis requiring a substantial number of market observations.[79] The operational value of the measure is the help it can give us in determining the optimum advertising budget level over the course of the budgetary period. This is extremely important Type B knowledge, and sometimes better than that, but it is acquired for relatively few brands.

Enough cases have been published to demonstrate conclusively, with Type A knowledge, that advertising *can* have a short-term effect. (Such an effect is of course not automatic and general, because some campaigns and/or appropriation levels and/or media plans do not work because of endemic weaknesses.) However, for examples of effectiveness, a number of cases involving campaign changes have yielded Type A knowledge that the response of sales to advertising can be immediate and very pronounced.[80]

There are also many published examples of sales increases which have resulted from increased advertising pressure but no campaign change. These rises in sales have also taken place without delay but have generally been much lower than with campaign changes. We have a number of pieces of Type B knowledge of the relatively low response of sales to increases in advertising pressure. Indeed, a brand with an average advertising elasticity (based on 128 cases) would require a 50 percent increase in advertising expenditure to bring about a short-term 10 percent boost in sales. In order to evaluate whether it pays to increase advertising, we must estimate the extra profit expected from the additional sales (including the lagged sales which come in later periods), and we must compare this profit with the cost of the advertising (Type A knowledge). In one instance of the reverse procedure (computation of the loss of profit from the sales reduction to be expected from an advertising cutback) "the model suggested that the resultant sales loss would diminish profits by 1.8 millions sterling."[81]

The Long-Term Effect of Advertising

The long-term effect of advertising can be demonstrated in at least five different ways.

First, there is the dynamic difference model mentioned in the section entitled "Advertising Budgets." This shows that, in 70 percent of a substantial sample of observed cases, there is an apparent causal relationship between a series of one-year changes in advertising pressure and a similar series of one-year changes in market share.[82] The regression provides Type A-2 knowledge (although in view of possible complications outside the model, its practical applications provide something weaker, or Type B knowledge). If the model fits, we can predict the effect on market share of a quantitative change in advertising. We can quantify the advertising-related scale economies of the larger and more successful brands in a market. We can also learn how to evaluate fairly well the effect of a campaign change on a year's sales.[83]

Second, there is the technique of the shifting demand curve. This is a relatively simple device borrowed from microeconomic theory. Only brands which sell at different prices (in different areas or at different but adjacent time periods) can be analyzed in this way, but the statistical technique is extremely easy to apply.[84] The operational value of the method is that it can enable us to make Type B estimates of the sales value (and marginal profit) yielded by the extra sales generated by a measured amount of advertising, and thus to quantify its productivity. This method is discussed in appendix A.

Third, there is the measurement of long-term advertising elasticity. The calculation calls for a large number of market observations. It does, however, make it possible to estimate the value of the repeat purchase of a brand, which can be derived from a comparison of the long-term with the short-term advertising elasticities.[85] This type of knowledge is somewhere between Types B and C. It is weaker than our knowledge of short-term elasticities, because the number of variables that have to be considered is greater, and there are also methodological problems.

The fourth method is a theoretical device for constructing families of advertising response functions, with the more efficient brands occupying a higher position on the diagram describing such functions: Brand O compared with Brand L in figure 10–2. Brand O could be a different and stronger brand than L. Alternatively, O could represent a strengthened version of L after it has received the benefit of repeat purchase and image-building advertising. The higher position of O represents the larger marginal advertising yield of the stronger brand, which is the result of its greater *overall* strength in the marketplace.[86] This method is, however, a technique with more analytical elegance than practical applicability—Type B knowledge at best.

The fifth method of evaluating the long-term effect of advertising is the adstock device, pioneered by Leo Burnett, which estimates advertising's carryover effect.[87] It is based on consumers' recall of an advertising campaign. The methodological problems of recall were raised in the discussion of day-after recall in the "Market Research" section. However, with adstock, the data are used only longitudinally and comparatively, so that the objections to recall as an evaluative device are not so serious. Adstock represents knowledge somewhere between Types B and C.

As with the techniques for short-term measurement, certain of the long-term measures can be operationally valuable. There is, how-

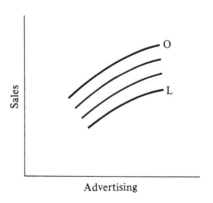

FIGURE 10–2

Advertising Response Functions for Different Brands in the Same Category

ever, one point of difference. The short-term effect of advertising, insofar as it can be efficiently isolated, is a function of the advertising alone. The long-term effect, on the other hand, is the result of the advertising working in conjunction with the added values of the brand. Indeed the reason why the advertising *has* a long-term effect different from (and invariably greater than) the short-term effect is repeat purchase, to which the added values make a major contribution. In other words, a given dose of advertising applied to different brands yields smaller or larger volumes of sales, depending on the innate strengths of the brands themselves. Larger sales results accrue to brands with more added values, and the acquisition of such added values is a long-term activity.

This concept is different from the notion that advertising may work better over the long term because when people see an advertisement for a brand, they are reminded of earlier advertisements for the same brand. Generally speaking, people, especially users of a brand, are more conscious of the brand than they are of the advertising for it. I therefore believe that an advertisement should be regarded realistically as a reminder of the brand itself, and not of previously seen advertisements. This is a contentious statement, and I would put it no higher than in the lower reaches of Type B knowledge.

The methods described in this section relate to the measurement of the advertising variable in isolation. If we wish to quantify the importance of the added values without any attempt to extract the contribution of the advertising, there are two extremely simple techniques which will do it neatly.

First, we can estimate the amount by which a successful brand's price exceeds the average of the prices of its competitors. This amount often changes over time, an increase accurately describing a strengthening of the brand. An important British brand of which I once had firsthand experience increased its price premium over the competition from 10 percent to 30 percent over the twenty-year period 1964 through 1984.[88] This device provides good Type B knowledge. And empirical work by Andrew Ehrenberg on the influence of brand differentiation on price sensitivity also provides respectable Type B evidence that strong branding reduces the price elasticity of demand for a brand.[89] This is a topic examined in appendix A.

The second and equally simple device is to carry out matched (blind and named) product tests. These enable the relative contribution of added values over and above the brand's functionality to be isolated and quantified. The measure used is the marginal extra number of consumers who discriminate in favor of the brand when it is named, beyond those who choose it blind (that is, because of its functional performance alone). This device also provides good Type B knowledge.[90]

How Does Advertising Work?

We can approach the problem of whether advertising works at a number of different levels. I shall concentrate on four (which cover part but not all of the ground) and comment on the state of our knowledge regarding each.

HOW DOES ADVERTISING WORK IN TERMS OF CONSUMER PSYCHOLOGY? We have nothing better than Type B knowledge of how advertising operates on the human mind, with the single exception of Type A knowledge that it does not work in any uniform fashion. One's first inclination is to try to find out more, although we have only Type B knowledge of what we would do with the information if we obtained it. It may help with research, and with education. But doubts remain about its potential operational value, which is why I do not put this branch of knowledge (or lack of knowledge) in the category of those things needing the most urgent attention.

There is Type B knowledge that learning, attitudes, and behavior can all be influenced in some way by advertising, although a single advertisement does not have to do all three things. But to get some real understanding of how advertising works, we need to know the order of events. This is another manifestation of the old problem of the direction of causality.

The earliest theory of psychological causality was based on a simple chain described by Charles Ramond as "learn-feel-do."[91] In this theory, people receive specific knowledge about a brand, as a result of which their attitudes toward the brand change and they develop a preference for it, and as a result of which they buy it. The term *hierarchy of effects* has been coined to describe the sequence. It has also been called the *learning hierarchy.* The theory is an old one. It has, however, been constantly disputed for a variety of reasons, the most serious of which are as follows:

1. There is Type B (perhaps Type A) evidence that communication also works in the reverse direction. Behavior influences attitudes, as people strive to reduce cognitive dissonance; indeed, probably the greatest single influence on attitudes toward a brand is people's use of it.[92] Behavior also influences learning, as a result of selective perception. In particular, users of a brand are normally those most conscious of its advertising (*pace* Rosser Reeves).

2. The theory concentrates exclusively on change (increase in learning, improvement in attitudes, and first purchase) and gives no attention to a generally unchanging pattern of consumer behavior driven mainly by repeat purchase. This pattern is general with the majority of brands (Type A knowledge).

3. The theory fails to enlighten us about certain well-established phenomena in the real world, such as the high failure rate of new brands and the continued existence of minor brands with small market shares and small advertising budgets. If change is so simple and sequential, why does it not happen more often?[93]

Perhaps most seriously, there have been only limited and artificial attempts to validate the theory empirically, and the results have not been in any way conclusive.[94] In the opinion of Michael Ray, who has been responsible for almost all the experimental work in this complex field, the learning hierarchy may possibly operate in cases in which "the audience is *involved* in the topic of the campaign and when there are clear differences between alternatives."[95] Our total state of knowledge regarding the learning hierarchy is that it may operate occasionally and in special circumstances in the real world (Type B knowledge at best).

A more pregnant theory than the learning hierarchy is the low-involvement hierarchy, first propounded in the mid-1960s by Herbert E. Krugman. This has been described as "learn-do-feel." The notion hinges on the concept of low involvement, as it applies to people's relationships to products, brands, and also media. Low involvement might be described as a lack of emotional commitment because of the essential triviality of the purchase decision for most low-price items. And with television advertising, there is a lack of consumer involvement in either brand or medium, and as a consequence, "perceptual defense may be absent. . . . persuasion as such, i.e. overcoming a resistant attitude, is not involved at all"; and commercials are received and responded to only as simple descriptions of brands. Decisions about buying are made as a result of consumers' being subjected merely to a "shifting [of] the relative salience of attributes."

This hierarchy proceeds, therefore, by changing awareness and knowledge of brands, in turn leading directly to a relatively casual purchase decision, which in turn leads to more knowledge and the development of attitudes stemming from brand use—a chain (in the words of the psychologist) of cognition-conation-affect: "With low involvement one might look for gradual shifts in perceptual structure, aided by repetition, activated by behavioral-choice situations, and *followed* at some time by attitude change."[96]

This theory is better than the learning hierarchy in two ways. First (and most important), it is compatible with the well-known fact that even if attitudes toward brands influence people's purchase of them, people's experience of brands (following purchase) has an equally important if not more important influence on their attitudes. In other words, the interaction between attitudes and behavior is two-way.

The second advantage of the Krugman theory is that it has at least some empirical basis, although this is rather flimsy. From experiments in an artificial environment carried out by Michael Ray and his colleagues on a reasonably large sample of respondents, using purchase intention and not direct behavioral measures, "it is clear that the 'Low Involvement' hierarchy occurs somewhat more often than the 'Learning' one."[97] All in all, we have Type B knowledge that the low-involvement hierarchy may operate in the cases of many packaged goods, at least in their launch phase, where the advertising has to achieve a basic cognitive result.

An extension of Krugman's hypothesis is the notion that the two hemispheres of the brain store different impressions and carry out different mental functions. The right hemisphere is supposedly concerned with pictorial impressions. The change in the salience of attributes (without the emotions' being committed), which is characteristic of low-involvement learning as described by Krugman, is thought to be essentially a right-brain function. On the other hand, verbal processes, including reading and speaking, are supposedly the function of the left brain; high involvement is concerned with the left brain. Our knowledge of the physical loci is at the lower end of Type B; but this knowledge is something which might eventually be relevant to the rather dubious sort of creative research which monitors brain waves.

In contrast to the learning hierarchy, which (if it operates at all) works with an involved consumer and clear differences between brands, the low-involvement hierarchy works with uninvolved consumers and where there are few obvious differences between the brand alternatives. But what of the cases where the functional differences between brands are of less importance than those based on *added values* which have been built by time and by advertising? In these cases, the low-involvement hierarchy does not tell the whole story.

But it does lead to a modification of the concept which has, I believe, widespread validity. This is the awareness–trial–reinforcement (ATR) theory, developed by Andrew Ehrenberg. It embraces advertising addressed to the existing user of a brand and aimed at reinforcing his or her preference for it, so that it will remain at least in its present position in the repertoire and perhaps be upgraded from occasional to regular use.

As the theory might have been described by Ramond, it is "do-feel-do," or mainly an interaction of the conative and affective processes among the existing users of a brand. A word borrowed from natural science, *resonance,* is an evocative way of expressing this continuous interaction of behavior and feelings. We have something between Type B and Type C knowledge that this effect is the norm with ongoing brands.

CAN ADVERTISING WORK WITH A SINGLE EXPOSURE? We have Type A evidence that this *can* happen in many cases.

First, there is the experience of direct response, which if it works at all, is effective with a single exposure, largely because it works as a complete advertising stimulus. This evidence is not in dispute, and it is one of the few effects of advertising we know about with Type A-1 certainty.[98]

Second, single exposures can be effective with other types of advertising. There is Type B evidence that one-exposure effectiveness may be widespread, especially with large brands. There is also Type B evidence that it is competition which may invalidate such an effect for smaller brands.

A number of informed practitioners support the possibility of advertising working on a "one-strike" basis.[99]

WHY THEN DO WE NEED TWO ADVERTISEMENTS OR MORE TO REGISTER A SALES EFFECT? Let us accept for the sake of argument that a number in excess of two strikes is required to achieve the optimum sales effect or even, in some cases, any sales effect at all. There is Type B evidence for this, as well as Type A evidence that such a conclusion is widely accepted in professional circles.

There are two logical explanations which can help us understand this phenomenon. They are separate, and in some ways they contradict one another.

The first line of reasoning is a body of psychological theory that advertising needs multiple exposure to the consumer if it is to work on his or her psyche. There is more than one expression of this theory, and the supporting evidence is respectable laboratory work on individuals' mental processes, that is, Type B knowledge.

Herbert E. Krugman developed a theory that three exposures are needed to do the following tasks, all of which, it is argued, are necessary if the advertising is to influence the consumer effectively:

1. To prompt the respondent to try to understand the nature of the stimulus, to ask the question "What is it?"
2. To prompt evaluation—"What of it?"—and recognition: "I've seen this before."
3. To remind (a stage which marks the beginning of disengagement). All the subsequent exposures function, in Krugman's theory, merely as repetitions of this third one.[100]

Krugman's work was underpinned by the extensive parallel experiments of Robert C. Grass of Du Pont, which were based on measures of respondents' attention to advertising, amounts learned, and generated attitudes: "attention increases and maximizes at two exposures, while the amount of learned information increases and maximizes at two or three exposures . . . generated attitudes are much more resistant to satiation effects than the recall of learned information."[101]

The second line of reasoning is more compatible with the possibility of single-exposure effectiveness. In fact, the argument actually stems from the assumed possibility of advertisements' working one exposure at a time. The idea is that the immediate effect of the single strike for one brand is sometimes blocked by the immediate effect of larger numbers of strikes for competing brands. The notion is expressed simply and clearly by Colin McDonald, who uses it to explain the reason for the extreme type of S-shaped response function demonstrated in a classic published case, in which the first advertising exposure triggered a negative response. The reason McDonald gives for the necessity of two exposures to achieve a positive sales effect is simply to break through the countervailing selling efforts of competitive advertising within the brand field. This is good Type B knowledge.[102]

The theory becomes very plausible if we are able to demonstrate that brands with large market shares and few competitors need less advertising frequency than do small brands with many competitors. There is some evidence that this is indeed the case.

One such piece of evidence comes from an important case using the Ad Tel split-cable television mechanism. Five brands were covered, and there is Type B evidence that the effectiveness of the first advertising strike is greater for large brands (which have little competition) than for smaller brands (which have substantial competition). This case also shows clearly that advertising for any brand has a greater effect on users than on nonusers. Since the large brand has more users than the small brand, it follows logically that, other things being equal, advertising for a large brand will have more effect than advertising for a small brand.[103]

Michael Naples demonstrated the reason why the advertising for large brands has a greater effect than the advertising for small ones.[104] This argument is based on the fact that most large brands have a share of market larger than their share of voice (that is, they underadvertise), a concept explored in chapter 5 of this book. It follows that the advertising for large brands is, dollar for dollar, more productive than that for small brands. I have estimated that in the toilet soap market, the advertising for Ivory is 3.5 times as productive as that for Tone. The inference of this conclusion (which is typical of many markets) is Type B knowledge, but the data are "hard," or Type A.

A related aspect of the greater efficiency of the advertising for large brands concerns the "penetration supercharge" (discussed in the section entitled "Products and Brands"), that is the tendency of a large brand to have a higher frequency of purchase and repurchase than a small brand has. This is the most accurate description of the concept of brand loyalty. The penetration supercharge can be described empirically, and there are Type A data for it.[105]

There are two additional pieces of Type B evidence which suggest that the factor which determines that the minimum frequency needed for a sales effect is what is necessary to break through the competitive advertising in a category.

One relates to experience in different countries. It is interesting that the inflection point in two British cases was at a low level of two or three "opportunities to see." In five American cases, it was invariably at a higher level, in most cases at about five opportunities to see. It is likely that the higher level of competitive advertising in the United States has dictated that more frequency is required to break through the amount of competitive "noise."[106]

The second point relates to experience of different media and is based on one specific case which compares radio with television. In this case, the inflection points for radio advertising are significantly higher than those for television. I believe that this disparity can be explained by the need for increased frequency to break through the high advertising clutter on radio, and also to compensate for the lower attention paid to radio than to television advertising. These effects are artifacts of competition.[107]

The argument in this section leads to the formulation of five hypotheses:

1. Single exposures have a demonstrable effect in the marketplace in very many cases; this is particularly true of larger brands. It follows that the psychological explanation that three exposures are required is not universally valid. (Type A knowledge.)

2. Three exposures may be necessary for new brands because of the psychological argument articulated by Krugman.

3. With continuous campaigns for repeat-purchase packaged goods, single exposures can be effective in psychological terms because they are in effect repeats of the result of the third advertising

exposure, which itself took place at the time of the launch. (Type B knowledge.)

4. Where a single exposure does *not* appear to work, McDonald and Naples plausibly argue that in effect it is being blocked or canceled by the parallel stimuli of advertisements for competitive brands. This is much less likely if the advertised brand has a large market share, and therefore few competitors. (Type B knowledge.)

5. The explanation in the fourth hypothesis also holds for those brands for which the first exposure may work, but additional exposures work more strongly (demonstrating increasing returns below the inflection point). This effect takes place because additional exposures work better, as they become cumulatively heavier in relation to the competition. (Type B knowledge.)

HOW CAN WE EXPLAIN THE INFLUENCE OF SHARE OF VOICE ON THE MARKET SHARES OF INDIVIDUAL BRANDS? The notion of a brand's advertising, being measured as the share of voice in a product category, is useful as an analytical tool. It is, however, misleading to expect this tool to help us understand how advertising works in human terms, that is, as a stimulus to consumers to buy a brand. People see too little advertising for individual brands and even product fields to be aware of changes in the levels of one brand in relation to others.

The way to make sense of the relationship between changes in advertising and changes in sales is to look on an advertising campaign for a brand as a large number of individual advertisements. The brand with a larger share of the advertising in a category will therefore expose more individual advertisements than a brand with a smaller advertising share. The proportions of the different numbers of advertisements will be more or less in line with the differences in the share of the total advertising.

This analysis suggests, therefore, that people respond to advertising in a very simple and direct way. They buy when they are reminded. They respond to individual exposures. The brand with a large share of voice has a schedule composed of a greater number of individual exposures, or stimuli to purchase, than a small brand has. And if changes in relative advertising pressure lead to changes in the sales of a brand, it is because there have been changes in the number of individual advertisements for that brand in comparison with its competitors. I believe this to be all Type B knowledge.

Advertising and Industry

A vast amount has been written during the past century on advertising's overall effect on the economy, on individual industries, and on typical individual manufacturers. There are, however, genuine difficulties in tracing cause-and-effect relationships, and there has been much contradiction in the findings of different investigations. The general state of knowledge is somewhere between Types B and C, confused by individual flickers of Type D.

Estimates of Advertising Expenditure

Estimates of total advertising volumes in the United States are published every year by *Advertising Age* and are the work of Robert Coen of McCann-Erickson. I shall include them in the Type A-2 category, although the quality of the estimates is better for some media than for others. The inaccuracies are, however, reasonably consistent, so that year-by-year comparisons can be regarded as robust.

International comparisons of advertising expenditures are confused by known difficulties of measurement. For instance, comparisons of United States volumes with those in other countries are normally Type D, and there is a methodological reason. The American estimates include figures for certain media (direct mail and a substantial "miscellaneous" category) which are not included in the estimates for other countries. As a result, international comparisons invariably inflate the American figures.[108] It is, however, easy to scale the American figures down (as I have done in chapter 2 of this book).

There are also deficiencies in the analyses of total advertising by category. Among the leading national advertisers in the United States (which together account for about 25 percent of all advertising), we have Type A knowledge that packaged goods account consistently for about 60 percent. But out of total advertising, this proportion probably comes down to under 40 percent (Type B knowledge). Our knowledge of the relative importance of other product fields in the advertising aggregates is equally hazy.

Advertising and Price, Advertising and Competition

These related subjects are discussed in detail in appendix A, so that it is superfluous to describe fully the main lines of the argument. Appendix A has a full bibliography, so that it is also unnecessary to detail the source material.

In summary, the state of knowledge is as follows:

1. Knowledge about advertising expenditures and advertising : sales (A:S) ratios within product categories is Type A; data on individual brands are Type B.
2. Knowledge regarding advertising's ability to raise prices over the short term is Type B.
3. Advertising's ability to make demand curves less elastic by stimulating oligopolistic differentiation is somewhere between Types B and C.
4. Knowledge of advertising's role in stimulating competition is Type B. What we know of the barriers to the entry of new competitors is also Type B. We have Type A knowledge of the stability of concentration ratios in most industries. This is presumptive evidence that entry barriers (of which advertising is not the most important) confine competitive activity to firms already established within the industry.
5. There is Type B knowledge of advertising's contribution to reducing prices over the long term by making possible the scale economies of large-scale production and marketing.
6. There is Type B knowledge of the Steiner effect: advertising's ability to increase demand elasticity at the retail level (the opposite of its effect at the manufacturer level), with a resultant downward pressure on retail margins and consumer prices.
7. There is impressionistic knowledge—between Types B and C—that advertising may be able to operate as efficiently as it does at present with lower levels of investment.
8. There is Type A evidence of advertising's subsidy to the media, and of the significant, although regressive, social benefit that flows from this subsidy.
9. There is Type B evidence that any macro effect of advertising is of minimal importance.

The economic effects of advertising are not a subject that has an immediate bearing on improving the efficiency of professional practice. It is nevertheless important that we advance our knowledge of it, for reasons beyond the (not unimportant) pursuit of truth. A firmer agreement than exists at present about advertising's contribution to competitive capitalism would make a considerable difference to the self-respect of the advertising industry. And talented and conscientious practitioners would need to spend less time and effort than many of them find it necessary to do at present in apologizing for their professional activities.

Advertising Agencies

We have Type A knowledge of the structure of the advertising agency market: the history of the business, the number of agencies, and their functions, sizes, international operations, types of organization, and profitability. I shall, however, concentrate in this section on four of the most sensitive and difficult issues[109]:

1. *Brand identity.* Advertising agencies, like advertised brands, have brand identities; and like advertised brands, they offer their clients an amalgam of functional and nonfunctional benefits. In most cases in the agency world, identity is extremely (and surprisingly) faint. My own observation, which is unscientific but based on reasonably broad experience (possibly Type B), suggests that the most senior clients in American companies (at the level, for example, of executive vice-president for marketing) perceive agencies as so similar to one another as to be almost a homogeneous mass. Such people virtually always deal with a repertoire of agencies and in most cases are knowledgeable about agencies as a result of experience from their present and previous jobs. The number of agencies which have managed to establish clear identities has been very small indeed, and in most cases they have not been able to maintain these permanently. This topic is discussed in chapter 4 of this book.

2. *Agency concentration.* There has been an increase in the concentration of the advertising agency business since the early 1970s. This was a well-established trend before the mid-1980s.[110] But the amalgamations of major agencies during the latter part of that decade naturally gave the movement a considerable boost. This is all

Type A evidence. The likely long-term effects on the agency business represent speculation rather than knowledge (Type C).

3. *Agency compensation*. The move away from the former standard 15 percent commission has been continuous, although there is still some way to go before this compensation level disappears. Official investigations among members of the Association of National Advertisers (ANA) show a continuous trend toward paying cut-rate commissions. A 1989 survey estimated that 29 percent of the members used this system, compared with 35 percent that used the full 15 percent commission and 24 percent that paid their agencies service fees based on the use of staff time. (The remaining 12 percent did not answer the question or paid their agencies in other ways.)[111] The majority of advertisers that work with cut-rate commissions or with fees pay their agencies *less* than they would have earned from 15 percent of the gross cost of space. These data are quite hard, that is, Type A, certainly as they apply to large advertisers. I have Type B evidence that there are no agencies in the United States that are still fortunate enough to maintain 15 percent commission from all their clients, although certain important clients (who must be nameless) still pay 15 percent.

The reasons the commission system will continue to erode are that it provides advantages only to large agencies and to small clients (although these are often charged substantial supplementary fees by their agencies). It is not in any way in the interest of either small agencies or large clients. And large clients, with their great bargaining power vis-à-vis their agencies, are the ones that are driving the system to the wall.

The likely effect on agencies of the continuous and (what will probably eventually be) the complete departure from 15 percent commissions is naturally a squeeze on profits. This is exacerbated by the relative reductions in above-the-line appropriations in favor of promotion below the line, the trend discussed in the section entitled "Products and Brands." Eventually, we can expect an increase in the pace of change in the advertising agency business as a whole. This may lead to an even greater emphasis on the creative product than there is at present. There will also probably be an increase in the (already Darwinian) ferocity of the competition among agencies. And great advantages will accrue to those agencies which *know* more than their competitors. These prognoses are all Type B and are partly based on my experience in Sweden, where the agency commission system had effectively broken down before the end of the 1960s.

There is Type A evidence that a handful of clients are experimenting with incentive compensation for their agencies.[112] Knowledge of its efficiency is Type C.

4. *The creative process.* I want to make three points about this:

First, it has always been surprising that creative people have always accounted for such a small proportion of an agency's staff. The normal range (estimated by head counting) is 25 percent to 28 percent. Since the agency is in the business of creating advertising, the obvious question is: What functions do the 72 percent to 75 percent of agency people who are not in creative departments actually perform? We have Type A data on their job descriptions, but our knowledge is Type C about whether agencies could make do with many fewer people in administration.

Second, agencies spend more time (and considerably more of the time of their senior staff) in evaluating advertising than in writing it. This is the natural result of the relatively small number of creative people. The recommendation of a major creative proposal to the client invariably involves disposing of a number of alternatives in favor of the selected offering. This disposal is made, on occasion, with the help of research, but far more often it is done on the basis of judgment alone. From what we know of the fallibility of human judgment about whether an advertisement will actually sell, it is certain that vast numbers of babies have been flushed away with the bathwater: enormous waste is involved.[113] This is Type B knowledge.

The commission system has in the past actively discouraged agencies from using better methods of discriminating between creative alternatives (for example, marketplace experimentation). The progressive reduction in rates of commission is providing even greater discouragement. This is Type B knowledge.

And third, opinion is widely expressed that there is a shortage of creative talent coming into the agency business. In my opinion, major agencies are using crude and essentially ineffective tools to locate such talent. The problem is the agencies' mind-set. Although they deplore the lack of fresh talent, they behave as if there were too much of it. They operate like account groups, by a process of discarding the bathwater, irrespective of the babies in it. This is also Type B knowledge.

Advertising and the Consumer

It would take a lifetime's study to cover even impressionistically the relationship between advertising and the consumer, on an overall or "macro" level. I shall consider only four issues.

Advertising's Power to Manipulate

There are isolated examples of people having been cheated by advertising, but these are sufficiently rare to suggest that there is Type B evidence that manipulation by advertising is very much the exception and not the rule. There are two pieces of presumptive evidence plus two arguments to support the case that advertising in most circumstances is not manipulative.

The presumptive evidence is that:

1. The rate of failure of new brand introductions is very high. This rate clearly suggests that advertising is not a strong enough force to create a consumer franchise on its own.[114]
2. Advertising is unable to compensate for relative functional deficiencies in existing brands. If a better competitor comes onto the market, existing brands will lose market share, despite the existence in many cases of substantial nonfunctional added values.[115]

The two arguments which suggest advertising to be nonmanipulative are, first, that people are exposed to very little of it for any individual brand. For most brands the average amount of exposure per consumer can be measured in *minutes* per year. Moreover, the human mind has a self-protective mechanism in selective perception: the brain unconsciously "zaps" more easily than the button on the television control. The second argument is that advertisements operate in a competitive environment, and the battle of competitive advertising stimuli tends to result in a mutual cancellation of their effect.

Advertising *can*, however, have power. But this is most commonly in its ability to reflect and reinforce consumers' perceptions of a brand, and it operates best with existing consumers. This ability has nothing much in common with manipulation. A better way of describing advertising is with the analogy in the well-known parable told by the pioneer market research Alfred Politz. This is very far from what manipulation is all about.[116] This is Type B knowledge.

Knowledge of "subliminal" advertising is clearly Type D (see chapter 3 in this book). There is Type A evidence that the widely reported original test in New Jersey never took place. Indeed there is Type B evidence that the movie house which was the site of the test never actually existed.

The Ethics of Advertising

Our awareness of the ethical issues involved in advertising—encouragement of materialism, absolute versus selective truth, and effects on vulnerable minorities—is reasonably complete (Type A), but our resolution of the issues is only (and *can* perhaps be only) Type B.

This is a world of value judgments, and the organizations best qualified to make value judgments are the churches. In the view of the more liberal branches of the Christian faith, such as the Anglicans, advertising is an ethically neutral issue.[117] the Jesuits, as might be expected, tend to adopt a more searching attitude, and they separate advertising's informative from its persuasive role. (This separation is actually rooted in classical economics.) Informative advertising is considered ethically neutral, but the persuasive variety is less than fully acceptable. There are two circumstances which can legitimize persuasive advertising from an ethical point of view. The first is its ineffectiveness: advertising is much weaker than many people think. Second, there must be no intention to mislead, even if persuasive advertising does in effect succeed in misleading through sins of commission or omission.[118] From my experience of advertising practice, I would expect many advertising people to share these views.

For a well-written and persuasive statement of the position of the most interested parties in the debate, advertising agencies, readers should look at an essay by Tom Corlett.[119] He concludes with an unanswerable argument: The more we accept the possibility that advertising can mislead, the more we must also accept the proposition that the business requires honest men to practice it.

Readers will note that I have not referred so far in this section to controls on advertising. These have a special and in some way paradoxical place in the debate about advertising and ethics.

Controls on Advertising

The problem with controls on advertising is that they are an implicit recognition that advertising can operate against the public interest. If it could not, controls would not be needed.

Regarding controls as a whole, we have Type A knowledge of their range of operation, Type B knowledge of their desirability, and Type C knowledge of their real efficiency.

Our Type A knowledge concerns the ramifications of the control systems in the United States:

- at the federal level
- at the state level
- self-regulation within the advertising industry
- individual action by consumers, journalists, and so on

Generally speaking, federal controls are exceedingly efficient, although selective in their operation. Federal Trade Commission (FTC) scrutiny of advertising is a fading power at the moment because of a shortage of staff in the Washington bureaucracy. FTC action operates as a force in the background, by threat rather than by active participation.

State regulations are (or were until recently) of peripheral importance. They are concerned with matters like the control of billboard advertising and small details of advertising copy, such as what store-opening times can be inserted in liquor advertisements. However, in a notable recent case of misleading advertising, a campaign for Volvo cars, legal proceedings were instituted by the attorney general of Texas. This is a dramatic instance of a state's stepping in because of the inaction of the FTC.[120] The activities of the Texas Attorney General appear not to be stopping with Volvo.

Self-regulation is of two sorts: first, regulation by the media (notably by the television networks, and also by a small number of influential magazines); second, post hoc regulation by the ramshackle edifice of the National Advertising Division (NAD)/National Advertising Review Board (NARB)/Better Business Bureaus. Of these two, the scrutiny by the networks is sharp and highly efficient. The second, which represents the advertising industry's self-proclaimed policing mechanism, is almost entirely ineffectual, judged by the small number of cases that are reviewed in any year.

From my own observation, individual action by consumers, especially when supported by journalists, is an efficient way of blowing the whistle on advertisers that operate flagrantly against the public interest.

This discussion has concentrated so far on the control systems that exist. I have not made any value judgment on the desirability of advertising regulations. Our knowledge of this issue is Type B at best. It can strongly be argued that regulation encourages potentially dishonest advertisers to sail close the wind, and that they would behave with greater probity if the law made it easier for consumers to sue for civil damages. But essentially, the whole question of advertising regulation is a matter of politics, concerned in the main with threats of legislation and how the advertising industry is able to duck away from them. Enoch Powell's contribution to this debate (appendix B of this book) is an important one.

Our knowledge of the effectiveness of the regulations is Type C. Only the television networks and certain of the major magazines take the trouble to scrutinize advertising *before* its appearance. All the other controls require the offending advertisement actually to have appeared and the damage to be done. They are therefore not so much controls as attempts to close stable doors. No estimates have been made of how many advertisements which appear in the American media can be construed as misleading in whole or in part. Estimates for the United Kingdom, based on sample surveys, suggest a range of 1 percent to 5 percent of all advertising.[121] This is a substantial total in absolute terms, but there is no evidence at all that the situation in the United States is even approximately similar.

Public Attitudes toward Advertising

There is reasonable information on public attitudes toward advertising. The source of the data is a series of surveys carried out by the Harvard Business School in 1964, 1967, and 1974. Since the findings are so out of date, it is difficult to classify them as better then

Type B.[122] But there are five more-or-less well-established points which judgment suggests may still hold.

First, advertising was not a salient issue to most people. When people were asked "which three or four items (on a prompt list) you and your friends talk about most" only about 14 percent in 1974 included advertising. Among issues at the top of people's minds, advertising took bottom place on the list.

Second, opinions about advertising were mixed, but favorable attitudes were rather more prevalent than unfavorable ones. There was a large group of people in the middle who apparently had no strong feelings, and this finding jibes with the point made already about the low saliency of advertising. Outright rejectors of advertising were in a minority: about 12 percent. And more people approved of advertising's informative function than of its role as a persuasive force.

Third, attitudes tended not to change much over time, although there was an indication in the 1970s that advertising was then creeping up in importance in people's attitudes, although it was still at a low level.

Fourth, there was a wide difference in acceptability among different advertisements. In a number of individual cases, two thirds and more of the respondents found the advertisement annoying. But in many other cases, the respondents tolerated them and, in some cases, even appeared to enjoy them.

Fifth, there is a gap in our knowledge. This concerns public attitudes toward advertising which is addressed to potentially vulnerable minorities, particularly children. Not much is known robustly about advertising for children. The best work is based on extrapolations from the studies of the cognitive psychologist Jean Piaget, which suggest that children become relatively sophisticated at an earlier age than many people think. Between the ages of eight and ten (sometimes even earlier), children are apparently capable of discriminating between television programs and television advertisements. Interestingly enough, the most thought-provoking analyses of the effects of television on children do not distinguish between the effects of television programs and television advertisements.[123] This is all Type B knowledge. However, the Type A knowledge that American children under the age of eleven view on average more than three hours of television per day is reasonable testimony that parents are not on the whole disturbed by their offspring's vulnerability to commercial exploitation.[124]

Summary

1. In this chapter I have dredged a pool and caused more than 170 objects to float to the surface. Many of these are similar to one another and are probably chips from the same submerged log.[125]

2. There is, in other words, much connection and duplication among the individual pieces of knowledge or lack of knowledge included in this inventory. And I have also made no attempt to weight the pieces of knowledge or lack of knowledge according to their relative importance. This is something that varies greatly, but many of the most important pieces of knowledge are in the categories of Types C and D.

3. For the reasons given in the last paragraph, and also because my classification of the data is subjective, I want to analyze the different pieces of knowledge only in an impressionistic way. Here is a percentage breakdown of the different categories, based on the total of 170 different pieces of knowledge. These percentages represent nothing more than orders of magnitude.

Type A	35%
Type B	46%
Type C	10%
Type D	7%
Type E	2%

4. Although, as explained, the totals are only approximate, 35 percent represents respectable knowledge (Type A), and 48 percent represents quasi-respectable knowledge (Types B and E). The remaining 17 percent of the total (Types C and D) is disreputable and needs urgent attention.

5. It is unrealistic to expect that all that needs to be done will be done over the short or medium term. In particular, I believe that the enormous Type B category can be tackled effectively only if the job is done slowly and progressively. However, immediate attention

should be directed to Types C, D, and E. These together represent about one fifth of the total.

6. Readers will remember that during the course of this chapter, I have flagged seven pieces of knowledge which, because of their importance, deserve our most urgent action. These are all in the Type C, D, and E categories.

    a. The unsatisfactory nature of the knowledge necessary to improve our success in new brand introductions.

    b. An inadequate formal understanding of the marketing and advertising implications of what is known about consumers' buying patterns in stationary markets.

    c. The lack of any reliable mechanism for forecasting the selling power of an advertisement.

    d. Our virtually complete lack of knowledge of the central process in developing creative ideas: the imaginative leap.

    e. The inadequacy of our knowledge of whether the craft rules which apply to direct response apply equally to general advertising.

    f. The scarcity of reliable knowledge of how consumers actually *use* media for information and entertainment. What is the relationship between the different media and their audiences?

    g. The patchiness of our knowledge of advertising's sales effects; the inadequacy of our methods of determining advertising budgets; and also the inadequacy of our techniques for planning the detailed patterns of advertising schedules (for example, the density of advertising flights).

These seven points provide a skeleton on which chapter 11 is partially constructed. That chapter deals with practical proposals for closing some of the gaps in our knowledge, as well as other ways of improving the efficiency of the advertising enterprise.

Fifty Proposals for Action

Madamina, il catalogo è questo . . .

Lorenzo da Ponte, Don Giovanni

This chapter is intended to be specific, forward-looking, and constructive. It contains fifty proposals for increasing the efficiency of advertising and thereby reducing waste. These are all rooted in conclusions drawn from the earlier chapters of this book. I have, however, tried to avoid another summary of these chapters' contents. Instead, I have aimed at a synthesis of the most important lessons that have emerged, and I have added thoughts to many of these in order to make them less academic and more easily actionable. In view of the length of the discussion in the earlier chapters, each of the points is made here relatively briefly. The majority of the recommendations are positive, that is, things to do; a minority are negative, that is, things to avoid doing. There is considerable emphasis on research and on various types of market experimentation.

The proposals in this chapter are numbered sequentially from 1 to 50, and they are broken down into nine separate sections. The first two of these are devoted to recommendations to advertisers and to agencies, respectively. The succeeding sections are addressed to the seven major gaps in our knowledge of advertising and its effects which emerged from the inventory in chapter 10. This method of presentation will make it easier for readers to locate the recommendations most relevant to them. I have not grouped my proposals according to my view of their relative importance, but I urge readers to pay particular attention to recommendations 9, 12, 13, 17, 39, and 47.

The majority of my recommendations have a substantial but un-

266 · How Much Is Enough?

stated price tag. A number of them propose employing more people, particularly in agencies. Even more of them suggest new and additional research. The present pressure on agency margins and the prevalent agency policy of reducing staff in order to maintain profit are obviously impediments to implementing the things I suggest. Nevertheless, if agencies were to succeed in moving to a remuneration system based on fees for the use of staff time (recommendation 12), I believe that this move would greatly improve their chances of boosting their income to cover specific planned expenditures. I must also emphasize that the reductions in waste that I visualize are intended to improve the efficiency of billions of dollars' worth of advertising. My proposals—extravagant as they are—would cost only a fraction of the anticipated savings.

Advice to Advertisers

1. Consumers and Competitors

Advertisers who have created major brands have done so invariably by concentrating on their existing and potential *consumers* (that is, their own consumers and also those of other brands in the category). There is a tendency today for advertisers to have their attention drawn away to their competitors in the marketplace, a change which has had serious ill effects.

In 1985, a major advertiser altered the formula of its best-selling brand to make it nearer to that of the closest competitor. This was done for fear of losing business to that competitor. The majority of the existing customers liked the existing formula and therefore did not take to the new one. The result was dire consequences for the advertiser (which was, of course, Coca-Cola).[1]

The vigorous response by competitors in a category to a single manufacturer that tries to establish a market niche has been the main cause of the astonishing fragmentation which has been such a feature of consumer goods marketing in the 1980s and early 1990s. This fragmentation—a doubling of the total number of brands and line extensions over the course of the decade—led to a splintering of consumer franchises and a loss of scale economies. It was a movement that was not always consumer-driven; indeed, in most cases, it was the result of "follow the leader," as one manufacturer imitated another.

2. *Two Purposes for Every Marketing Activity*

The first aim of every marketing activity should be to generate long-term profit. This is generally (although not invariably) the result of advertising's influence on sales. In addition, however, there should always be a second objective: increased knowledge. This means that every marketing program—brand launch, restaging, advertising campaign, and promotion—should be evaluated with the help of good research, and a best estimate should be made of its short- and long-term productivity. If this productivity is zero or negative, this may be discouraging, but it is itself an important and usable piece of knowledge.

3. *Brand Stewardship*

The manufacturer is the custodian and steward of every brand it markets, although with advertising-intensive brands, the agency often develops over time a role almost as important as that of the manufacturing company. But the company must assume the ultimate role as guardian of the brand, in view of its fiduciary responsibility to its stockholders. Because of the ability of established brands to generate long-term as well as short-term profit, such brands should not be lightly abandoned, nor should they be neglected because of the allure of new ventures. Custody of the brand implies that the manufacturer should assemble, codify, and *use* in marketing the accumulated knowledge generated by the brand.

4. *Expectations for Advertising*

a. The manufacturer should develop a series of realistic, experience-based guidelines for what its advertising can be expected to accomplish, and the specific ways in which this advertising can be anticipated to do its job. This procedure will help to set targets against which advertising performance can be judged.

b. Ideally the manufacturer should be able to make an approximate quantitative estimate of how much a brand's sales variability can be attributed to defined increments of advertising.

c. It should also be possible to estimate (again quantitatively) the degree to which advertising is able to influence surrogates for sales measures, notably impressions in the consumer's mind of the brand name and the brand's image attributes.

d. In all circumstances, the manufacturer should understand that advertising must be integrated with all other parts of the marketing mix. Advertising is gravely handicapped if it does not work in cooperation with the other stimuli to sales of the brand.

5. Judgment and Research

Market research unconnected with marketing judgment is dangerous. But judgment unsupported by research is generally worse. The advertiser should devote much attention to recognizing the degree to which decisions should depend on research, including what research the advertiser believes in. The planned balance of judgment and research should be inoculated into the company bloodstream. Most manufacturers should be prepared to spend more money than they do at present on research. This is a general recommendation, and many of the proposals in this chapter deal with specific types of research for defined problems.

Equally important, I believe that businesspeople should spend more time than they do at present in *thinking*. As a person who came to academe after a business career, I am astonished when I look back at the high proportion of their time that my clients and colleagues used to spend on "busy work" (for example, attending meetings, dictating letters and memoranda, traveling, and entertaining), and how little they spent coolly and objectively contemplating their businesses and where these were going. Such contemplation is all too often relegated to unplanned intervals during journeys—and even then, businesspeople often have to plod through a turgid mound of reports and briefing papers.

The situation is worse in America than in Europe, although Europe is catching up with the worst of American practice. The hour at which the ambitious American businessman arrives at his desk in the morning—normally shortly after dawn—has always struck me essentially as a symbol of personal superiority, even of virility. It is a statement about the businessman himself, and hardly a discipline that automatically ensures high performance.

6. *Preconceptions about Styles of Advertising*

The advertiser has a right to expect that its advertising will achieve certain predetermined objectives. The advertiser should, however, avoid rigid preconceptions of *how* particular types of advertisement will do their job. In particular, the advertiser should resist the temptation to force its agency to follow a particular style (for example, slice of life, product demonstration, or unique selling proposition). One of the things we know with certainty is that advertising does not operate in a uniform way. Therefore for a manufacturer to assume that a single style of advertising is always the best one is to narrow its own thinking and to make its agency operate in blinkers.

7. *The Client's Role and the Agency's Role*

The relative roles of client and agency should be worked out and specified in every contract between advertiser and agency. There are many areas of responsibility that are traditionally ill defined, for example: Who should be responsible for developmental research and who for evaluative research? How much should the agency be involved in new product development? Who should take the initiative in contingency planning? The financial difficulties which stem from an unclear division of responsibilities would become much simpler if agencies were to succeed in moving to fee-based compensation (see recommendation 12). I believe that the points made in this paragraph are more important than the rather trivial details often written into agency contracts. These documents would generally benefit by being made much simpler than many of them are at present.

8. *How Manufacturers Should Manage Advertising*

Advertisers should make a serious effort to solve the deep-seated organizational problem of managing their advertising. This often relates to an unclear definition of who the real advertising decision makers are in any organization. Brand managers, who can say no but are not empowered to say yes, are invariably forced to steer advertising proposals through many ascending steps in a company's hierarchy. This is a system notorious for diffusing the initial focus of an advertising idea and encouraging safe rather than bold solutions to advertising problems. It has also encouraged the use of spurious quantitative measures of advertising efficacy. Understandably, the system has been widely criticized.

A small number of advertisers have experimented with new management systems, with partial although not complete success. In some cases, a senior staff adviser specializing in advertising content is consulted by brand managers whenever the agency presents creative proposals. In other cases, senior managers who are empowered to approve recommendations must attend major presentations by the agency.

However, the organizational control of advertising by most advertisers is unsatisfactory, and even worse is their lack of awareness that their system is often bad enough to be counterproductive.

9. Integrated Communications

The 1980s witnessed the quiet (initially almost imperceptible) spread of a far-reaching change in marketing practice. This was the broadening of the spectrum of communications planned centrally to encompass advertising, direct response, data base marketing, consumer promotions, trade promotions, public relations, and corporate communications. Such a broadening is entirely harmonious with how consumers view a brand: as a totality.

Manufacturers in the 1990s not only should be conscious of what is happening but should be geared organizationally to exploit the synergies of integrated communications. This means a change in their mind-set, and this is something that must also be reflected and echoed by the agency (it goes far beyond cross-selling a range of agency services to individual clients). The concept of integrated communications is a gestalt, that is, a method of looking at a brand's communications strategy in aggregate or global terms, rather than as a group of coordinated strategies for individual activities.

10. Contingency Planning (Development of Alternatives)

Advertising campaigns (with extremely rare exceptions) have a finite life. Campaigns should not however be changed until they stop "pulling": or, to be more precise, until a very short while *before* this happens. But the client and agency then need an alternative. This means that they should have carried out contingency planning while the current campaign was running with apparently full effect.

Such contingency planning is extremely rare in the real world. But it is by no means unknown. Brooke Bond Oxo, an important British food company acquired by Unilever a few years ago, began in the 1960s to commission its agency to generate alternative advertising ideas for its Oxo brand of bouillon cubes. Not only have these advertising ideas been developed to the stage of finished commercials, but alternative campaigns have been exposed and evaluated in area tests while the main campaign has run in the rest of the country. This expensive and in some ways disheartening policy has paid off in an astonishing way during the long and successful history of the brand.[2]

11. *The Company as a Brand*

Many manufacturers have allowed an unclear relationship to develop between their brand name(s) and their company name. The majority of companies concentrate more attention on each individual brand name, since this name normally has its own reasonably well-defined consumer franchise. There are nevertheless advantages in exploiting the favorable associations of the company name. These associations are complicated. For instance, it is usually unwise to try to save advertising money by launching new products under an "umbrella" name. Yet a company or umbrella name can provide the manufacturer with some advantages with consumers and considerable advantages vis à-vis the retail trade. Manufacturers should develop a clear policy on this matter, which has an operational bearing on packaging and also on advertising. The eventual objective of a successful integration of brand name(s) and company name is the type of synergism possessed by companies like Hershey, S. C. Johnson, and Kellogg's.

Advice to Agencies

12. *Fees versus Commission*

There was a strong move during the 1980s for clients to pay their agencies at reduced rates of commission (often on a sliding scale).

This is a pernicious arrangement. It enables clients to curtail what they see as the excessive profitability to agencies of the traditional 15 percent commission level. However, reduced commission puts a large—and often progressive—bite on agency profits, and it forces agencies to cut into the fat and eventually into the muscle of their staff, often by getting rid of people whose productivity becomes manifest only over the long term, but who may nonetheless be important contributors to the business. Commission also provides agencies with no safety net at all in the event of reductions in client billings. This is a very common situation in today's marketplace; indeed stagnation or even decline in real terms is the most likely long-term prospect for the advertising business as a whole (although some sectors of the business are likely to grow at the expense of others).

It seems to me pressingly important for agencies to persuade each of their clients to pay them service fees according to the time that the staff spends on the client's business and also to cover out-of-pocket expenses. Reasonable profit can be included in such fees. And the small number of clients who are experimenting with incentive systems, by which agencies receive extra pay for superior work, would probably permit this experimentation to continue in a fee-based arrangement. Fee systems are invariably difficult to work out, but the even greater problems associated with reduced commissions should force agencies to bite the bullet and work at solving the difficulties of fee remuneration.

A move to service fees is a very important recommendation, because I believe that many agencies are at the moment understaffed in specific departments, notably the creative department and also for strategic planning (the function which is called *account planning* in Britain, but which is hardly carried out at all in American agencies). Service fees are used by only about one fourth of the major clients in the United States. But a more general spread of this system is in my opinion the key to making it possible for agencies to increase significantly the depth and efficiency of service which they need to provide their clients.

One major and long-established New York agency (whose name I am not allowed to disclose) has succeeded in persuading most of its clients to accept service fees, so that 80 percent of its income currently comes from fees and only 20 percent from commission. This is the only agency I know which, in the early 1990s, is reasonably optimistic about the future.

13. Sales Effects of Advertising: Part One
(see also Recommendation 47)

Agencies must pay more than pay lip service to the notion that advertising sells brands. It is still extremely common for agencies (and clients) to be unable to demonstrate statistically the results of the advertising they expose. When they are challenged about this, there is a tendency for agencies to respond defensively about building images, changing consumer perceptions, and generating long-term sales. My own experience has taught me that without a short-term effect, advertising will never have a long-term effect.

Agencies should not shy away from accountability. Specifically, they should look for some or all of the following marketplace effects:

a. An immediate influence of advertising on the brand's penetration (that is, user base). An increase in penetration will normally mean an increase in sales. The maintenance of constant penetration in a shrinking category will boost the brand's market share.

b. An immediate influence of advertising on the brand's purchase frequency. An increase in purchase frequency will generally mean an increase in sales. Holding a constant level of purchase frequency in a declining category will increase a brand's market share.

c. An immediate sales response, insofar as it can be robustly attributed to advertising. Such an assessment often, but not always, calls for an econometric analysis of sales.

d. A gradual increase in the price consumers are willing to pay for the brand. This is often expressed by the manufacturer's ability to reduce gradually the proportion of total sales made with promotions. The influence on price is an important but long-term effect of advertising and is invariably preceded by one or more of the short-term effects described in the three preceding paragraphs.

14. Historical Data

Clients are obviously the custodians of the historical data relating to their own brands. Agencies, which generally have a broader experience of markets than their clients have individually, should be repositories of an extremely wide range of historical data, in particular about the effects of previous advertising on the sales of the range of brands they handle. There are also great possibilities of cross-fertilization of experience between brands in sometimes completely unconnected fields. Despite the value of historical information, in practice it is only rarely looked at and virtually never used by agencies. A senior executive of a major agency recently told me that in his organization every effort to establish principles based on past experience—or even to persuade people working on accounts to examine relevant historical data—had been quite unavailing. This is a sad commentary on the corporate culture of that agency. The situation is sometimes better in smaller agencies.

The coming of the agency conglomerates in the 1980s actively discouraged the valuable but laborious process of learning from the past. As an example, when the WPP Group acquired J. Walter Thompson, WPP immediately dismantled both the company archive and the management committee concerned with studying how advertising works and planning educational programs for the staff. And when WPP bought Ogilvy & Mather, it was not long before the Ogilvy Center for Research and Development was disbanded. It is difficult to think of more striking examples of short-term thinking—of eating the seed corn.

15. Advertising Strategy

One obvious method of increasing the efficiency of advertising—or rather of improving the chances of generating effective advertising—is to write the best possible strategy for the brand advertised. Without going into details (which will be found in chapters 7 and 8), I shall only remind readers that the advertising strategy describes where the brand is to be found on its competitive map. The strategy describes the brand's source of business in terms of the brand(s) that the target group are now using, giving due attention to current and lapsed users of the brand itself. It then isolates the brand's functional motivators and discriminators, as well as its nonfunctional discriminators, those that describe its personality. In addition, the strategy outlines the specific role of the advertising.

Most agencies do not make a good job of writing strategy on the basis of a thorough analysis of their clients' businesses, and their work is growing worse as the pressures on agency profit cause the work load of each staff member to become greater. It is ironic and also unfair that clients should complain that agencies are becoming weaker in strategic thinking: "Agencies are bad strategy partners. They don't immerse themselves in our business."[3] Yet it is the reductions in agency income forced by the clients themselves which have caused agency staffs to be so thinly stretched that agencies are unable to find the time to evaluate their clients' brands objectively and rigorously before they start writing advertisements for them.

It is no coincidence that London agencies, which employ account planners (people thoroughly imbued with the strategic relationship between the brand and its consumers), are also more often paid by service fees than American agencies are.[4] This wider use of fees carries an obvious lesson for United States practice.

I am not necessarily recommending the appointment of account planners on the British model in American agencies (although the system might work in a few of the smaller U.S. organizations). The culture of American agencies, certainly the longer established ones, encourages account executives to be the people most concerned with strategy development. The point I am making is that the job needs to be done much better than it is at present. Agencies are much more concerned with the short than with the long term. I believe that they should direct their thoughts much more to the latter, and they have to be paid for it. Again, fees based on the time spent by the staff will be the key.

16. *Volume of Creative Output*

The best advice I ever received when I was new to the advertising agency business was "Underpromise and overdeliver."

If agencies are to carry out more contingency planning than at present, and if they will also be required to generate an increased number of alternative ideas as a result of a more rigorous evaluation of running campaigns, then agencies will have to add to their pool of creative talent. Adding more creative staff again forces us to return to the present pressures on agency profits. It is in the clients' interests for their agencies to provide a richer creative service as well as a better standard of strategic thinking. In order to pay for such services, clients must be persuaded that fees based on the time spent by the staff are the most equitable arrangement for agencies and the best system to ensure that agencies will deliver the goods.

17. Creative Recruitment

Agencies find it particularly difficult to locate and recruit talented newcomers for their creative departments. One of the problems is that there are vast numbers of applicants with a widely varying range of talent, and agencies are inefficient in sifting this applicant pool.

For the initial screening of applicants' portfolios, many agencies employ "creative managers," specialized staff who, strangely enough, are not themselves creative people. The first cut is invariably based on the applicants' ability to produce professional-looking press advertisements. Ninety percent of applicants are rejected at this initial stage. I believe that these 90 percent often include the most promising conceptual thinkers. The initial selection is made according to the wrong criteria: the finish and craft displayed by the layouts in the portfolio. Potential art directors stand a better chance of selection than potential copywriters do.

Most agencies are reluctant to experiment with alternative systems, but a few are successful at it. J. Walter Thompson, New York, has had remarkable success with a copy test open to anybody (answers are sent in by mail). My own teaching experience has encouraged me to believe that a few typical pieces of a student's written work (not necessarily advertising copy) will provide good evidence of whether the writer has anything new to say.

J. Walter Thompson, Scandinavia, developed a system by which the agency would experiment with promising but unproven talent by getting these people to work on real creative assignments. The newcomers would operate for a day or two as members of the agency's creative department. It was a system that worked.

It is trite but nevertheless true to say that the health of the advertising business has always depended on the agencies' capacity to generate effective advertising. Locating and nurturing new supplies of creative talent is the only way by which agencies can ensure that they will have a prosperous future. They must do a better job of this than they do at present.

18. Research for Advertising Development

Qualitative research during the development of campaigns does not guarantee that the campaigns will be successful. Nevertheless, such research is very effective in locating problems and sharpening and improving creative ideas. Agencies should make it a firm rule that they should not finalize any major creative recommendation without an input from the consumer through qualitative research. It is in the agency's as well as the client's interest to use research, and carrying it out should be an agency initiative.

19. Agency Culture

A recognizable culture results in a strong agency. But there are dangers in a culture that is too dominating. In particular, it is counterproductive for an agency to dictate a uniform style of advertising and/or a uniform media strategy and/or a single type of research for all its clients. A good rule to follow is that the agency culture should be concerned with ends and not means. This concern is harmonious with the nature of advertisements themselves. It is appropriate for an agency to have clear ideas about what its advertising should accomplish and how it should do its job, for example, achieve an immediate behavioral effect, or build added values to encourage repeat purchase, or reflect the psychographics of the target group. It narrows the agency's thinking if the agency culture grows so strong that it dictates (explicitly or implicitly) that these tasks can be accomplished only by one particular creative or media approach, or by a single type of planning procedure.

The culture of the agency should also not act as a barrier to recruiting people who are bold enough to question it. The culture should not be allowed to stifle or to make life so uncomfortable for mavericks that they will quit the agency in frustration.

New Brand Development

20. New Brands versus Existing Brands

It is an almost universal rule that existing brands are more important to manufacturers than new brands are. Existing brands are a source of repeat business and scale economies. New brands are a hazardous venture, with a greater chance of failure than success.

New brand launches always mean a trade-off of resources and management time between an uncertain future with the new brands and the (often) very profitable present with existing brands. This trade-off is especially evident with line extensions—brand stretching—by which new products using an existing brand name can endanger the strength and integrity of the original brand. Line extensions have led directly to the fragmentation of brand franchises which has been such a devastating feature of consumer markets since the early 1980s.

My first and strongest recommendation in this section is that manufacturers restrain their enthusiasm for new brand activity, and in particular their urge to follow their competitors into every market niche that opens up.

21. Brand Development versus Brand Exploitation

The development stage of a new brand includes locating the market opportunity, doing the laboratory work on the formula, doing the fundamental design work, positioning the brand, producing trial batches, testing the product, and designing and researching the packaging. The exploitation stage includes advertising, promotions, test marketing, and rolling the brand out into a wider market.

It has been traditional with most manufacturing companies in the United States for the exploitation stage to be treated as more important than the initial development.[5] In view of the high failure rate of new brands, a very strong case can be made for reversing these priorities.

22. Demonstrable Functional Performance

The most important single cause of the failure of new brands is an inability to provide functional superiority over the brands from which it is hoped to take business.[6]

I therefore repeat the recommendation of A. C. Nielsen that no new brand be launched without a minimum preference in blind product testing of 60:40 (ideally 65:35) over the direct competition. It is normally impossible to achieve this ratio in overall preference covering all aspects of the brand, but it should be a required measure for the key functional characteristics of the new brand that will be exploited in the advertising.

23. Protection of Existing Brands

A manufacturer's existing brands are potentially vulnerable to successful new brands from competitors. It is therefore in the manufacturer's interest to maintain the *relative* functional excellence of its existing brands. This means continuously upgrading their performance. The best discipline to focus attention on this upgrading is to carry out regular blind product tests of the manufacturer's brand against its main competitors (also on occasion to conduct similar tests of the existing formula of the manufacturer's brand against the original formula).

24. Study of New Brands by Comparisons of Successes and Failures

Manufacturers and their agencies should be in a position to locate and isolate substantial numbers of new brand successes, both their own and their competitors'. Alongside the successes, even larger numbers of failures should also be available for examination.

With this data base, what should now be done is to work backward. By comparing successes and failures—how they were planned and exploited—it should not be too difficult to isolate factors which have had a decisive influence on success or failure. Some high-level mathematics may be called for, although a commonsense interpretation of the data will probably reveal the most salient points. Working backward in the way recommended here has a good chance of providing usable findings. Published work by Peckham[7] and Davidson,[8] carried our along similar lines, has given us some of our best clues to the factors that have exercised the strongest influence on successful new brands. Peckham's and Davidson's conclusions are of course general, and not specifically related to any particular manufacturer's business.

This type of post hoc research aimed at uncovering general lessons must be carried out by disinterested and appropriately qualified people, and this recommendation implies that manufacturers and agencies must consider the matter important enough to commit the necessary resources. The existing failure rate for new brands is a powerful argument in favor of this recommendation.

Stationary Markets

25. The Role of Habit

Clients and agencies should accept the habit plays a leading role in maintaining the sales levels of most repeat-purchase packaged goods. It explains why stationary markets are so commonly found in the real world and why advertising acts so often as a reinforcement—in accordance with the weak force theory. Creatively, such advertising should address existing users and should concentrate mainly on the nonfunctional discriminators of the brand, since its functional features will already be familiar to users.

26. Tracking Studies: Part One
(see also Recommendation 34)

The best way of assessing how well advertising reinforces a brand's image attributes is by carrying out regularly repeated research (generally every twelve months) covering awareness, trial, and repeat purchase of all brands in the category. This research should explore consumers' brand awareness, how much consumers associate individual brands with specific functional and nonfunctional qualities, and which brands they buy regularly and infrequently.

This research does not establish precisely whether awareness of image attributes—and in particular a strengthening of these attributes in consumers' minds—is a result of advertising, or brand purchasing, or both. However, it is a reasonable confirmation that the advertising is working effectively if any of the following take place:

a. Sales remain reasonably constant while the image attributes in general improve.

b. There are improvements in public awareness of the specific qualities of the brand that are featured in the advertising.

c. There are improvements in qualities communicated implicitly rather than directly by the advertising, for example, consumers' belief that Andrex toilet tissue provides good value for money (see chapter 9).

d. There is an increase in repeat purchase.

When a new brand is introduced successfully into a stationary market, or when an existing brand is restaged with a very large sales improvement (both relatively uncommon phenomena), a temporary nonstationary element is introduced into the category. After the market has shaken down to accommodate the innovation, stationary conditions are likely to return. The same happens in a reverse direction when an existing brand declines significantly.

The way to trace the dynamics of the processes of growth and decline is to track, via research repeated at regular intervals, the penetration and purchase frequency of the brands in the category. Stable brands, whose advertising is operating according to the weak theory, will have a stable penetration and a constant or slightly increasing purchase frequency. Growing or declining brands will have a penetration that is trending upward or downward, respectively. If the trend is upward, the advertising will be acting as a strong force, and the creative content of the campaign should concentrate on the functional features of the brand in order to persuade nonusers to become infrequent users.

One phenomenon to look out for is what I have described as *penetration supercharge:* the tendency for brands which have a high penetration to benefit also from an above-average purchase frequency, particularly as the period examined is lengthened.

The market research industry in the United States is some way short of offering "single-source" data on a national scale, and the practical difficulties in the way of this important development should not be underestimated. Nevertheless, this methodology offers a very alluring prospect of our being able to relate behavioral effects to individuals' exposure to advertising.

27. *Advertising Research: "Horses for Courses"*

It follows from recommendation 26 that advertising research aimed at measuring an advertisement's power to change—to be intrusive, to be recalled, to persuade—is relevant only to the minority of advertising that operates according to the strong theory. In the United States, the method predominantly used for such research is quantitative copy testing. There are considerable problems with this method (see recommendation 32).

For the larger amount of advertising that operates according to the weak theory, advertising should be researched for its ability to reinforce the image of the brand, especially among existing users. Qualitative techniques are most appropriate for this kind of research.

28. *Composition of the Brand Repertoire*

Good data are available from Mediamark Research Inc. and Simmons describing the brands that are frequently and infrequently bought by consumers. The former tend to be the preferred brands in homemakers' buying repertoires.

The striking feature of the penetration figures published by these well-known and reputable research organizations is the relatively small size of the average penetration figures. For instance, as we saw in chapter 7, a very large brand of breakfast cereals, Kellogg's Corn Flakes, has 20.4 million female buyers. A smaller but still important brand, Lucky Charms, has only 6.5 million. I concluded in chapter 7 that the advertising for these two brands should be addressed mainly to these existing users. The raw numbers for the two brands represent, respectively, 24.5 percent and 7.8 percent of all female homemakers (that is, the brands are *not* bought by 75.5 percent and 92.2 percent, respectively, of all housewives). Both brands use television advertising, despite the conspicuous waste in addressing these two relatively small user groups with unselective mass media, such as network television. A strong case can be made for experimenting with the most tightly targeted media available. Specifically, the manufacturers of these two brands should be building a data base of users and focusing particular marketing attention on them. This procedure has a direct application to promotions, but the advertising implications should also not be ignored.

29. *The Brand Life Cycle*

Inertia—the continuation of existing buying habits—is a major obstacle to the disappearance of brands. Penetration only rarely declines in absolute terms. Brands in a downward trend lose purchase frequency, generally because competitive brands perform better. Even more seriously, declining brands run the risk of being delisted by the retail trade if they continue to be neglected by their manufacturers.

This description of typical brands in decline emphasizes the fact that the downward phase of the brand life cycle is a managed and self-fulfilling process. A brand's decline is caused by lack of care and attention, in particular by the manufacturer's permitting it to be superseded functionally by its competitors, and by making large advertising reductions and so allowing the salience of the brand to fade in the minds of consumers. Manufacturers of declining brands often maintain promotions at a competitive rate, primarily to maintain retail interest. This support is rarely powerful enough to save such brands in the long run.

Manufacturers and agencies should work on the assumption that the inevitability of the decline phase of the life cycle is a fallacy.

Forecasting Advertising's Selling Power

30. *Single versus Multiple Creative Proposals*

There is direct evidence and powerful indirect evidence (from the relatively small number of campaigns that are demonstrably successful) that judgment is a weak guide to forecasting the selling power of an advertisement. It is therefore dangerous and potentially very wasteful for agencies to concentrate on a single creative solution to an advertising problem, and to reject any alternatives on the basis of judgment alone. When creative proposals are taken forward to the stage of research, campaign alternatives should always be included. This recommendation holds even if the testing is carried out monadically.

The argument can be taken further. When the client and agency's preferred campaign is put into the marketplace, at least one creative alternative should be put concurrently into test in a different area. I have expressed this point to many advertisers and agencies. In reply, they have invariably made strong objections based on the cost and time involved. My response has always been that it is less wasteful to sacrifice substantial sums for two or more alternative films and running them and evaluating them in separate market tests, than it is to commit perhaps ten times as much money on screen time for a single but ultimately unsuccessful campaign.

31. *Advertising Research:*
Before or after Advertising Exposure?

There are considerable limitations on all types of research on advertisements before they reach the marketplace. Far more is to be learned about the effectiveness of advertising from tracking conducted *after* the advertising has been exposed, although such research, being retrospective, cannot be used to forecast the effectiveness of new campaigns. Research carried out after campaign exposure should explore consumer knowledge, attitudes, and behavior and the relationship among these three variables. Such research has a great advantage in that it evaluates advertising as it actually works—in cooperation with all other stimuli on sales of the brand. This procedure is obviously of no help to us in evaluating a particular advertisement in order to improve it. But it is the best tool we have available to improve our overall knowledge of advertising for a brand.

32. *Quantitative Copy Testing*

Most major consumer goods companies in the United States have spent large amounts of time and money on quantitative copy testing of their advertisements. (I shall not explore the opportunity cost involved in screening commercials that tested well but that were often ineffective, nor that involved in the rejection of commercials that tested badly but might well have been effective in use).

It seems sensible, to say the least, for companies to scrutinize their batteries of test data and to apply their best judgment to the task of comparing each test score with the marketplace effectiveness of the tested commercial. The object would be to trace any relationship between advertisements which tested well and performed well; between those which had average scores and achieved an average performance; and between those with low scores and a low performance.

My own experience has convinced me that there is no simple correlation, except in the isolated case of very low-scoring commercials. (These are likely anyway to be rejected by the advertiser on grounds unrelated to test scores.) If advertisers examine their own experience in the way proposed in the last paragraph, and if their conclusions parallel my own, they should ask themselves frankly why they should commit further money and time to quantitative copy testing.

There has been more than one broad-scale evaluation of quantitative copy testing. As long ago as the 1960s, two British researchers looked at a large number of commercials which had been subjected to a then-fashionable method of forecasting a commercial's selling power, the Schwerin "Relative Competitive Preference." The scores from many Schwerin tests were compared with the actual sales performance of the commercials, and very little connection was found between the two.[9] It is perhaps no coincidence that Schwerin shortly afterward went out of business.

33. Study of Campaigns by Comparisons of Successes and Failures

This recommendation is similar to recommendation 24. Manufacturers and agencies should work backward by isolating those campaigns for which there appear to be signals of marketplace success and those that have been failures. It is important to exclude from further evaluation those campaigns which were ineffective for reasons unconnected with the advertising, for example, because of problems with product functionality, price, or distribution.

The campaigns that remain should now be subjected to intensive analysis (possibly involving complex mathematics if the sample sizes are large enough). The aim would be to isolate the qualities that may make a critical difference between failure and success. In relatively rare cases, the variables determining success or failure are connected with whether the strategy was right or wrong. However, in most circumstances, the clues to the factors that decide success or failure will be much more difficult to find. It is useful at this stage to involve researchers with an education in psychology and experience in copy testing, because advertising often operates in subtle ways; detecting these ways is a skilled—even an artistic—endeavor.

In comparisons of successful and unsuccessful campaigns, one of the elements that should be looked for is the forecasting ability of any developmental and "quality-control" research that was carried out before the advertising was exposed, in particular whether research provided any warning signals about the failures.

If readers are skeptical of the value of such a laborious exercise, they should refer to a published case which provides a parallel. In this case, the problem was to locate the quality or qualities that distinguish a company that is highly regarded by the public from a company that is not well regarded. An analysis similar to that recommended here was carried out, and an unexpected conclusion emerged: The quality of a company's communications is a decisive discriminator determining how well it is perceived.[10]

34. Tracking Studies: Part Two
(see also Recommendation 26)

A commonsense analysis of tracking studies covering brand awareness, brand image associations, and brand purchasing can isolate the
most effective campaigns and can also give valuable clues about how
they worked in terms of consumer perceptions. Even recall of advertisements—normally a misleading measure—can be helpful if the
scores are tracked longitudinally. With the important British brand
Oxo, fading recall of the long-lasting and (during its early years)
highly successful "Katie" campaign gave a clue that the campaign
was losing its salience with consumers. This piece of evidence made
an important contribution to the decision to abandon Katie, a decision which had very beneficial consequences for the brand.[11]

Not enough work has been done on the interrelationship of different types of tracking studies.[12] We need to examine more fully the
circumstances in which improvements in image attributes *precede*
sales increases, with some estimation of the time lags. We also need
to know the circumstances in which it is sales that govern changes in
attitudes. The mutual interaction of changes in image attributes and
changes in sales is likely to differ according to the size and development of the brand.

The Imaginative Leap

35. Size of the Target Group

I have already demonstrated (in recommendation 28) that the number of people to whom advertising campaigns are directed is often
quite small. An important *creative* lesson follows from this fact.

In most cases, the advertiser and the agency should direct a sharply
focused message to a small group of people, in preference to a more
general (and probably anodyne) message to a large group of people.

This principle should encourage creative people to direct their
thoughts to the functional and nonfunctional *discriminators* of the
advertised brand. This is possible only if the agency studies the brand
rigorously and develops a tight and productive advertising strategy
(see recommendation 15).

Using this strategy, the creative people should absorb themselves in the brand and in the priorities that have been set and should then allow their subconscious to process the data and throw up ideas. This procedure is described in James Webb Young's classic monograph, *A Technique for Producing Ideas.*[13]

36. Gurus

Agencies have made their living for almost a century from generating advertising ideas. Yet no, or at least very few, agencies have committed time and money to exploring how ideas are actually produced and developed. Surprisingly, most of the serious study of this fascinating process has taken place *outside* the advertising field. I propose that major agencies should now play their part. Well-established agencies have the incomparable benefit of having, in their campaigns, a large store of ideas—some effective and some ineffective in the marketplace—that provide an empirical base which can be studied. Ideas are a necessary but not sufficient basis for successful advertising. Young people in the agency business must be stimulated to generate ideas, but they should also be encouraged to direct themselves toward sales-generating (as opposed to award-winning) ideas.

Such an educational task would be a wonderful job for a seasoned creative person reaching the end of his or her career. I have come across many such men and women, creative people who are still fascinated with advertising and who manage to maintain the youthful freshness of their approach to the creative process—a realization that "young" ideas are as valuable as, or even more valuable than, campaign classics.

Every agency should find such a person, relieve him or her of all other executive responsibility and hand the person a double charge: (a) to study the generation of ideas, and (b) to steer the young people in the agency through training programs focused on the creative process. Gurus in different agencies will want to compare notes, and this should be encouraged.[14]

37. Research among Creative People

Since agencies find group discussions so helpful in developing (and to some extent also in generating) creative ideas, it seems logical to use the same technique to explore how different creative talents produce and sift ideas. If the best creative people in a large agency are put together into a half-dozen groups, and if the discussion within these groups is efficiently moderated, it will disclose rich insights into how the creative imagination works. Groups are the ideal technique for this research. Creative people tend to interact well with their peers, and the production of ideas is both their professional endeavor and their personal preoccupation.

38. *Laboratory Experiments*

I believe it would be worthwhile to set up experiments in a psychology laboratory to explore a number of the specifics of idea generation. There is no limit to the topics that might be covered in such experiments, but there are four questions at the top of my own mind, all connected in various ways with direct personal experience:

a. How important is it for an advertising idea to be *incomplete?* How much of a gap does the receiver of the advertising message have to fill in to make the advertisement generate mental engagement and a behavioral response? We need to be surer than we are at present that the audience will "get it."

b. What is the role of *unexpectedness* in a successful advertising idea? How much will it attract attention? If an advertisement catches a person unawares, will that person be disillusioned to discover that he or she has been tricked into paying attention to it?

c. What advantage is there in presenting consumers with a brand's *deficiencies?* How much will honesty about deficiencies increase the credibility of the positive claims in the advertisement?

d. In what specific circumstances does "comparison advertising"—naming names—actually work? There is evidence that the traditional view—that comparison advertising is unsuitable for market leaders—is not always valid. We need to increase our stock of case studies to cover a wider range of specific examples of the technique in action.

Lessons from Direct Response

39. *Direct Response and the Culture of the General Agency*

There is a divide separating the majority of general advertising agencies from direct agencies, whose work now encompasses a variety of data base marketing in addition to traditional direct-response advertising. The possibility that there may be lessons for general practice from direct response is culturally unacceptable to the average senior person in consumer goods agencies. Direct response is seen to be at the lower end of the advertising profession: the realm of the huckster and not the artist.

It should not be necessary to emphasize that such preconceptions are both wrong and counterproductive. Brand building (the objective of above-the-line activity) is complementary to and not competitive with brand exploitation (the aim of below-the-line action). The notable characteristic of direct response is its measurability, and who can deny the advantages to general advertising if it managed to achieve a similar ability to gauge results? If it were to be robustly established that at least some general advertising works by the same psychological processes as direct response, then what is *known* about direct response could be applied to this general advertising, to the great benefit of the latter. But a process of this sort will be impossible unless and until people in general agencies overcome their distaste for what they see at present as direct response's "tackiness".

An important supplementary point is that consumer targets for brands of consumer goods will probably become narrower in the future (see recommendation 28). Direct-response advertising may therefore become an important medium in its own right for packaged goods, beyond being a device used to help improve the general advertising for those products.

40. *Matched Testing: Television Advertising*

It is normally perfectly possible to convert a television advertisement for a general brand of fast moving consumer goods (FMCG) into a direct-response advertisement, although the spot would need to be lengthened, from 30 seconds to possibly as much as 120 seconds. Such an adaptation provides a good basis for marketplace experimentation. The adapted film should be run in one or two cities at low frequency (to compensate for the greater screen-time cost of the longer spot in comparison with the shorter one). Response should be geared to a special offer or some other type of tactical marketing device.

The agency should now follow the standard direct-response practice of running the advertisement, analyzing the replies, improving the advertisement, analyzing the further replies, improving the advertisement again, and so on. This procedure will yield productive lessons about the most important elements of the advertisement—and these conclusions can be applied to the *general* campaign.

41. *Matched Testing: Print Advertising*

It is often difficult to convert a television advertisement for an FMCG brand into a direct-response print advertisement. There is a larger gap between a general television advertisement and a direct-response print advertisement than there is between general and direct-response advertisements when they are both on television.

The experiment is nevertheless worth carrying out. Print advertising is simpler, more flexible, and less costly than television advertising, so that running experimental print advertisements for FMCG brands is a simple and inexpensive process. These advantages go a long way toward balancing the negative point that the advertising delivery of print is different from that of television. The lessons which emerge will be—at the very least—an aid to judgment.

An additional advantage of experimentation with print advertising is that it will direct attention to advertising craft: well-argued and persuasive copy, readable typography, and good design. All direct-response experience tells us that well-crafted advertisements pull better than badly crafted ones.

The Advertising Audience and the Media

42. *How Consumers Use Media*

Consumers use media similarly to how they use goods and services. Media provide a range of specific rewards in use. If we learn to understand better the ways in which various groups of people use individual media, we should be able to use those media more efficiently to reach and sell to our target audiences.

Specifically, we need to know how and in what circumstances people view, read, or listen to particular media and media vehicles. We need to explore the psychological affinities between members of the public and particular media and vehicles. We need to gauge how much attention people pay, and whether they doing anything else when they are viewing, reading, or listening.

This information can be collected by quantitative research, supplemented as necessary by selective qualitative research. The purpose to which it can be put is to provide additional criteria to guide media selection; it will be a further and more subtle research input to add to the viewership and readership data which are used exclusively at present as the statistical basis for media planning.

Common sense strongly suggests that there are large differences in attention value between media vehicles, for example, television day parts. To be able in some way to quantify these differences would be immediately valuable. Of longer range value would be the insights that might eventually be gained from comparisons *across* media (for example, between television and magazines). This is at the moment a substantially unexplored field. I am optimistic enough to believe that research techniques will eventually improve enough to make such exploration possible.

43. *Media Evolution*

Many if not most of the important innovations that have been made in advertising have been connected with the media. It is safe to predict that the media will change during the 1990s no less than during any previous decade. The changes that can be anticipated to take place are related to the fragmentation of consumer goods categories. Whether we like it or not, niche marketing is here to stay, and niche brands are demanding and will continue to require targeted media. We can therefore expect:

a. a general narrowing of focus, as the formerly monolithic media (notably the television networks) continue to erode and give way to more sharply defined media and vehicles;

b. a continued development of data base media, for example, direct-response catalogs;

c. a continued development of interactive media;

d. a further shrinkage of many (although not all) newspapers and larger magazines.

The advertising industry needs better published research than is available at present to monitor existing—and unanticipated—media trends. (Too little is known, for instance, of the composition of the audience of many audiovisual media.) The integration of communications (see recommendation 9) is a development that has already made great impact and will unquestionably grow even more important in the future.

44. Media Links

Advertising campaigns commonly use more than one advertising medium. They do this for two reasons: either (a) to even out coverage, that is, to get to members of the target group not effectively reached by one medium (for example, the use of magazines to cover light television viewers), or (b) to reinforce the impression made by the campaign on the *same* people.

Both objectives involve uncertainties. We do not know much about whether the same campaign, tailored for different media, works in the same way in each. To throw light on this question, the advertising prepared for each medium should be researched qualitatively and comparatively, so that the advertiser can ensure that the same advertising strategy will be executed with reasonably equal efficiency everywhere.

The other possibility is regional testing. If the main campaign uses national media, there are great practical problems involved in media experimentation in different areas, although with ingenuity something can be done. It is worth the effort to experiment as far as is practicable with varying the amounts of the different media in at least a few areas. These tests should be prolonged, and the effect on consumer perceptions of the brand must be evaluated by tracking studies.

45. Brand Competition and Media Strategy

In the majority of cases, directly competitive brands use substantially the same combination of media for their campaigns. The possibility of competing by using *different* media is very rarely contemplated by advertisers, which almost invariably follow one another dutifully in their media strategy. Using different media should be an increasingly relevant consideration as the media themselves become more frag-

mented. The obvious way of examining this proposal is by area testing (despite the practical difficulties).

46. Passive Meters

I do not need to emphasize the importance of developing the technology of "passive" meters, so that the advertising industry will be able
to calculate with greater precision than at present the composition of
the audience for television commercials.

Sales Effects, Budgeting, and Budgetary Deployment

47. Sales Effects of Advertising: Part Two
(see also Recommendation 13)

This is the most important of all the recommendations in this chapter. The point I am making here is separate from that in recommendation 13. I now wish to emphasize the tactical and strategic *action*
that follows campaign evaluation.

I believe that advertisers and agencies should study campaign evaluation almost as energetically as they tackle the more exciting task of
developing the campaigns that are going to be evaluated. As stated in
recommendation 13, it should be automatically expected that all advertising will yield a short-term sales return, to be followed in most
cases by an additional long-term effect related to the repeat purchase
that follows the initial sales.

If there is no obvious short-term sales effect, the immediate action
needed is to improve the mathematics of measurement. If improved
measurement does not show something happening to sales, tactical
changes (for example, increased advertising weight or alterations in
the media mix) should be carried out in a renewed effort to swing the
sales needle. If nothing happens even then, the advertiser and the
agency should immediately consider changing the campaign.

The mathematical techniques involved in the comprehensive monitoring of campaign effects include regression analysis and model
building, on top of simpler measures such as consumer sales via retail
audits, consumer purchases via diary studies (in particular single-
source data), and continuous tracking of consumers' perceptions of
the advertised brand and its competitors.

In the 1970s, a British brand with which I was closely familiar was subjected to eight separate measures (some simple, others sophisticated) to evaluate the effects of the advertising. It is no coincidence that this brand has been the market leader in its category (which is an important one) for three decades.

48. Multiple Influences on the Advertising Budget

This recommendation reiterates the argument in chapter 5. The budgetary process involves the optimization of a number of different variables. The most important of these are the measures that relate to the market in which the brand competes: experience of previous expenditure levels, average share of voice, and so on. "Affordability"—measures based on the brand's cost structure—should enter the budgetary process at a later stage. If the measures relating to the market suggest that the advertising budget should be larger than the brand can afford over the short term, this calls for a medium-term analysis of the brand's profitability year by year, and a delayed payout should be contemplated. *It is more economic to spend more on advertising than the brand can immediately afford than to spend what the brand can afford in the certain knowledge that this will be too little to be effective.*

49. Sales and Profit

Manufacturers are in business for profit. They generally (although not always) boost their profit by increasing their sales. Paradoxically (see chapter 6), many businesses tend to pay more attention to sales than to profit. This is a dangerous misjudgment of priorities.

Sales and profit are both yardsticks of efficiency—and they are also rewards for doing an effective job in satisfying consumers and making progress in the marketplace. Satisfying consumers should be a more important objective than short-term profit (profit can be increased in the short run by reducing costs, and this may make it harder to satisfy consumers in the long run). But when manufacturers deploy resources (for example, on advertising and promotions) to strengthen their position in the market, they should judge the efficiency of this deployment by the criterion of profit as well as by that of sales. As a broad generalization, advertising often (although not invariably) yields small but profitable sales increases, while sales promotions tend to provide large but unprofitable sales increases. Cynical observers of business practice sometimes describe large and increasing promotional programs as a behavioral expression of the death wish.

As we saw in chapter 6, a promotion has a better chance of being profitable if the resultant sales offtake is very high. There is evidence that only a very small proportion—perhaps a mere 20 percent—of the population is aware of any promotion.[15] It seems sensible therefore for every promotion to be advertised in order to boost awareness to a more productive level. This will increase the cost, but it may ensure that the unprofitability of the promotion will not be as severe as it would be without the advertising.

50. Flights versus Drip Feeding

The conventional wisdom of advertising tells us that a minimal level of advertising pressure is necessary to cross an effectiveness threshold and stimulate a short-term sales increase (that is, there is an *S*-shaped response curve, which demonstrates some increasing returns over the short term). This is sometimes but not always true; and it tends to be less true for brands with large market shares than for those with small shares.[16] Yet the media schedules for virtually all brands of packaged goods compress the advertising into flights in order to cross this assumed threshold. With finite budgets, flights can generally be bought only at the expense of continuity in the schedule; that is, a schedule with flights also normally contain gaps. For a brand which sells equally well at all times of the year, gaps in the schedule represent a major weakness.

For any brand, there is a way of finding out whether there is an *S*-shaped response curve, with a threshold of effectiveness. This method is to carry out a drip-feed test in a single television area. (This suggestion is of course predicated on the assumption that the main campaign does not use network advertising.) At the end of a year, the advertiser should look for a difference in sales between the drip-feed area of continuous low-pressure advertising and in the other areas which have had a normal flighted schedule. Such a difference in sales does not always happen, but I have personal experience of such an experiment (the brand was the same one referred to at the end of recommendation 47). In the area of the drip-feed test, sales ended the first year 5 percent ahead of the national level. In the early 1990s, thirteen years after the original experiment, this brand is still advertised by drip feed. It is also still the market leader.

Appendix A

Advertising and the Economic System

It is not necessary to advertise food to hungry people, fuel to cold people, or houses to the homeless.

John Kenneth Galbraith

Some Basic Concepts

The subject of this appendix is controversial. Despite the interest and importance of the topic, much of the plentiful debate that it generates falls regrettably into one of two types of error (and sometimes even into both!). It either oversimplifies, or it overcomplicates. In an attempt to steer a course between these unattractive alternatives, I shall guide readers over the extensive ground in rather a decisive way. The purpose of this approach is to prevent readers from getting lost, although it is probably too much to expect that they will gain an appreciation of all the subtleties of this dense and complex subject.

Let me start with a value judgment: The greatest effect of advertising on society is in the realm of economics. Many people with first-hand knowledge of advertising's workings will share this view, although journalistic and academic commentators who believe that advertising has a powerful social and cultural influence (and a generally negative one at that) may dispute the predominance of its economic role. Since the focus of this book is managerial and professional, I make no excuses here for emphasizing advertising's economic importance. The major concentration will be on its microeconomic effects—how advertising influences the individual brand and the firm that manufactures it—rather than on how it affects the economy as a whole. I shall, however, discuss the last point—advertising and macroeconomics—in a special section at the end of this appendix.

The science of economics is built on the foundation of a number of technical assumptions whose meaning and limits are precisely understood. The conditions of their operation are always indicated by the qualification "other things being equal." This appendix must start by taking a quick look at four of these assumptions, assumptions which are all directly relevant to advertising's specific role in the marketplace.

Equilibrium

Microeconomics is concerned essentially with markets in a state of equilibrium. Complete equilibrium never occurs in the real world, a place of flux, although not necessarily random instability. This generalization is true for economically liberal countries like the United States. In countries subject to greater economic management, there tends to be less movement. The direction in which markets progress is toward equilibrium, a state which is in fact never reached because additional changes always get in the way. The subtlety of the discipline of microeconomics is that by studying equilibrium, we can more easily isolate for study those forces which lead toward it. Such a study provides much enlightenment. However, since equilibrium is never reached, economics is open to some criticism because it does not describe the world literally as it is.

In some circumstances, advertising is a force for stability and continuity, and in others, a force for change. In any market, the advertising of some brands will aim toward the maintenance of the same buying patterns; the advertising of other brands will aim toward the introduction of new patterns. The central process of competition implies change, or rather attempts at change; this is because the offensive marketing of some brands is usually countered by the defensive activity of others, so that the two often cancel out. Offensive action in markets means product differentiation; differentiation requires the diffusion of information.[1] Advertising contributes to both these things. Offensive action is dynamic; it is not aimed toward equilibrium. It is therefore not possible to understand advertising according to the "ideal" conditions of perfect equilibrium. The more that markets fall short of this, the greater the role that advertising plays in their functioning.

Consumer Prices

Microeconomics is, more than anything else, a study of the price mechanism. The analysis assumes that consumers will buy goods at the cheapest price possible. When consumers behave in this rational way, their welfare will be maximized because their income will be used with the highest degree of efficiency.

There are, however, two problems in this appealing concept:

1. In reality, people's knowledge of the actual prices ruling in any market is imperfect. Consumers' ability to find goods at the lowest prices is therefore, to some extent, a matter of blind chance, or else the result of laborious search. In the latter case, advertising can of course be a helpful tool. The role of advertising in reducing search costs is an important field of study by contemporary economists.[2] I shall return to it in a later section of this appendix when I discuss the influence of advertising on the distributors' margin.

2. An even more important point is that it is extremely common for consumers to buy goods at prices higher than those at the bottom end of the market. This is even true when there may be little to choose functionally between goods at different prices. Low prices signal to some consumers a low quality (that may not in reality be present), and this will depress demand. Another factor is also at work. Branded goods provide both functional and nonfunctional benefits, and consumers are perfectly willing to pay higher prices for greater amounts of the latter. Advertising is an important source of those intangible, psychological rewards that come from owning and using brands. It is therefore in this context a factor contributing to higher prices.

Profit Maximization

All microeconomic descriptions of the production process assume that businesspeople have as their sole goal the maximization of the firm's profit. This is far more generally true than untrue, but there are a number of important qualifications and exceptions to this rule:

1. There is often a severe dissonance between immediate and long-term profit, although manufacturers are obviously concerned about both. In one very important marketing activity, new product introductions (in which advertising has an important role), manufacturers generally sacrifice profit deliberately for perhaps three years or more by investing in advertising and promotions, in the hope (although never the certainty) that the brand will eventually break even, then earn enough to recoup earlier losses, and eventually begin a profitable existence.

2. It is common for large firms, especially those which hold substantial shares of their markets, to develop organizational inefficiencies, a type of bureaucratic sloth (often described in the economic literature as diseconomies of scale). What such firms are in effect doing is exchanging the chance of earning the maximum profit with much effort for the certainty of earning a lower profit accompanied by a quiet life. In such circumstances, competition between firms is more commonly driven by the sheer volume of advertising and promotions than by innovation in ideas. Advertising weight that will maintain the status quo is often seen as preferable to new brand development, which calls for energy, free-ranging imagination, and good research.

3. In the same way that consumers have a less than perfect knowledge of prices, manufacturers have an imperfect knowledge of their costs and therefore their profits. Maximum production efficiency for a manufacturer is described in economic terms as when the marginal cost (that is, the cost of the last, incremental, unit of goods produced) equals the marginal revenue (that is, the price earned by this unit). In the real world, manufacturers have only the crudest knowledge of their marginal cost and marginal revenue, although they have an accurate enough knowledge of their *average* cost and *average* revenue. Advertising represents a significant element of cost, but accurate and detailed knowledge of its total yield, let alone its immediate marginal productivity, is generally so faint as to be nonexistent. (This is even more true of its long-term, lagged effect.) Readers will, however, remember the published data on advertising elasticity dis-

cussed in chapter 6; but such information is not available for the general run of brands.

Competition

Microeconomic analysis describes competition between manufacturers as being of three main types (with certain additional refinements, which it is not necessary to discuss here):

1. *Pure or atomistic competition.* In this, there is a large number of producers in a market, none of whom is individually large enough to influence price. At the existing ruling price in the market, they can sell all they want to. An individual manufacturer cannot raise price at all because it will then lose all its sales; and there is simply no point in reducing its price since it can sell all it wishes at the ruling price. It is also assumed that the product of all manufacturers is homogeneous, that there is free entry into the market, and that there is perfect knowledge on the part of all consumers. These are heroic assumptions.

If atomistic competition ever existed in any markets for consumer goods, it was when economies were primitive, incomes were low, and consumers purchased commodities and not brands. As John Kenneth Galbraith reminds us in the quotation that prefaces this appendix, advertising has no role in such circumstances. It is relevant and effective only in relatively affluent societies. Advertising is a tool that influences only the distribution of discretionary income, something that hardly exists in undeveloped economies.

2. *Oligopoly.* This assumes a relatively small number of producers whose importance is measured by the concentration ratio, that is, the proportion of sales that is in the hands of a defined number of manufacturers (commonly four, five, or six). Since each manufacturer is large, it influences the market by its actions. If it increases its price, the demand for its goods goes down and vice versa. And if it increases its sales, its price goes down and vice versa. The responsiveness, or elasticity, of demand to change in price can be measured by the coefficient of price elasticity, or the percentage increase in sales which results from a 1 percent drop in price, or the percentage reduction in sales that results from a 1 percent increase in price. As

discussed in chapter 6, it is not easy to work this sum out, but the calculation has been made hundreds of times.

A manufacturer normally wishes to reduce the elasticity of demand for its goods, so that it can increase its price without much reduction in demand. Generally, an oligopolist can control either its price or its output, but not both. If it changes it price, demand will adjust to the new price, and the degree of responsiveness of demand depends, of course, on price elasticity.

Competition in oligopolistic markets is intense because manufacturers worry about the effect of their actions not only on their customers but on their competitors also. The heat of the competition in such markets is generated mainly by manufacturers' reacting to one another's tactics. But the paradoxical outcome is that much of the mutual reaction is self-canceling, so that the result is stability—although a stability that conceals underlying ferment.

3. *Monopoly.* This assumes the existence of a single manufacturer, which exercises substantial control of its market. If the goods it makes are necessities of life, it has absolute control both of its price and of its sales level. If it produces goods that some people are prepared to stop buying (or to reduce the quantity they buy), the monopolist—rather more strongly than the oligopolist—can control either its price or the quantity it sells, but not both.

Of these three competitive states, the one that plays the largest part in the economic literature is the equilibrium of perfect competition. Such competition is regarded as an ideal state, in which the prices are the lowest possible, and the output is produced with the greatest theoretical efficiency. These conclusions, based on sound logic, lead to the inevitable conclusion that perfect competition is the condition in which the economic welfare of the public is maximized.

Perfect competition has always been an alluring idea. And because it is so attractive, it tends to blind people to past and present reality. The fact is that perfect competition is and has always been extremely rare; nor is there the faintest possibility that it will ever become more widespread in the future. Something approaching perfect competition can be found in the markets for certain agricultural commodities and for company stock traded on the exchanges. But outside these markets, which are highly specialized despite their importance, conditions of perfect competition do not exist in the real world. In perfectly competitive markets, advertising would not be necessary because of the complete diffusion of knowledge and the homogeneity of the product. It is with consumer goods sold directly to the public that advertising is of first importance. As far as these are concerned—and this goes both for products like soap and refrigerators and for services like airlines and credit cards—all the markets are organized oligopolistically.

The present oligopoly structure emerged in no general pattern. Different markets evolved in different ways. In some cases (beer, hard liquor, soap, and soft drinks), there was originally a fairly large number of producers, and this number became smaller by the emergence of strong market leaders and by mergers and acquisitions. In other cases (airlines, breakfast cereals, margarine, and motor cars), there were originally only a few manufacturers, which became even fewer by amalgamation.

In yet other cases (instant coffee, frozen food, phonograph records, and razors and blades), the first manufacturer was for a while a monopolist because it held a patent. Oligopoly emerged quickly because competitive manufacturers were ingenious enough to copy the monopolist, without infringing the legal protection originally acquired.

In none of these cases was there ever a myriad of manufacturers and a homogeneous product. Consumer goods markets have almost always been oligopolistic; they have merely changed in their degree of concentration—and this only during their early development. Oligopolistic competition as it exists today can best be described as a situation of apparent stasis, often described as maturity. This means stagnation in total market size. And as has already been mentioned, there is also little apparent change in market shares, since the intense activity as competitor fights competitor tends to be self-canceling. Although there is considerable stability over the short and medium term, in many instances the major individual manufacturers' market shares move up and down over the long term. But even when this happens, the changes balance out, so that the overall concentration ratio in a mature market tends to remain unchanged.

Oligopoly does not offer the same theoretical advantages as pure competition; in particular, prices are higher. Nevertheless, oligopoly is a system that provides considerable social benefits, many of which are discussed in this appendix. These include economies of scale in production and marketing (with the realistic possibility of reductions in consumer prices). There is a good deal of product and brand innovation. And the markets are generally characterized by an intense degree of price and nonprice competition between large manufacturers: something which almost invariably operates in the public interest.

Readers will remember the point made earlier that if an oligopolist pushes up its price, it will lose sales, and that the actual loss of sales depends on the elasticity of demand for the brand. A high elasticity means a large loss of sales in response to a price increase. This can be illustrated diagrammatically. In figure A–1, demand curve $D1$ is elastic; $D2$ is much less so. In order to minimize the loss of sales resulting from a price increase, the oligopolist will wish to tilt the curve from $D1$ to $D2$, as indicated by the dotted line.

How well the oligopolist can actually change its demand curve depends on how easily consumers judge its output and that of its competitors to be substitutes for one another. If when it increases its price, demand is elastic, and substitution is easy, it will lose much business. If demand is inelastic and substitution is difficult, it will lose less. The oligopolist will therefore increase its advantage by reducing the degree of substitution between its brand and its competitors, and how well it can do this depends on how distinctive it can make its brand. Ideally the brand should be functionally unique, and also unique in its psychological rewards and associations.

Readers will readily appreciate the importance of the manufac-

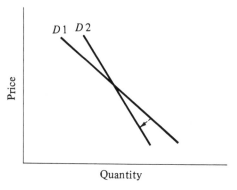

FIGURE A–1

The Oligopolist's Objective

turer's advertising campaign both in demonstrating the brand's functional distinctiveness and in nourishing its nonfunctional values in the minds of existing and new consumers.[3]

I shall call the distinctiveness of the oligopolist's brand *oligopolistic differentiation.* Rather importantly, it is the quality that enables the oligopolist to charge and receive a price that is above that ruling in the theoretical model of perfect competition.

Six Aspects of Advertising and Microeconomics

The argument on which I shall now embark represents a continuous thread. To simplify readers' progress along it, it will be covered in six stages. These are individually free-standing, but they are all connected and follow a sequence.

The first topic is *advertising and price over the short term.* The difficulty here is to isolate the short-term effects of the advertising for an individual brand or product—to freeze them before the rest of the market responds. To do this, we have to find some rather special examples. These demonstrate that advertising can increase demand and that increased demand can raise prices.

Higher prices stimulate new and additional output in the market. This comes partly from existing manufacturers, and also from new competitors. The second subject we discuss is therefore *advertising and competition.* How much does advertising stimulate competition? How much does it facilitate innovation? On the other hand, what barriers does it erect to the emergence of new competitors?

The entry of new competitors into the market influences the degree of concentration among manufacturers. My third subject, *advertising and industrial concentration,* examines changes in the degree of oligopoly within markets.

Concentration is also something that happens in the retail trade. This means that retailers can become increasingly strong vis-à-vis manufacturers. Consumer goods sold through the retail trade carry substantial markups. Are these increasing or decreasing? Theoretically, they will decrease if advertising improves consumers' knowledge of prices and helps bring about a single ruling consumer price in a market, which will of course be the lowest one. Advertising also stimulates consumer demand, thereby making the retailer's job easier, especially if there are large and increasing volumes of merchandise involved. My fourth topic is therefore *manufacturers' advertising and retail margins.*

Increased production has an important influence on prices in the long run: it is a force that reduces them. The extent to which prices will actually come down depends substantially on the degree to which the additional production manages to tap into the scale economies of large output. The fifth topic is therefore *advertising, scale economies, and long-term price.*

The sixth point is a digression, but it covers the clearest and most unambiguous illustration of advertising's power to reduce prices. It is *advertising and the price of the media.*

As is obvious from this summary, the argument in this appendix revolves around how advertising influences consumer prices. This is consonant with what was said about consumer prices at the beginning of this appendix, that social welfare is maximized if prices are at their lowest. There is no dispute that the short-run intention of advertising is to increase prices. But it is very important to examine whether advertising goes on pushing prices up, or whether it provides a countervailing force to bring them down in the long run.

Advertising and Price Over the Short Term

The most immediate and obvious effect of advertising on price is that the price the consumer pays for any advertised product or service must include the cost of its advertising. If the goods were formerly unadvertised and are now advertised for the first time, the advertising can be funded only by an increase in price or a reduction in profit, or both.

The cost of the advertising to the manufacturer is generally a small although significant proportion of the total cost. The figure is generally expressed not as a proportion of the consumer price of the brand, but as a percentage of its net sales value, and it is described as the brand's advertising to sales (A:S) ratio. There are published data describing the average A:S ratios for 200 different industries, some of which are more important than others.

Table A–1 presents the figures for twenty consumer goods industries in which advertising is a relatively important sales-generating

TABLE A–1

A:S Ratios by Industry, 1989

Industry	A:S Ratio (%)
Sugar and confectionery products	10.6
Perfume, cosmetics, related toilet articles	10.4
Malt beverages	8.4
Soap, detergent, related toilet preparations	7.7
Canned/frozen preserves, fruit, vegetables	6.9
Ice cream and frozen desserts	6.9
Sausage, other prepared meat products	6.9
Pharmaceutical preparations	6.8
Cigarettes	5.7
Greeting cards	5.1
Cookies and crackers	4.8
Dairy products	4.7
Photographic equipment and supplies	3.6
Poultry slaughter and processing	3.1
Bottled and canned soft drinks, water	2.9
Department stores	2.9
Canned fruit, vegetables, preserves, jams, jellies	2.2
Scheduled air transport	1.8
Motor vehicles and car bodies	1.7
Personal credit institutions	1.5

Source: "Advertising-to-Sales Ratios, 1989" *Advertising Age* November 13, 1989, p. 32. The data came originally from Schonfeld & Associates.

activity. In the table these have been ranked according to the size of the A:S ratio, from the highest to the lowest.

There are three points to be made about this table. First, the figures are averages and there are brands in any market whose ratios greatly exceed these. This is especially true of new introductions. Second, the important mail-order category (which is not covered in table A–1, since it embraces a large number of product fields, some small) is characterized by A:S ratios generally above 10 percent, sometimes a good deal higher. This is compensation for the fact that there are no wholesale and retail margins in mail-order trading; the advertising does the job normally done by the store. Third, in many product fields where A:S ratios are low, these ratios translate into large absolute sums which are in effect paid by consumers. A striking example is the motor car industry, for which the advertising cost commonly exceeds $200 per car, and even larger sums for new model introductions.

In addition to the expenditure on advertising above the line, the manufacturer will make similar (or, more commonly, greater) expenditures on promotions below the line. These mostly take the form of price reductions to the retail trade and the consumer. Promotional outlays therefore influence the price of a brand differently from how advertising affects it, since a large slice of the promotional cost finds its way directly back to the consumer.

The cost of the advertising campaign is not the only cause of short-term price increases. An even more important one is the operation of the campaign itself, insofar as it has any real effect in increasing demand (something that cannot be universally assumed). When advertising does boost demand, this boost can be described in the microeconomic model (figure A–2) by the demand schedule's being pushed to the right (from $D1$ to $D2$). The higher price draws onto the market additional (higher cost) production, by existing manufacturers working over capacity, and also by new, less efficient producers deciding to manufacturer. The new equilibrium ($P2$) is at a higher price and with a greater output than before ($P1$). This is strictly a short-term effect, and we shall not pursue for the moment any long-term

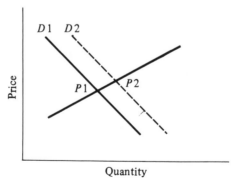

FIGURE A–2
Effect of Increased Demand

response from existing and new competitive manufacturers to the new higher price.

In order to demonstrate the short-term response of price to advertising-generated demand, we must look for examples in which the demand increase is frozen as in figure A–2. These must demonstrate ways of holding back the natural response of the market to increased price.

HOW AVOCADO FARMERS BOOSTED THEIR INCOMES: CALIFORNIA AVOCADO ADVISORY BOARD. The main point about most agricultural products is that they have no direct competition. If total demand for avocados can be increased by advertising, there are no obvious competitors to move in in response to the extra demand; consumers will buy only a limited extra quantity of grapefruit and dips and other salad vegetables.

This causes the demand for avocados to be inelastic. (This demand is described diagrammatically by a steeply falling demand curve.) Extra supplies in a good growing year are not easily absorbed by the market, and when this happens, prices can fall dramatically. The main avocado producers in the United States, the California farmers, had suffered from such sluggishness of demand in the 1950s, when every heavy crop had a disastrous effect on farm incomes.[4]

The 1959–60 season produced an enormous crop of fruit which had the expected effect on prices and incomes, and as a result the farmers got together to set up a cooperatively funded advertising and publicity campaign aimed at helping to stabilize the market. The intention was to increase the primary demand (that is, the demand for all avocados, not just particular types or fruit from certain regions), first, by encouraging existing users to buy more (for example, by showing recipes in the advertising), and second, by bringing new buyers into the market.

Just as the demand for avocados is inelastic, the supply is also inelastic (portrayed by a steeply rising supply curve). As with all agricultural products, the size of the crop is governed by the forces of nature, and because avocados are perishable, they cannot be stored so that stocks can be carried forward from year to year. All avocados grown during the season have to be eaten or thrown away. If advertising pushes up demand, the price will increase without any short-term response in increased output. This characteristic of the market enables us to freeze the effect of advertising on price.

Theory would lead us to expect sharply increasing prices as a measure of advertising's success in boosting consumer demand. Table A–2 averages the figures for a sequence of five five-year periods (in order to even out short-term fluctuations). There was no advertising and promotion during the first two periods; the campaign began in 1960.

From the period of lowest prices, and using the average price during this period as a base index of 100, average returns per acre increased to 128 during 1960–65; to 227 during 1965–70; and to 425 during 1970–75. These increases are uncorrected for inflation, but they are greater than any increase that inflation alone would have brought about (this is especially true of the huge increases in 1965–70 and 1970–75). Essentially, the only change that took place in the marketing of avocados before the price rise was the advertising and publicity campaign, so that the price increase can be reliably attributed to this campaign. The number of households purchasing avocados increased during the period, and so did the average household purchases of the fruit. Significantly, purchases went up most among older households, those to which the advertising campaign was mainly directed.

The increased income from the crop also had a long-term outcome, which is now described briefly. (A fuller discussion of the general long-term effects of advertising is introduced later in this appendix.) The higher income that the farmers were now receiving induced them to bring more acres into avocado cultivation (up from 21,000 in 1959–60 to 23,000 in 1974–75). This increase in acreage, accompanied by superior farming methods which significantly lifted the av-

TABLE A–2

Average Value of California Avocados ($ per Acre)

1950–51 through 1954–55	$588
1955–56 through 1959–60	$413
1960–61 through 1964–65	$529
1965–66 through 1969–70	$938
1970–71 through 1974–75	$1756

ocado production per acre, led to a large increase in the quantity of avocados grown (up from 140 million pounds in 1959–60 to 207 million pounds in 1974–75). Despite this greater quantity for the market to absorb, the increase in demand was so great and so continuous that price was pushed up by the large amounts seen in table A–2.

Agricultural production differs from manufacturing production in an important way that affects this analysis. Unlike a farmer, a manufacturer can change its price and can adjust its production accordingly. As already described, the manufacturer generally wishes to make demand inelastic by making it difficult for its competitors to substitute their brands for its, so that it can lift its price without losing much business.

The agricultural producer, on the other hand, has much less control over its destiny. If the demand is reasonably constant, the price will depend on output, which is governed by nature. This means that if production varies erratically year by year (as do most agricultural crops), there is the danger that this variation will cause continuous variations in price. If the producer wants to stabilize the price, the demand must be made more elastic. This means that it will move up immediately when a large crop brings price down, the extra volume being absorbed without continued pressure to reduce price further. This situation is described in figure A–3, by the demand curve's being tilted to make it more elastic, from D1 to D2, following the direction indicated by the dotted line.

There is evidence that the advertising for avocados did something

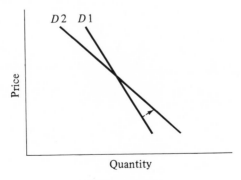

FIGURE A–3
The Farmers' Objective

to tilt the demand curve in the way described in figure A–3. It did this by suggesting additional uses for the fruit and by flagging the lower prices as soon as they came down, so that buyers were encouraged to increase their consumption soon after a large crop hit the market.

In 1959–60 (before the advertising began), the crop had been 36 percent larger than in the previous year. This caused the price to fall by 35 percent, a drop suggesting that at this level of production, each percentage point by which the harvest was above the previous year would cause the price to drop by about one percentage point. In 1974–75, the increase in the crop was 93 percent above that of the preceding season. But the price did not drop by anything like 93 percent. It fell by 44 percent—a severe reduction, but not as catastrophic for the farmers as a 93 percent drop would have been. Demand had obviously been expanded more easily in 1974–75, and the more flexible demand meant that the drop in price was relatively less than in 1959–60.

If we now use microeconomic analysis to describe what happened in the avocado market, we can see that the following changes took place in figure A–4:

1. Advertising boosted demand, shifting the curve from D1 to D2.
2. After a long delay, the arrival of fruit from the extra acreage planted, as well as the larger quantity of avocados per acre

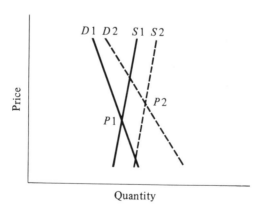

FIGURE A–4

Long-Term Movements in the Avocado Market

resulting from improved agricultural methods, caused the supply curve to shift to the right (from S1 to S2).

3. Advertising changed the slope of the demand curve, by making it rather more elastic (that is, D2 is less steep than D1).

4. The increased demand had an even greater effect on the market than the greater output because price (P2) was now well ahead of where it had been fifteen years before (P1). Table A–2 provides decisive confirmation of this analysis. And this increase in price occurred despite the greater production of fruit that had taken place over the fifteen year span of this case. Note that in the model, the first demand curve is highly inelastic and the second one less so, and that both supply curves are highly inelastic.

AN OBSERVED DEMAND CURVE: BRAND ALPHA. As explained, farmers cannot exercise any control over their output in the short run. They are also unable to differentiate it from that of competitive producers. These are important conditions for the development of an oligopoly. Our next example is a manufactured product, a brand of consumer packaged goods sold in Britain. The brand name is familiar to British consumers, but its manufacturer only permitted the details of the case to be published anonymously.[5]

Brand Alpha is a market leader. With more than 30 percent of consumer sales, its share is high by the standards of most consumer goods markets in developed countries. What is even more unusual is that it is more than three times the size of any competitive manufacturer's brand. In fact, the market comprises Brand Alpha, which is a powerful market leader, followed by a long tail of inexpensive minor labels and store brands. The concentration ratio in the market is therefore rather low.

It is the strength of Alpha that has led to a lack of competitors that are comparable with it either in functional terms or in the richness and density of their nonfunctional added values. This means that for this analysis, as with avocados, we can freeze the effect of advertising. There is not enough effective competition to come into the market in immediate response to the increase in demand and price engineered by Alpha's advertising.

As might be expected from the number of cheap brands on sale, the market is oriented to heavy promotional price cutting. Alpha is quite heavily promoted, but it is also the only substantial advertiser in the market. As we shall see, this advertising has had a demonstrable effect. All manufacturers in the category run different promotions (with different expenditures) in different regions of Britain, which result in the various brands' being differently priced (at least temporarily) in different parts of the country. By means of retail audit research, it was possible in the late 1970s to isolate the different regional sales levels of Alpha and to associate them with the different prices in effect. From this information, Alpha's demand curve could be constructed. The price in each region was determined for Alpha on a comparative basis, as the difference between it and the average price for all brands. This use of comparative prices compensated for price changes over time caused by inflation.

A year after the first demand curve was drawn up—and after the exposure of heavy advertising—another demand curve was put together. What happened is described in figure A–5. Following the advertising campaign (which was judged successful also by other criteria), the demand curve had shifted significantly to the right (from D1 to D2.)

The second position of the demand curve D2 demonstrates clearly that, in comparison with D1, a given level of output now commanded a strikingly higher price. The only important change in the marketing mix during the period between D1 and D2 was the exposure of the advertising campaign. This means that the rise in Alpha's

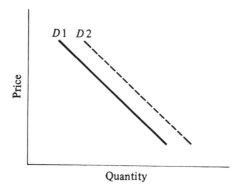

FIGURE A–5

Shift in Demand Curve for Brand Alpha

price in the second period can be reliably attributed to advertising's ability to make the brand more valuable to consumers by the successful communication of its functional and nonfunctional values. One operational advantage of this analysis to the manufacturer was that it enabled it to estimate the specific cost–benefit ratio of the advertising, a sophisticated and extremely useful procedure.

Advertising and Competition

The important point about avocados and Brand Alpha is that they have little direct competition. In contrast, for the vast majority of goods and services sold today, there are existing competitive brands and also latent competition in the wings that is easily lured forward in response to any significant price increase that takes place in the market. I shall shortly examine what happens to prices when this happens. But before I do so, we must consider a related but different question: Does advertising itself influence the extent of this latent competition? Does it make it more difficult or easier for new competitors to come into the market?

The most striking feature of advertising in consumer goods markets is that there is a great deal of it. Competition between brands operates in all parts of the marketing mix; advertising is no exception. Brands compete with one another in the persuasiveness of their advertising campaigns and also in the weight put behind these campaigns. This presents an immediate problem for a new brand entering a market.

The problem occurs, not only because there are high expenditures to compete with, but also because of the phenomenon discussed in chapter 5, which will be repeated here: The average advertising expenditure put behind a small brand has to be relatively larger than that devoted to a large brand.[6] This point is illustrated in the advertising-intensiveness curve (see figure A–6). In this curve, the comparison of the relative expenditures of different-sized brands is based on each brand's contribution to the total advertising in its market, or share of voice (SOV). A brand's share of voice can be compared with its share of the sales of all brands in a market: its share of market (SOM). When a brand's share of voice is larger than its share of market, it is investing at a higher than average rate. Figure A–6

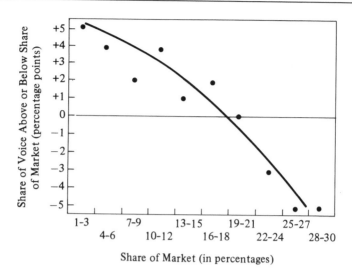

FIGURE A-6

Advertising-Intensiveness Curve

shows very clearly that this is normal for small brands. In fact, the smaller the brand, the higher the relative advertising investment that it is likely to make. This conclusion is based on the average figures for a substantial number of brands—a total of 666 different packaged goods. These averages set standards in markets; they suggest the size of the entrance fee which new brands coming into a market are obliged to pay.

This entrance fee—the investment level required for a new brand to compete realistically—is dictated by the size of the market and by the amount of advertising activity within it. In the United States, the sums are generally in the millions of dollars. And the investments have to be continued until the advertised brand becomes profitable, a period rarely less than three years.

For a small manufacturer, there is a further difficulty. Large manufacturers are able to obtain price reductions from owners of advertising media because of the size of their investments. The reason is that large expenditures earn considerable officially defined quantity rebates, and also that big manufacturers can use their superior bargaining power, that is, their ability to force down media prices below the published rate-card costs. As a result, large advertisers are often able to buy television and radio time and newspaper and magazine space 5 percent to 10 percent more cheaply than small advertisers can—a saving in the $25-million to $50-million range on an aggregate advertising budget of $500 million.[7] The small competitor's relative weakness in media buying "clout" is less marked if the manufacturer of the new brand has other important brands in this or other markets, the size of whose budgets would strengthen the manufacturer's hand with the media.

These two factors—the relatively lower advertising-intensiveness of large brands and the relatively cheaper prices that large advertisers pay the media—mean that large existing firms have a double advertising-related advantage over their small competitors. From the point of view of small new manufacturers, this advantage represents a twin hurdle that they will have to surmount. But this is not the only barrier, nor is it even the most important one faced by potential new competitors in a market.

The large manufacturer is also able to manufacture its output more efficiently—at lower cost—because it produces on a larger scale than its small rival can. It has a larger sales force carrying more lines, which means that it probably incurs a lower selling cost per unit sold. It is able to bargain more effectively with the retail trade and may be able to offer lower "slotting allowances" and other discounts. It is able to buy its raw materials with greater expertise and probably more cheaply. It is able to generate more research and development (R & D)—perhaps of higher quality—more cheaply than the small firm can.

The large manufacturer benefits, then, from a number of different types of scale economy. Its advertising-related economies are significant, but they are certainly not the most important advantages the large manufacturer has over its smaller rivals.

The barriers faced by new competitors entering developed consumer goods markets have been erected essentially by the efficiency of existing firms. These firms do not use illegal or unfair means to raise the barriers. Existing manufacturers in such markets keep alive by producing the goods that consumers want at prices that the public is prepared to pay. The barriers against new manufacturers entering the market are the difficulties they face in providing comparable (or better) goods, at similar (or lower) prices. Existing manufacturers have unquestionably created advantages for themselves. But since these are the result of their ability to satisfy consumer demand efficiently, the resultant exclusivity of markets is not devoid of social benefits. And although new manufacturers inevitably find it difficult to satisfy consumer demand as efficiently and cheaply as existing firms can, the strength of the competitive impulse does not inhibit new producers from trying to enter markets—and very occasionally succeeding. But the success rate is low, and the talent, resources, and effort required are very great. The barriers to entry represent in effect the main reason why most new competition in any market tends to be confined to existing manufacturers within that market. This is a topic discussed in the next section.

New competition—competition from outside the market but more commonly from within it—needs all the help it can get. There is, however, one obvious weapon available to make this endeavor easier, a weapon of considerable value if used skillfully. But whether or not it is used with the necessary finesse and knowledge, it is universally regarded as indispensable to the competitive process.

This weapon is, of course, consumer advertising. It is impossible to visualize how any new brand could be introduced at all without the speed and weight of coverage provided by advertising in the main media. Advertising is the most *practical* means of communicating to a large market. Advertising has three roles in the introduction of new brands. First, it spreads the news of the brand to the public. Second, it is an essential support to the sales efforts of the retail trade; indeed stores normally refuse to stock a new brand unless there is a promise of strong consumer advertising for it. The third role is that advertising is the main source of a brand's nonfunctional added values, and any brand must quickly build a store of these if it is to compete in the market on a long-term basis.

These three factors are all important. But surprisingly, the first point is not quite as dominant as common sense suggests it should be. The reason is that consumers normally hear about new brands from shop display and word of mouth more than from advertisements.[8] From a long-run point of view, the third point is the key. Added values, especially if they are constantly refreshed, operating in conjunction with continuous improvements in the brand's functional performance—improvements necessary to maintain its differentiation from its competitors—are the way to achieve stable and possibly improving sales.

These arguments have power. Readers may, however, detect that there is something circular about them. Markets have to some degree been created by advertising. Existing brands have been established as a result (at least partly) of their advertising campaigns, which also continue to protect and boost these brands' market shares. Advertising also lubricates the competitive process. This means that new brands must follow the same route as existing brands; they cannot be effectively launched without advertising. It follows that the part that advertising plays in markets is, to a large extent, self-perpetuating.

But what about a market that may at the moment by unadvertised? Is it in any way possible that advertising, which has until now been unnecessary, offers any economic advantages to justify its cost? Many people would deny this on logical grounds. We do, however, have some good evidence which demonstrates that advertising can play a beneficial role.

PRICE WITH AND WITHOUT ADVERTISING: THE CASE OF EYEGLASSES. The interesting feature of this case is that we are able to compare the influence of advertising on the price of eyeglasses by looking at the American states where eyeglasses are legally allowed to be advertised, and at the states where advertising was not allowed at the time the research took place.[9] In table A–3, the data have been slightly simplified.

The researcher who published these figures, Lee Benham, drew the obvious inference: "Prices were found to be substantially lower in states which allowed advertising."[10] The reason was partly because advertising gave optometrists more sales and thereby reduced their

TABLE A–3

The Price of Eyeglasses with and without Advertising, 1963

	Six States with Complete Advertising Restrictions		Twelve States with No Advertising Restrictions	
	Sample of Buyers	Average Price Paid	Sample of Buyers	Average Price Paid
Eyeglasses alone	50	$33.04	127	$26.34
Eyeglasses and eye examinations combined	121	$40.96	261	$37.10

cost per sale. More important, it also provided a sharp impetus to competition, particularly by increasing consumers' knowledge of where the lowest prices were to be found and thereby reducing consumer search costs. (This is a point to which we shall return.) An interesting footnote is that Benham, without disclosing his information, asked a number of professors of economics and of marketing at the University of Chicago what effect advertising would have on prices. Four in ten of the economists and all the marketing professors got the answer wrong.

Advertising and Industrial Concentration

I have already argued in this appendix that advertising makes it easier for manufacturers to make a success of their innovations by spreading news of new brands, by helping persuade the retail trade to stock them, and by building nonfunctional added values. It is possible to test how well advertising carries out these tasks by examining advertising-intensive markets and finding out how much competition there is to be found in them. One reasonable (although not perfect) way of doing this is by examining the degree of fragmentation in such markets. Fragmentation is the measure of how many brands are on the market and what their shares are; high fragmentation means, prima facie, a high degree of competition. A second way of measuring competition is by looking at the degree of fragmentation (or its opposite: concentration) from the standpoint of the firm. Falling market shares of some existing firms without a compensating increase in the shares of others mean a reduction in the concentration ratio, and vice versa.

The question of *brand fragmentation* has been studied by a number of observers, and they have all reached substantially similar conclusions.

Using A. C. Nielsen retail audit data, James O. Peckham, Sr., examined eight different packaged-goods markets.[11] In two cases he looked at trends over a decade; in five cases, over two decades; and in one case, over more than four decades. What his data demonstrated is significant new brand activity: a successful launch of more than fifty new brands in the eight markets, which in turn led to a significant reduction in the average shares of the existing brands in these markets. Because of the generally high failure rate of new brands, this total of fifty successes meant the probable launch of at least one hundred new brands and maybe as many as five hundred. Peckham's data unfortunately do not examine whether the rate of innovation was increasing over time, but the picture he showed certainly points to a high absolute level of competitive activity.

Jules Backman published in 1967 an extensive review of brand proliferation in food and drug markets, with evidence of a significant increase in the number of brands over the long term. Among his many examples is an examination of nine important grocery fields. Aggregating these, Backman counted 913 different brands in 1950 and 1,812 in 1963.[12]

Lord Heyworth, then chairman of Unilever, published in 1958 figures demonstrating the importance of new products to his company.[13] He measured this importance by the share of sales in 1957 represented by brands launched since 1951. Twenty-five specific markets were examined, covering seven different countries. In these markets, new products represented fifty percent or more of sales in nine cases, 25 percent to 49 percent in seven cases, and less than 25 percent in nine cases.

I published case studies of nineteen different brands in 1989. There was evidence of increasing fragmentation in fourteen of the nineteen markets studied.[14] These were all important product categories, covering both the United States and overseas.

In chapter 2, I referred to William M. Weilbacher's striking evidence of an increasing fragmentation of brands.[15] For example:

- There were 7 large ($1 million plus) brands of toothpaste in 1979 and 31 (at 1979 prices) in 1989.
- There were 33 large ($1 million plus) brands of coffee in 1979 and 52 (at 1979 prices) in 1989.
- There were 7 models of Ford cars in 1960 and 28 in 1989.
- There were 3 Oldsmobile models in 1960 and 19 in 1989.

These different sets of data are consistent, but they are patchy. The most persuasive evidence of the increasing diversification of markets is, however, to be found from everyday personal observation. If the shopper's memory is reasonably long, evidence of the growth in brand plurality can be seen on every supermarket shelf. A recent survey in a popular magazine claimed that there were 13,000 items in the average supermarket in 1979, a number that had grown to 26,000 in 1989.[16]

When we move from the fragmentation of brands to the *fragmentation of markets among firms,* is there evidence of the same splintering? The answer is no; the best available data seem to be negative. In mature markets, the overall concentration ratios in markets seem not to change very much over time, although this lack of change does not preclude individual manufacturers' market shares from going up or down.

Backman's 1967 study analyzed concentration in nineteen markets and quoted a summary of an additional sixty-seven markets reviewed about the same time by Stanley Solson.[17] These examples, which all relate to mature advertising-intensive product categories, show that there was very little change in the concentration ratio of any market over a medium-term span (five to ten years). Furthermore, the number of cases of increased concentration was balanced almost precisely by the number of reductions. In other words, Backman found that concentration ratios remained, in the aggregate, highly stable. The data are strong although old. More up-to-date figures have been published piecemeal, and these consistently confirm no growth at all in concentration ratios—just as Backman noted in 1967.[18]

What emerges from this analysis is that there is a tendency for *brands* to fragment, but for concentration ratios of the leading *firms* to remain stable, in the aggregate. We can draw a clear inference. It seems that there is a good deal of innovation within markets through the launch of new brands, the majority of which are unsuccessful but a few of which succeed. But most of these unsuccessful and successful new brands come from existing manufacturers in the market. Successes do no more than cause shifts in existing manufacturers' market shares—some going up and some down—leaving the total share of the main manufacturers added together relatively unchanged, in other words, making no change in the concentration ratios.

The factor that keeps outside manufacturers from entering a market is the scale economies and expertise already enjoyed by the firms successfully operating within it. These include scale effects attributable to advertising, although these are probably relatively unimportant in comparison with economies in production, purchasing, sales force employment, and R & D.

The relative unimportance of advertising is confirmed by two published examinations of the relationship between industrial concentration and advertising expenditures, intended to throw light on a commonly held view that advertising creates such amounts of goodwill for existing brands that new competitors are effectively prevented from competing against them. These two investigations refute this view rather emphatically.

In 1988, Robert B. Ekelund, Jr., and David S. Saurman published a review of ten multibrand studies that had examined statistical relationships between advertising levels and concentration ratios. The authors found a positive association in only three of the ten, a finding that drew the following observation from them: "At worst, one might conclude that the evidence suggests that the notion that advertising causes concentration is uncertain, with the preponderance of evidence suggesting no causal relationship at all."[19]

The European analyst Jean-Jacques Lambin, writing in the mid-1970s and basing his study on six regressions calculated from a total sample of 436 different brands, concluded even more strongly that "no statistically significant association is observed between measures of market concentration and measures of advertising intensity."[20]

Manufacturers' Advertising and Retail Margins

The leading contributor to the debate on the effect of advertising on retail margins is the economist Robert L. Steiner. In a seminal paper published in 1973, Steiner examined a business in which he had extensive personal experience, children's toys.[21] During his early years in the business, toys had been mainly unadvertised. However, the period which Steiner covered in his article was the fifteen years 1955–70, when television advertising expenditures in the toy market were growing strongly, leveling off at about $80 million per annum at the beginning of the 1970s.

When Steiner surveyed the market to evaluate the effect of this advertising, he made two discoveries; the first was interesting enough, and the second was very remarkable indeed:

1. The cost of the advertising for the average manufacturer, estimated at between 3 percent and 5 percent of net sales value (NSV),

was more than compensated for by offsetting savings in the production cost of the toys. This was an example of the economies of large-scale production, and the savings came at least partly as a result of a growth in the size of manufacturers, which led to an increase in the concentration ratio in the industry. The gain from the lower production cost, after the advertising was paid for, represented an average net reduction of approximately 5 percent of NSV. (Steiner did not mention the possibility of further scale economies that might become available in the long run. We shall shortly see that these are a realistic possibility.)

2. The even more striking discovery was that the advertising stimulated a large reduction in the distributors' margin. Measuring this as a proportion of retail prices, Steiner estimated that the margin had dropped from an average of 49 percent in 1947–58 to 33 percent in the early 1970s.

Steiner also published data demonstrating that margins for the best-selling merchandise were even lower than the overall averages, which were of course below what they had been before the advertising. He also demonstrated that the reduction in margins occurred in both the United States and Canada, and that the same thing was also beginning to happen in 1973 in Britain and Australia.

The reasons for the reduction in distributors' margin are rather complex. Advertised brands are familiar to the public because of the very fact of their advertising. The public is therefore more conscious of the prices of advertised than of unadvertised brands. These prices are evident in the store and do not necessarily have to be featured in the advertising. Because of the public's familiarity with the prices of advertised brands, there is less variation in the prices in different retail outlets than is the case with unadvertised brands. Individual retailers are unable to get away with higher prices; the cheapest price becomes the ruling price in the market. Even the retailers that normally charge the highest prices are forced to adopt this lowest ruling price, and even if they find it unprofitable, they will probably carry the low-priced brand as a "traffic builder" or "loss leader" because the brand is a big seller. In any event, the advertising that has built the brand makes the retailer's selling job easier and thus makes the retailer more comfortable with a lower margin.

The overall result of this process is a general shrinking in the distributors' margin for advertised brands. Moreover, if any retailer attempts to increase the price it will lose business, so that there is also *an increase in the elasticity of demand at the retail level.* This is all brought about by advertising, information, familiarity, and an overall reduction in search costs for the consumer. These factors together prevent any individual retailer from pushing up its price and padding its margin.

This increase in the elasticity of demand to the retailer operates alongside the reduction in the elasticity of demand which advertising provides to the manufacturer through the process of increasing oligopolistic differentiation, that is, the impediments created by advertising to the substitution of competitive brands for the advertised brand. The publicity—the advertising that builds added values—which brings about this differentiation is the very factor that increases retail elasticity of demand and reduces the retail margin. The double effect of advertising on demand elasticity—a reduction to the manufacturer but an increase to the retailer—has been called the *Steiner effect.*[22] It mitigates advertising's upward pressure on manufacturers' prices by imposing a countervailing downward pressure on retailers' prices.

When Robert Steiner published his article, the toy market was unlike many other consumer goods markets. It was showing strong growth. There were no manufacturers with large individual market shares, although (as has already been mentioned) the concentration ratio in the industry was growing. Most important, the average retail margin before the introduction of television advertising was high—far higher than in, for example, the food trade. These differences naturally raise the question of whether the Steiner effect applies generally to advertised brands or whether it is unique to the rather untypical toy market.

In order to examine this and other questions, the British economist W. Duncan Reekie undertook an investigation on behalf of the Advertising Association, the leading British professional organization in the advertising field. He published his report in 1979.[23] It contains the following examples, all of which confirm the Steiner effect fully and consistently:

1. Reekie examined data relating to twenty-five product categories (all food) sold in a leading British national grocery chain. There

was clear evidence of lower retail margins for the largest selling and most heavily advertised categories: a 6 percent average margin, compared with 12.5 percent for the poorest selling and least advertised categories.

2. He presented national data for two frequently purchased non-food grocery product categories. In one, he found that the average retail margin for the best-selling brands was a little more than half the average retail margin of the poorest selling brands. In the other case, the average retail margin of the most heavily advertised brands was even lower: approximately half that of the brands supported by the least amounts of advertising. He also examined temporary price reductions (TPRs), and found that they were more common with best-sellers and the most heavily advertised brands than in the market as a whole.

3. Quoting a British government report, Reekie showed that the basic distributors' margins for proprietary medicines were in the 15 percent to 20 percent range for nationally advertised brands from leading manufacturers, and in the 20 percent to 27 percent range for unadvertised, slow-moving brands.

4. Referring to another government report, dealing this time with the furniture, domestic electrical appliance, and footwear industries, Reekie noted that the domestic electrical appliance trade was the one with the most advertising. It was also the one with the lowest distributors' markups.

5. Referring to the discussion of the footwear industry in this same government report, Reekie quoted the following conclusion (retaining the emphasis in the original): "*Lower mark-ups are applied to nationally advertised brands* of shoes than to others."[24]

6. From yet another British government report, dealing with the paint industry, Reekie repeated the conclusion from the original that "Advertising appears to create a level of sales which enables the manufacturer to lower his unit production costs and encourages the retailer to accept lower gross margins."[25]

One additional effect was noted by Reekie as an indirect confirmation of the Steiner effect. Advertised food brands in Britain rose in price at a below-average rate over a period of more than two decades. Between 1955 and 1965, the prices of advertised brands went up by 14 percent (all food brands advertised and unadvertised rising by 30 percent). During the inflationary conditions between 1964 and 1978, the prices of advertised food brands increased by 220 percent (all food brands rising by 309 percent).

In the section "Advertising and Industrial Concentration," it was argued that industrial concentration ratios appear to have become stable in mature markets. Has this same trend applied also to the retail field? There is a good deal of evidence that this is not the case, and that in retailing, concentration is still increasing.[26] As discussed in chapter 2, this is essentially a regional phenomenon in the United States; for geographical reasons the degree of national concentration is still not as great as it is in some European countries.

We would logically expect increasing concentration in the retail trade to push up margins as a result of the pressure applied by retailers to manufacturers, and there is evidence that this has indeed happened. At least we can infer it from the rise that has taken place in manufacturers' promotional expenditures, which act substantially as a device to augment retail margins.[27]

The influence of this increasing retail concentration on the *relative* margins of advertised and unadvertised brands has not been explored specifically, and there is need for this to be done. However, judgment suggests that the Steiner effect is still operating, and a case can be made that greater retail concentration may even have strengthened it. The reason is that stronger brands (which are mostly the most heavily advertised ones) are those that are most indispensable to the retail trade. It is therefore futile and even dangerous for retailers to try to increase their margins on these, and they have a far greater chance to boost their margins on weaker brands. As a result, we might expect no weakening of the Steiner effect—indeed, probably the opposite.

Advertising, Scale Economies, and Long-Term Price

We now return to the main line of argument about advertising and price. Readers will remember the theoretical model and the cases supporting it, which demonstrate advertising's effectiveness in lifting demand, which in turn produces an immediate increase in price. The higher price immediately draws into the market new (higher cost, less efficiently produced) output, leading to a new market equilibrium at a higher price and a greater supply of goods than before.

I will now continue the argument to describe the long-term out-come of this second equilibrium. The newly expanded market will persuade manufacturers to begin the search for ways of improving their methods of production. This search will lead, all else being equal, to greater long-term efficiency and reduction of costs and will bring about more output, indicated by an eventual shift in the supply curve, and a reduction in price, a situation, incidentally, with obviously favorable implications for social welfare. This theoretical progress is plotted in figure A–7. In this figure, demand stimulated by advertising increases from D1 to D2, causing price to rise from P1 to P2. The higher price triggers a long-term response from existing and new manufacturers (shifting the supply curve from S1 to S2), which brings about a reduction in price to a new long-run level of equilibrium (P3).

This theoretical model is neat, optimistic, and relatively simple to comprehend. We must, however, now face the difficult task of testing it empirically.

The first and most important difficulty concerns the scale economies and the concomitant cost reductions which are brought into play by the increased output. Such economies are a commonplace of industrial production, especially in capital-intensive product fields where levels of output have been pushed up. Many cases have been published to demonstrate the operation of such scale economies, although industries which are not capital-intensive can achieve scale

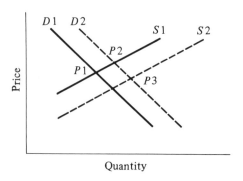

FIGURE A–7

Long-Term Response of Supply to a Short-Term Increase in Demand

economies without huge output and the stimulus of large-scale advertising.[28]

More difficult is the question of whether the benefit of the lower costs is actually passed to the public in the form of lower prices. How much this will actually happen depends on the degree of competition in the market and the relative strength of individual oligopolists.

Most packaged-goods markets are characterized by intense oligopolistic competition, which in effect forces manufacturers to pass at least a proportion of the cost savings on to the consumer. Table A–4 presents old but authoritative evidence for such a transfer of cost savings: the prices of a wide range of important and typical Unilever brands in 1957 in comparison with their prices in 1938 (with appropriate corrections for inflation).[29]

The data in table A–4 are very striking and relatively consistent. It should be emphasized that the brands in the table were all important and were typical of Unilever's portfolio. Out of the total of twenty-nine different brands, twenty-two declined in price (corrected for inflation) over the two decades covered. Moreover, the price reductions were accompanied by many significant improvements in the brands' functional performance. The history of these brands indicates clearly that scale economies made themselves felt and that they were passed on to the consumer. However, there is no indication from this table that the degree of oligopolistic differentiation changed over time. As the brands became stronger, it is probable that it increased over the two decades. It is unlikely to have been reduced.

Oligopolistic differentiation can theoretically be measured by the higher price of the brand, and also (although not quite so reliably) by the higher profit earned by its manufacturer. We should now look at any facts that can be brought to bear on the prices of advertised brands (and the profits of their manufacturers) in comparison with unadvertised brands (and the profits of those who make them).

The relationship between consumer prices and advertising has been examined in a number of broadly based studies. The results are frankly contradictory.[30] Nevertheless, one surprisingly obvious piece of everyday observation amply confirms that oligopolistic differentiation indeed carries with it a significant price for the consumer to pay. This observation is a comparison between the prices of branded goods and of unbranded generics—a study that can be made by

Prices of Unilever Brands, Adjusted for Inflation

	1938 (Index)	1957 (Index)
United Kingdom		
Persil laundry detergent	100	56
Lux soap flakes	100	102
Vim scourer	100	65
Lux Toilet soap	100	85
Stork margarine	100	99
Wall's sausages	100	83
Wall's icecream	100	57
Netherlands		
Sunlight soap	100	95
Radion laundry detergent	100	87
Vim scourer	100	72
Lux Toilet soap	100	88
Blue Band margarine	100	86
Belgium		
Sunlight soap	100	86
Soleil soap powder	100	58
Vim scourer	100	61
Lux Toilet soap	100	67
Solo margarine	100	61
France		
Persil laundry detergent	100	84
Lux Toilet soap	100	115
Germany		
Sunlight soap	100	117
Vim scourer	100	103
United States		
Lux Toilet soap	100	82
Lifebuoy soap	100	103
Rinso laundry detergent	100	92
Australia		
Sunlight soap	100	108
Velvet soap	100	95
Rinso laundry detergent	100	81
India		
Sunlight soap	100	118
Lux Toilet soap	100	66

spending a half hour in any supermarket. The consumer prices of branded goods are at least 20 percent higher than generics (although this figure should be reduced to, maybe, 10 percent to compensate for the somewhat lower product quality of the generics). The higher price of branded goods tips the balance rather decisively in favor of the view that oligopolistic differentiation contributes to lifting consumer prices. The literature in the field provides real although sporadic support for the contention that advertising can make demand more inelastic and can thus increase "the capacity for the firm to charge higher prices."[31]

Like studies of advertising and price, investigations of the relationship between manufacturers' profits and their advertising levels are also contradictory. If we accept the strong likelihood that the consumer has to pay higher prices for the oligopolistic differentiation, we would be led to expect manufacturers of advertised brands to earn higher profits than manufacturers of unadvertised goods. This was the conclusion of William S. Comanor and Thomas A. Wilson, from the first (but certainly not the last) examination of the connection between advertising and manufacturing profitability. The following summary was based on the experience of forty-one industries: "Advertising has a statistically significant and quantitatively important impact upon profit rates."[32]

If we look at the balance between scale economies (one of the major forces in the market that reduces prices) and oligopolistic differentiation (the most important force that increases them), the latter seems to be the stronger. This theory is confirmed by the widely remarked phenomenon that strongly advertised brands commonly command premium prices.

In 1987, an investigation carried out by J. Walter Thompson, New York, examined 389 large advertised brands (the data being provided by twenty-three different countries). These brands were generally well established and successful. Of these brands, 32 percent were sold at a premium price, and 17 percent were sold at a below-average price.[33]

A 1989 publication by the American Association of Advertising Agencies claimed that "Businesses that are superior in relative perceived quality and spend more than competitors (as a percentage of sales) command prices that are 9 percent higher than businesses that offer inferior product or service quality and spend less than competitors on advertising."[34]

David N. Martin, an advertising professional, wrote in 1989:

> Even established products can add value by giving an old song a new arrangement. Jello did it with chocolate pudding by calling it chocolate mousse and tacking 30 cents onto its retail price. . . . [Campbell's] targeted weight-conscious working women with a low calorie dinner that could easily be heated in a microwave oven. They gave it an upscale name and package. Campbell's glop is much the same as Swanson's, but it sells for twice as much.[35]

These quotations are frank, and they are typical of what is said by experienced practitioners about the price of advertised merchandise. They do, however, illustrate the intrinsically contradictory nature of the beliefs about advertising and price which are held in the professional world (sometimes by the same people at the same time!). Advertising is supposedly able to boost prices and make brands more profitable to manufacturers. It is also supposedly able to benefit society through long-term price reductions caused by huge production runs which are made economically feasible through the demand stimulated by advertising! Both views cannot be right; or at least they cannot both apply simultaneously. I shall shortly examine how much the economic pros and cons of advertising balance out.

One question that must be considered is the truth, or otherwise, of the statement that "Campbell's glop is much the same as Swanson's." To an individual observer this might appear to be the truth. However, blind product tests in this and other brand categories carried out among substantial numbers of consumers confirm quite emphatically that there are wide differences in consumer perceptions of the functional performance of competing brands. This is even more true of branded goods versus generics. In the latter comparisons, the differences perceived by consumers are underscored by the opinions of food chemists and store managers, who all generally agree that generics vary greatly in their functional quality, depending on who supplies them.

Any attempt at a *quantitative* evaluation of the various contradictory influences of advertising on price is extremely crude and heavily judgmental. The effort is nevertheless worth making because an order of magnitude, no matter how imprecise, is far better than anything we have at present, which is nothing beyond a number of opposing partisan views and the even more plentiful opinions of people who cannot make up their minds on the issue.

There are five factors to take into account if we are to attempt to put some numbers into our arguments. Two of these factors push prices up; two bring them down; the fifth factor does not operate directly on price, but it provides an indirect (but demonstrable) social benefit which is funded by advertising:

1. The direct cost of advertising increases prices. Typical A:S ratios (calculated on the manufacturer's NSV) are in the 4 percent to 8 percent range. Such expenditures lift consumer prices by about 5 percent.

2. Oligopolistic differentiation also increases prices. Offsetting immediate economies of scale (although allowing that further ones may begin to operate in the long run), the maximum net amount by which price may be elevated by oligopolistic differentiation may be about 20 percent. This is a premium similar to that carried by many branded goods over generic products. This percentage should, however, be scaled down—perhaps to about 10 percent—to compensate for the significantly lower functional quality of the generics.

3. The scale economies in manufacturing and marketing branded goods may bring additional downward pressures on prices in the long run (as illustrated by the Unilever experience). This reduction may be of the order of 10 percent for typical large-volume packaged goods. However, in some more technically oriented consumer goods fields (for example, ballpoint pens, pocket calculators, and miniature radios), the scale economies have in the past been very much greater and have led to spectacular long-range reductions in consumer prices. These possibilities have, however, been excluded from my calculations.

4. The reduction in retail margins associated with the Steiner effect probably accounts for a minimum price reduction of about 5 percent.

5. There is the question of the subsidy to the media, which (as we shall see in the next section) provides an indirect income to virtually all members of society. This can be estimated at about $260 per capita per annum.

These five sums, crude though they are, suggest that the various influences of advertising on price tend more or less to balance out—or at the very least to counter and trim back the extreme effect of any of the influences operating individually. Another way of expressing this point is that the net economic cost of advertising is relatively small, if we take into account the long-term reactions and corrections that the competitive market stimulates. It should of course be added that advertising is a lubricant of the economic system rather than a prime mover. The engine—the force that drives competition into its responses to market forces—is businesspeople's self-interest. The social benefits that flow from this competition, in particular the way in which consumers are protected from extortionate prices, are as significant today as they were two centuries ago, when they were described, in Adam Smith's powerful metaphor, as being engineered by an "invisible hand."

Three points must be made in concluding this section. First, if we were to abolish advertising and thereby to eliminate the first of the five elements from the above calculation, the net effect of the reduction would be unpredictable. The reason is that every one of the other four variables would be affected, and we have no way of knowing what the eventual outcome would be.

Second, oligopolistic capitalism offers very major economic advantages, which include income growth, innovation, a rapid response to consumer needs, and a far higher degree of efficiency than the economic systems permitted by noncapitalist political regimes. It is striking that in view of advertising's contribution to the economy of a country like the United States, its net cost is so small.

The third point is the most important one. The way in which the advertising business is organized and operated is open to much criticism for its wastefulness. It is virtually certain that the beneficial effects of advertising could be obtained for far less cost. But in order to make this happen, the business needs to operate with considerably greater skill and knowledge than it now does. If such an improvement were ever to be made, the cost equation of advertising might eventually show a credit balance, rather than an approximate break-even.

Advertising and the Price of the Media

In 1990, the amount spent by advertisers in the main media in the United States was over $77 billion. Table A–5 shows how this sum was broken down into its component elements.

TABLE A–5

Volume of Advertising in the United States, 1990

	Gross Expenditures ($ billion)	Expenditures Excluding Commission ($ billion)
All media	77.3	65.6
Newspapers	32.3	27.4
Television	28.4	24.1
Radio	8.7	7.4
Consumer magazines	6.8	5.8
Outdoor	1.1	0.9

Adapted from "U.S. Advertising Volume" Advertising Age, May 6, 1991, p. 16. Used with permission.

The figures in table A–5 give some measure of the extent to which advertising provides a subsidy, a transfer payment, to users of the media, a group that effectively comprises all members of society. The figures must however be scaled down to eliminate the cost of planning, writing, running, and supervising the advertising, and we can estimate this cost, very approximately, as 15 percent of the gross cost of media budgets (reflecting the traditional, although not universally applied, level of agency commissions). The second column of figures in table A–5 takes this cost into account. Thus it can be seen that the overall net value of the subsidy to media users totals a little over $65 billion, or about $260 for every man, woman, and child in the United States.

The subsidy is spread widely, although not entirely evenly, over the population as a whole; there is a skew toward those people who use the largest numbers and amounts of media. Television and radio have a virtually universal coverage, but this is not true of newspapers and magazines. The effective per capita subsidy to the 70 percent of the population who have newspaper subscriptions in addition to television and radio is the equivalent of about $280 from these three media alone.[36] Note that the transfer payment to users of these media is different in one important particular from how society implements other income readjustments, such as those engineered by fiscal policy. The payment to media users is regressive. Better educated and higher income people, who are above-average users of the media, receive a larger subsidy than the less well educated and those with lower incomes.

The media subsidy applies to newspapers, television, radio, and magazines, but not of course to outdoor advertising, since this does not try to secure its audience's attention by providing entertainment and news to accompany the advertisements. As far as the four most important media are concerned, advertising provides the funding for all television on network stations and their local affiliates, although not everywhere for the small but influential stations of the Public Broadcasting System (PBS). It funds all local radio stations, except National Public Radio (NPR) affiliates. To virtually the total population, this means that there is no "admission fee" for what is clearly their major source of entertainment (judged by the length of time the average family watches television, more than seven hours per day.)[37]

As for the print media, advertising provides, on average, a 40 percent subsidy of the price of a newspaper (so that without advertising, a 50-cent issue would cost the newspaper buyer 85 cents) and a 50 percent subsidy of the price of a magazine (causing the cost of a nominally $2.50 title to come down to $1.25).[38]

It is therefore literally true that advertising reduces the price of one significant item of household expenditure: the mass media of entertainment. Therefore it is legitimate to include the media subsidy of $260 per capita in the estimated computation of the economic cost of advertising which was made in the preceding section of this appendix. And readers will remember that the media subsidy appeared on the positive side of the balance, as a factor yielding a significant social benefit to set against the cost of advertising.

Advertising and Macroeconomics

The final topic I shall examine is the macroeconomic effect of advertising, that is, advertising's influence on the overall volume of sales in individual product categories. Does a high volume of advertising increase the size of a category? Does a reduced volume of advertising decrease it?

In the description of the campaign of the California Avocado Advisory Board, we have already examined a case in which advertising succeeded in increasing primary demand, that is, the total demand in a product field. However, the difference between this and most categories of consumer goods is that in the latter, much of advertising's successful stimulation of the demand for one specific brand is countered by the advertising and promotion of competitive brands. It can therefore be argued that the advertising and promotional efforts of individual brands cancel out to some extent, and this canceling out inhibits the effect of the campaigns for individual brands on the total size of any category.

The relatively small amount of research in this field tends to support this view. There are at least no strong data to support the notion that advertising has a significant macro effect on competitive markets.

In 1976, Lambin published details of ten cases in which he estimated the advertising elasticity of category (as opposed to brand) sales.[39] In only four of the ten cases (two covering soft drinks and one each covering hairspray and transportation) was it possible to find a statistically significant advertising elasticity relating to markets as a whole. These were at a very low level of significance (25 percent). And the elasticities themselves were also small; in three of the four cases, they were below what is (apparently) the average advertising elasticity for brands in competitive markets.[40]

Even more important, Lambin admitted that the four cases were examples of developing markets, "where product-related social, economic and technological forces are favorable to the spontaneous expansion of demand."[41]

In 1970, the economist Julian L. Simon published an examination of advertising and the "propensity to consume," using an interesting and original array of empirical sources.[42] Simon admitted the imperfections of most of his data, and the result of his evaluation was that he found the overall macroeffect of advertising to be indeterminate. There was no clear effect either way.

This conclusion is no great distance away from Neil Borden's, in the first serious examination of the economic effects of advertising, which was published half a century ago: "Basic trends of demand for products, which are determined by underlying social and environmental conditions, are more significant in determining the expansion or contraction of primary demand than is the use or lack of use of advertising."[43] Borden's conclusion relates specifically to the more mature markets, in which advertising arguments tend to be extremely discriminating (that is, brand-specific) rather than motivating (that is, selling general product benefits). Mature markets are of course the rule and not the exception in the United States in the 1990s.

Evidence from actual markets during the past decade or so provides general confirmation of advertising's weak or nonexistent macroeffect. As described in chapter 2, by the end of the 1970s, the number of consumer goods markets in the United States that had flattened had overtaken the number that were still growing. Today, in the early part of the 1990s, I estimate that 90 percent of all expenditure on consumer goods takes place in markets which no longer show growth beyond the annual increment of 1 or 2 percent caused by population increase. It is obvious from this situation that high expenditures on advertising and promotions have not succeeded in stimulating any continuation in market growth. The stagnation seems to have been brought about by a general saturation in consumption levels, certainly in packaged-goods categories. And advertising has apparently been unable to affect the situation.

An interesting parallel conclusion can be drawn from the progress of sales in the cigarette market. In this market, overall consumption began to decline only in 1981,[44] a decade after the major reduction in advertising expenditures that followed the removal of cigarette advertising from the television screen in early 1971. This decade was also a time of massive and uniformly unfavorable publicity about the effects of smoking on health. Not only is the stability of cigarette consumption evidence of the lack of responsiveness of demand to negative persuasion, but it also shows that advertising has little macroeffect in a downward direction. Reduced advertising does not depress category sales. Similarly, high levels of advertising do not increase them.

During the 1960s, the Unilever operating company in Sweden detected a flattening in total sales of toilet soap—a stagnation in average consumption per capita at a level below that in other developed markets, notably the United States. A special advertising campaign was mounted to try to get the total market moving again. It failed.[45]

If advertising has no macroeffect on individual product categories, it therefore has no macroeffect on the economy as a whole. It cannot be used as a tool for economic management, for example, as a device to control the overall propensity to consume.

Summary

1. The majority of consumer goods markets are oligopolies, and the economic effects of advertising can best be understood from an examination of the conditions of oligopolistic competition. Under oligopoly, the competition between firms is real and active, and it embraces both price and nonprice competition. An important aspect of nonprice competition is that the oligopolist uses advertising to differentiate its brand in order to reduce its elasticity of demand. This means that the oligopolist is better able to increase its price.

2. All advertising must be paid for, out of either the price charged or the profit earned (or both.) The A:S ratio of a brand is normally a small, although significant, element in its cost, commonly a figure representing 4 percent to 8 percent of NSV.

3. The main object of advertising is to increase demand (illustrated by a shift of demand curves to the right). Increased demand elevates price, and there is evidence that advertising *can* increase demand. But this does not mean that advertising is always efficient enough to work in this way.

4. Higher prices generally stimulate competition. The structure of capitalist industry has erected barriers against new entrants into any product field. These barriers are the result of scale economies in all aspects of business, including manufacture, raw material purchasing, marketing, and R & D. High advertising expenditure is one of these barriers, although not the most important one.

5. On the other hand, advertising is an essential dynamic of the competitive process. There can be no effective competition without it. There is evidence that on the rare occasions when advertising is begun in formerly unadvertised fields, it can actually cause prices to come down.

6. There is a demonstrably high level of innovation in most consumer goods markets. This is far more the work of existing firms in the field than of new firms coming in from outside. These are generally kept out by the barriers discussed in point 4. The proof of this conclusion comes from the continuous stability of concentration ratios in most markets.

7. The increased production that is made possible by improved manufacturing methods, and that is drawn onto the market by the higher price stimulated by advertising, causes a downward pressure on price in the long run. How much price is actually reduced depends

on the scale economies that are now made possible by the larger volume of output. There is evidence that such scale economies exist, and that they can bring prices down.

8. An additional downward pressure on consumer prices is the tendency, described as the Steiner effect, of strongly advertised brands to carry reduced retail margins.

9. The amounts by which advertising causes prices to rise seem to be balanced approximately by the amounts by which it causes them to fall. Overall, the influence of advertising on price is relatively neutral.

10. Advertising is an important part of the competitive capitalist system, and oligopolistic competition could not operate without it. However, it is perfectly true that if advertising were more efficient, its cost could be reduced, and that this reduction would in turn yield an improvement in social welfare.

11. A side benefit of advertising is that it provides a transfer payment, estimated to average $260 per capita in 1990, to all users of the communications media in the United States, in effect, all members of American society.

12. There is very little evidence that advertising has any macroeffect. It has no demonstrable influence on the total level of demand for specific goods and services. And as an extension of this point, it has little effect on the economy as a whole, beyond the sum of its microeffects on individual brands and firms. It is too weak to be used as a tool of economic management.

Appendix B

A Politician's View of Advertising: A Speech by Enoch Powell

He is the only man who is for ever apologizing for his occupation.

H. L. Mencken (talking about the typical businessman)

Enoch Powell is a prominent British politician. He was born in 1912, was educated as a classical scholar, and during the 1930s taught the Greek and Latin classics at the Universities of Cambridge and Sydney. On the outbreak of World War II, he joined the British army as a private soldier and within five years had become a brigadier on the general staff.

After the war, he went into politics and was elected to the House of Commons in 1950. He was a Member of Parliament for almost forty years and was a Minister of the Crown between 1955 and 1963, successively under Anthony Eden and Harold Macmillan. He declined to serve under Sir Alec Douglas-Home, who became leader of the Conservative Party in 1963 after Macmillan.

Enoch Powell was never again in government but remained an influential Member of Parliament and from the back benches expressed powerful and persuasive views on many important public issues. He was and is a controversial figure and has espoused a number of unpopular causes. He is nevertheless universally known for the strength of his principles and is widely respected for his moral and intellectual integrity.

He is a prolific writer and has published on a wide variety of political topics, and on the Greek and Latin classics. He has also published three volumes of poetry.

He delivered the speech that is republished in this appendix on

June 26, 1969. His audience was the Advertising Association, the most important British organization representing the interests of advertisers, advertising agencies, and the advertising media.

Two points must be made to explain the relevance of this speech to the content of this book.

First, Enoch Powell explains that advertising is an important part of competitive capitalism, and that it yields a positive net return to society when we balance its advantages and disadvantages. This view is entirely harmonious with everything that is said in this book.

Second, he emphasizes the robust nature of capitalism. When he reminds us that advertisers should respond trenchantly to criticisms of what they do, he underscores the fact that advertising is itself often conducted in a soft, unaggressive, "civilized" manner. On occasion there is a good reason for this. Advertisers and their agencies sometimes judge understatement and soft selling to be more effective than overstatement and hard selling, because understatement by the advertiser can be an effective technique in achieving a psychological response from the audience.

More often, however, soft selling is an excuse for something else. In my direct personal experience, I have come across at least three different forces at work which in effect emasculate the strength of advertising claims:

1. The fear of competitive retaliation often trims and mutes the power and directness of an advertising message.
2. There have been cases in which the media have explicitly refused to carry strongly competitive advertising for fear of losing business from competitive brands.
3. It is not uncommon for competitors in a product category to visualize themselves as members of an exclusive club. When they feel this way, the very act of being beastly to their "friendly competitors" (*sic:* these words are often used) would result in a disturbingly uncomfortable life. This means an uncomfortable life for them, but not for the public.

In 1776, Adam Smith said: "People of the same trade seldom meet together, even for merriment and diversion, but the conversation ends in a conspiracy against the public, or in some contrivance to raise prices."

This book has argued that advertising's essential contribution to society is its role in the competitive process. Enoch Powell's speech is an implicit reminder that the greater the vigor of the advertising, the greater will be the ensuing benefit to society as a whole.

His speech is quoted verbatim:

"Any guest is under an obligation not merely to say 'thank you' to his hosts, but if possible to repay them. I should like to discharge this obligation to your Association, because I am specially honored by being made your guest of honor. The natural coin with which a professional can repay the members of another profession is advice, advice from the area where he is (or at any rate is supposed to be) expert and they are not. But this advice, in order to be of any use, must be unwelcome advice. There is no merit in welcome advice: if it is wrong (which advice often is anyhow), it merely confirms the recipients in their error; if it is right, it is superfluous, because the recipients knew it already. Hence my intention this afternoon is to offer what I hope and trust will be unwelcome advice.

"Advertising is under constant attack, political attack, moral attack, all sorts of attack. Now, the members of any trade or profession thus under attack are prone to fall into certain, absolutely classic lines of error in reacting; and if, to their misfortune, they are combined in, or still worse—horrible idea!—'represented' by, an Association there seems to be no possibility whatsoever of their avoiding those errors. The first is to defend themselves; the second is to get hold of 'a hair of the dog that bit them.' Pardon me, but advertisers and their spokesmen—it is rarely advisable for businessmen to have spokesmen; they should 'spoke' themselves, if at all—react to attack in precisely these two predictable ways.

"Advertising is under attack for promoting superfluous and synthetic desires, for encouraging the sale and consumption of goods and services which are positively undesirable, for causing economic waste by differentiating products and thus reducing the scope for economies of scale in manufacture and marketing, for being itself wasteful in that it conveys partial information to the public at unnecessarily high cost. I have quoted some typical specimens of the attack. Sure enough, the spokesmen of advertising rush headlong into defending themselves against them. They adopt what Demosthenes called the Thracian style of boxing—to put one's hand over the place where the last blow fell. There is, as the phrase is, 'no future' in this.

"Watch a professional instead; watch a politician engaged in his trade, a man who lives his whole life 'where the knocks are hardest.' He, you will notice, spends as little time as possible answering the attacks upon him, and as much as possible assailing his opponents. This is not because he is by nature pugnacious or devious—though I wouldn't deny that necessarily—it is because experience and operation of natural selection have taught him that this is his best way to survive. There is an underlying logic about these tactics. Most charges or criticisms are not absolutely without foundation, and therefore can never be disposed of one hundred percent, whereas all practical life consists in choosing between more or less imperfect and unsatisfactory alternatives, so that the act of judgment is normally an act of comparison—a mental process wonderfully stimulated by exercising one's own ability to give the other fellow a black eye.

"Now take advertising. There is some truth in every one of the charges I enumerated. It is impossible to deny that sometimes, if not frequently, an article could be provided cheaper if not differentiated for the purposes of market promotion or that much of the information conveyed by expensive advertising could be imparted at barely any cost at all by a label. These assertions, however, are only relevant if the particular case is looked at in isolation. They cease to be so immediately we look at the whole environment, and inquire what is the alternative.

"The alternative is some state or at least public authority which would organize a system of consumer information and advice. The alternative is an authority which would decide how many variations and therefore what variations in the goods and services to be provided shall be permitted. Remove advertising, disable a person or a firm from preconizing its wares and their merits, and the whole of society and of the economy is transformed. The enemies of advertising are the enemies of freedom—a good serviceable battle cry, and one which indicates the only safe tactic: to carry the war into the opponent's territory. There is no need to claim for advertising, any more than for any other aspect of the market, that it is perfect or perfectible. By all means admit that it involves what may be discerned, after the event, to have been waste of economic resources. Never forget, however, what is the alternative, and the only alternative to the market: an enforced and arbitrary control over the actions of the individual, and a limitation of his choices.

"Of course I recognize at least one of the reasons why the members of a trade or profession, or their 'spokesmen,' are so reluctant to do battle upon this favorable ground—indeed the only ground on which victory is technically possible. 'But,' they say, 'this argument is political, and we are nonpolitical, our case has nothing to do with politics.' When I hear this, I am reminded of nothing so much as the high-pitched and pitiable note which the fly emits when the spider gets it into its clutches on the edge of the web. No doubt it, too, is protesting that it is nonpolitical. 'Nonpolitical,' my foot! The whole question is one of politics, and only capable of being politically decided: it is the question of the sort, and organization, of the economy and of society which one is prepared to accept. Political attack can only be repelled on political grounds, to meet a political assault with nonpolitical arguments is to descend naked into the gladiatorial arena.

"It is possible, however, to go still further, and while stripping oneself of defense, to present a weapon to one's opponents. This is done by adopting the principle of 'a hair of a dog that bit you.' The profession or trade which is under attack says to its attacker, 'All right, but we will discipline ourselves so as to remove the causes of offense,' thereby instantly conceding both the validity of the offense and the necessity for control (called 'discipline'). The case for the market, operating freely within the general law, is thus given away at the outset and, what is more sinister still, the very 'representatives' and 'spokesmen' of the profession or trade volunteer to be the janitors and prison warders of its members; they enlist, though in a subordinate capacity, in the ranks of the enemy.

"Consider a recent publication by a body which includes the word *Christian* in its description. The publication bears the innuendo-laden title *Ten Years of Advertising Alcohol.* Its object of course is to pretend 'that the growing rate of drunkenness particularly among the young' is partly due to 'the efforts of the drink trade to boost sales by widespread and intensive advertising,' though it does not explicitly claim more than that the two things 'cannot be completely divorced.' I want to draw your attention to the following statement in the preface: 'It is obvious that Parliament will soon find itself bound to intervene unless the trade disciplines itself. Control by Act of Parliament,

346 · *Appendix B*

however, is nothing like so satisfactory as would be the full and free acknowledgment by the trade of its responsibilities, and the adoption of a strict code of alcohol advertising ethics.'

"This is precisely the trap and it is baited with that word *ethics,* which attracts all professions and their 'spokesmen' like moths from miles away. There is only one safe answer and it is this. If Parliament, in its wisdom or unwisdom, legislates, then there will be law applied and interpreted by the courts, known and public, applying to all alike. In that event, we will, of course, comply like other law-abiding citizens, and the consequences, good or bad, will be upon the heads of those who made the law. But do not ask us to admit by implication what we deny, and to plead guilty to what we do not recognize as an offense. Unless and until the law requires otherwise, we have the same right as other citizens to conduct our affairs, and to earn our profits, as we think fit. The pretension of a public authority to decide that it shall not be lawful to advertise what it is lawful to sell, that in itself leads to consequences which we do not accept and do not believe our fellow countrymen would accept. It is several degrees worse still if such a claim were to be advanced by a private body, even though that body purported to 'represent' us."

Notes

Chapter 1

1. See, for instance, Frank Whitehead, "Advertising" in *The Three Faces of Advertising,* ed. Michael Barnes (London: Advertising Association, 1975), 35–55. Many other examples could be chosen to illustrate this point.
2. Editorial, "Catch Them Young," *The Economist* (January 27, 1990).
3. Robert E. Hite and Cynthia Fraser, "International Advertising Strategies of Multinational Corporations," *Journal of Advertising Research* (August/September 1988): 9–17.
4. See, for instance, John Philip Jones, *What's in a Name? Advertising and the Concept of Brands* (Lexington, MA: Lexington Books, 1986), 64–66.
5. Magid M. Abraham and Leonard M. Lodish, "Getting the Most out of Advertising and Promotions," *Harvard Business Review* 90 (May–June 1990): 50–60.
6. Callaghan OHerlihy, "How to Test the Sales Effects of Advertising," *Admap* (January 1980): 32–35.
7. John Philip Jones, *Does It Pay to Advertise? Cases Illustrating Successful Brand Advertising* (Lexington, MA: Lexington Books, 1989), 294–300.
8. A number of hypothetical examples that demonstrate this phenomenon are to be found in Jones, *Does It Pay,* 323–328.
9. Various calculations demonstrating the unprofitability of promotions are to be found in John Philip Jones, "Promotions—A Game of Double Jeopardy," *Harvard Business Review* 90 (September–October 1990): 145–52.
10. R. S. Woods, "Forgetting Brand Loyalty, or Why 85% of Advertising Is Wasted," *Advertising Age* (March 5, 1990): 22.
11. I am indebted to my friend Harold F. Clark, Jr., for stressing the importance of this factor.
12. G. Robert Cox and Edward J. McGee, *The Ad Game: Playing to Win* (Englewood Cliffs, NJ: Prentice-Hall, 1990), 21–22.
13. Al Ries and Jack Trout, *Positioning: The Battle for Your Mind* (New York: Warner Books, 1981), 218–219.
14. John Lyons, *Guts: Advertising from the Inside Out* (New York: Amacon, American Management Association, 1989), 113.
15. William M. Weilbacher, *Current Advertiser Practices in Compensating Their*

Advertising Agencies (New York: Association of National Advertisers, 1989). Also John Micklethwait, "The Advertising Industry" (Survey), *The Economist* (June 9, 1990): 16–17.

Chapter 2

1. Quoted in Nancy Giges, "Through Eyes of Wall Street," in "The House That Ivory Built: 150 Years of Procter & Gamble," *Advertising Age* (August 29, 1987): 26.
2. Ibid., 24.
3. R. Craig Endicott, "Hundred Leading National Advertisers," *Advertising Age* (September 27, 1989): 106; R. Craig Endicott, "Hundred Leading National Advertisers," *Advertising Age* (September 25, 1991): 58.
4. John Maynard Keynes, *The General Theory of Employment, Interest and Money* (New York: Harcourt Brace Jovanovich, 1964), 29–30. Official figures for the United States provide some oblique confirmation of this hypothesis. For instance, the proportion of personal consumption expenditure that was spent on nondurable goods (that is, where there was no element of saving involved) went down from 38 percent in 1980 to 35 percent in 1988. There was a corresponding increase in the value of consumer expenditure on certain consumer durables, notably automobiles and television sets. (In neither case was there any increase in the size of the market measured in volume, merely increases in the average prices of cars and television equipment.) *Statistical Abstract of the United States* (Washington, DC: Bureau of the Census, 1990).
5. Neil H. Borden, *The Economic Effects of Advertising* (Chicago: Richard D. Irwin, 1942), 433.
6. I selected these categories on the basis of their large size and whether they are characterized by obvious market activity; 150 categories represents a large sample: 33 percent of the 450 covered by MRI.
7. The data collected by the Census of Manufactures are put together in large categories, some of which comprise many subcategories. The fifty fields I have examined represent virtually the total number of consumer goods categories; my data are based not so much on a sample as on a census.
8. J. O. Peckham, Sr., *The Wheel of Marketing,* 2nd ed. (privately published, and available through A. C. Nielsen), 89–91.
9. See, for instance, "Brand Stretching Can Be Fun—and Dangerous," *The Economist* (May 5, 1990).
10. William J. Hampton and James R. Norman, "General Motors: What Went Wrong," *Business Week* (March 16, 1987): 102–110; also Raymond Serafin and Wayne Walley, "GM Slices $1m. in Ads," *Advertising Age* (January 15, 1990): 1, 50; also Raymond Serafin & Heather Hunt, "The Life and Times of GM under Smith," *Advertising Age* (July 23, 1990): S-4.
11. Peckham, *Wheel of Marketing,* 77.
12. Quoted by William M. Weilbacher, *How Consumers' View of Media Can*

Lead to Better Media Planning (Evanston, IL: Northwestern University's Fifth Annual Media Symposium, 1990).

13. See, for instance, *Niche Marketing, Identifying Opportunity Markets with Syndicated Consumer Research* (New York, Mediamark Research Inc., 1988).

14. Weilbacher, *Better Media Planning*, 11.

15. John Philip Jones, *Does It Pay to Advertise? Cases Illustrating Successful Brand Advertising* (Lexington, MA: Lexington Books, 1989), 301.

16. Shirley Young, "Copy Testing Without Magic Numbers," *Journal of Advertising Research* (February 1972): 3–12.

17. Estimates made by Robert J. Coen of McCann-Erickson, "Coen: Little Ad Growth," *Advertising Age* (May 6, 1991): 1, 16.

18. The econometric evaluation of advertising performance is an important topic that will be discussed in chapter 10. The process has developed much further in Europe than in the United States since the early 1980s. This development suggests (to optimistic observers) the possibility of rapid advances in the United States in the near future, through the use of techniques pioneered in Europe.

19. John Philip Jones, "Is Total Advertising Going Up or Down?" *International Journal of Advertising* 4 (1985): 47–64.

20. The deficiencies of recall testing are discussed in John Philip Jones, *What's in a Name? Advertising and the Concept of Brands* (Lexington, MA: Lexington Books, 1986), ch. 6.

21. This subtle and important point was made in personal conversation, in September 1990, by the well-known advertising researcher Edward Rosenstein.

22. See, for instance, Richard Zoglin, "Days of Distress at CBS," *Time Magazine* (December 25, 1989).

23. Gary Levin & Jon Lafayette, "Agency Employment Decline Continues," *Advertising Age* (May 14, 1990): 16.

24. See, for instance, Kathleen Barnes, "Nestlé Exec Criticizes Sluggish Global Shops," *Advertising Age* (November 13, 1989): 86; also Jon Lafayette, "Smaller Agencies Hook Big Fish," *Advertising Age* (November 13, 1989): 28; also Joseph M. Winski, "Confidence in Ad Agencies Slips," *Advertising Age* (March 12, 1990): 20.

25. John Philip Jones, "Cure the Industry with More Creativity," *New York Times* (September 10, 1989): Section 3, p. 3.

26. See an extremely interesting article on five of the most prominent small, thrusting agencies in New York City: Randall Rothenberg, "Advertising's Antic Upstarts," *New York Times* (March 31, 1991): Section 3, pp. 1–3. Two of the young people whose work is described in this article are former students of mine.

27. Packaged goods represent approximately 40 percent of all advertising volume in the United States (and about 60 percent of the volume of the 100 largest advertisers). There is evidence that promotions are also playing an increasing part in other product fields, for example, financial services and the various automotive categories.

28. Don E. Schultz and Robert D. Dewar, "Retailers in Control: The Impact of

Retail Trade Concentration," *Journal of Consumer Marketing* 1, no. 2 (1983–84): 81–89.

Chapter 3

1. Fred Danzig, Editor of *Advertising Age,* "Advertising and Progress," *Advertising Age,* Special Issue (November 9, 1988).
2. Philip Kotler, *Marketing Management, Analysis, Planning and Control,* 5th ed. (Englewood Cliffs, NJ: Prentice-Hall, 1984), 658.
3. Arthur A. Winters and Shirley F. Milton, *The Creative Connection* (New York: Fairchild Publications, 1982), 4.
4. John Kenneth Galbraith, *The New Industrial State,* 2nd ed. (Harmondsworth, Middlesex, U.K.: Penguin Books, 1978), 213.
5. Frank Whitehead, "Advertising," in *The Three Faces of Advertising,* ed. Michael Barnes (London: Advertising Association, 1975), 54.
6. Joan Robinson, *The Economics of Imperfect Competition* (London: Macmillan, 1950), 90.
7. I am grateful to Professor Andrew Ehrenberg of the London Business School for the arresting notion that a belief in the power of advertising is pretty well the sole point of agreement uniting many of its protoganists and antagonists. Professor Ehrenberg made this point at a seminar in Geneva, Switzerland, in October 1988 in which we both participated. His name will appear again in this chapter.
8. I once heard advertising referred to by a thoughtful and educated member of the public as "psychological engineering," a description he intended other people to take entirely seriously.

   Of all the common misconceptions about advertising, the most delightful is surely the notion of "subliminal" effects, the supposed ability of advertising to sell by flashing words onto a cinema or television screen so rapidly that viewers are not conscious that the eye has picked them up. This "technique" was first described in an article in the *Sunday Times* of London in 1956 and was given wide publicity in the United States by Vance Packard in 1957. See Vance Packard, *The Hidden Persuaders* (Harmondsworth, Middlesex, UK: Penguin Books, 1979), 41–42. Interest in subliminal effects has never flagged since; as a result, they have become all but universally believed in by the public.

   At an early stage in the history of subliminal advertising, however, skeptics pressed its proponents for evidence of its effectiveness. Under rigorous scrutiny, it was discovered that the original "test" of subliminal advertising in a New Jersey cinema never in fact took place. Indeed, the cinema in which it was supposedly held never existed. The whole thing was a journalistic hoax, a minor Piltdown man. The report of the proceedings of the 1987 Conference of the American Academy of Advertising contains a perfectly serious paper on subliminal advertising, which includes fifty footnotes referring to papers on the subject in academic journals. See also note 19.

9. The ancient adage "No one ever lost money by underestimating public taste" is one of the better known catch phrases associated with advertising.

10. Stephen King, *Advertising as a Barrier to Market Entry* (London: Advertising Association, 1980), 15.

11. John Philip Jones, *What's in a Name? Advertising and the Concept of Brands* (Lexington, MA: Lexington Books, 1986), 64–66.

12. Ibid. 83–92.

13. This has been Ehrenberg's main field of study. He has assembled and synthesized a formidable volume of data covering consumers' purchasing habits in more than thirty different product fields in a number of different countries over a thirty-year time span. The regularity of the purchasing patterns he discovered enabled him to model them mathematically, and the models have been widely and successfully used for prediction. Ehrenberg's work is sponsored financially by many of the largest and most skilled manufacturers of consumer goods in the United States and Europe. The operational applications of Ehrenberg's work are described and discussed in Jones, *What's in a Name?* ch. 5.

14. See for instance editorial, "The Ad 'Crash' of '85," *Advertising Age* (October 17, 1988). See also Jones, *What's in a Name?* ch. 11.

15. The reader should note that the word *marginal* is used here and in the following paragraph in its precise meaning (which originated in microeconomics), that is, "at the margin," or "incremental," particularly as it describes a dependent incremental change following an incremental change in an independent stimulus. It does not necessarily mean a small change.

16. See John Philip Jones, *Does It Pay to Advertise? Cases Illustrating Successful Brand Advertising* (Lexington, MA: Lexington Books, 1989).

17. Advertising does, however, have a secondary, or lagged, effect. But this is the result of repeat purchase which follows the initial purchase stimulated in the first place by an advertisement.

18. In one investigation, covering the relationships between advertisers and their agencies over the five years 1981–85, it was found that at least half the advertisers in every one of the product fields examined had changed agencies at least once. In most fields the rate of change was much higher. Paul Michell, "Account Switching," *Journal of Advertising Research* (June–July 1988): 38.

19. Here is one example (from among many I could have chosen) to illustrate this point. American professors who teach advertising belong to an organization called the American Academy of Advertising. In the proceedings of the 1988 Conference of this body, forty-two papers were published: (a) not a *single paper* includes data on the sales effect of any specific advertising campaign; (b) there is no reference at all to the possibility that advertising may ever work according to the weak theory; and (c) in the 620 source references in the published papers, Ehrenberg's name appears only once (as a coauthor of a technical paper dealing with the duplication of television viewing between stations). Because of the absence of any references to Ehrenberg's most important work, we could never guess that he is one of the most widely

published and respected authors in the marketing and advertising fields, having
been responsible for six books and more than two hundred papers that have
appeared in professional and research journals.

20. It has always been true that a large number of entrants into the advertising
business have been graduates in the liberal arts. The proportion of new
entrants who come from this source does not appear to be declining.

Chapter 4

1. Marvin Bower, former managing director of McKinsey & Company. Quoted
   in Terence E. Deal and Allan A. Kennedy, *Corporate Cultures: the Rites and
   Rituals of Corporate Life* (Reading, MA: Addison-Wesley Publishing
   Company, 1982), 4.

2. Sir David Orr, Foreword, in John Philip Jones, *Does It Pay to Advertise? Cases
   Illustrating Successful Brand Advertising* (Lexington, MA: Lexington Books,
   1989), xxi.

3. Deal and Kennedy, *Corporate Cultures*. Cynthia G. Swank, of the Inlook
   Group, P.O. Box 405, Portsmouth, NH 03802-0405, has assembled a helpful
   bibliography of books and articles that discuss corporate culture.

4. Denis Lanigan, former vice-chairman of J. Walter Thompson, private
   communication, August 1989. I am grateful to Mr. Lanigan for this and a
   number of other important contributions to the argument in this chapter.

5. Simon Broadbent, vice-chairman of Leo Burnett, London, private
   communication, August 1989.

6. Denis Lanigan, private communication, August 1989.

7. This distinction has been strongly emphasized to me by William M.
   Weilbacher, who has extensive experience of both account-driven and
   creative-driven agencies in the United States.

8. Personal conversation in June 1985. In his published work, David Ogilvy gives
   another figure, but not of a completely different order of magnitude: "in my
   long career as a copywriter I have not had more than 20 [big ideas]." David
   Ogilvy, *Ogilvy on Advertising* (New York: Crown Publishing Inc., 1983), 16.

9. I am grateful to my friend David Wheeler, former director-general of the
   Institute of Practitioners in Advertising, London, for this striking thought.

10. A favorite expression of Bill Hinks, who was managing director of the London
    office of J. Walter Thompson in the 1950s, and chairman in the early 1960s.

11. This charming quotation was retailed by my friend Harold F. Clark, Jr., who
    has also made a number of other important contributions to this chapter.

12. John Philip Jones, "Cure the Industry with More Creativity," *New York Times*
    (September 10, 1989): Section 3, p. 3.

13. David Ogilvy, *Confessions of an Advertising Man,* 8th printing (New York:
    Atheneum, 1984), 89–90.

14. Rosser Reeves, *Reality in Advertising* (New York: Alfred A. Knopf, 1961).

15. Kim B. Rotzoll, "The Starch and Ted Bates Correlative Measures of Ad-

vertising Effectiveness," *Journal of Advertising Research* (March 1964): 22–24.

16. William M. Weilbacher, *Current Advertiser Practices in Compensating Their Advertising Agencies* (New York: Association of National Advertisers, 1989).

17. I can think of perhaps a score of former colleagues who either resigned or were fired from JWT London for reasons connected with the agency's culture, and who went on to make extraordinary careers in other organizations or as individual entrepreneurs. In a few cases, they became (almost) household names. JWT's inability to exploit the talents of these people is a failing that is difficult to explain away.

Chapter 5

1. Claude C. Hopkins, *My Life in Advertising* (Chicago: Crain Books, 1966), 3.
2. David Ogilvy, *Ogilvy on Advertising* (New York: Crown Publishers, 1983), 103.
3. Randall Rothenberg, "Advertising. An Iconoclast Looks at the Future," *New York Times* (August 1, 1989): D17.
4. Randall Rothenberg, "Advertising. A Critic Gets Forceful Responses," *New York Times* (August 22, 1989): D21.
5. The prevalence of such methods is described in Andre J. San Augustine and William F. Foley, "How Large Advertisers Set Budgets," *Journal of Advertising Research* (October 1975): 11–16.
6. The sample in postal surveys is always uncontrolled (that is, we cannot decide who will reply). In mitigation of this circumstance, however, I can confirm that the majority of people who were contacted completed their questionnaires. And the resultant coverage of total JWT business was large—about 25 percent of the product categories in which the agency operates.
7. Argentina, Australia, Austria, Brazil, Canada, Chile, Colombia, France, Germany, Greece, Hong Kong, India, Italy, Japan, Malaysia, Mexico, the Philippines, Portugal, South Africa, Sri Lanka, Thailand, the United Kingdom, and the United States.
8. Stationary market conditions have been explored in great detail, with the use of data from the United States and other countries, by Andrew Ehrenberg of the London Business School, who has published widely on the subject. The advertising implications of such conditions are examined in John Philip Jones, *What's in a Name? Advertising and the Concept of Brands* (Lexington, MA: Lexington Books, 1986), ch. 5. See also ch. 3 of the present book.
9. There is one mathematical quirk which must be understood. It stems from the fact that there are some brands in every market that are unadvertised. This means that the average share of voice (shared among fewer brands) is, for mathematical reasons, *above* the average share of market (shared among more brands). Thus it is not quite true to say that the normal and stable relationship for any brand is a parity of share of market and share of voice. The normal

relationship for an advertised brand is in fact a brand's share of market and a *higher* share of voice. In some markets the difference is only fractional, but in others, where there are many substantial but unadvertised store brands, the difference may be quite large. However, in all circumstances, if a brand spends the same share of voice as its share of market, it is (at least slightly) underspending.

10. James O. Peckham, Sr., *The Wheel of Marketing,* 2nd ed. (privately published but available through A. C. Nielsen, 1981), 100–103.

11. See for instance Nariman K. Dhalla and Sonia Yuspeh, "Forget the Product Life Cycle Concept," *Harvard Business Review* 54 (January-February 1976): 102–112.

12. Jones, *What's in a Name?* 86, 114, 126, 233.

13. These markets were picked out by examining each packaged-goods category in turn and selecting and more normal ones that contain at least four advertised brands, and which are not dominated by any brands with exceptionally large shares. This process reduced the number of markets examined to 117 (48 percent of the total sample) and the number of brands to 666 (61 percent of the total sample).

14. The AIC was first described (although not named AIC) in John Philip Jones, *Does It Pay to Advertise? Cases Illustrating Successful Brand Advertising* (Lexington, MA: Lexington Books, 1989), 294–300. Its operational uses were not widely discussed in this book.

15. This case is described in ibid., ch. 6.

16. In the United States and Canada, 58 percent of brands of packaged goods have market shares of 6 percent or less. In the rest of the world, the figure is 38 percent. Ibid., 301.

17. The key importance of share of voice in determining the effects of advertising expenditure by individual brands is discussed in Jones, *What's in a Name?* ch. 10.

Chapter 6

1. Thomas W. Wilson Jr., *Achieving a Sustainable Competitive Advantage* (New York: Association of National Advertisers New Product Marketing Workshop, 1982), 7. During the nine continuous years of highest inflation, 1974–82, aggregate corporate profit was static in real terms in 1979 and declined in 1974, 1975, 1980, 1981, and 1982. *Statistical Abstract of the United States* (Washington, DC: U.S. Department of Commerce, Bureau of the Census, 1989).

2. Peter F. Drucker, *Managing in Turbulent Times* (New York: Harper Colophon Books, 1980), 11, 29.

3. Nancy Koch, *The Changing Marketplace Ahead and Implications for Advertisers* (New York: Association of National Advertisers, 1983), 5.

4. There is some evidence to support this hypothesis. Gerard J. Tellis, "The

Prince Elasticity of Selective Demand: A Meta-Analysis of Econometric Models of Sales," *Journal of Marketing Research* (November 1988): 331–341.

5. This was when I was a young account executive at J. Walter Thompson, London. My client at the time was Chesebrough-Pond's (now part of Unilever); the brand on which we used price elasticity as an operational tool was Vaseline Petroleum Jelly.

6. Tellis, "Price Elasticity."

7. Gerard J. Tellis, "Point of View: Interpreting Advertising and Price Elasticities," *Journal of Advertising Research* (August–September 1989): 40–43.

8. The British analyst Broadbent worked out an average price elasticity of −1.32 in 1980. Simon Broadbent, "Price and Advertising: Volume and Profit," *Admap* (November 1980): 536. Another Englishman, Roberts, working from a smaller sample than Broadbent's, calculated an average figure of −1.67. Andrew Roberts, "The Decision between Above- and Below-the-Line," *Admap* (December 1980): 590. Tellis suggests that price elasticities in Europe may be less negative than in the United States. Tellis, "Price Elasticity," 339.

9. Estimates have been published of advertising-to-sales ratios for the main industries in the United States. These have been presented according to advertising's percentage of sales and its percentage of margin (i.e. indirect cost.) From these data, it is possible to extrapolate the average ratios of variable cost by industry. "Advertising-to-Sales-Ratios, 1989," *Advertising Age* (November 13, 1989): 32.

10. Retail concentration, especially in the food trade, is a widely discussed characteristic of the distributional system. As pointed out in chapter 2, it is mainly a regional phenomenon in the United States and has not developed nationally as extensively as in certain European countries, such as the United Kingdom and Sweden; the reason is largely geographical. See Wilson, *Sustainable Competitive Advantage, 6.* In Europe, retail concentration has been the major cause of increases in promotional expenditures since the early 1970s, as well as of the squeeze on the relative size of theme advertising budgets.

11. This evidence comes from Nielsen. There is an exceptional circumstance— when a brand is on a strongly rising sales trend—in which a promotion can end with sales remaining a notch higher than at the beginning. However, in the vast majority of circumstances, "The consumer sales effect is limited to the time period of the promotion itself," James O. Peckham Sr., *The Wheel of Marketing,* 2nd ed. (privately published but available through A. C. Nielsen, 1981), 69.

12. I am grateful to Boris Wilenkin of Unilever for providing this neat and accurate image.

13. See, for instance, Robert M. Prentice, "How to Split Your Marketing Funds between Advertising and Promotion," *Advertising Age* (January 10, 1977): 41–44.

14. See for instance, John Philip Jones, *Does It Pay to Advertise? Cases Illustrating*

Successful Brand Advertising (Lexington, MA: Lexington Books, 1989). ch.
20. Also The Ogilvy Center for Research and Development, *Advertising, Sales
Promotion and the Bottom Line* (San Francisco: The Ogilvy Center for
Research & Development, 1989).

15. John Philip Jones, *What's in a Name? Advertising and the Concept of Brands*
(Lexington, MA: Lexington Books, 1986), ch 2.

16. Peckham, *Wheel of Marketing,* 62.

17. I am grateful to Boris Wilenkin for reminding me of the promotion-
commotion-demotion adage.

18. Gert Assmus, John U. Farlet, and Donald R. Lehmann, "How Advertising
Affects Sales: Meta-Analysis of Econometric Results," *Journal of Marketing
Research* 21 (February 1984): 65–74.

19. See, for instance, Broadbent, "Price and Advertising," and Roberts, "Decision
between Above- and Below-the-Line."

20. This point has been argued and illustrated trenchantly by Broadbent. Simon
Broadbent, "Point of View: What is a 'Small' Advertising Elasticity?" *Journal
of Advertising Research* (August–September 1989): 37–39. This publication
also includes a reply by Tellis, a rejoinder from Broadbent, and an editorial
note on the controversy (noting that it is unusually good-tempered!). I am
extremely grateful to Simon Broadbent for many perceptive observations on
drafts of this chapter.

21. A well-known British analyst claims that 95 percent of all advertising-pressure
tests fail. I believe that this failure is very often due to too low an expenditure
unplift, compounded by poor analysis stemming from the mathematical
difficulty of disentangling the small effect of the extra advertising from other
influences on sales: seasonality, promotions, and random factors. See
Callaghan OHerlihy, "How to Test the Sales Effects of Advertising," *Admap*
(January 1980): 32–35.

Chapter 7

1. Denis Higgins, ed., *The Art of Writing Advertising* (Chicago: Advertising
Publications Inc., 1965), 43.

2. H. W. Fowler and F. G. Fowler, eds., *The Concise Oxford Dictionary of
Current English,* 5th ed. (Oxford: Oxford University Press, 1964).

3. The principles of military strategy discussed in this chapter are derived from B.
H. Liddell Hart, "Strategy Re-Framed," in *The British Way in Warfare*
(London: Faber & Faber, 1932), 93–114.

4. E. Jerome McCarthy, *Basic Marketing: A Managerial Approach,* 7th ed.
(Homewood, IL: Richard D. Irwin, 1981), 42.

5. Distribution is measured by the percentage of stores carrying a brand.
Numerical distribution is based on a simple count of the stores, unweighted for
their size. Effective (or weighted or dollar) distribution gives extra emphasis to
the larger stores and less emphasis to the smaller ones. One makes this
calculation by aggregating the sales volumes of all stores of the appropriate

type in the relevant geographic area (*A*); aggregating the sales volumes of the stores carrying the brand being measured (*B*); and then calculating the percentage that *B* is of *A*.

6. Stephen A. Greyser, ed., "Exercise in Television and Print Campaign Analysis," in *Cases in Advertising and Communications Management,* 2nd ed. (Englewood Cliffs, NJ: Prentice-Hall, 1982), 323–340.

7. A contemporary example demonstrates confusion of an even more profound order: the notion of *bottom-up marketing,* much discussed in the advertising trade press. The idea is that tactics supposedly governs strategy. Since the concept is not so much original as wrong—being based on a misunderstanding of the meaning of the words—it is not productive or even necessary to discuss it.

8. An observation made in personal conversation by the well-known advertising researcher Edward Rosenstein, August 1990.

9. There is much controversy about whether the effects of advertising are felt on the consumer's psyche before or after brand purchase. This matter is discussed in John Philip Jones, *What's in a Name? Advertising and the Concept of Brands* (Lexington, MA: Lexington Books, 1986), ch. 6.

10. *Annual Consumer Surveys* (New York: Mediamark Research Inc.).

11. *Annual Consumer Surveys* (New York: Simmons Market Research Bureau).

12. The market had matured by 1990, in which year the aggregate growth slowed to 1 percent. Kathleen M. Berry, "The Snap Has Turned to Slog," *New York Times Business Section* (November 18, 1990): 5.

13. John C. Maxwell Jr., "Marketers Milk Cold Cereal Sales," *Advertising Age* (September 26, 1988): 64.

14. *Statistical Abstract of the United States* (Washington, DC: U.S. Department of Commerce, Bureau of the Census, 1989), 17.

15. Arnold Mitchell, *The Nine American Lifestyles: Who We Are and Where We Are Going* (New York: Macmillan, 1983). The VALS grouping is described and quantified in chapters 1 and 4.

Chapter 8

1. (Ed.) Denis Higgins, *The Art of Writing Advertising* (Chicago: Advertising Publications Inc., 1965), 44.

2. James Webb Young, *How to Become an Advertising Man* (Chicago: Advertising Publications Inc., 1963), 19.

3. Martin Mayer, *Madison Avenue, USA* (New York: Harper & Brothers, 1958), 35–70.

4. John Philip Jones, *Does It Pay to Advertise? Cases Illustrating Successful Brand Advertising* (Lexington, MA: Lexington Books, 1989), 105.

5. I have counted six separate brands in the family orientation segment. Two of these, Jergens Aloe & Lanolin and Palmolive Green, contain skin-care ingredients, but these ingredients are not appropriate to the beauty orientation segment. Moreover, the soaps do not have a heavy perfume.

6. The Campbell's and Korvette's research was carried out by Brouillard Communications, New York. I carried out the Ronzoni investigation in cooperation with students at Syracuse University.

7. Personal information from Edward Rosenstein. I am also very grateful to Mr. Rosenstein for other contributions to chapters 7, 8 and 9.

8. Arnold Mitchell, *The Nine American Lifestyles: Who We Are and Where We Are Going* (New York: Macmillan, 1983), 65–149.

9. Stephen King, "Practical Progress for a Theory of Advertisements," *Admap* (October 1975): 338–343.

10. I have relied on the extensive experience of my friend Harold F. Clark, Jr., in defining the stages of the King continuum.

11. See for example, Jones, *Does It Pay to Advertise?* ch. 19, "The United States Marine Corps."

12. Philip Levine, "Commercials That Name Competing Brands," *Journal of Advertising Research* (December 1976): 7–14.

13. Firsthand information from an experienced food chemist.

Chapter 9

1. Martin Mayer, *Madison Avenue, USA* (New York: Harper & Brothers, 1958), 223.

2. See for example Leo Bogart, B. Stuart Tolley, and Frank Orenstein, "What One Little Ad Can Do," *Journal of Advertising Research* (August 1970): 3–13. Also Graeme McCorkell, "When Experts Can Get It Wrong," *Campaign* (February 15, 1985): 55–56.

3. The problems involved are discussed in John Philip Jones, *What's in a Name? Advertising and the Concept of Brands* (Lexington, MA: Lexington Books, 1986). ch. 6.

4. A well-known example of proposition testing, for Helena Rubinstein's Deep Cleanser, was published by David Ogilvy, *Confessions of an Advertising Man* (New York: Atheneum, 1984), 116–118.

5. The example of upstream research presented in this chapter, and all other research examples quoted here, come from British sources, solely because there are more *published* examples in the United Kingdom than in the United States. Evidence of American interest in upstream research can be found in Ronald Dean Wilcox, *Investigation of Client and Agency Attitudes to Copytesting,* unpublished master's thesis, Syracuse University, 1990, pp. 66–74. Ron Wilcox, who works for a major packaged goods advertising agency in the United States, carried out this investigation through qualitative interviews with thirty informed observers and users of advertising research: agency colleagues and clients. This outstandingly interesting piece of work cannot be published because of the confidential and proprietary nature of the views expressed by the respondents. Quotations in this book have been veiled to conceal the research practices of the named clients.

6. Terry Prue, "Crown Solo, the Paint that Rewrites the Rules," in *Advertising*

Works 6: Paper from the I.P.A. Advertising Effectiveness Awards, Paul Feldwick, ed. (Henley-on-Thames, U.K.: NTC Publications, 1991): 191–208.

7. David Schwartz, *Concept Testing: How to Test New Product Ideas before You Go to Market* (New York: AMACOM, American Management Association, 1987), 5.

8. Sev D'Souza, "Red Mountain: Ground Coffee Taste Without the Grind," in *Advertising Works 5: Papers from the I.P.A. Advertising Effectiveness Awards, 1988,* Paul Feldwick, ed. (London: Cassell, 1990), 196–216.

9. David Baker (Account Planning director, J. Walter Thompson, London), personal communication, November 1990.

10. Leslie Butterfield, "Creative Development Research," in *How to Plan Advertising,* Don Cowley, ed. (London: Cassell, in association with the Account Planning Group, 1989), 100–109.

11. Wilcox, *Client and Agency Attitudes,* 62–64.

12. Ibid, 63.

13. Peter Sampson, "Qualitative Research and Motivation Research," in *Consumer Market Research Handbook,* 2nd ed. Robert M. Worcester and John Downham, eds., (London: Van Nostrand Reinhold Company, 1978), 25.

14. Wilcox, *Client and Agency Attitudes,* 49–50.

15. Thomas L. Greenbaum, *The Practical Handbook and Guide to Focus Group Research* (Lexington, MA: Lexington Books, 1988). ch. 7. Also private information.

16. This point was made (independently) by two of my friends, Edward Rosenstein and William M. Weilbacher. They also contributed other helpful observations which led to improvements in the argument in this chapter.

17. Tony McGuinness, "The Repositioning of Mazola," in *Advertising Works 4: Papers from the I.P.A. Advertising Effectiveness Awards, 1986,* Charles Channon, ed. (London: Cassell, 1987), 198–200.

18. Evelyn Jenkins and Christopher Timms, "The Andrex Story—A Soft, Strong and Very Long-Term Success," in *Advertising Works 4,* Channon, ed., 180–183.

19. Wilcox, *Client and Agency Attitudes,* 56.

20. Butterfield, "Creative Development Research," 107–120.

21. Wilcox, *Client and Agency Attitudes,* 56–57.

22. Stephen A. Greyser, ed., "Northwestern Mutual Life Insurance Company (B)," *Cases in Advertising and Communications Management,* 3rd ed. (Englewood Cliffs, NJ: Prentice-Hall, 1992), 235–264.

23. Wilcox, *Client and Agency Attitudes,* 53.

24. Sampson, "Qualitative Research and Motivation Research," 25. However, it should be noted that margins of error are very rarely quoted in the reports of quantitative copy tests.

25. See reference in note 3.

26. Wilcox, *Client and Agency Attitudes,* 5, 9.

27. Ibid., 4.

28. Jones, *What's in a Name?* 138–139.

29. Ibid.
30. John Philip Jones, *Does It Pay to Advertise? Cases Illustrating Successful Brand Advertising* (Lexington, MA: Lexington Book, 1989), 300–302. Also John Philip Jones, "Why European Ads Are More Amusing," *New York Times Business Section* (October 7, 1990), 13.
31. Wilcox, *Client and Agency Attitudes,* 39.
32. Ibid., 43–44.

Chapter 10

1. Rosser Reeves, *Reality in Advertising* (New York: Alfred A. Knopf, 1961), 145.
2. Ibid., 4.
3. Ibid., 32.
4. Ibid., 41.
5. Kim B. Rotzoll, "The Starch and Ted Bates Correlative Measures of Advertising Effectiveness," *Journal of Advertising Research* (March 1964): 22–24.
6. Andrew Ehrenberg, "Repetitive Advertising and the Consumer," *Journal of Advertising Research* (April 1974): 25–33.
7. Timothy Joyce, "What Do We Know about How Advertising Works?" in *How Advertising Works,* (London: J. Walter Thompson Company, Ltd., 1974), 1–31.
8. Reeves, *Reality in Advertising,* 44.
9. James O. Peckham, Sr., *The Wheel of Marketing,* 2nd ed. (privately published, 1981, and available through the A. C. Nielsen Company), 108.
10. Colin McDonald, "Myths, Evidence and Evaluation," *Admap* (November 1980): 546–555.
11. John Maynard Keynes, *The General Theory of Employment, Interest, and Money* (New York: Harcourt Brace Jovanovich, 1964), 3.
12. John Philip Jones, *What's in a Name? Advertising and the Concept of Brands* (Lexington, MA: Lexington Books, 1986), ch. 1, 2. These chapters include extensive endnotes which refer to additional sources.
13. Ibid., ch. 2, also Neil Hopper Borden, *The Economic Effects of Advertising* (Chicago: Richard D. Irwin, 1942), 49–51; also Lord Kaldor, "The Economic Aspects of Advertising," *Review of Economic Studies* 18 (1950–51): 1–27, reprinted in Michael Barnes, ed., *The Three Faces of Advertising* (London: Advertising Association, 1975).
14. Stephen King, *Developing New Brands* (London: Pitman Publishing, 1973), 1–2; also John Madell, "New Products: How to Succeed When the Odds Are against You," *Marketing Week* (February 22, 1980): 20–22.
15. J. Hugh Davidson, "Why Most New Consumer Brands Fail," *Harvard Business Review* 54 (March–April 1976): 117–122; also Peckham, *Wheel of Marketing,* 76, 92.

16. Stephen King, *Advertising as a Barrier to Market Entry* (London: Advertising Association, 1980); also, Peckham, *Wheel of Marketing*, 15–16.
17. Peckham, *Wheel of Marketing*, 77–81; also John Davis, *The Sales Curves of New Products* (London: J. Walter Thompson Company, 1965).
18. Andrew Ehrenberg and G. L. Goodhardt, *Seventeen Essays on Understanding Buying Behavior* (New York: J. Walter Thompson Company and the Market Research Corporation of America, 1977–80), essay number 4.
19. Peckham, *Wheel of Marketing*, 89–91.
20. King, *Developing New Brands*, 161–167.
21. Davidson, "Why Most New Consumer Brands Fail."
22. Peckham, *Wheel of Marketing*, 77.
23. Ibid., 95–96.
24. Booz, Allen and Hamilton, *New Product Management for the 1980s* (privately published, 1982).
25. Andrew Ehrenberg, *Repeat-Buying, Theory and Applications* (Amsterdam: North-Holland Publishing Company, 1972).
26. See, for instance, Jones, *What's in a Name?* ch. 5.
27. Ibid.
28. Ehrenberg and Goodhardt, *Understanding Buying Behavior*, essay number 3.
29. Ibid., 2.14–2.15.
30. Ibid., essay number 2.
31. Peckham, *Wheel of Marketing*, 71–73.
32. Peter Carter and Roz Hatt, "How Far Does Advertising Protect the Brand Franchise?" *Admap* (May 1983): 261–280.
33. Peckham, *Wheel of Marketing*, 26–28.
34. Andre Gabor and C. W. J. Granger, "Price Sensitivity of the Consumer," *Journal of Advertising Research* (December 1964): 42.
35. Gerard J. Tellis, "The Price Elasticity of Selective Demand: A Meta-Analysis of Econometric Models of Sales," *Journal of Marketing Research* (November 1988): 331–341.
36. Jones, *What's in a Name?* ch. 11.
37. Peckham, *Wheel of Marketing*, 61, 63, 67.
38. Don E. Schultz and R. D. Dewar, "Retailers in Control: The Impact of Retail Trade Concentration," *Journal of Consumer Marketing* 1 (1983–84): 81–89; also T. W. Wilson, Jr., *Achieving a Sustainable Competitive Advantage* (New York: Association of National Advertisers, 1982); also Nancy Koch, *The Changing Marketplace Ahead and Implications for Advertisers* (New York: Association of National Advertisers, 1983); also R. D. Miller, vice president for marketing, Best Foods North America—CPC, personal communication, November 19, 1984.
39. Miller, personal communication, November 19, 1984.
40. Jack Frantz, executive vice-president of Grey Advertising, New York, personal communication, January 13, 1984.
41. William Phillips, former chairman of Ogilvy & Mather, personal communication, July 19, 1985.

42. King, *Developing New Brands,* 2–6; also Nariman K. Dhalla and Sonia Yuspeh, "Forget the Product Life Cycle Concept," *Harvard Business Review* 54, (January–February 1976): 102–112; also Sir David Orr, Foreword to John Philip Jones, *Does It Pay to Advertise? Cases Illustrating Successful Brand Advertising* (Lexington, MA: Lexington Books, 1989), xx.

43. Tom Corlett, "Consumer Purchasing Patterns: A Different Perspective," *How Advertising Works,* 111–119. (London: J. Walter Thompson Company, Ltd., 1974).

44. Martin Collins, "Sampling," in *Consumer Market Research Handbook,* 2nd ed., 74–90, Robert Worcester and John Downham, eds. (Woking, UK: Van Nostrand Reinhold Company Ltd., 1978). Includes bibliography.

45. For two examples (from many that could have been chosen) to illustrate the positive dangers of asking the wrong questions in market research, see Jones, *Does It Pay to Advertise?* 105, 237–241.

46. Judie Lannon and Peter Cooper, "Humanistic Advertising: A Holistic Cultural Perspective," *International Journal of Advertising* 2 (July–September 1983): 195–213.

47. Barbara Coe and James MacLachlan, "How Major TV Advertisers Evaluate Commercials," *Journal of Advertising Research* (December 1980): 51–54.

48. Shirley Young, "Copy Testing without Magic Numbers," *Journal of Advertising Research* (February 1972): 3–12; also Art Shulman, "On-Air Recall by Time of Day," *Journal of Advertising Research* (February 1972): 21–23; also Sonia Yuspeh, "The Medium versus the Message: The Effects of Program Environment on the Performance of Commercials," *A.M.A. Tenth Attitude Research Conference,* Hilton Head, SC (American Marketing Association, 1979).

49. Jack B. Haskins, "Factual Recall as a Measure of Advertising Effectiveness," *Journal of Advertising Research* (March 1964): 2–8.

50. Darrell B. Lucas, "The ABCs of A.R.F.'s P.A.R.M." [*sic*], *Journal of Marketing* (July 1960): 9–20; also W. A. Twyman, *The Measurement of Page and Advertisement Exposure—A Review of Progress of the A.R.C.* (London: Agencies Research Consortium, 1972); also D. Morgan Neu, "Measuring Advertisement Recognition," *Journal of Advertising Research* (December 1961): 17–22; also J. S. Karslake, "The Purdue Eye Camera: A Practical Apparatus for Studying the Attention Value of Advertisements," *Journal of Applied Psychology,* 24 (1940): 417–40; also J. J. McNamara, "A New Method of Testing Effectiveness through Eye Movement Photographs," *The Psychological Record* (Bloomington, IN, September 1941): 399–460; also David R. Aitchison, "Some Thoughts on the Readership of Advertisements," *Admap World Advertising Workshop* (1970); also Robert Fletcher and Bill Mabey, "Reading and Noting Revived!" *Admap* (December 1971): 422–28.

51. See, for example, Stephen A. Greyser, *Cases in Advertising and Communications Management,* 3rd ed. (Englewood Cliffs, NJ: Prentice-Hall, 1992), 84–103.

52. Edward de Bono, *Lateral Thinking* (New York: Harper Colophon Books, 1973), 39–45.
53. Mark Lovell and Jack Potter, *Assessing the Effectiveness of Advertising* (London: Business Books, 1975).
54. Stephen King, "How Useful Is Proposition Testing?" *Advertising Quarterly* (Winter 1965–66): 24–34.
55. Leo Bogart, B. Stuart Tolley, and Frank Orenstein, "What One Little Ad Can Do," *Journal of Advertising Research* (August 1970): 3–13; also Graeme McCorkell, chief executive of MSW Rapp and Collins, "When Experts Can Get It Wrong," *Campaign* (February 15, 1985): 55–56.
56. James Webb Young, *A Technique for Producing Ideas* (Chicago: Crain Communications Inc., 1972).
57. Arthur Koestler, *The Act of Creation* (New York: Macmillan, 1964), 49–62.
58. Young, *Technique*, 25.
59. Koestler, *Act of Creation*, 337–340.
60. Joyce, "What Do We Know?"
61. See, for example, de Bono, *Lateral Thinking*.
62. Roger von Oech, *A Whack on the Side of the Head* (New York: Warner Books, 1983).
63. Jean Currie, *The Advertisers' Recipe Book* (London: J. Walter Thompson Company Ltd., 1980). This book was based on considerable research carried out by J. Walter Thompson, London, during the 1970s.
64. John Caples, *Tested Advertising Methods* (Englewood Cliffs, NJ: Prentice-Hall, 1974); also Claude C. Hopkins, *Scientific Advertising* (Chicago: Crain Books, 1966); also David Ogilvy, *Confessions of an Advertising Man* (New York: Atheneum, 1984).
65. Thomas J. Amico, *Breaking the Rules: An Examination of Magazine Advertising Effectiveness and the Principles Which Govern It*, unpublished undergraduate honors thesis, Syracuse University, 1982.
66. Robert Potter, promotions director, Time-Life Books, a number of personal communications, 1984 and 1985.
67. Andre J. San Augustine and William F. Foley, "How Large Advertisers Set Budgets," *Journal of Advertising Research* (October 1975): 11–16; also Steven E. Permut, "How European Managers Set Advertising Budgets," *Journal of Advertising Research* (October 1977): 75–79.
68. Harry Henry, *Cranfield Broadsheet Number 2: Deciding How Much to Spend on Advertising* (Cranfield, UK: Cranfield School of Management, 1979).
69. David A. Aaker and James M. Carman, "Are You Overadvertising?" *Journal of Advertising Research* (August–September 1982): 57–70.
70. H. R. Kropp, Stanley D. Canter, and Andrew Kershaw, *Determining How Much to Spend for Advertising—Without Experimental Testing* and *Marketing Implications of Media Expenditures* (New York: Association of National Advertisers Research and media Workshops, 1974 and 1971).
71. Peckham, *Wheel of Marketing*, 108–132.
72. The average of 128 advertising elasticities is published in Gert Asmuss, John

U. Farlet, and Donald R. Lehmann, "How Advertising Affects Sales: Meta-Analysis of Econometric Results," *Journal of Marketing Research* 21 (February 1984): 65–74.

73. John A. Quelch, "It's Time to Make Trade Promotions More Productive," *Harvard Business Review* 61 (May–June 1983): 130–136. Also Tellis, "Price Elasticity."

74. J. Walter Thompson, *Women's Use of Media, A Report on a Behavioral Study* (London: J. Walter Thompson Company Ltd., 1975).

75. Unpublished estimate made in 1990 by William M. Weilbacher, a closely informed observer of the media scene in the United States.

76. Magid M. Abraham and Leonard M. Lodish, "Getting the Most Out of Advertising and Promotions," *Harvard Business Review* 90 (May–June 1990): 50–60; also Callahan OHerlihy, "How to Test the Sales Effects of Advertising," *Admap* (January 1980): 32–35.

77. Jones, *What's in a Name?* chs. 8, 9. Note the many source references in the endnotes.

78. Ibid., 221–222.

79. Asmuss, Farlet, and Lehmann, "How Advertising Affects Sales."

80. Jones, *What's in a Name?* ch. 7.

81. Stephen King, personal communication, May 22, 1984.

82. Peckham, *Wheel of Marketing,* 108–132.

83. Jeremy Elliott, "Kellogg's Rice Krispies: The Effect of a New Creative Execution," *Advertising Works, Papers from the I.P.A. Effectiveness Awards,* Simon Broadbent, ed. (London: Holt, Rinehart & Winston, 1981), 86–87.

84. Tom Corlett, "How to Make Sense of Market Analysis," *Campaign* (May 26, 1978).

85. Nariman K. Dhalla, "Assessing the Long-Term Value of Advertising," *Harvard Business Review* 56 (January–February 1978): 87–95. There is a methodological flaw in Dhalla's work. His long-term effect is based on a dependent variable derived from the short-term sales increase.

86. Julian L. Simon and Johan Arndt, "The Shape of the Advertising Response Function," *Journal of Advertising Research* (August 1980): 21–22.

87. Simon Broadbent, ed., *The Leo Burnett Book of Advertising* (London: Business Books, 1984), 91–94.

88. Stephen King, personal communication, January 3, 1985.

89. Andrew Ehrenberg, *Pricing and Brand Differentiation* (London: London Business School, 1985).

90. Jones, *What's in a Name?* 32.

91. Charles Ramond, *Advertising Research: The State of the Art* (New York: Association of National Advertisers, 1976), 14–22.

92. Leon Festinger, "Cognitive Dissonance," *Scientific American* (October 1962): 93–102.

93. Ehrenberg, "Repetitive Advertising and the Consumer."

94. Henry Assael and George S. Day, "Attitudes and Awareness as Predictors of Market Share," *Journal of Advertising Research* (December 1968): 3–10;

also Terrence O'Brien, "Stages in Consumer Decision Making," *Journal of Marketing Research* (August 1971): 283–289.

95. Michael L. Ray, Alan G. Sawyer, Michael L. Rothschild, Roger M. Heeler, Edward C. Strong, and Jerome B. Reed "Marketing Communication and the Hierarchy of Effects," in *New Models for Mass Communication Research,* Peter Clarke, ed. (Beverly Hills, CA: Sage Publications, 1973), 151.

96. Herbert E. Krugman, "The Impact of Television Advertising: Learning without Involvement," *Public Opinion Quarterly* 29 (1965): 350–356.

97. Ray, Sawyer, Rothschild, Heeler, Strong, and Reed, "Marketing Communication."

98. Julian L. Simon, *Issues in the Economics of Advertising* (Urbana: University of Illinois Press, 1970), 11–14.

99. David Ogilvy, personal communication, April 29, 1985; also Stephen King, personal communication, January 3, 1985; also Michael Naples, ed., *Effective Frequency: The Relationship between Frequency and Advertising Effectiveness* (New York: Association of National Advertisers, 1979), 84; also Gus Priemer, "Are We Doing the Wrong Things Right?" *Media Decisions* (May 1979): 152; also Reeves, *Reality in Advertising,* 124–125.

100. Herbert E. Krugman, "Why Three Exposures May Be Enough," *Journal of Advertising Research* (December 1972): 11–14; also Herbert E. Krugman, "What Makes Advertising Effective?" *Harvard Business Review* 53 (March–April 1975): 96–103.

101. Naples, *Effective Frequency,* 20–24.

102. Ibid., ch. 3 and app. A.

103. Ibid., ch. 5.

104. Ibid., 76–78.

105. Jones, *What's in a Name?* 114–126.

106. Ibid., chs. 8, 9.

107. Naples, *Effective Frequency,* app. B.

108. David Dunbar, "Trends in Total Advertising Expenditure in 29 Countries, 1970–1980," *International Journal of Advertising* 1 (1982): 57–87.

109. William M. Weilbacher, *Advertising,* 2nd ed. (New York: Macmillan, 1984), 66–73; also Sandra J. Smith, *Advertising Agencies: An Analysis of Industry Structure,* unpublished paper, Michigan State University, 1985; also *Advertising Age:* regular estimates of aggregate expenditures; expenditures of 100 leading advertisers; size, clients, and so on of leading advertising agencies; estimates of advertising agency profitability.

110. Smith, *Advertising Agencies.*

111. William M. Weilbacher, *Current Advertiser Practices in Compensating Their Advertising Agencies* (New York: Association of National Advertisers, 1989).

112. See for instance Julie Liesse, "Kraft G.F. Shifts Agencies, Pay," *Advertising Age* (October 22, 1990): 1, 58; also Pat Sloan and Jon Lafayette, "Chesebrough adds bonuses for agencies," *Advertising Age* (January 13, 1992): 2.

113. Bogart, Tolley, and Orenstein, "What One Little Ad Can Do."

114. King, *Developing New Brands,* 1–2.

115. Peckham, *Wheel of Marketing*, 71–76.
116. Alfred Politz's parable: There were once three rooms, all opening on the same beautiful view. However, when a person entered any of the rooms, he could not see the view directly: it was possible to see only a mirror in which the view was reflected. In the first room, the looking glass was old and cracked; in the second, it was a lovely eighteenth-century artifact framed in ormolu; in the third, the whole wall was a plate glass mirror. A man entered the first room, and what he saw was a beautiful view reflected in a cracked mirror. A man entered the second room, and what he saw was a beautiful view reflected in a beautiful mirror. A man entered the third room and what he saw was a beautiful view.

     For *view* read *brand*. For *mirror* read *advertising*. Politz inhabits the third room. And so do I. See *The Politz Papers*, Hugh S. Hardy, ed. (Chicago: American Marketing Association, 1990), 40.
117. Canon Roy McKay, former head of religious broadcasting, BBC, private communication, 1979.
118. Thomas M. Garrett, S.J., *An Introduction to Some Ethical Problems of Modern American Advertising* (Rome, Italy: Gregorian University Press, 1961).
119. Tom Corlett, *Advertising—Is This the Sort of Work That an Honest Man Can Take Pride In?* (London: J. Walter Thompson Company Ltd., 1974).
120. Barry Meier, "New Volvo Ad Calls Old One a Phony," *New York Times* (November 6, 1990): D1, D17.
121. These estimates were made during the 1970s by J. Walter Thompson Company Ltd., London.
122. Weilbacher, *Advertising*, 42–57.
123. See for instance Kate Moody, *Growing Up on Television* (New York: Times Books, 1980); also Edward L. Palmer, *Television and America's Children* (New York: Oxford University Press, 1988); also Marie Winn, *The Plug-In Drug: Television, Children, and the Family* (New York: Penguin Books, 1985).
124. John A. Howard and James Hulbert, *Advertising and the Public Interest, A Staff Report to the F.T.C.*, unpublished paper, 1973.
125. In this inventory, certain pieces of knowledge fall between two categories. In classifying these cases, I have put such a piece of knowledge in the lower of the two groups; for example, if it falls between A and B, I have put it in B.

Chapter 11

1. John Philip Jones, *What's In a Name? Advertising and the Concept of Brands* (Lexington, MA: Lexington Books, 1986), 40–41.
2. John Philip Jones, *Does It Pay to Advertise? Cases Illustrating Successful Brand Advertising* (Lexington, MA: Lexington Books, 1989), ch. 8.
3. Words of a senior marketing executive, quoted by William M. Weilbacher, *Managing Agency Relations: Maximizing the Effectiveness* (New York: Association of National Advertisers, 1991), 23.

4. Based on discussions in November 1990 with the Institute of Practitioners in Advertising, London, and J. Walter Thompson, London.
5. Booz, Allen and Hamilton, *New Product Management for the 1980s* (privately published, 1982).
6. Jones, *What's in a Name?* 51–53.
7. James O. Peckham, Sr., *The Wheel of Marketing,* 2nd ed. (privately published, 1981, and available through the A. C. Nielsen Company), 76, 92.
8. J. Hugh Davidson, "Why Most New Consumer Brands Fail," *Harvard Business Review* 54 (March–April 1976): 117–122.
9. J. E. Fothergill and A. S. C. Ehrenberg, "On the Schwerin Analyses of Advertising Effectiveness," *Journal of Marketing Research* (August 1965): 298–306.
10. Jones, *Does It Pay to Advertise?* 237–243.
11. Ibid., 119.
12. See for instance Andrew Roberts, "Improving Advertising Content: Tracking Studies or Pre-Testing," *Admap* (April 1987): 44–46.
13. James Webb Young, *A Technique for Producing Ideas.*
14. The relatively new discipline of account planning, which is now in almost universal use in London agencies, suggests an indirect parallel with what I have in mind for how the creative process should be studied. Account planning was started in each agency by an individual. It grew, as it were, by osmosis and reached a stage by which account planners eventually formed a professional association called the Account Planning Group, with a current membership of 550. This group assembles and propagates the doctrines and procedures of account planning, so that a synergy develops among account planners in different London agencies. Some of these planners have even managed to infiltrate the agency scene in the United States, and they have in turn formed an American Account Planning Group that meets regularly.
15. Peter Holloway, *Maximizing Communicational Effectiveness—How Research Can Help* (Amsterdam, Netherlands: European Society for Opinion and Marketing Research Seminar on How Advertising Works and How Promotions Work, April 22–24, 1991), Proceedings, 149–158.
16. This complex matter is discussed in Jones, *What's in a Name?* chs. 8, 9, 10.

Appendix A

1. The most perceptive and realistic description of competition in the real world was written by the Nobel Laureate Friedrich von Hayek, "The Meaning of Competition," *Individualism and Economic Order* (Chicago: University of Chicago Press, 1948), 92–106.
2. For review, see Robert B. Ekelund, Jr., and David S. Saurman, *Advertising and the Market Process: A Modern Economic View* (San Francisco: Pacific Research Institute for Public Policy, 1988), ch. 4.
3. There is some generalized marketplace evidence that advertising can reduce the elasticity of demand for brands. Andrew Ehrenberg, *Pricing and Brand Differentiation* (London: London Business School, 1985).

4. All the data on this case come from "California Avocado Advisory Board," in Stephen A. Greyser, ed., *Cases in Advertising and Communications Management,* 2nd ed. (Englewood Cliffs, NJ: Prentice-Hall, 1981), 23–61.

5. This case was originally published by Tom Corlett, "How to Make Sense of Market Analysis," *Campaign* (May 26, 1978). In this article, price is set out on the horizontal and output on the vertical axis, the opposite of how it is set out in conventional price theory. This format does not affect the analysis. Jeremy Elliott published a similar analysis for Kellogg's Rice Krispies in the United Kingdom. Jeremy Elliott, "Kellogg's Rice Krispies, The Effect of a New Creative Execution," in *Advertising Works: Papers from the I.P.A. Advertising Effectiveness Awards,* Simon Broadbent, ed., (London, UK: Holt, Rinehart & Winston, 1981), 84–85.

6. John Philip Jones, *Does It Pay to Advertise? Cases Illustrating Successful Brand Advertising* (Lexington, MA: Lexington Books, 1989), 299.

7. Unpublished estimate made in 1990 by William M. Weilbacher, a closely informed observer of the media scene in the United States.

8. Stephen King, *Advertising as a Barrier to Market Entry* (London, UK: Advertising Association, 1980), 15.

9. Lee Benham, "The Effect of Advertising on the Price of Eyeglasses," *Journal of Law and Economics* 15 (1972): 337–352.

10. Ibid., 352.

11. James O. Peckham, Sr., *The Wheel of Marketing,* 2nd ed. (privately published but available through A. C. Nielsen, 1981), 74–75.

12. Jules Backman, *Advertising and Competition* (New York: New York University Press, 1967), 61–81.

13. Lord Heyworth, *Advertising (Statement Accompanying Unilever Annual Report)* (London, UK: Unilever Ltd., 1958), app. 1.

14. Jones, *Does It Pay to Advertise?* especially pp. 3–4. Of particular interest is the market for soft drinks; see p. 144.

15. William M. Weilbacher, *How Consumers' View of Media Can Lead to Better Media Planning* (Evanston, IL: Northwestern University's Fifth Annual Media Symposium, 1990).

16. Bernice Kanner, "Shelf Control," *New York* (January 22, 1990): 22–23.

17. Backman, *Advertising and Competition,* 96–114.

18. Five random examples:

   a. *Breakfast cereals.* In 1964, six manufacturers "held almost all the breakfast cereal market" (Backman, *Advertising and Competition,* note, pp. 74–76). In 1985, the six-firm concentration ratio was 94.6 percent; in 1986, 94.6 percent; in 1987, 94.6 percent (*Advertising Age,* September 26, 1988, p. 64).

   b. *Soft drinks.* In 1964, the six-firm concentration ratio was 89.7 percent (Backman, *Advertising and Competition,* 107). In 1988, it was 86.4 percent (*New York Times,* January 15, 1989).

   c. *Pet food.* In 1979, the five-firm concentration ratio was 64.8 percent (*Advertising Age Yearbook,* Chicago: Crain Books, 1982, p. 273). In 1985, it was 62.4 percent (*Advertising Age,* August 18, 1986).

   d. *Regular coffee.* The five-firm concentration ratio was 71.9 percent in

1976 and 70.1 percent in 1979 (*Advertising Age Yearbook,* Chicago: Crain Books, 1981, p. 178).

e. *Instant coffee.* The five-firm concentration ratio was 89.5 percent in 1976 and 89.7 percent in 1979 (*Advertising Age Yearbook,* 1981, p. 178).

19. Ekelund and Saurman, *Advertising and the Market Process,* 101.

20. Jean-Jacques Lambin, *Advertising, Competition and Market Conduct in Oligopoly over Time* (New York: American Elsevier Publishing Company, 1976), 134.

21. Robert L. Steiner, "Does Advertising Lower Consumer Prices?" *Journal of Marketing* 37 (October 1973): 19–27.

22. Michael Lynch, *The "Steiner Effect": A Prediction from a Monopolistically Competitive Model Inconsistent with Any Combination of Pure Monopoly or Competition* (Washington, DC: Bureau of Economics, Federal Trade Commission, 1986): unpublished.

23. W. Duncan Reekie, *Advertising and Price* (London: The Advertising Association, 1979).

24. Ibid., 43.

25. Ibid., 41–42.

26. Don E. Schultz and Robert D. Dewar, "Retailers in Control: The Impact of Retail Trade Concentration," *Journal of Consumer Marketing* 1, no. 2 (1984): 81–89; also Thomas W. Wilson, Jr., "Achieving a Sustainable Competitive Advantage" (New York: Association of National Advertisers New Product Marketing Workshop, 1982).

27. As discussed in chapter 2, promotions below the line accounted in 1989 for 66 percent of manufacturers' total expenditure above and below the line, compared with 58 percent in 1976.

28. Scale effects are illustrated in Reekie, *Advertising and Price,* 9–19. The cases quoted by Reekie actually demonstrate that the cost savings from large output were substantially passed on in the form of lower prices. Also Steiner, "Does Advertising Lower Consumer Prices?" 23. See Neil Borden, *The Economic Effects of Advertising* (Chicago: Richard D. Irwin, 1942), 854–857, which discusses the situation in industries that are not capital-intensive.

29. Heyworth, *Advertising,* app. 2.

30. See, for instance, Mark S. Albion and Paul W. Farris, *The Advertising Controversy: Evidence of the Economic Effects of Advertising* (Boston: Auburn House, 1981), 167–170.

31. Lambin, *Advertising, Competition and Market Conduct,* 138. For evidence of advertising's ability to reduce the elasticity of demand, see endnote 3.

32. William S. Comanor and Thomas A. Wilson, "Advertising, Market Structure and Performance," *Review of Economics and Statistics* (November 1967): 423–440.

33. Jones, *Does It Pay to Advertise?* 297.

34. *The Value Side of Productivity* (New York: American Association of Advertising Agencies, 1989), 30.

35. David N. Martin, *Romancing the Brand* (New York: Amacon, American Management Association, 1989), 23.

36. Melvin L. DeFleur, "How Massive Are the Mass Media? Implications for

Communications Education and Research," *Syracuse Scholar* (Spring 1990): 14–34.

37. Ibid.
38. Ben H. Bagdikian, *The Media Monopoly,* 3rd ed. (Boston: Beacon Press, 1990), 132, 147.
39. Lambin, *Advertising, Competition and Market Conduct,* 136–138.
40. Average advertising elasticities were published by Gert Assmus, John U. Farlet, and Donald R. Lehmann, "How Advertising Affects Sales: Meta Analysis of Econometric Results," *Journal of Marketing Research* 21 (February 1984): 65–74.
41. Lambin, *Advertising, Competition and Market Conduct,* 136.
42. Julian L. Simon, "The Effect of Advertising upon the Propensity to Consume," *Issues in the Economics of Advertising* (Urbana: University of Illinois Press, 1970), 193–217.
43. Borden, *Economic Effects of Advertising,* 433; see also Lester G. Telser, "Advertising and Cigarettes," *Journal of Political Economy* (October 1962): 471–499.
44. Hilary Stout, "Cigarettes: Still Big Business," *New York Times* (June 12, 1988).
45. Private information, which dates from the five-year period (1967–72) when I was responsible for the advertising for the largest brand of bar soap in Sweden.

Acknowledgments

I am extremely grateful for material used in this book and for perceptive comments on the whole manuscript or parts of it from the following friends, colleagues, and former colleagues: David Baker (director of J. Walter Thompson, London), Simon Broadbent (vice-chairman of Leo Burnett, London), Harold F. Clark, Jr. (former director of J. Walter Thompson), Jack Cronin (former director of J. Walter Thompson), Melvin DeFleur (Syracuse University), Arthur Ecker (formerly of University Hospital, Syracuse), Andrew Ehrenberg (London Business School), Stuart Hyatt (former executive vice-president of Omnicon), Don Johnston (former chairman/CEO of J. Walter Thompson), Timothy Joyce (former chairman of Mediamark Research Inc.), Sattar Khan (planning director of J. Walter Thompson, Hong Kong), Stephen King (former director of J. Walter Thompson, London), Denis Lanigan (former president of J. Walter Thompson), Keith McKerracher (former president of the Institute of Canadian Advertising), Denis Pelli (Syracuse University), Terry Prue (director of J. Walter Thompson, London), Edward Rosenstein (former director of Saatchi & Saatchi, New York), Julian Simon (University of Maryland), Robert Steiner (formerly of the Federal Trade Commission), William M. Weilbacher (former vice-chairman of Dancer, Fitzgerald, Sample), David Wheeler (former director-general of the Institute of Practitioners in Advertising, London), Ronald Wilcox (art director of D'Arcy, Masius, Benton & Bowles, St. Louis), and Boris Wilenkin (formerly of Unilever Marketing Division).

The sharpest critic of the content and form of my writing is my wife, Wendy, who also performed the formidably laborious task of feeding the (sometimes illegible) drafts of the manuscript into a word processor. Without her contribution, there would have been no book.

Journal articles based on some of the material used in chapters of this book have appeared in the following publications:

Chapter 2, *Le Temps Stratégique*
Chapter 3, *Admap, International Journal of Advertising, Marketing and Research Today,* and *Syracuse Scholar*
Chapters 5 and 6, *Harvard Business Review*

The articles in the *Harvard Business Review* used for Chapters 5 and 6 were entitled, respectively, "Ad Spending: Maintaining Market Share," which appeared in the issue of January–February 1990, copyright © President and Fellows of Harvard College, and "The Double Jeopardy of Sales Promotions," which appeared in the issue of September–October 1990, copyright © President and Fellows of Harvard College.

Chapter 3 was the basis of a presentation I made to the 1991 Conference of the European Society for Opinion and Marketing Research. Chapter 5 formed the substance of a presentation to the Asian Advertising Congress in 1989. Chapter 6 provided a skeleton for a speech to the Institute of Canadian Advertising in 1990 and a presentation to the Advertising Research Foundation in 1991. Chapter 5 contains empirical material collected by J. Walter Thompson, Hong Kong, with which I worked in processing and interpreting it. Chapter 10 is extracted from a study I carried out for the Ogilvy Center for Research and Development, and it is reproduced with their permission.

Index

Aaker, David A., 363
Abraham, Magid M., 10, 347, 364
Account planning, 74, 272, 275, 367
Account versus creative orientation of an advertising agency, 65, 72–74, 77–78, 81
Adams, John, 205
Added values, advertising-related, 124, 162–72, 175, 186
Adell Chemical, 14
Adstock, 242
Ad Tel split-cable television mechanism, 249
Advertising Age, 35, 45, 252, 335
Advertising
  agency concentration, 254
  agency's and client's roles in developing, 269
  expectations for, 33, 267–68
  misleading, 260
  public attitudes toward, 260–62
Advertising agencies, confused identity of, 254
Advertising Association (UK), 325
Advertising/brand awareness measures, 280
Advertising-intensiveness (average share of voice), 89–90, 98
Advertising-intensiveness curve (AIC), 93–94, 96–98, 100, 232, 315–16
Advertising rebates, 104
Advertising Research System (ARS), 200
Advertising styles, preconceptions about, 269
Advertising versus advertisements, 185–86
After Eight chocolates, 164
Aitchison, David R., 362
Albion, Mark S., 369
Alcohol advertising, 345
American Association of Advertising Agencies, 331

Amico, Thomas J., 228–29, 363
Andrex toilet tissue, 196, 280
Arbitron, 221
Arndt, Johan, 364
Asmuss, Gert, 356, 363, 364, 370
Assael, Henry, 364
Association of National Advertisers (ANA), 255

Backer, Spielvogel, Bates, 79, 96
Backman, Jules, 321–22, 368
Bagdikian, Ben H., 370
Baker, David, 359
Barnes, Kathleen, 349
Barnes, Michael, 347, 350, 360
Bates, Ted, 78, 79
Batten, Barton, Durstine & Osborn (BBDO), 166
Benham, Lee, 319–20, 368
Bernbach, Bill, 38, 73, 77, 82
Berry, Kathleen M., 357
Bisociative fusion, 226
Bogart, Leo, 358, 363, 365
Booz, Allen & Hamilton, 361, 366
Borden, Neil H., 337, 348, 360, 369, 370
Bower, Marvin, 63, 352
Brand
  company as a, 271
  concept of the, 74, 156, 175, 209–16
Brand extension/stretching *see* Names, umbrella versus new
Brand, Jonathan, 68–70
Brand management, 202, 222, 269–70
Brand positioning, 79, 133–35
Brand repertoire, 51, 212, 282
Brands, second and third in a category, 79, 211
Brand stewardship, 267, 279
British Broadcasting Corporation (BBC), 5
Broadbent, Simon, 352, 355, 356, 364, 368

Brooke Bond Oxo, 190, 271
Brouillard Communications, 357
Budgets, advertising, 17, 55, 62, 85–100, 230–33, 263, 294
Bullmore, Jeremy, 185
Burger King, 109
Burke Day-After Recall, 200
Burnett, Leo, 77, 78, 79, 82, 96, 119, 129, 155, 242
Butterfield, Leslie, 359

Cake mixes, 157
California Avocado Advisory Board, 309–13, 336
Campbell's soup, 164
Canter, Stanley D., 363
Caples, John, 363
Carman, James M., 363
Carter, Peter, 361
Case rate budgeting, 86–87, 100, 232
Categories of consumer goods
  declining, 23, 26
  growing, 24–26, 28
Cereals, breakfast, 24, 28, 131–52
Channon, Charles, 359
Cheer detergent, 77
Chicago, University of, 320
Cigarette advertising, 23, 338
Citrus Hill, 27
Clark, Harold F., Jr., 347, 352, 358
Clarke, Peter, 365
Client dissatisfaction with agencies, 38
Coca-Cola, 31, 266
Coe, Barbara, 362
Coen, Robert J., 252, 349
Coffee, instant, 157
Cognitive and affective results of advertising, 47, 49, 74
Colgate-Palmolive, 57, 161, 171
Collins, Martin, 362
Colman, Prentis & Varley (CPV), 66–67, 81
Comanor, William S., 331, 369
Commission system, agency, versus fees, 5, 15–16, 19, 38, 39, 43, 70, 81, 255, 266, 271–72
Communications, integrated, 270
Comparison advertising, 135, 176, 288
Competition
  influence of advertising on, 4, 253, 305, 315–20, 339, 343
  pure or atomistic, 301

Competitive pressure and advertising budgets, 13–14
Competitors, advertisers' concentration on, 122–23, 135, 266–67, 342
Concentration, industrial, influence of advertising on, 305, 320–23, 339
Consumer, advertising and the, 257–62
Consumer orientation of marketing, 266
Consumer panel research, 219–20
Consumer purchasing patterns, 51–52, 212–13, 263
Consumers who claim to be uninfluenced by advertising, 50
Contingency planning, 270–71, 275
Controls on advertising, 259–60
Cooper, Peter, 362
Corlett, Tom, 258–59, 362, 364, 366, 367
Cost structure of brands, 99–100, 231–32, 294
Coupons, 104, 108
Cowley, Don, 359
Cox, G. Robert, 347
Craft skills, advertising, 119, 227–29
Creative executions, research into, 188, 190–92
Creative organization in advertising agencies, 256
Creative output of advertising agencies, volume of, 275
Creative recruitment, 276
Creative revival during 1960s, 38, 43, 73, 77
Crown Paints, 188–90, 198
Culture, agency, 13, 17, 63–83, 277
Currie, Jean, 363

Danzig, Fred, 350
da Ponte, Lorenzo, 265
Davidson, J. Hugh, 279, 360, 361, 367
Davis, John, 361
Day-after recall testing (DART), 37, 200, 218, 222–24, 228
Day, George S., 364
Deal, Terence E., 352
de Bono, Edward, 227, 362, 363
Deficiencies admitted in advertising, 288
DeFleur, Melvin, L., 369
Demand curve, moving, 241, 313–15
Demographics, 30, 124, 141–49, 153, 178
de Tocqueville, Alexis, 205
Dewar, Robert D., 349, 361, 369
Dhalla, Nariman K., 354, 361, 364
Dial Corporation, 160, 171

Diapers, disposable, 97
Direct response advertising, 7–8, 18, 85, 228–29, 263, 282, 288–90, 291
Discriminating claims in advertising, 31–32, 161–62, 179, 286
Dishwashing liquid, 156–57
Display incentives, 104
Distribution, retail, 125, 210, 214
Donnelley Marketing, 40–41
Downham, John, 359–362
Drip feeding of advertising, 295–96
Drucker, Peter F., 354
D'Souza, Sev, 359
Dunbar, David, 365
Durables, consumer, 21, 24
Dynamic difference, 232–241

Economist, The, 7
Education, advertising, in universities, 56–60, 62
Effects of advertising, long-term, 241–44, 273, 294, 339–40
Effects of advertising, short-term, 237–41, 273, 293–94, 295, 339
Ehrenberg, Andrew, 48, 52–53, 57, 212, 243, 247, 350, 351, 353, 360, 361, 364, 367
Ekelund, Robert B., Jr., 323, 367, 369
Elasticity
    advertising, 10, 98–99, 110–12, 114–17, 240, 241
    price, 103–06, 113–16, 214
Elasticity of demand curves, influence of advertising on, 243, 253, 273
    see also Oligopolistic differentiation
Elliott, Jeremy, 364, 368
Employment, reduced, in agencies, 38, 54, 59, 82
Endicott, R. Craig, 348
Equilibrium in economic analysis, 298–99
Ethics of advertising, 258–59, 346
European advertising styles, 32
Expenditure on advertising, aggregate, 22, 27, 34–39, 42–43, 52, 54, 252
Exposure, low levels of advertising, 257
Eyeglasses, advertising, 319–20

Fa soap, 160
Farlet, John U., 356, 363, 364, 370
Farris, Paul W., 369
Fast moving consumer goods (FMCG), *See* Repeat purchase packaged goods
Federal Trade Commission (FTC), 259

Feldwick, Paul, 359
Festinger, Leon, 364
Fletcher, Robert, 362
Focus groups, 194–99, 204
Foley, William F., 353, 363
Foote, Cone & Belding, 166
Forced exposure, 198
Forced purchase, 212
Fothergill, J.E., 367
Fowler, F.G., 356
Fowler, H.W., 356
Fragmentation of brands, 29, 278, 320–22
Fragmentation of markets, 22, 26–27, 28–33, 37, 42–43, 266, 322
Frantz, Jack, 361
Fraser, Cynthia, 347
"Fresh Eggs" parable, 177
Frequency distribution of purchases, 212
Functional differentiation of brands, 32, 124, 156–62, 215, 257, 278

Gabor, Andre, 361
Galbraith, John Kenneth, 297, 301, 350
Gallup & Robinson, 223
Garrett, Thomas M, S.J., 366
General Foods, 57, 138
General Mills, 57, 138
General Motors, 15, 29
Giges, Nancy, 348
Global advertising, 8–9, 18, 27, 38
Godwin, Mary Wollstonecraft, 45
Goodhardt, G.L., 361
Granger, C.W.J., 361
Grass, Robert C., 248
Greenbaum, Thomas L., 359
Greyser, Stephen A., 357, 359, 362, 367
"Gurus," advertising, 287

Hamton, William J., 348
Hard core of regular buyers, 213
Hard selling, 48, 53, 58–59, 342
Hardy, Hugh S., 366
Harvard Business School, 261
Haskins, Jack B., 362
Hatt, Roz, 361
Health drinks, 158
Heeler, Roger M., 364, 365
Hendry model, 231
Henkel (detergent manufacturer), 160
Henry, Harry, 363
Hershey, 271
Heyworth, Lord, 321, 368, 369
Hierarchy theories, 48, 244–47

Higgins, Denis, 356, 357
Hinks, Bill, 352
Historical studies of advertising effectiveness, 273–74, 279, 285
Hite, Robert E., 347
Hi-tech goods, 21
Holloway, Peter, 367
Hopkins, Claude C., 85–86, 353, 363
Howard, John A., 366
Hulbert, James, 366
Hunt, Heather, 348

Idea generation, 119, 224–27, 263
Ignorance/knowledge of advertising effects, 13, 19, 45, 55, 58, 62, 83, 206, 233, 239, 262, 267
Incompleteness in advertising, 288
Inflexion point, 238
Investment brands, 90–92
Invisible hand, 3, 334

Jenkins, Ev, 359
Johnson, S.C., 271
Johnston, Don, 75
Jones, John Philip, 347, 349, 351, 352, 353, 354, 355, 356, 357, 358, 360, 361, 362, 364, 365, 366, 367, 368, 369
Joyce, Timothy, 226, 360, 363
Judgment, use of, in evaluation of research, 268

Kaldor, Lord, 360
Kanner, Bernice, 368
Karslake, J.S., 362
"Katie," heroine of Oxo campaign, 286
Kellogg Company, 271
Kellogg's Corn Flakes, 138–47, 151–52, 174, 177, 180–81, 282
Kennedy, Allan A., 352
Kershaw, Andrew, 363
Keynes, Maynard, 22, 209, 348, 360
King continuum, 172–75, 179
King, Stephen, 120, 172, 351, 358, 360, 361, 363, 364, 365, 368
Knowledge of advertising, classification, 13, 206, 262
Knowledge of advertising effects, *see* Ignorance/knowledge of advertising effects
Koch, Nancy, 354, 361
Koestler, Arthur, 226, 363
Korvette's stores, 165
Kotler, Philip, 350

Kropp, H.R., 363
Krugman, Herbert E., 245–47, 248, 250, 365

Lafayette, Jon, 349, 365
Lambin, Jean-Jacques, 323, 337, 369, 370
Lanigan, Denis, 352
Lannon, Judie, 362
Leaky bucket theory, 213
Lehmann, Donald R., 356, 363, 364, 370
Lestoil, 14
Lever Brothers, 171
Leverhulme, Lord, 12
Levin, Gary, 349
Levin, Philip, 358
Liddell Hart, B.H., 356
Liesse, Julie, 365
Life cycle theory, 215–16, 282–83
Lodish, Leonard M., 10, 347, 364
London Business School, 48
Longley, Alice Beebe, 21
Lovell, Mark, 363
Low involvement, 53
Lucas, Darrell B., 362
Lucky Charms, 138–49, 151–52, 177, 181–82, 282
Lux Toilet soap, 95, 115, 164
Lynch, Michael, 369
Lyons, John, 347

Mabey, Bill, 362
MacLachlan, James, 362
Macro effect of advertising, 22–23, 253, 336–38, 340
Madell, John, 360
M. & M. Mars, 57
Margins, retail, advertising's influence on, 306, 323–27, 333, 340
Market-leading brands, 79
Market maturity, 21–27, 35–37, 42, 49, 101, 116, 132–33, 338
Martin, David N., 332, 369
Matrix system of agency organization, 64–65
Maxwell, John C., Jr., 357
Mayer, Martin, 156, 185, 357, 358
Mazola corn oil, 195–96
McCann-Erickson, 252
McCarthy, E. Jerome, 356
McCollum/Spielman, 200
McCorkell, Graeme, 358, 363
McDonald, Colin, 249, 251, 360
McDonald's, 109

McGee, Edward J., 347
McGuinness, Tony, 359
McKay, Roy, 366
McKinsey & Company, 63
McNamara, J.J., 362
Media
  advertising subsidy to, 5–7, 253, 306,
    333–36, 340
  consumers' use of, 234–35, 263, 290–91
  evolution, 291
  fragmentation, 37, 291
  links between, 292–93
Media buying scale economies, 236, 316–
  17
Mediamark Research Inc. (MRI), 24, 29,
  131–49, 153, 158–62, 170–72, 178,
  220–21, 282, 357
Media planning, 79
Media research, 220–21
Media strategy, 233–36
Media tactics, 236
Meier, Barry, 366
Mergers in the advertising business/agency
  conglomerates, 27, 38, 54, 71
Michell, Paul, 351
Micklethwait, John, 348
"Milking," 90–91
Miller, R.D., 361
Milton, Shirley, F., 350
Mitchell, Arnold, 357, 358
Monopoly, 302
Moody, Kate, 366
Morris, Philip, 138
Motivating claims in advertising, 31–32,
  161, 179
Motivation Learning Potential (MLP), 200
Multi-brand buying patterns, 212

Names, umbrella versus new, 28, 210
Naples, Michael, 249, 251, 365
National Advertising Division (NAD), 260
National Advertising Review Board
  (NARB), 260
National Public Radio (NPR), 336
Neu, D. Morgan, 362
New Products and brands, 9–10, 18, 50,
  51, 209–12, 215, 257, 263, 277–78
Niche marketing, 30
Nielsen, A.C. 28, 67, 90, 108, 220–21,
  320
Norman, James R., 348

O'Brien, Terrence, 364

Ogilvy & Mather, 39, 77–78, 79, 231,
  274
Ogilvy Center for Research and Develop-
  ment, 274, 356
Ogilvy, David, 38, 69, 73, 77, 79, 82, 83,
  85, 352, 353, 358, 363, 365
OHerlihy, Callaghan, 347, 356, 364
Oligopolistic differentiation, 253, 304–05,
  333
Oligopoly, 301–05, 339–40
On Air Lab (OAL), 200
One-on-ones (individual interviews), 194–
  99, 204
Optimism of advertising practitioners, 14–
  15, 19, 85
Orenstein, Frank, 358, 363, 365
Orr, Sir David, 63, 352, 362
Oxo bouillon cubes, 271, 286

Packard, Vance, 350
Palmer, Edward L., 366
Passive meters, 220, 293
Peckham, James O., Sr. 279, 320, 348,
  354, 355, 356, 360, 361, 363, 364,
  365, 367, 368
Penetration, 132–47, 152–53, 212–13,
  273
Penetration supercharge, 92, 213, 281
People meters, 220
Perceptual mapping, 169–72, 179
Permut, Steven E., 363
Persuasion measures, advertising, 37
Phillips, William, 361
Picture sorting, 166–68
Planning Cycle, 120–21, 186
Politz, Alfred, 365–66
Post Fruit & Fibre, 138–49, 152, 177,
  182–83
Potter, Jack, 363
Potter, Robert, 363
Powell, Enoch, 18, 260, 341–46
Preemptive arguments in advertising, 157
Prentice, Robert M., 355
Pressure testing, advertising, 10, 51, 214
Price, general influence of advertising on,
  253, 305, 306–15, 339–40
Pricing, brand, 108, 124–25, 210–11,
  214, 243, 273, 299
Priemer, Gus, 365
Pringles, 27
Procter & Gamble, 14, 21–22, 27, 29, 57,
  77, 160–61, 171, 215, 232
Product demonstration, 269

Production, advertising, 2
Product tests, matched, 244
Professional mainstream, agency staff in, 76, 256
Profitability, loss of respect for, by business, 102
Profit, importance of in advertising and promotional evaluation, 107, 112, 116, 294–95
Profit, industrial, influence of advertising on, 331
Profit maximization in economic analysis, 299–301
Profit-taking brands, 90–92
Projective research techniques, 166–68
Promotions, sales, 6, 11–12, 19, 22, 27, 34–37, 39–42, 101–10, 116–17, 125, 214–15
    encouragement of retaliation, 108–09, 116
    general absence of long-term, 107–08, 116
    influence on brand images, 109, 116
    limited franchise-building, 108
    mortgaging effect, 108, 116
Proposition, advertising, 129–30, 155–72, 178–79, 186
Prue, Terry, 358
Psychographics, 124, 149–53, 161–72, 277
Psychology, consumer, and advertising, 244–52
Public Broadcasting System, (PBS), 336
Purchase frequency, 131–38, 152–53, 212–13, 273

Qualitative advertising research, 17, 74, 80, 187–99, 222, 276–77, 281–82, 285
Qualitative advertising research, stimulus material, 192–93
Quantitative copy testing, 32, 37, 199–203, 204, 222–24, 228, 281–82, 285
Quelch, John A., 364

Ramond, Charles, 244, 247, 364
Ratios, advertising-to-sales, 89, 253, 306–08, 333, 339
Ray, Michael L., 245–46, 364, 365
Recall, advertising (see also Day-after recall testing), 286
Recipe advertising, 228
Reculer pour mieux sauter, 187
Red Mountain instant coffee, 190–92, 198

Reed, Jerome B., 364, 365
Reekie, W., Duncan 325–27, 369
Reeves, Rosser, 77–78, 79, 82, 156, 207–08, 245, 352, 360, 365
Reith, Lord, 5
Repeat buying patterns, 51–52, 212–13
Repeat purchase packaged goods (fast moving consumer goods), 21, 51–52, 212–16, 329
Research
    advertising, carried out in universities, 57–58, 60, 62
    among creative people, 287–88
    laboratory, 288
    market, general problems with, 10, 216–19
    syndicated, 131
    weakness in forecasting advertising's selling power, 186, 221–24, 263, 283–85
    "What is a Brand?" technique, 163–66
Resor, Stanley, 71, 73
Response functions, advertising, 237–40, 242
Response orientation in agency philosophy, 79–80, 83, 176
Retail audit research, 219–20
Retail concentration, 41, 215
Ries, Al, 347
Roberts, Andrew, 355, 356, 367
Robinson, Joan, 350
Ronzoni spaghetti, 165
Rosenstein, Edward, 166, 349, 357, 358, 359
Rothenberg, Randall, 349, 353
Rothschild, Michael L., 364, 365
Rotzoll, Kim B., 352, 360
Rubican, Raymond, 82

Saatchi & Saatchi (Compton), 79, 166
Sainsbury formula, 221
Sales, advertising's general influence on, 4, 7, 263
Sales Area Marketing Inc. (SAMI), 30
Sampson, Peter, 359
San Augustine, Andre J., 353, 363
Saurman, David S., 323, 367, 369
Save, increasing marginal propensity to, 22
Sawyer, Alan G., 364, 365
Scale economies, advertising-related, 87–96, 213, 315–17
Scale economies, industrial, influence of advertising on, 306, 327–34, 339–40
Schultz, Don E., 349, 361, 369

Schumpeter, Joseph A., 101
Schwartz, David, 359
Schwerin Relative Competitive Preference, 284–85
Segments, market, 124, 133–35, 178, 210
Selective perception, 49, 56, 82, 257
Serafin, Raymond, 348
Services, consumer, 21
Share of voice and its effect, 51, 55, 89–97, 251–52
Shulman, Art, 362
Simmons Market Research Bureau (SMRB), 131, 153, 178, 220–21, 282, 357
Simon, Julian L., 337, 364, 365, 370
Single exposure effectiveness, 53, 247–51
Single-source data, 13, 220, 281
Slice of life television technique, 218, 269
Sloan, Pat, 365
Slotting allowances, 41, 104
Smith, Adam, 3, 334, 342
Smith, Sandra J., 365
Soft drinks, 24, 28, 97
Soft selling, 342
Solson, Stanley, 322
Split-cable television testing, 10, 249
Stability, lack of, in client-agency relationships, 54
Starch readership research, 223
Stationary conditions in markets, 52, 212–16, 263, 280–81
Steiner effect, *see* Steiner, Robert L.
Steiner, Robert L., 253, 323–26, 333, 340, 369
Stout, Hilary, 370
Strategy
  advertising, 2, 17, 74, 125–83, 225, 228, 274–75
  advertising, research into, 187–90, 203–04, 225
  business plan, 123–24, 152
  general, 119–83
  marketing, 124–25, 152
  military, 122–23
Strong, Edward C., 364, 365
Strong force theory of advertising, 17, 46–48, 58–62
Subliminal advertising, 48, 53, 258, 350
Swank, Cynthia G., 352
Sweden, toilet soap market, 338, 370

Tactics, military, 123
Target groups in advertising, 17, 53, 56, 62, 129–53, 178, 180, 181, 182, 282, 286
Television advertising
  agency bias toward, 75, 79, 228
  large increase after 1950, 5
Television, cable, 221
Tellis, Gerard J., 105, 354, 355, 356, 361
Telser, Lester G., 370
Temporary price reductions (TPRs), 104, 108
Test market reliability, 211
Texas, attorney general, 259
Thompson, J. Walter
  Amsterdam office, 68
  London office, 68, 71–76, 79, 164, 185, 234
  New York office, 71, 73–75, 88, 164, 274, 276, 331
  Scandinavian office, 67–71, 81, 276
"Thompson man," 72–73
"Three rooms" parable, 258, 365–66
Tide detergent, 29, 168
Timms, Christopher, 359
Tinker, Jack, 38, 73, 82
Toilet soap market, 158–62, 170–72
Tolley, B. Stuart, 358, 363, 365
Tone of voice, advertising, 56, 62
Top hat effect of promotions, 108
Tracking studies, 280–81, 284, 286
Trends, marketplace, as component in advertising budgeting, 98, 100
Trout, Jack, 347

Uneconomic returns to advertising, 2, 10–11, 19, 111
Unexpectedness in advertising, 288
Unilever, 63, 95, 109, 190, 321, 329–30, 333, 338, 368
Unique selling proposition (USP), 78, 156, 161, 269
United States Department of Commerce, 26, 35
University of Southern California, 105
Usage-pull, 78

Vail, Theodore N., 1
Values and Lifestyles (VALS), 150–51, 168–69, 180, 181, 182
Volvo cars, 259
von Hayek, Friedrich, 367
von Oech, Roger, 227, 363

Walley, Wayne, 348

Wanamaker, John, 12
Waste in advertising, quantification, 12
Ways in which advertising campaign
    should work, 130, 172–77, 179, 180–
    81, 182, 183
Weak force theory of advertising, 17, 48–
    62, 258
Weasel words, 157
Weilbacher, William M., 31, 321, 347,
    348, 349, 352, 353, 359, 364, 365,
    366, 368
Wells, Mary, 38, 73, 77, 82
Wheeler, David J., 352
Whitehead, Frank, 347, 350
Wilcox, Ronald Dean, 358, 359, 360
Wilenkin, Boris, 355, 356
Wilson, Thomas A., 331, 369

Wilson, Thomas W., Jr., 354, 355, 361,
    369
Winn, Marie, 366
Winski, Joseph M., 349
Winters, Arthur A., 350
Woods, R.S., 347
Worcester, Robert M., 359, 362
Wordsworth, William, 155
WPP Group, 274

Young, James Webb, 155, 174, 226–27,
    287, 357, 363
Young, Shirley, 349, 362
Yuspeh, Sonia, 354, 361–62

Zapping, 221, 257
Zoglin, Richard, 349

About the Author

John Philip Jones was born in Wales in 1930 and graduated in economics from Cambridge University (B.A. with Honors; M.A.).

From 1953 to 1980 he worked in the advertising agency field. This experience included twenty-five years with J. Walter Thompson, as a market research executive in London (1953–55); advertising account executive in London (1957–65); account supervisor and head of television in Amsterdam (1965–67); account director and head of client service in Scandinavia, based in Copenhagen (1967–72); and account director in London (1972–80). He worked on a wide variety of packaged-goods accounts, including many brands from Unilever and brands marketed by Beecham, Chesebrough-Pond's, Gillette, Nestlé, Pepsi-Cola, Quaker Oats, Scott Paper, and other major consumer-goods companies. He was international account director on Lux Toilet Soap (the largest selling bar soap in the world) from 1972 to 1980. He was also involved in a wide range of management education both within and outside the agency.

He joined Syracuse University at the end of 1980 and is currently a tenured full professor in the Newhouse School of Public Communications. He was for seven years chairman of the Advertising Department at the Newhouse School, and for three years editor of the university's interdisciplinary journal of ideas, the *Syracuse Scholar*. He was a member of the Mellon Foundation project team which for two years explored the interconnections between liberal and professional education. (A book, *Contesting the Boundaries of Liberal and Professional Education*, was published by the Syracuse University Press in 1988.) He was a member of the Chancellor's Panel on the Future of Syracuse University, which reported following a two-year study in 1988.

Professor Jones has published many articles in professional journals, including *Admap*, the *Harvard Business Review*, and the *Inter-*

national Journal of Advertising. He has also written a number of pieces of national and international journalism, and his comments on the marketing scene are frequently quoted in the press. His books *What's in a Name? Advertising and the Concept of Brands* (Lexington Books, 1986) and *Does It Pay to Advertise? Cases Illustrating Successful Brand Advertising* (Lexington Books, 1989) have gone through many printings and are used by advertising and marketing professionals all over the world.

He is employed as a consultant by many major consumer-goods companies and advertising agencies in the United States and abroad, and he travels widely in connection with this activity.

In 1991, Professor Jones was named by the American Advertising Federation as the Distinguished Advertising Educator of the Year.